Designing the User Interface: Strategies for Effective Human-Computer Interaction

BEN SHNEIDERMAN
The University of Maryland

Illustrations by Carol Wald

ADDISON-WESLEY PUBLISHING COMPANY

READING, MASSACHUSETTS • MENLO PARK, CALIFORNIA
DON MILLS, ONTARIO • WOKINGHAM, ENGLAND • AMSTERDAM
SYDNEY • SINGAPORE • TOKYO • MADRID • BOGOTÁ
SANTIAGO • SAN JUAN

Library of Congress Cataloging-in-Publication Data
Shneiderman, Ben.
    Designing the User Interface: Strategies for Effective Human-Computer
    Interaction

    Bibliography: p.
    Includes indexes.
    1. Interactive computer systems. 2. System design.
I. Title.
QA76.9.I58S47 1987   004.6   85–28765
ISBN 0–201–16505–8

Reprinted with corrections May, 1987

Text reproduced by Addison-Wesley from camera-ready materials provided by the author. Cover and chapter opening illustrations ©Carol Wald.

EFGHIJ-HA–898

Dedication

For my wife Nancy and
our children Sara and Anna.

PREFACE

FIGHTING FOR THE USER

Frustration and anxiety are a part of daily life for many users of computerized information systems. They struggle to learn command language or menu selection systems that are supposed to help them do their job. Some people encounter such serious cases of computer shock, terminal terror, or network neurosis that they avoid using computerized systems. These electronic-age maladies are growing more common; but help is on the way!

Researchers have shown that redesign of the human-computer interface can make a substantial difference in learning time, performance speed, error rates, and user satisfaction. Information and computer scientists have been testing design alternatives for their impact on these human performance measures. Commercial designers recognize that systems that are easier to use will have a competitive edge in information retrieval, office automation, and personal computing.

Programmers and quality assurance teams are becoming more cautious and paying greater attention to the implementation issues that guarantee high quality user interfaces. Computer center managers are realizing that they must play an active role in ensuring that the software and hardware facilities provide high quality service to their users.

In short, the diverse use of computers in homes, offices, factories, hospitals, electric power control centers, hotels, banks, and so on is stimulating widespread interest in human factors issues. Human engineering, which was seen as the paint put on at the end of a project, is now understood to be the steel frame on which the structure is built.

However, an awareness of the problems and a desire to do well are not sufficient. Designers, managers, and programmers must be willing to step forward and fight for the user. The enemies include inconsistent command languages, confusing operation sequences, chaotic display formats, inconsistent terminology, incomplete instructions, complex error recovery procedures, and misleading or threatening error messages.

I believe that progress in serving users will be rapid because as examples of excellence proliferate, users' expectations will rise. The designers, managers, and researchers who are dedicated to quality and to nurturing the user community will have the satisfaction of doing a good job and the appreciation of the users they serve.

The battle will not be won by angry argumentation over the "user friendliness" of competing systems or by biased claims that "my design is more natural than your design." Victory will come to people who take a disciplined, iterative, and empirical approach to the study of human performance in the use of interactive systems. More and more, system developers, maintainers, and managers are collecting performance data from users, distributing subjective satisfaction surveys, inviting users to participate in design teams, conducting repeated field trials for novel proposals, and using field study data to support organizational decision making.

Marsall McLuhan observed that "the medium is the message." Designers send a message to the users by the design of interactive systems. In the past, the message was often an unfriendly and unpleasant one. I believe, however, that it is possible to send a much more positive message that conveys the genuine concern a designer has for the users. If the users feel competent in using the system, can easily correct errors, and can accomplish their tasks, then they will pass on the message of quality to the people they serve, to their colleagues, and to their friends and families. In this way, each designer has the possibility of making the world a little bit warmer, wiser, safer, and more compassionate.

WHOM THIS BOOK IS FOR

Designing the User Interface was written primarily for designers, managers, and evaluators of interactive systems. It presents a broad survey of the issues in designing, implementing, managing, maintaining, training, and refining the user interface of interactive systems. The book's second audience is researchers in human performance with interactive systems. These researchers may have their background in computer science, psychology, human factors, ergonomics, education, management information systems, information science, or industrial engineering, but they all share a desire to understand the complex interaction of people and machines. Students in these fields will also benefit from the contents of this book. It is my hope that this book will stimulate the introduction of courses on user interface design in all of these disciplines. Finally, serious users of interactive systems may benefit by a more thorough understanding of the design questions for user interfaces.

My goals are to encourage greater attention to the user interface and to help develop a more rigorous science of user interface design. *Designing the User Interface* presents design issues, offers experimental evidence where available, and makes reasonable recommendations where suitable. The book begins with a motivating review and a presentation of frameworks for thinking about systems: theories, models, principles, and guidelines. Then, Part II covers the primary interaction styles: menu selection, form fill-in, command languages, natural language interaction, and direct manipulation. Part III includes a set of vital issues, such as the hardware devices, reponse time, display rate, system messages, screen design, color, windows, printed manuals, online help, and tutorials. Part IV describes assessment methods, iterative design, testing, evaluation, management strategies, and social and individual impacts.

The topic of interactive systems has grown enormously in the five years it took to write this book, making it impossible to cover all the vital issues with sufficient depth. Therefore, many references, presented at the end of each chapter, can guide the interested reader to further sources.

Two major areas are covered only briefly: the discussion of human cognitive skills, personality styles, and perceptual abilities, and the description of the dialog management systems (also known as User Interface Management Systems) and formal specifications. Each deserves an entire book.

ACKNOWLEDGMENTS

My goal in writing *Designing the User Interface* was to integrate experimental evidence, practical experience, and theories from computer science, psychology, education, management, and commercial applications into one comprehensive book. Some of the material appeared as early forms in journals. Editors, reviewers, and readers provided guidance in making further changes for the versions that appear here. These articles include:

The psychology of serving the user community: Management strategies for interactive systems, *Journal of Capacity Management 1*, 4, (1983), 328–343.

Direct manipulation: A step beyond programming languages, *IEEE Computer 16*, 8, (August 1983), 57–69.

Response time and display rate in human performance with computers, *ACM Computing Surveys 16*, 3, (September 1984), 265–285.

Correct, complete operations and other principles of interaction, In Salvendy, G., Editor, *Human-Computer Interaction*, Elsevier Science Publishers, Amsterdam, (1984), 135–147.

Human factors issues of manuals, online help, and tutorials, In Agrawal, J. C. and Zunde, P., Editors, *Empirical Foundations of Information and Software Science*, Elsevier Science Publishers B. V., Amsterdam, (1985), 253–275.

Designing menu selection systems, *Journal of the American Society for Information Science 37*, 2, (March 1986), 57–70.

The feedback from colleagues, students, practitioners, and managers from many disciplines was extremely helpful. Integrating the divergent and prolific sets of advice was a profound challenge. Those who contributed their opinions include:

Phil Barnard, Cambridge University;
James H. Baroff, University of Maryland;

Patricia A. Billingsley, Digital Equipment Corporation;
Christine Borgman, UCLA;
Alphonse Chapanis, Independent consultant;
Susan Flynn, University of Maryland;
James Foley, George Washington University and
   Computer Graphics Consultants;
John Gannon, University of Maryland;
Charles Grantham, Honeywell Corporation;
Thomas Green, Cambridge University;
Stephen J. Hanson, Bell Communications Research;
Deborah Hix, Virginia Tech;
Susanne Humphrey, National Library of Medicine;
Robert J. K. Jacob, Naval Research Laboratory;
John Kohl, Independent consultant;
Charles B. Kreitzberg, Cognetics Corporation;
Henry Ledgard, Independent consultant;
Clayton Lewis, University of Colorado at Boulder;
Charles MacArthur, University of Maryland;
Janis Morariu, University of Maryland;
Dard Nelson, IBM Federal Systems Division;
Kent Norman, University of Maryland;
John J. O'Hare, Office of Naval Research;
Glenn Ricart, University of Maryland;
Richard Rubinstein, Digital Equipment Corporation;
Suzanne Stevenson, University of Maryland;
John C. Thomas, IBM, Yorktown Heights, NY;
Thomas S. Tullis, McDonnell Douglas Astronautics;
Jerry J. Vaske, Honeywell Corporation;
Anthony I. Wasserman, University of California at San Francisco;
Mark Weiser, University of Maryland;
Linda Weldon, University of Maryland.

   My thanks also to the following people who helped with the
illustrations:

Jack Callahan
Robert J. K. Jacob

Steve Miller
Stan Rifkin
Barbara Young.

Many other people contributed to making this book. Carol Wald's original artwork is a valuable addition. Deborah Stoffel and her staff in the Publications Office of the University of Maryland Computer Science Center worked diligently to typeset the manuscript. Mildred Johnson handled the large secretarial load with her usual efficiency, effectiveness, and good cheer. Grace Sheldrick of Wordsworth Associates handled the copyediting and proofreading. Peter Gordon, Helen Goldstein, Carolyn Berry, and Mary Coffey of Addison-Wesley Publishing Company helped bring the project to fruition.

Even with these professional supports, an author's work is highly personal and sometimes lonely. That isolation is softened by family and friends who must put up with the author's struggle. In this connection, I thank my wife, Nancy, and children, Sara and Anna, for cheering me on, accepting my intense involvement in writing, and showing me the beauty in living and loving.

B.S.
College Park, Maryland

CONTENTS

SPECIAL COLOR SECTION

PART I

MOTIVATIONS AND FOUNDATIONS

CHAPTER 1

HUMAN FACTORS OF INTERACTIVE SOFTWARE

Designing an object to be simple and clear takes at least twice as long as the usual way. It requires concentration at the outset on how a clear and simple system would work, followed by the steps required to make it come out that way—steps which are often much harder and more complex than the ordinary ones. It also requires relentless pursuit of that simplicity even when obstacles appear which would seem to stand in the way of that simplicity.

T. H. Nelson, *The Home Computer Revolution*, 1977

1.1 INTRODUCTION

New technologies provide remarkable, almost supernatural, powers to those who master them. Computer systems are a new technology in the early stages of dissemination and refinement. Great excitement now exists as designers provide remarkable functions in simple and elegant interactive systems. The opportunities for system builders and entrepreneurs are substantial since only a fraction of the potential functions and market has been explored.

Like early photography or automobiles, computers are available only to people who devote extensive effort to mastering the technology. Harnessing the computer's power is a task for designers who understand the technology and are sensitive to human capacities and needs.

Human performance in the use of computer and information systems will remain a rapidly expanding research and development topic in the coming decades. This interdisciplinary journey of discovery combines the experimental methods and intellectual framework of cognitive psychology with the powerful and widely used tools developed from computer science. Contributions also accrue from educational psychologists, instructional designers, graphic artists, technical writers, and traditional areas of human factors or ergonomics.

Applications developers who apply human factors principles and processes are producing exciting interactive systems. Provocative ideas emerge in the pages of the numerous computer magazines, the shelves of the proliferating computer stores, and the menus of the expanding computer networks.

There is a growing interest in the human factors issues of computer use with systems (Figure 1.1) such as:

- text editors, word processors, and document formatters
- electronic mail and computer conferencing
- expert systems and science workstations
- electronic spreadsheets and decision support systems
- personal, home, and educational computing
- bibliographic and database systems

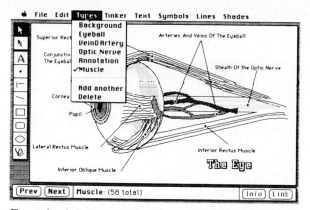

Figure 1.1a: Eye physiology explanation with pull-down menu in Business Filevision®. (Telos Software Products' Filevision®)

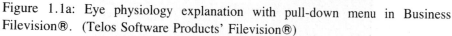
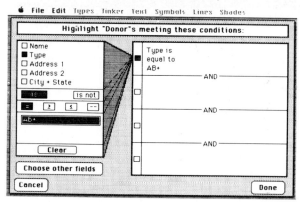

Figure 1.1b: Database search for blood donors. Written for American Red Cross by Stan Rifkin using Business Filevision®. (Telos Software Products' Filevision®)

Figure 1.1c: The Print Shop, personal computer graphics editing system for the Apple II computer. (The Print Shop is a trademark of Broderbund Software, Inc.)

5

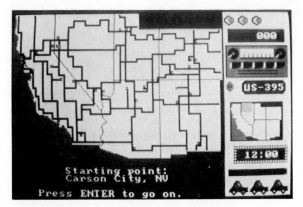

Figure 1.1d: Educational game, Road Rally USA, for Apple II and IBM PC computers. (Courtesy of Bantam Electronic Publishing)

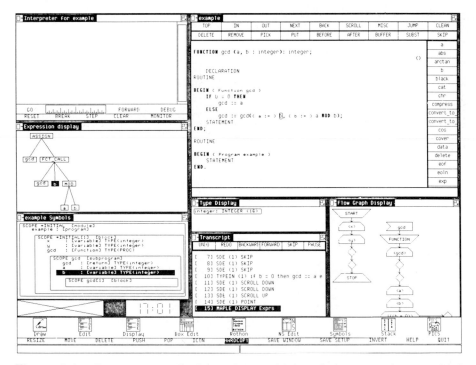

Figure 1.1e: Large-screen display using multiple windows to show multiple views of a program. (Courtesy of Steven Reiss, Brown University.)

Figure 1.1f: Air traffic controllers must take extensive training to become familiar with the tasks and the computer-related aspects of their job. They must work rapidly and reliably under stress, integrating knowledge procedures with information from computer displays, maps, handwritten notes, and voice contacts. (Courtesy of Raytheon Company, Lexington, MA)

- commercial systems, such as inventory, personnel, and reservations
- air traffic and electric utility control
- programming environments and tools
- computer-assisted design and manufacturing
- art and entertainment.

Practitioners and researchers in many fields are making vital contributions. Academic and industrial experimenters and theorists in computer science, psychology, and human factors are studying cognitive theories and models of human performance; novice versus expert user differences; individual differences, such as cognitive style, personality, or gender; and experimental methodologies for evaluation.

Software designers and researchers are exploring:

- menu selection techniques
- command, parametric, and query languages
- use of graphics, animation, and color

- direct manipulation
- natural language facilities
- error handling, messages, and prevention
- screen formatting.

Hardware developers and system builders are offering novel approaches to:

- keyboard design
- large, high resolution displays
- rapid response time
- fast display rates
- novel pointing devices
- speech input and output.

Developers with an orientation toward educational psychology, instructional design, and technical writing are coping with online tutorials, effective training and reference manuals, online manuals and assistance, classroom and individual training methods, and lectures versus experiential training.

Sociologists, philosophers, policy makers, and managers are dealing with organizational impact, computer anxiety, job redesign, retraining, and work-at-home, and long-term societal changes.

This is an exciting time for developers of interactive computer systems. The hardware and software foundations for the bridges and tunnels have been built. Now, the roadway can be laid and the stripes painted to make way for the heavy traffic of eager users.

1.2   PRIMARY DESIGN GOALS

Every designer wants to build a high quality interactive system that is admired by colleagues, celebrated by users, circulated widely, and frequently imitated. Appreciation comes, not from flamboyant promises or stylish advertising brochures, but from inherent quality features that are achieved by thoughtful planning, sensitivity to user needs, careful attention to detail in design and development, and diligent testing. Multiple design alternatives are raised for consideration, and the leading contenders subjected to further development and testing. Evaluation of designs refines the understanding of appropriateness for each choice.

Successful designers go beyond the vague notion of "user friendliness" and probe deeper than a checklist of subjective guidelines. They must have a thorough understanding of the diverse community of users and the tasks that must be accomplished. Moreover, they must have a deep commitment to serving the users.

Effective systems generate positive feelings of success, competence, and clarity in the user community. The users are not encumbered by the computer and can predict what happens with each of their actions. When an interactive system is well designed, it almost disappears, enabling the users to concentrate on their work or pleasure. Creating an environment in which tasks are carried out almost effortlessly, requires a great deal of hard work for the designer.

1.2.1 Proper functionality

The first step is to ascertain the necessary functionality—what tasks and subtasks must be carried out. The frequent tasks are easy to determine, but the occasional tasks, the exceptional tasks for emergency conditions, and the repair tasks to cope with errors in use of the system are more difficult to discover. Task analysis is central, because systems with inadequate functionality frustrate the user and are often rejected or underutilized (Bailey, 1982). If the functionality is inadequate, it doesn't matter how well the human interface is designed. Excessive functionality is also a danger, and probably the more common mistake of designers, because the clutter and complexity make implementation, maintenance, learning, and usage more difficult.

A related issue is compatibility with other computer and noncomputer systems that the users may be using. Slight differences among systems can lead to annoying and dangerous errors. Gross differences among systems require substantial retraining and burden the users. Incompatible storage formats, hardware, and software versions cause frustration and delay. Designers must decide whether the improvements they offer are enough to offset the disruption to the users.

1.2.2 Reliability, availability, security, and integrity

The second step is ensuring proper system reliability. The software architecture and hardware support must ensure high availability, ease of maintenance, and correct performance. If the system is not functioning or introduces errors, then it doesn't matter how well the human interface is designed. Attention must also be paid to ensuring privacy, security, and information integrity. Protection must be provided from unwarranted access, inadvertent destruction of data, or malicious tampering.

1.2.3 Schedules and budgets

The third step is to plan carefully to be on schedule and within budget. Delayed delivery or cost overruns can threaten a system because the confrontive political atmosphere in a company or the competitive market environment contains potentially overwhelming forces. If an in-house system is late, then other projects are affected, and the disruption may cause managers to choose an alternative. If a commercial system is too costly, customer resistance may emerge to prevent widespread acceptance, allowing competitors to capture the market.

Proper attention to human factors principles and testing often leads to reductions in the cost and time for development. A carefully tested design generates fewer changes during implementation and after release of new systems.

1.3   HUMAN FACTORS DESIGN GOALS

If adequate functionality has been chosen, reliability is ensured, and schedule plus budgetary planning is complete, then attention can be focused on the design and testing process. The multiple design alternatives must be evaluated for specific user communities and for specific benchmark sets of tasks. A clever design for one community of users may be inappropriate for another community. An efficient design for one class of tasks may be inefficient for another class.

1.3.1 The Library of Congress experience

The relativity of design played a central role in the evolution of information services at the Library of Congress. Two of the major uses of computer systems were cataloging new books and searching the online book catalog. Separate systems for these tasks were created that optimized the design for one task and made the complementary task difficult. It would be impossible to say which was better, because they were both fine systems, but serving different needs. It would be like asking whether the New York Philharmonic Orchestra was better than the New York Yankees baseball team.

The bibliographic search system, SCORPIO (Figure 1.2), was very successfully used by the staffs of the Library of Congress, the Congressional Research Service (CRS), and the Senate and House of Representatives. They could do bibliographic searching and used the same system to locate and read CRS reports, to view events recorded in the bill status system, and much more. The professional staff members took a three- to six-hour training course and then could use terminals in their office, where more experienced colleagues could help out with problems and where adequate consultants were usually available.

Then, in January 1981, the Library of Congress stopped entering new book information in the manual card catalogs, thus requiring the general public to use one of the eighteen terminals in the main reading room to locate new books. For even a computer-knowledgeable individual, learning to use the commands, understanding the cataloging rules, and formulating a search strategy would be a challenging task. The reference librarians claimed that they could teach a willing adult the basic features in fifteen minutes. But fifteen minutes per patron would overwhelm the staff and, more importantly, most people are not interested in investing

```
bgns lccc
TUESDAY, 12/10/85  09:23 A.M.
***LCCC- THE LIBRARY OF CONGRESS COMPUTERIZED CATALOG
        is now available for your search.
        The Term Index was updated on 12/09/85.

        To learn about the contents of this file, type
        SHOW FILE and transmit.
        For a description of available commands, type
        SHOW COMMANDS and transmit.

    LCCC lists books cataloged at LC beginning with language and date indicated
    ENGLISH  1973    OTHER EUROPEAN 1976-1977    NON-EUROPEAN 1978-1979

        New items are added every two weeks.  Some books listed are not
    actually in the Library.  You may search by author, subject heading,
    title, card number and partial call number.

    READY FOR NEW COMMAND:

show file

                                                    LAST UPDATED:10/26/83

TITLE: LIBRARY OF CONGRESS COMPUTERIZED CATALOG (LCCC)

                FOR INFORMATION ABOUT:       TYPE THIS:

                Contents of the file         XDESC
                Searching                    XSLCT
                Displaying                   XDSPL
                Limiting                     XLIMT


PAGE 1 OF 1. READY FOR NEW COMMAND OR NEW OPTION:

show commands

    Every step of a search requires a command.  With commands, you search
    a file for the information you want.  This list shows the available
    commands and their abbreviations.  Always put a space after a command.

    BEGIN    - BGNS    EXECUTE - EXEC    NEXT       - N      SELECT - S
    BROWSE   - B       EXPAND  - EXPN    PRINT      - P      SET
    COMBINE  - C       FIND    - F       RELEASE    - RLSE   SHOW
    DISPLAY  - D       KEEP              RETRIEVE   - R
    DROP               LIMIT   - LIMT    SAVE
    ENDS     - END     LIVT              SCAN

    For more information on a command, type: SHOW COMMAND command-name
              Example:   SHOW COMMAND BROWSE

    SHOW0002  Ready for new command:

browse sachs, marilyn

BRWS TERM FILE: LCCC ENTRY TERM:SACHS, MARILYN
B01 SACHS, LORRAINE P//(AUTH=1)
B02 SACHS, LOTHAR//(AUTH=5)
B03 SACHS, MARGARET//(AUTH=2)
B04 SACHS, MARIANNE//(AUTH=1)
B05 SACHS, MARIE//(AUTH=1)
B06+SACHS, MARILYN//(AUTH=24)
B07 SACHS, MARVIN L//(AUTH=1)
B08 SACHS, MARY PARMLY (KQUES)//(AUTH=1)
B09 SACHS, MAURICE--//(AUTH=3; INDX=4)
```

Figure 1.2: The Library of Congress's SCORPIO system can access many databases, including the Library of Congress Computerized Card Catalog. User-typed commands are underscored. Abbreviated forms of the commands are

```
B10 SACHS, MENDEL//(AUTH=6)
B11 SACHS, MICHAEL//(AUTH=3)
B12 SACHS, MICHAEL H//(AUTH=1)
B13 SACHS, MICHAEL JEHIEL//(AUTH=1)
B14 SACHS, MICHAEL L//(AUTH=2)
B15 SACHS, MOSHE Y//(AUTH=3)
B16 SACHS, MURRAY//(AUTH=2)
B17 SACHS, MURRAY B//(AUTH=1)
B18 SACHS, NELLY--//(AUTH=9; INDX=8)
B19 SACHS, NORMAN//(AUTH=1)
B20 SACHS, PAUL JOSEPH--//(AUTH=2; INDX=1)
READY FOR NEW COMMAND (FOR NEXT PAGE, XMIT ONLY):
select b06

SET   1          24: SLCT AUTH/SACHS, MARILYN



READY FOR NEW COMMAND:
display 1

FILE:LCCC; TITLE/LINE--SET 1                              ITEMS 1-7 OF 24

1. 66-8827:Sachs, Marilyn.  Amy and Laura.  Garden City, N.Y, Doubleday, 1966
    .   189 p, illus, 22 cm.
    LC CALL NUMBER: PZ7.S1187 Am
2. ac68-1610: (IS NOT IN FILE OR FILE IS NOT CURRENTLY AVAILABLE).
3. 68-11813:Sachs, Marilyn.  Veronica Ganz.  Garden City, N.Y, Doubleday,
    1968.  156 p, illus, 22 cm.
    LC CALL NUMBER: PZ7.S1187 Ve
4. 69-12226:Sachs, Marilyn.  Peter and Veronica.  Garden City, N.Y, Doubleday,
    1969.  174 p, illus, 22 cm.
    LC CALL NUMBER: PZ7.S1187 Pe
5. 72-89128:Sachs, Marilyn.  The truth about Mary Rose.  Garden City, N.Y,
    Doubleday, 1973.  159 p, illus, 22 cm.
    LC CALL NUMBER: PZ7.S1187 Tr
6. 73-79708:Sachs, Marilyn.  A pocket full of seeds.  Garden City, N.Y,
    Doubleday, 1973.  137 p, illus, 22 cm.
    LC CALL NUMBER: PZ7.S1187 Po
7. 73-116250:Sachs, Marilyn.  Marv.  Garden City, N.Y, Doubleday, 1970.  160
    p, illus, 22 cm.
    LC CALL NUMBER: PZ7.S1187 Mar
READY FOR NEW COMMAND OR NEW ITEM NBR (FOR NEXT PAGE, XMIT ONLY):


FILE:LCCC; TITLE/LINE--SET 1                              ITEMS 8-13 OF 24

8. 74-10932:Sachs, Marilyn.  Matt's mitt.  Garden City, N.Y, Doubleday, 1975.
32 p, col. illus, 20 x 24 cm.
    LC CALL NUMBER: PZ7.S1187 Mat
9. 74-33688:Sachs, Marilyn.  Dorrie's book /.  Garden City, N.Y, Doubleday,
    1975.  136 p, ill., 22 cm.
    LC CALL NUMBER: PZ7.S1187 Do
10. 76-7697:Sachs, Marilyn.  A December tale /.  Garden City, N.Y, Doubleday,
    c1976.  87 p., 22 cm.
    LC CALL NUMBER: PZ7.S1187 De
11. 76-56330:Sachs, Marilyn.  Fleet-footed Florence /.  Garden City, N.Y,
    Doubleday, c1981.  48 p, ill., 27 cm.
    LC CALL NUMBER: PZ7.S1187 Fl
12. 76-157621:Sachs, Marilyn.  The bears' house.  Garden City, N.Y, Doubleday,
    1971.  81 p, illus, 22 cm.
    LC CALL NUMBER: PZ7.S1187 Be
13. 77-25606:Sachs, Marilyn.  A secret friend /.  Garden City, N.Y, Doubleday,
    c1978.  111 p., 22 cm.
    LC CALL NUMBER: PZ7.S1187 Se
READY FOR NEW COMMAND OR NEW ITEM NBR (FOR NEXT PAGE, XMIT ONLY):
```

available. This search shows a browse command for the author "sachs, marilyn", selection of the set of books by the author, and a display of two pages of the brief card catalog entries.

even fifteen minutes in learning to use a computer system. Library patrons have work to do and often perceive the computer as an intrusion or interference with their work. The SCORPIO system that worked so well for one community of users was inappropriate for this new community.

The system designers revised the online messages to provide more supportive and constructive feedback, offered extensive online tutorial material, and began to explore the use of menu selection approaches for the novice users. In short, a new community of users demanded substantial redesign of the human interface.

1.3.2 Measurable human factors goals

Once a determination has been made of the user community and the benchmark set of tasks, then the human factors goals can be examined. For each user and each task, precise measurable objectives guide the designer, evaluator, purchaser, or manager. These five measurable human factors are central to evaluation:

- *time to learn*. How long does it take for typical members of the target community to learn how to use the commands relevant to a set of tasks?

- *speed of performance*. How long does it take to carry out the benchmark set of tasks?

- *rate of errors by users*. How many and what kinds of errors are made in carrying out the benchmark set of tasks? Although time to make and correct errors might be incorporated into the speed of performance, error making is such a critical component of system usage that it deserves extensive study.

- *subjective satisfaction*. How much did users like using aspects of the system? This can be ascertained by interview or written surveys that include satisfaction scales and space for free-form comments.

- *retention over time.* How well do users maintain their knowledge after an hour, a day, or a week? Retention may be closely linked to time to learn; frequency of use plays an important role.

Every designer would like to succeed in every category, but there are often forced tradeoffs. If lengthy learning is permitted, then task performance speed may be reduced by use of complex abbreviations and shortcuts. If the rate of errors is to be kept extremely low, then speed of performance may have to be sacrificed. In some applications, subjective satisfaction may be the key determinant of success, while in others short learning times or rapid performance may be paramount. Project managers and designers must be aware of the tradeoffs and make their choices explicit and public. Requirements documents and marketing brochures should make clear which goals are primary.

After multiple design alternatives are raised, the leading possibilities should be reviewed by designers and users. Paper mockups are useful, but online protoype verions of the system create a more realistic environment for review. After extensive testing of design goals, the final design should be written down. The user manual and the technical reference manual can be written before the implementation to provide another review and perspective on the design. Then the implementation can be carried out; this should be a modest effort if the design is complete and precise. Finally, the acceptance test certifies that the delivered system meets the goals of the designers and customers. The development and evaluation process is described in greater detail in Chapter 10.

1.4   MOTIVATIONS FOR HUMAN FACTORS IN DESIGN

The enormous interest in human factors of interactive systems arises from the complementary recognition of how poorly designed many current systems are and the genuine desire to create elegant systems that effectively serve the users. This increased concern emanates from four primary sources: life-critical systems; industrial/commercial uses; office, home, and entertainment applications; and exploratory, creative, and expert systems.

1.4.1 Life-critical systems

Life-critical systems include air traffic, nuclear reactor, or power utility control; medical intensive care or surgery; manned spacecraft; police or fire dispatch; and military operations. In these applications, high costs are expected, but they should yield high reliability and effectiveness. Lengthy training periods may be acceptable to obtain rapid, error-free performance. Subjective satisfaction is less of an issue because the users are well motivated and paid. Retention is obtained by frequent use of common functions and practice sessions for emergency actions.

1.4.2 Industrial/commercial uses

Typical industrial/commercial uses include banking, insurance, order entry, inventory management, airline, hotel, or car rental, utility billing, credit card management, and point-of-sales terminals. In these cases, costs shape many judgments; lower cost may be preferred even if there is some sacrifice in reliability. Operator training time is expensive, so ease of learning is important. The tradeoffs for speed of performance and error rates are decided by the total cost over the system's lifetime. Subjective satisfaction is of modest importance, and, again, retention is obtained by frequent use. Speed of performance becomes central for most of these applications because of the high volume of transactions. Trimming 10 percent off the mean transaction time means 10 percent fewer operators, 10 percent fewer terminal workstations, and possibly a 10 percent reduction in hardware costs. A 1982 study by a leading motel chain reported that a 1-second reduction in the 150-second mean time per reservation would save $40,000 per year.

1.4.3 Office, home, and entertainment applications

The rapid expansion of office, home, and entertainment applications is the third source of interest in human factors. Personal computing applications include word processing, automated teller machines, video games, educational packages, information retrieval, electronic mail, computer conferencing, and small business management. For these systems, ease of learning, low error rates, and subjective satisfaction are paramount because use is frequently discretionary and competition is fierce. If the users can't succeed quickly, they will abandon the use of a computer or try a competing package. In cases where use is intermittent, retention is important, so online assistance becomes very important.

Choosing the right functionality is difficult. Novices are best served by a constrained simple set of actions; but as experience increases, so does the desire for more functionality. A layered or level structured design is one approach to graceful evolution from novice to expert usage. As users gain competence, their desire for more rapid performance and extensive functionality grows. Low cost is important because of lively competition, but extensive design and testing can be amortized over the large number of users.

1.4.4 Exploratory, creative, and expert systems

An increasing fraction of computer use is to support human intellectual and creative enterprises. Electronic encyclopedias, database browsing, statistical hypothesis formation, business decision-making, and graphical presentation of scientific simulation results are examples of exploratory environments. Creative environments include writer's toolkits or workbenches, architecture or automobile design systems, artist or programmer workstations, and music composing systems. Expert systems aid knowledgeable users in medical diagnosis, financial decision-making, oil-well log data analysis, satellite orbit maneuvering, and military advising.

In these systems, the users may be knowledgeable in the task domain but novices in the underlying computer concepts. Their motivation is often high, but so are their expectations. Benchmark tasks are more difficult to describe because of the exploratory nature of these applications. Usage can range from occasional to frequent. In short, it is difficult to design and evaluate these systems.

1.5   ACCOMMODATING HUMAN DIVERSITY

The remarkable diversity of human abilities, backgrounds, motivations, personalities, and workstyles challenges interactive system designers. A right-handed male designer with computer training and a desire for rapid interaction using densely packed screens may have a hard time developing a successful workstation for left-handed women artists with a more leisurely and free-form work style. Understanding the physical, intellectual, and personality differences among users is vital.

1.5.1 Physical abilities and physical workplaces

Accommodating the diverse human motor and perceptual abilities is a challenge to every designer. Fortunately, there is much literature reporting research and experience from design projects with automobiles, aircraft, typewriters, home appliances, and so on that can be applied to the design of interactive computer systems (Van Cott & Kinkade, 1972; Tichauer, 1978). In a sense, the presence of a computer is only incidental to the design; human needs and abilities are the guiding forces.

Basic data about human dimensions comes from research in anthropometry (Dreyfus, 1967; Roebuck et al., 1975). Thousands of measures of hundreds of features of males and females, children and adults, Europeans and Asians, underweight and overweight, and tall and short individuals provide data to construct means and 5 to 95 percentile groupings. Head, mouth, nose, neck, shoulder, chest, arm, hand, finger, leg, and foot sizes have been carefully catalogued for a variety of populations. The great diversity in these static measures reminds us that there can be no image of an "average" user, and that compromises must be made or multiple versions of a system must be constructed.

The choice of keyboard design parameters (see Section 6.2) evolved to meet the physical abilities of users in terms of distance between keys, size of keys, and required pressure. People with especially large or small hands may have difficulty in using standard keyboards, but a substantial fraction of the population is well served by one design. On the other hand, since screen brightness preferences vary substantially, designers must provide a knob to enable user control. Chair height and back controls or display screen angle controls also allow individual adjustment. When a single design cannot accommodate a large fraction of the population is well served by one design. When a single design cannot accommodate a large fraction of the population, then multiple versions or adjustment controls are helpful.

Physical measures of static human dimensions are not enough. Measures of dynamic actions, such as reach distances while seated, speed of finger-presses, or strength of lifting, are also necessary (Bailey, 1982; Kantowitz & Sorkin, 1983).

Since so much of work is related to perception, designers need to be aware of the ranges of human perceptual abilities (Schiff, 1980). Vision is especially important and has been thoroughly studied (Wickens, 1984). Concerns about perception include:

- response time to varying visual stimuli
- capacity to identify an object in context
- reading text
- color vision and deficiencies
- spectral range and sensitivity
- peripheral vision
- flicker sensitivity
- contrast sensitivity
- low-light or night vision and adaptation times
- bright light vision
- motion sensitivity
- 3-D vision and depth perception
- appropriate viewing distances and angles

- impact of glare
- visual fatigue
- eye disorders, damage, and diseases
- corrective lenses.

Other senses are also important: touch for keyboard or touchscreen entry and hearing for audible cues, tones, and speech input/output (see Chapter 6). Pain, temperature sensitivity, taste, and smell are rarely used for input/output in interactive systems, but there is room for imaginative applications.

These physical abilities influence elements of the interactive system design. They also play a prominent role in the design of the workplace or workstation (or playstation). The American National Standard for Human Factors Engineering of Visual Display Workstations lists these concerns:

- work-surface height
- clearance under work surface for legs
- posture
- adjustable heights and angles for chairs and work-surfaces
- seating depth and angle
- back rest height and lumbar support
- armrests, foot rests, and palm rests
- work-surface width and depth
- chair castors.

Work-place design is important in ensuring job satisfaction, high performance, and low error rates. Incorrect table heights, uncomfortable chairs, or inadequate space to place documents can substantially impede work. The Standard document also addresses such issues as:

- illumination levels (200 to 500 lux)
- glare minimization (antiglare coatings, baffles, positioning)

- luminance balance
- equipment reflectivity
- acoustic noise
- vibration
- air temperature, humidity, and movement
- equipment temperature.

The most elegant screen design or command language can be compromised by a noisy environment or a stuffy room that eventually lowers performance, raises error rates, and discourages even motivated users.

Another physical environment question involves room layout and the sociology of human interaction. With multiple workstations for a classroom or office, alternate layouts can encourage or limit social interaction, cooperative work, and assistance with problems. Because users can often quickly help each other with minor problems, there may be an advantage to layouts that group several terminals closely together or that enable supervisors or teachers to view all screens at once from behind. On the other hand, programmers or reservations clerks may appreciate the quiet and privacy of their own workspace.

The physical design of workplaces is often discussed under the term *ergonomics*. Anthropometry, sociology, industrial psychology, organizational behavior, and even anthropology may offer useful insights in this area.

1.5.2 Cognitive and perceptual abilities

A vital foundation for interactive systems designers is an understanding of the cognitive and perceptual abilities of the users (Kantowitz & Sorkin, 1983; Wickens, 1984). The human ability to interpret sensory input rapidly and to initiate complex actions makes modern computer systems possible. In milliseconds, users recognize slight changes on their displays and begin to issue a stream of commands. The journal

Ergonomics Abstracts offers this classification of human "central processes":

- short-term memory
- long-term memory, learning
- problem solving
- decision making
- attention and set
- search and scanning
- time perception

and this set of "factors affecting perceptual motor performance":

- arousal and vigilance
- fatigue
- perceptual (mental) load
- knowledge of results
- monotony and boredom
- sensory deprivation
- sleep deprivation
- anxiety and fear
- isolation
- aging
- drugs and alcohol
- circadian rhythm.

These vital issues are not discussed in depth in this book, but they have a profound influence on the design of most interactive systems. The term *intelligence* is not included in this list, because of its controversial nature and the difficulty of measuring pure intelligence.

In any application, background experience and knowledge in the task domain and the computer domain (see Section 2.2) play a key role in learning and performance. Task or computer skill inventories can be helpful in predicting performance.

1.5.3 Personality differences

Some people dislike or are made anxious by computers; others are attracted to or are eager to use computers. Often, members of these divergent groups disapprove or are suspicious of members of the other community. Even people who enjoy using computers may have very different preferences for interaction styles, pace of interaction, graphics versus tabular presentations, dense versus sparse data presentation, step-by-step work versus all-at-once work, and so on.

These differences are important. A clearer understanding of personality and cognitive styles can be helpful in designing systems for a specific community of users.

A fundamental difference is between men and women, but no clear pattern of preferences has been documented. It is often pointed out that the preponderance of video arcade game players are young males, and so are the designers. Women will play Pacman and its variants, plus a few other games such as Donkey Kong or Centipede. One female commentator labeled Pacman "oral aggressive" and could appreciate the female style of play. Other women have identified the compulsive cleaning up of every dot as an attraction. These games are distinguished by their less violent action and sound track. Also, the board is fully visible, characters with personality appear, softer color patterns are used, and there is a sense of closure and completeness. Can these informal conjectures be converted to measurable criteria and then validated? Can designers become aware of the needs and desires of women and create video games that will be more attractive to women than to men?

Turning from games to office automation, the largely male designers may not realize the impact on women users when the command names require the users to KILL a file or ABORT a program. These and other unfortunate mismatches between the user interface and the user might be avoided by more thoughtful attention to individual differences among users. Unfortunately, there is no simple taxonomy of user personality types. An increasingly popular technique is to use the Myers-Briggs Type Indicator (MBTI) (Shneiderman, 1980) that is based on Carl Jung's theories of personality types. Jung conjectured that there were four dichotomies:

- *extroversion/introversion:* extroverts focus on external stimuli and like variety and action. Introverts prefer familiar patterns, rely on their inner ideas, and work contentedly alone.
- *sensing/intuition*: sensing types are attracted to established routines, are good at precise work, and enjoy applying known skills. Intuitive types like solving new problems and discovering new relations but dislike taking time for precision.
- *perceptive/judging*: perceptive types like to learn about new situations but may have trouble making decisions. Judging types like to make a careful plan and seek to carry it through even if new facts may change the goal.
- *feeling/thinking*: feeling types are aware of other people's feelings, seek to please others, and relate well to most people. Thinking people are unemotional, may treat people impersonally, and like to put things in logical order.

The theory behind the MBTI provides portraits of the relationships between professions and personality types and between people of different personality types. It has been applied to testing user communities and providing guidance to designers.

Many hundreds of psychological scales have been developed, including:

- risk taking/risk avoidance
- internal/external locus of control
- reflective/implusive
- convergent/divergent
- high/low anxiety
- high/low tolerance for stress
- high/low tolerance for ambiguity
- field dependence/independence
- assertive/passive
- high/low motivation

- high/low compulsiveness
- left/right brain orientation.

As designers explore computer applications for home, education, art, music, and entertainment, it seems clear that greater attention to personality types will be a great benefit.

Another perspective on individual differences has to do with cultural, ethnic, racial, or linguistic background. It seems obvious that users who were raised learning Japanese or Chinese will scan a screen in a different manner than users who were raised learning English or French. Users from cultures that have a more reflective style may prefer different interfaces than users from cultures with a more action-oriented style. Very little is known about computer users from different cultures.

1.6 INFORMATION RESOURCES

There is an enormous volume of literature in computer science, psychology, human factors, and other areas that might be relevant; some sources are especially rich. Two prominent journals that focus on questions of human performance with computers are:

Behaviour and Information Technology
International Journal of Man-Machine Studies

Other journals regularly carry articles of interest:

ACM Computing Surveys
Communications of the ACM
ACM Transactions on Office Information Systems
Ergonomics
Human Factors
IBM Systems Journal
IEEE Computer
IEEE Computer Graphics and Applications
IEEE Transactions on Systems, Man, and Cybernetics
Journal of Applied Psychology

The Association for Computing Machinery (ACM) has a Special Interest Group on Computer & Human Interaction (SIGCHI) that publishes a quarterly newsletter and holds regularly scheduled conferences. The American Society for Information Science (ASIS) has a Special Interest Group on User Online Interaction (SIGUOI) that publishes a quarterly newsletter and participates by organizing sessions at the annual ASIS convention. The International Federation for Information Processing has a working group WG 6.3 on human computer interaction that publishes a quarterly newsletter called *Interact*. The Human Factors Society also has a Computer Systems Group with a quarterly newsletter.

Conferences, such as the ones held by the ACM, IEEE, ASIS, National Computer Conference Board of AFIPS, Human Factors Society, and IFIP, often have relevant papers presented and published in the proceedings.

The list of guidelines documents and books at the end of this chapter is a starting point to the large and growing literature in this area. Gerald Weinberg's 1971 book, *The Psychology of Computer Programming*, is a continuing inspiration to thinking about how people interact with computers. James Martin provided a thoughtful and useful survey of interactive systems in his 1973 book, *Design of Man-Computer Dialogues*. My 1980 book, *Software Psychology: Human Factors in Computer and Information Systems* (Shneiderman, 1980), attempts to promote the use of controlled experimental techniques and the reductionist scientific method. Rubinstein and Hersh, *The Human Factor: Designing Computer Systems for People* (1984), offers an appealing introduction and many useful guidelines. The parade of books has been more regular in recent years, with more books appearing monthly.

1.7 THREE GOALS

Clear goals are useful, not only for system development, but also for educational and professional enterprises. Workers in human-computer interaction have three primary goals: (1) influencing academic and industrial researchers, (2) providing tools, techniques, and knowledge for commercial systems implementors, and (3) raising the consciousness of the general public.

1.7.1 Influencing academic and industrial researchers

Early research in human-computer interaction was done largely by introspection and intuition, but this approach suffered from lack of validity, generality, and precision. The techniques of controlled psychologically oriented experimentation can lead to a deeper understanding of the fundamental principles of human interaction with computers.

The reductionist scientific method has this basic outline:

- lucid statement of a testable hypothesis
- manipulation of a small number of independent variables
- measurement of specific dependent variables
- careful selection and assignment of subjects
- control for biasing
- application of statistical tests.

Materials and methods must be tested by pilot experiments and results must be validated by replication in variant situations.

Of course, the highly developed and structured method of controlled experimentation has its weaknesses. It may be difficult or expensive to find adequate subjects, and laboratory-like conditions may distort the situation so much that the conclusions have no application. When results for large groups of subjects are arrived at by statistical aggregation, extremely good or poor performance by individuals may be overlooked. Furthermore, anecdotal evidence or individual insights may be given too little emphasis because of the authoritative impact of statistics.

In spite of these concerns, controlled experimentation provides a productive basis that can be modified to suit the situation. Anecdotal

experiences and subjective reactions should be recorded, thinking aloud
or protocol approaches should be employed, field or case studies with
extensive performance data collection should be carried out, and the
individual insights of researchers, designers, and experimental participants
should be captured.

Within computer science, there is a growing awareness of the need for
greater attention to human factors issues. Researchers who propose new
programming language or data structure constructs are more aware of the
need to match human cognitive skills. Developers of advanced graphics
systems, robots, computer-assisted design systems, or artificial
intelligence applications increasingly recognize that the success of their
proposals depends on the construction of a suitable human interface.
Researchers in these and other areas are making efforts to understand and
measure human performance.

In psychology, there is a grand opportunity to apply the knowledge and
techniques of traditional psychology and such recent subfields as
cognitive psychology to the study of human-computer interaction.
Psychologists are investigating human problem-solving with computers to
gain an understanding of cognitive processes and memory structures. The
benefit to psychology is great, but psychologists also have the golden
opportunity to influence dramatically an important and widely used
technology.

Researchers in information science, business and management,
education, sociology, and in other disciplines are benefitting and
contributing by their study of human-computer interaction. There are so
many fruitful directions for research that any list can only be a
provocative starting point. Here are several potential research directions:

1. *Reducing anxiety and fear of computer usage*. Although
computers are widely used, they still serve only a fraction
of the population. Many people avoid using such
computerized devices as bank terminals or word processors
because they are anxious or even fearful of breaking the
computer, making an embarrassing mistake, or being
incapable of succeeding. Interviews with nonusers of
computers would help determine the sources of this anxiety

and lead to design guidelines to alleviate the fear. Tests could be run to determine the effectiveness of redesign of systems and of improved training procedures.

2. *Graceful evolution.* Although novices may begin with menu selection, they may wish to evolve to faster or more powerful facilities. Methods for smoothing the transition from novice to intermittent knowledgeable user to frequent expert could be studied. The differing needs of novice and experts in prompting, error messages, online assistance, display complexity, locus of control, pacing, and informative feedback all need investigation.

3. *Menu selection.* Menu selection is offered on many systems for novice users, but there is little data to support design guidelines. The content, number, placement, and phrasing of menu choices could be studied with attention to titling of menu frames, effectiveness of instructions, availability of type-ahead strategies or menu shortcuts, backtracking, and graphic design to show hierarchical organization (Chapter 3). Much progress could be made in this area with modest experimental efforts. An opportunity also exists to investigate software architectures for menu management systems that dramatically reduce the amount of code while permitting end users to develop and maintain their own menus.

4. *Command languages.* This traditional style of interaction is another excellent candidate for research to understand the importance of consistency in syntactic format, congruent pairings of commands, hierarchical structure, choice of familiar command names and parameters, suitable abbreviated forms, automatic command completion, and interference from multiple routes to accomplish the same task (Chapter 4). The impact of response time and novel hardware display and entry devices on the command set is another worthy topic.

5. *Direct manipulation.* Visual interfaces in which the user operates on a representation of the objects of interest are

extremely attractive in computer-assisted design and manufacturing, video games, database query, electronic spreadsheets, display editors, and so on (Chapter 5). Empirical studies would refine our understanding of what is an appropriate analogical representation and the role of rapid, incremental, reversible operations.

6. *Hardware devices.* The plethora of keyboards, displays, and pointing devices presents opportunities and challenges to system designers (Chapter 6). The heated discussions about the relative merits of lightpens, touchscreens, the mouse, voice input, function keys, or high resolution displays could be resolved through extensive experimentation with multiple tasks and user communities. Underlying issues include speed, accuracy, fatigue, error correction, and subjective satisfaction.

7. *Response time, display rates, and operator productivity.* Many computer professionals believe in the simple principle that faster is always better. Evidence from several IBM studies and other sources suggests that programmers are more productive when system response time is kept within the 1-second range or even faster (Chapter 7). On the other hand, isolated studies have shown that in some business decision-making tasks, computer-assisted instruction, complex order entry, and introductory sessions with novices, rapid performance leads to poorer learning, less effective decisions, higher error rates, and occasionally decreased satisfaction. A thorough study of multiple tasks with a variety of user communities would shed light on which situations would be improved with shorter response times or faster display rates. Understanding psychological issues of short-term memory load, decision-making strategies, and information overload would help in preparing design guidelines for system implementers.

8. *Online assistance.* Although many systems offer some help or tutorial information online, there is limited understanding of what constitutes effective design for novices, intermittent

knowledgeable users, and experts (Chapter 9). The role of these aids and online user consultants could be studied to assess their impact on user success and satisfaction. The utility of a separate display or window for assistance or tutorials should be contrasted with the common approach of entering a separate subsystem that displaces the current display of work.

9. *Specification and implementation of interaction.* Most interactive systems are constructed with traditional procedural languages, but novel techniques could reduce implementation times by an order of magnitude. Specification languages and dialog management systems have been proposed and some commercial packages are available. Advanced research on tools to aid interactive systems designers and implementers might have substantial payoff in reducing costs and improving quality.

1.7.2 Tools and techniques for systems developers

Commercial systems managers, designers, and implementers are emerging from benign neglect of human engineering. There is a great thirst for knowledge, software tools, design guidelines, and testing techniques. New dialog management software packages provide support for rapid prototyping and system development while aiding design consistency and simplifying evolutionary refinement.

Guidelines documents are being written for general audiences and for specific applications. Many projects are taking the productive route of writing their own guidelines specifically tied to the problems of their application environment. These guidelines are constructed from experimental results, experience with actual systems, and some knowledgeable guesswork.

Pilot, iterative, and acceptance testing is appropriate during system development. Once the initial system is available, refinements can be made on the basis of online or printed surveys, individual or group interviews, or more controlled empirical tests of novel strategies (see Chapter 10).

Feedback from users during the development process and for evolutionary refinement can provide useful insights and guidance. An online electronic mail facility allows users to send comments directly to the designers. Online user consultants and telephone "hot line" workers can provide not only prompt assistance but also much information about the activities and problems of the user community.

1.7.3 Raising the consciousness of the general public

The media is so filled with stories about computers that raising public consciousness may seem unnecessary. In fact, however, many people are uncomfortable with computers. When they do finally use a bank terminal or word processor, they may be fearful of making mistakes, anxious about damaging the equipment, worried about feeling incompetent, or threatened by the computer "being smarter than I am." These fears are generated, in part, by poor designs that have complex commands, hostile and vague error messages, tortuous and unfamiliar sequences of actions, or a deceptive anthropomorphic style.

One of my goals is to encourage users to translate their internal fears into action. Instead of feeling guilty when they get a message like SYNTAX ERROR, they should express their anger at the system designer who was so inconsiderate and thoughtless. Instead of feeling inadequate or foolish because they can't remember a complex sequence of commands, they should complain to the designer who didn't provide a more convenient mechanism or should seek another product that does.

As examples of successful and satisfying systems become more visible, the crude designs will appear increasingly archaic and become commercial failures. As designers improve interactive systems, some of these fears will recede and the positive experience of competence, mastery, and satisfaction will flow in. Then the image of computer scientists and data processing professionals will change in the public's view. The machine-oriented and technical image will give way to one of personal warmth, sensitivity, and concern for the user.

1.8   PRACTITIONER'S SUMMARY

If you are designing an interactive system, a thorough task analysis can provide the information for a proper functional design. Attention should be paid to reliability, availability, security, integrity, and the administrative issues of schedules and budgets. As design alternatives are proposed, they can be evaluated for their role in providing short learning times, rapid task performance, low error rates, high user satisfaction, and ease of retention. As the design is refined and implemented, you can test for accomplishment of these goals with pilot studies and acceptance tests. The rapidly growing literature and sets of design guidelines may be of assistance in developing your project standards and practices.

1.9   RESEARCHER'S AGENDA

The opportunities for researchers are unlimited (National Research Council, 1983). There are so many interesting, important, and do-able projects that it may be hard to choose a direction. Begin by understanding the practical background of the problem; consider the fundamental psychological principles of human behavior; and propose a lucid, testable hypothesis. Then consider the appropriate research methodology, collect the data, and analyze the results. Finally, return to the practical application area with specific recommendations and refine your model of human performance. Each chapter of this book ends with specific research proposals.

GUIDELINES DOCUMENTS

Banks, William W., Gertman, David I., and Petersen, Rohn J., Human Engineering Design Considerations for Cathode Ray Tube-Generated Displays, NUREG/CR–2496, U. S. Nuclear Regulatory Commission, Washington, DC, (April 1982).

—Detailed information and extensive references emphasizing perceptual issues and physical devices. It cites other guidelines documents and contains extensive appendices with experimental data about human visual performance.

Banks, William W., Gilmore, Walter E., Blackman, Harold S., and Gertman, David I., Human Engineering Design Considerations for Cathode Ray Tube-Generated Displays: Volume II, NUREG/CR–3003, U. S. Nuclear Regulatory Commission, Washington, DC, (July 1983).

—Thoughtful set of screen design guidelines with examples from graphic displays. Covers screen layout, symbol selection, and font design.

Engel, Stephen E. and Granda, Richard E., Guidelines for Man/Display Interfaces, Technical Report TR 00.2720, IBM, Poughkeepsie, N.Y. (December 1975).

—An early and influential document that is the basis for several of the other guidelines documents.

Smith, Sid L. and Mosier, Jane N., Design Guidelines for User-System Interface Software Report ESD-TR–84–190, The MITRE Corporation, Bedford, MA 01730, Electronic Systems Division, (September 1984), 448 pages. Available from National Technical Information Service, Springfield, VA.

—This thorough document, which is regularly revised, begins with a good discussion of human factors issues in design and then covers data entry, data display, and sequence control. Guidelines are offered with comments, examples, exceptions, and references.

Human Engineering Design Criteria for Military Systems, Equipment and Facilities, Military Standard MIL-STD–1472C, U.S. Government Printing Office, (May 2, 1981).

—Almost three hundred pages, largely on traditional ergonometric or anthropometric issues, but this latest edition has a ten-page addition on "Personnel-computer interface."

Human Factors Review of Electric Power Dispatch Control Centers: Volume 2: Detailed Survey Results, Prepared by Lockheed Missiles and Space Company for the Electric Power Research Institute, 3412 Hillview Avenue, Palo Alto, CA 94304, 1981.

—Well-researched and thoghful comments about electric power control centers, with many generally applicable conclusions.

Human Factors of Work Stations with Display Terminals, IBM Document G320–6102–1, San Jose, CA 95193 (1979).

—Informative and readable discussion about terminal design.

Human Factors Engineering Criteria for Information Processing Systems, Lockheed Missiles and Space Company, Inc., Sunnyvale, CA, 94086 (September 1982).

—Well-written and precise guidelines with numerous examples on display format, data entry, language and coding, interaction sequence control, error handling procedures, online guidance, and color displays.

Guidelines for Control Room Reviews, NUREG–0700, U. S. Nuclear Regulatory Commission, Washington, DC, (September 1981).

—Detailed checklist and issues for evaluating nuclear reactor control rooms, with many items of interest to other control room or workstation designers.

BOOKS

Bailey, Robert W., *Human Performance Engineering: A Guide for System Designers*, Prentice-Hall, Inc., Englewood Cliffs, NJ, (1982), 656 pages.

Bolt, Richard A., *The Human Interface: Where People and Computers Meet*, Lifelong Learning Publications, Belmont, CA, (1984), 113 pages.

Cakir, A., Hart, D. J., and Stewart, T. F. M., *Visual Display Terminals: A Manual Covering Ergonomics, Workplace Design, Health and Safety, Task Organization*, John Wiley and Sons, New York, NY, (1980).

Card, Stuart K., Moran, Thomas P., and Newell, Allen, *The Psychology of Human-Computer Interaction*, Lawrence Erlbaum Associates, Hillsdale, NJ, (1983), 469 pages.

Dreyfus, W., *The Measure of Man: Human Factors in Design*, (Second Edition), Whitney Library of Design, New York, NY, (1967).

Foley, James D., and Van Dam, Andries, *Fundamentals of Interactive Computer Graphics*, Addison-Wesley Publishing Co., Reading, MA, (1982).

Galitz, Wilbert O., *Human Factors in Office Automation*, Life Office Management Association, 100 Colony Square, Atlanta, GA 30361, (1980), 237 pages.

Galitz, Wilbert O., *Handbook of Screen Format Design*, Q. E. D. Information Sciences, Inc., 180 Linden Street, Wellesley, MA 02181, (1981), 212 pages.

Heckel, Paul, *The Elements of Friendly Software Design*, Warner Books, New York, (1982), 205 pages.

Hiltz, Starr Roxanne, *Online Communities: A Case Study of the Office of the Future*, Ablex Publishing Corporation, Norwood, NJ, (1984), 261 pages.

Hiltz, Starr Roxanne, and Turoff, Murray, *The Network Nation: Human Communication via Computer*, Addison-Wesley Publishing Co., Reading, MA, (1978).

Kantowitz, Barry H., and Sorkin, Robert D., *Human Factors: Understanding People-System Relationships*, John Wiley & Sons, New York, NY, (1983), 699 pages.

Martin, James, *Design of Man-Computer Dialogues*, Prentice-Hall, Inc., Englewood Cliffs, NJ, (1973), 509 pages.

McCormick, Ernest J., and Sanders, M. S., *Human Factors in Engineering and Design*, McGraw-Hill Book Company, New York, NY, (1982).

Mehlmann, Marilyn, *When People Use Computers: An Approach to Developing an Interface*, Prentice-Hall, Inc., Englewood Cliffs, NJ, (1981).

National Research Council, Committee on Human Factors, *Research Needs for Human Factors*, National Academy Press, Washington, DC, (1983), 160 pages.

Roebuck, J. A., Kroemer, K. H. E., and Thomson, W. G., *Engineering Anthropometry Methods*, Wiley, New York, NY, (1975).

Rubinstein, Richard, and Hersh, Harry, *The Human Factor: Designing Computer Systems for People*, Digital Press, Maynard, MA, (1984), 249 pages.

Schiff, W., *Perception: An Applied Approach*, Houghton Mifflin, New York, NY, (1980).

Sheridan, T. B., and Ferrel, W. R., *Man-Machine Systems: Information, Control, and Decision Models of Human Performance*, MIT Press, Cambridge, MA, (1974).

Shneiderman, Ben, *Software Psychology: Human Factors in Computer and Information Systems*, Little, Brown and Co., Boston, MA, (1980), 320 pages.

Tichauer, E. R., *The Mechanical Basis of Ergonomics*, John Wiley and Sons, New York, NY, (1978).

Van Cott, H. P., and Kinkade, R. G., (Editors), *Human Engineering Guide to Equipment Design*, U. S. Superintendent of Documents, Washington, DC, (1972).

Weinberg, Gerald M., *The Psychology of Computer Programming*, Van Nostrand Reinhold, New York, NY, (1971), 288 pages.

Wickens, Christopher D., *Engineering Psychology and Human Performance*, Charles E. Merrill Publishing Co., Columbus, OH, (1984), 513 pages.

COLLECTIONS

Proceedings Human Factors in Computer Systems, Available from Washington, DC, Chapter of the ACM (March 15–17, 1982), 399 pages.

Proceedings ACM CHI '83 Conference: Human Factors in Computing Systems, Available from ACM Order Dept., P. O. Box 64145, Baltimore, MD 21264, (1983), 295 pages.

Proceedings ACM CHI '85 Conference: Human Factors in Computing Systems, Available from ACM Order Dept., P. O. Box 64145, Baltimore, MD 21264, (1985), 231 pages.

Proceedings ACM CHI '86 Conference: Human Factors in Computing

Systems, Available from ACM Order Dept., P. O. Box 64145, Baltimore, MD 21264, (1986).

INTERACT '84: First IFIP International Conference on Human-Computer Interaction, North-Holland Publishing Co., Amsterdam, (September 1984).

Badre, Albert, and Shneiderman, Ben (Editors), *Directions in Human-Computer Interaction,* Ablex Publishing Co., Norwood, NJ, (1980), 225 pages.

Blaser, A., and Zoeppritz, M. (Editors), *Enduser Systems and Their Human Factors,* Springer-Verlag, Berlin, (1983), 138 pages.

Coombs, M. J. and Alty, J. L. (Editors), *Computing Skills and the User Interface,* Academic Press, New York, NY, (1981).

Curtis, Bill, *Tutorial: Human Factors in Software Development,* IEEE Computer Society, Los Angeles, CA, (1981), 641 pages.

Guedj, R. A., Hagen, P. J. W., Hopgood, F. R. A., Tucker, H. A., and Duce, D. A. (Editors), *Methodology of Interaction,* North-Holland Publishing Co., Amsterdam, (1980), 408 pages.

Hartson, H. Rex, *Advances in Human-Computer Interaction: Volume 1,* Ablex Publishing Corporation, Norwood, NJ, (1985), 290 pages.

Larson, James A. (Editor), *Tutorial: End User Facilities in the 1980's,* IEEE Computer Society Press (EHO 198–2), New York, NY, (1982).

Monk, Andrew (Editor), *Fundamentals of Human-Computer Interaction,* Academic Press, London, (1984), 293 pages.

Muckler, Frederick A., *Human Factors Review: 1984,* The Human Factors Society, Inc., Santa Monica, CA, (1984), 345 pages.

Norman, Donald A., and Draper, Stephen W. (Editors), *User Centered System Design: New Perspectives on Human-Computer Interaction,* Lawrence Erlbaum Associates, Hillsdale, NJ, (1986).

Salvendy, Gavriel (Editor), *Human-Computer Interaction,* Proceedings of the First USA-Japan Conference on Human-Computer Interaction, August 18–20, 1984, Elsevier Science Publishers, Amsterdam, (1984), 470 pages.

Shackel, Brian (Editor), *Man-Computer Interaction: Human Factors Aspects of Computers and People.* Sijthoff and Noordhoof Publishers, The Netherlands, (1981), 560 pages.

Sime, M., and Coombs, M. (Editors), *Designing for Human-Computer Communication*, Academic Press, New York, NY, (1983), 332 pages.

Smith, H.T., and Green, T. R. G. (Editors), *Human Interaction with Computers*, Academic Press, New York, NY, (1980).

Thomas, John C., and Schneider, Michael L. (Editors), *Human Factors in Computer Systems*, Ablex Publishing Corporation, Norwood, NJ, (1984), 276 pages.

Vassiliou, Yannis (Editor), *Human Factors and Interactive Computer Systems*, Ablex Publishing Corporation, Norwood, NJ, (1984), 287 pages.

CHAPTER 2

THEORIES, PRINCIPLES, AND GUIDELINES

We want principles,
not only developed,—the work of the closet,—
but applied; which is the work of life.

Horace Mann, *Thoughts*, 1867

2.1 INTRODUCTION

Successful designers of interactive systems know that they can and must go beyond intuitive judgments made hastily when a design problem emerges. Fortunately, guidance for designers is beginning to emerge in the form of:

- high-level theories or models
- middle-level principles
- specific and practical guidelines and
- strategies for testing.

The theories or models offer a way to organize the design process, whereas the middle-level principles are useful in weighing alternatives. The practical guidelines provide helpful reminders of rules uncovered by previous designers. Early prototype evaluation encourages exploration and enables iterative design to correct inappropriate decisions. Acceptance testing is the trial-by-fire to determine whether a system is ready for distribution; its presence may be seen as a challenge, but it is also a gift to designers since it establishes clear measures of success.

In many contemporary systems, there is a grand opportunity to improve the human interface. The cluttered and multiple displays, complex and tedious procedures, inadequate command languages, inconsistent sequences of actions, and insufficient informative feedback can generate debilitating stress and anxiety that lead to poor performance, frequent minor and occasional serious errors, and job dissatisfaction.

This chapter begins with a review of theories, concentrating on the syntactic/semantic model. Section 2.3 then deals with frequency of use, task profiles, and interaction styles. Eight principles of interaction are offered in Section 2.4. Strategies for preventing errors are described in Section 2.5. Specific guidelines for data entry and display appear in Sections 2.6 and 2.7. Testing strategies are presented in Section 2.8 and covered in detail in Chapter 10. Section 2.9 attempts to deal with the difficult question of the balance between automation and human control.

2.2   A HIGH-LEVEL THEORY: SYNTACTIC/
SEMANTIC MODEL OF USER KNOWLEDGE

Distinctions between syntax and semantics have long been made by compiler writers who sought to separate out the parsing of input text from the operations that were invoked by the text. Interactive system designers can benefit from a syntactic/semantic model of user knowledge. In outline, this explanatory model suggests that users have syntactic knowledge about device-dependent details and semantic knowledge about concepts. The semantic knowledge is separated into task concepts (objects and actions) and computer concepts (objects and actions) (see Figure 2.1). A person can be an expert in the computer concepts, but a novice in the task, and vice versa.

The syntactic/semantic model of user behavior was originated to describe programming (Shneiderman & Mayer, 1979; Shneiderman,

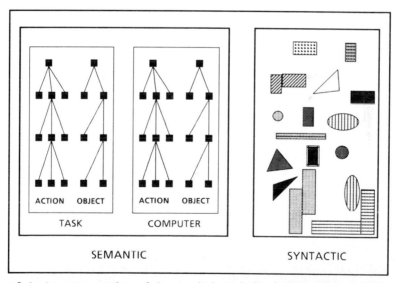

Figure 2.1: A representation of the user's knowledge in long-term memory. The syntactic knowledge is varied, device dependent, acquired by rote memorization, and easily forgotten. The semantic knowledge is separated into the computer and task domains. Within these domains, knowledge is divided into actions and objects. Semantic knowledge is structured, device independent, acquired by meaningful learning, and stable in memory.

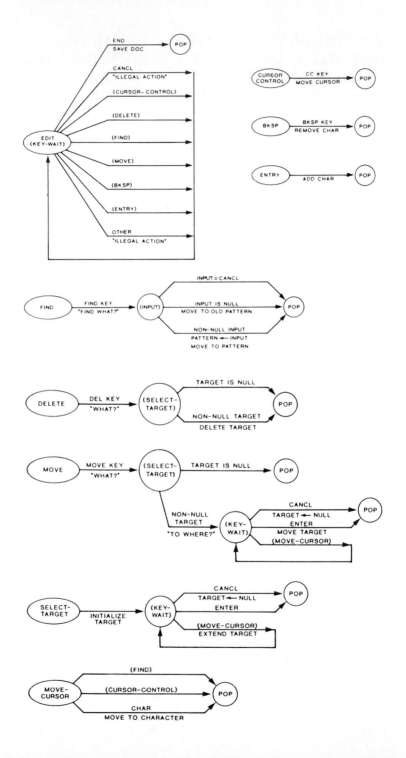

libsys

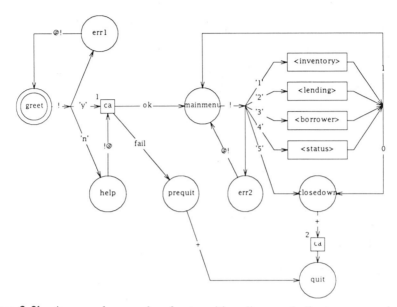

Figure 2.2b: A second example of a transition diagram indicates user actions on the arrows and computer responses or states in the boxes and circles. (Source: Transition   diagram   editor   from   Interactive   Development)

1980) and has been applied to database manipulation facilities (Shneiderman, 1981) as well as to direct manipulation (Shneiderman, 1983).

Other strategies for modeling interactive system usage involve transition diagrams (Kieras & Polson, 1985) (Figure 2.2). These diagrams are helpful during design, for instruction, and as a predictor of learning time, performance time, and errors.

Figure 2.2a: This generalized transition network for the Displaywriter shows the sequence of permissible actions. If the users begin at the EDIT state and issue a FIND command, they follow the paths in the FIND subdiagram. (Kieras and Polson, "An approach to the formal analysis of user complexity," *International Journal of Man-Machine Studies 22* [1985], 365–394. Used by permission of Academic Press Inc. [London] Limited.)

Other theories include the four-level approach of Foley and Van Dam (1982):

1. The highest level is the conceptual model or the user's mental model of the interactive system. Two conceptual models for text editing are line editors and screen editors.

2. The semantic level describes the meanings conveyed by the user's command input and by the computer's output display.

3. The syntax level defines how the units (words) that convey semantics are assembled into a complete sentence that instructs the computer to perform a certain task.

4. The lexical level deals with device dependencies and the precise mechanism by which a user specifies the syntax.

Card, Moran, and Newell (1980, 1983) proposed the GOMS (goals, operators, methods, and selection rules) model and the keystroke-level model. They postulated that users formulate goals and subgoals that are achieved by methods or procedures for accomplishing each goal. The operators are "elementary perceptual, motor, or cognitive acts, whose execution is necessary to change any aspect of the user's mental state or to affect the task environment" (Card, Moran & Newell, 1983: 144). The selection rules are the control structure for choosing among the several methods available for accomplishing a goal.

The keystroke-level model is an attempt to predict performance times for error-free expert performance of tasks by summing up the time for keystroking, pointing, homing, drawing, thinking, and waiting for the system to respond. These models concentrate on expert users and error-free performance, with less emphasis on learning, problem-solving, error handling, subjective satisfaction, and retention.

Kieras and Polson (1985) used production rules to describe the conditions and actions in an interactive text editor. The number and complexity of production rules gave accurate predictions of learning and performance times for five text editing operations: insert, delete, copy, move, and transpose.

Norman (1984) offers a stages and levels model of human-computer interaction. The four stages of an interaction are:

1. Forming an intention: internal mental characterization of a goal.
2. Selecting an action: review possible actions and select most appropriate.
3. Executing the action: carry out the action using the computer.
4. Evaluating the outcome: check the results of executing the action.

Norman's levels correspond roughly to Foley and Van Dam's separation of concerns, that is, the user forms a conceptual intention, reformulates it into the semantics of several commands, and eventually produces the action of moving the mouse to select a point on the screen. Norman describes how errors often occur as intentions are reformulated to lower levels.

Refinements to these theories and more detailed models will undoubtedly emerge. There is a need for many theories about the multiple aspects of interactive systems. The next section expands on the syntactic/semantic model of user behavior.

2.2.1 Syntactic knowledge

When using a computer system, users must maintain a profusion of device-dependent details in their human memory. These low-level syntactic details include the knowledge of which key erases a character (delete, backspace, CTRL-H, rightmost mouse button, or ESCAPE), what command inserts a new line after the third line of a text file (CTRL-I, INSERT key, I3, I 3, or 3I), which icon to click on to scroll text forward, which abbreviations are permissible, and which of the numbered function keys produces the previous screen.

The learning, use, and retention of this knowledge is hampered by two problems. First, these details vary across systems in an unpredictable manner.   Second, acquiring syntactic knowledge is often a struggle because the arbitrariness of these minor design features greatly reduces the effectiveness of paired-associate learning.   Rote memorization requires repeated rehearsals to reach competence, and retention over time is poor unless the knowledge is frequently applied.   Syntactic knowledge is usually conveyed by example and repeated usage.   Formal notations, such as Backus-Naur Form, are useful for knowledgeable computer scientists but confusing to most users.

A further problem with syntactic knowledge, in some cases, is the difficulty of providing a hierarchical structure or even a modular structure to cope with the complexity.   For example, how is a user to remember these details of using an electronic mail system: Press RETURN to terminate a paragraph, CTRL-D to terminate a letter, Q to quit the electronic mail subsystem, and logout to terminate the session.   The knowledgeable computer user understands these four forms of termination as commands in the context of the full system, but the novice may be confused by four seemingly similar situations that have radically different syntactic forms.

A final difficulty is that syntactic knowledge is system dependent.   A user who switches from one machine to another may face different keyboard layouts, commands, function key usage, and sequences of actions.   To be sure, there may be some overlap.   For example, arithmetic expressions might be the same in two languages; but unfortunately, small differences can be the most annoying.   One system uses K to keep a file and another uses K to kill the file, or S to save versus S to send.

Expert frequent users can overcome these difficulties and they are less troubled by syntactic knowledge problems.   Novices and intermittent users, however, are especially troubled by syntactic irregularities.   Their burden can be lightened by using menus (see Chapter 3), a reduction in the arbitrariness of the keypresses, use of consistent patterns of commands, meaningful command names and labels on keys, and fewer details that must be memorized (see Chapter 4).

In summary, syntactic knowledge is arbitrary, system dependent, and ill-structured.   It must be acquired by rote memorization and repetition.   Unless it is regularly used, it fades from memory.

2.2.2 Semantic knowledge—computer concepts

Semantic knowledge in human long-term memory has two components: computer concepts and task concepts (Figure 2.1). Semantic knowledge has a hierarchical structure ranging from low-level actions to middle-level strategies to high-level goals (Shneiderman & Mayer, 1979; Soloway et al., 1982; Card et al., 1983). This presentation enhances the earlier syntactic/semantic model and other models by decoupling computer concepts from task concepts. This enhancement accommodates the two most common forms of expertness: task experts who may be novice computer users and computer user experts who may be new to a task. Different training materials are suggested for task or computer experts. Novices in both domains need yet a third form of training.

Semantic knowledge is conveyed by showing examples of use, offering a general theory or pattern, relating the concepts to previous knowledge by analogy, describing a concrete or abstract model, and by indicating examples of incorrect use. There is an attraction to showing incorrect use to indicate clearly the bounds of a concept, but there is also a danger since the learner may confuse correct and incorrect use. Pictures are often helpful in showing the relationships among semantic knowledge concepts.

Computer concepts include *objects* and *actions* at high and low levels. For example, a central set of *computer object* concepts deals with storage. Users come to understand the high-level concept that computers store information. The concept of stored information can be refined into the object concepts of the directory and the files of information. In turn, the directory object is refined into a set of directory entries that each have a name, length, date of creation, owner, access control, and so on. Each file is an object that has a lower level structure consisting of lines, fields, characters, pointers, binary numbers, and so on.

The *computer actions* are also decomposable into lower level actions. The high-level actions or goals, such as creating a text data file, may require load, insertion, and save actions. The mid-level action of saving a file is refined into the actions of storing a file and backup file on one of many disks, of applying access control rights, of overwriting previous versions, of assigning a name to the file, and so on. Then, there are many low-level details about permissible file types or sizes, error conditions such as shortage of storage space, or responses to hardware or software errors. Finally, there is the low-level action of issuing a specific command, carried out by the syntactic detail of pressing the RETURN key.

These computer concepts were designed by highly trained experts in the hope that they were logical, or at least "made sense" to the designers. Unfortunately, the logic may be a very complex product of underlying hardware, software, or performance constraints, or it might be just poorly chosen. Users are often confronted with computer concepts that they have great difficulty absorbing; but hopefully, designers are improving and computer literacy training is raising knowledge levels. For example, the action of terminating a command by pressing RETURN is more and more widely known, even by nonprogrammers.

Users can learn computer concepts by seeing a demonstration of commands, hearing an explanation of features, or by trial and error. A common practice is to create a model of concepts, either abstract, concrete, or analogical, to convey the computer action. For example, with the file-saving concept, an instructor might draw a picture of a disk drive and a directory to show where the file goes and how the directory references the file. Alternatively, the instructor might make a library analogy and describe how the card catalog acts as a directory for books saved in the library.

Since semantic knowledge about computer concepts has a logical structure and since it can be anchored to familiar concepts, this knowledge is expected to be relatively stable in memory. If you remember the high-level concept about saving a file, you will be able to conclude that the file must have a name, a size, and a storage location. The linkage to other objects and the potential for a visual presentation support the memorability of this knowledge.

These computer concepts were once novel and known to only a small number of scientists, engineers, and data processing professionals. Now, these concepts are taught at the elementary school level, argued over during coffee breaks in the office, and exchanged in the aisles of corporate jets. When educators talk of computer literacy, part of their plans cover these computer concepts.

In summary, the user must acquire semantic knowledge about computer concepts. These concepts are hierarchically organized, acquired by meaningful learning or analogy, independent of the syntactic details, hopefully transferable across different computer systems, and relatively stable in memory. Computer concepts can be usefully sorted out into objects and actions.

2.2.3 Semantic knowledge—task concepts

The primary way for people to deal with large and complex problems is to decompose them into several smaller problems in a hierarchical manner until each subproblem is manageable. Thus, a book is decomposed into the task objects of chapters, the chapters into sections, the sections into paragraphs, and the paragraphs into sentences. Each sentence is approximately one unit of thought for both the author and the reader. Most designed objects have similar decompositions: computer programs, buildings, television sets, cities, paintings, and plays, for example. Some objects are more neatly and easily decomposed than others; some objects are easier to understand than others.

Similarly, task actions can be decomposed into smaller actions. A construction plan can be reduced to a series of steps; a baseball game has innings, outs, and pitches; and creating a business letter involves creating an address, date, addressee, body, signature, and so on.

In writing a business letter with a computer, the user has to integrate smoothly the three forms of knowledge. The user must have the high-level concept of writing (task action) a letter (task object), recognize that the letter will be stored as a file (computer object), and know the details of the save command (computer action and syntactic knowledge). The user must be fluent with the middle-level concept of composing a sentence and must recognize the mechanism for beginning, writing, and ending a sentence. Finally, the user must know the proper low-level details of spelling each word (task), comprehend the motion of the cursor on the screen (computer concept), and know which keys to press for each letter (syntactic knowledge).

Integrating the three forms of knowledge, the objects and actions, and the multiple levels of semantic knowledge is a substantial challenge that takes great motivation and concentration. Learning materials that facilitate the acquisition of this knowledge are difficult to design, especially because of the diversity of background knowledge and motivation levels of typical learners. The syntactic/semantic model of user knowledge can provide a guide to educational designers by highlighting the different kinds of knowledge that users need to acquire (see Chapter 9).

Designers of interactive systems can apply the syntactic/semantic model to systematize their efforts. Where possible, the semantics of the task objects should be made explicit and the user's task actions should be laid out clearly. Then the computer objects and actions can be identified, leaving the syntactic details for the end. In this way, designs appear to be more comprehensible to users and more independent of specific hardware.

2.3   PRINCIPLES: RECOGNIZE THE DIVERSITY

The remarkable diversity of human abilities, backgrounds, cognitive styles, and personalities challenges the interactive system designer. When multiplied by the wide range of situations, tasks, and frequencies of use, the set of possibilities becomes enormous. The designer can respond by choosing from a spectrum of interaction styles.

A preschooler playing a graphic computer game is a long way from a reference librarian doing bibliographic searches for anxious and hurried patrons. Similarly, a professional programmer using a new operating system is a long way from a highly trained and experienced air traffic controller. Finally, a student learning from a computer-assisted instruction lesson is a long way from a hotel reservations clerk serving customers for many hours a day.

These sketches of users highlight the differences in background knowledge, training in the use of the system, frequency of use, goals of the user, and the impact of a user error. No single design could satisfy all these users and situations, so before beginning a design, the characterization of the users and the situation must be precise and complete.

2.3.1 Usage profiles

"Know the user" was the first principle in Hansen's (1971) list of user engineering principles. It's a simple idea, but a difficult goal and, unfortunately, an often undervalued goal. No one would argue against this principle, but many designers assume that they understand the users and their tasks. Successful designers are aware that other people learn, think, and solve problems in very different ways (see Section 1.5). Some users really do have an easier time with tables than graphs, with words instead of numbers, with slower rather than faster display rates, or with a rigid structure rather than an open-ended form.

It is difficult for most designers to know whether boolean expressions are too difficult a concept for library patrons at a junior college, fourth graders learning programming, or professional electric power utility controllers.

All design should begin with an understanding of the intended users, including profiles of their age, sex, physical abilities, education, cultural or ethnic background, training, motivation, goals, and personality. There are often several communities of users for a system, so the design effort is multiplied. In addition to these profiles, users might be tested for such skills as comprehension of boolean expressions, knowledge of set theory, fluency in a foreign language, or skills in human relationships. Other tests might cover such task-specific abilities as knowledge of airport city codes, stockbrokerage terminology, insurance claims concepts, or map icons.

The process of knowing the user is never ending, because there is so much to know and because the users keep changing. Every step in understanding the users and in recognizing them as individuals whose outlook is different from the designer's own is likely to be a step closer to a successful design.

For example, a generic separation into novice, knowledgeable intermittent, and frequent users might lead to these differing design goals:

Novice users: This community is assumed to have no syntactic knowledge about using the system and probably little semantic knowledge of computer issues. They may even have shallow knowledge of the task and, worse still, they may arrive with anxiety about using computers that inhibits learning. Overcoming these limitations is a serious challenge to the designer. Restricting vocabulary to a small number of familiar, consistently used terms is essential to begin developing the user's knowledge of the system. The number of possibilities should be kept small and the novice user should be able to carry out a few simple tasks to build confidence, reduce anxiety, and gain positive reinforcement from success. Informative feedback about the accomplishment of each task is helpful, and constructive, specific error messages should be provided when errors do occur. Carefully designed paper manuals and step-by-step online tutorials may be effective.

Knowledgeable intermittent users: Many people will be knowledgeable but intermittent users of a variety of systems. They will be able to maintain the semantic knowledge of the task and the computer concepts, but they will have difficulty maintaining the syntactic knowledge. The burden of memory will be lightened by simple and consistent structure in the command language, menus, terminology, and so on, and by the use of recognition rather than recall. Consistent sequences of actions, meaningful messages, and frequent prompts will all help to assure knowledgeable intermittent users that they are performing their tasks properly. Protection from danger is necessary to support relaxed exploration of features or attempts to invoke a partially forgotten command. These users will benefit from online help screens to fill in missing pieces of syntactic or computer semantic knowledge. Well-organized reference manuals will also be useful.

Frequent users: The knowledgeable "power" users are thoroughly familiar with the syntactic and semantic aspects of the system and seek to get their work done rapidly. They demand rapid response times, brief and less distracting feedback, and the capacity to carry out actions with just a few keystrokes or selections. When a sequence of three or four commands is performed regularly, the frequent user is eager to create a macro or other abbreviated form to reduce the number of steps. Strings of commands, shortcuts through menus, abbreviations, and other accelerators are requirements.

These characteristics of these three classes of usage must be refined for each environment. Designing for one class is easy; designing for several is much more difficult.

When multiple usage classes must be accommodated in one system, the basic strategy is to permit a level-structured (some times called layered or spiral approach) to learning. Novices can be taught a minimal subset of objects and actions with which to get started. After gaining confidence from hands-on experience, the users can progress to ever greater levels of semantic concepts and the accompanying syntax. The learning plan should be governed by the progress through the task semantics. For users with strong knowledge of the task and computer semantics, rapid presentation of syntactic details is possible.

For example, novice users of a bibliographic search system might be taught author or title searches first, followed by subject searches that require boolean combinations of queries. The progress is governed by the task domain, not by commands.

The level-structured approach must be carried out not only in the design of the software, but also in the user manuals, help screens, error messages, and tutorials.

Another approach to accommodating different usage classes is to permit user control of the density of informative feedback that the system provides. Novices want more informative feedback to confirm their actions, whereas frequent users want less distracting feedback. Similarly, it seems that frequent users prefer more densely packed displays than do novices. Finally, the pace of interaction may be varied from slow for novices to fast for frequent users.

2.3.2 Task profiles

After carefully drawing the user profile, the tasks must be identified. Task analysis has a long, but mixed history (Bailey, 1982). Every designer would agree that the set of tasks must be decided on before design can proceed, but too often the task analysis is done informally or implicitly. If implementers find that another command can be added, the designer is often tempted to include the command in the hope that some users will find it helpful. Design or implementation convenience should not dictate system functionality or command features.

High-level task actions can be decomposed into multiple middle-level task actions that can be further refined into atomic actions that the user executes with a single command, menu selection, and so on. Choosing the most appropriate set of atomic actions is a difficult task. If the atomic actions are too small, the users will become frustrated by the large number of actions necessary to accomplish a higher level task. If the atomic actions are too large and elaborate, the users will need many such actions with special options, or they will not be able to get exactly what they want from the system.

The relative task frequencies will be important in shaping a set of commands, a menu tree, etc. Frequently performed tasks should be simple and quick to carry out, even at the expense of lengthening some infrequent tasks.

Relative frequency of use is one of the bases for making architectural design decisions. For example, in a text editor:

1. Frequent actions might be performed by special keys, such as the four cursor arrows, the INSERT, and the DELETE key.

2. Intermediate frequency actions might be performed by a single letter plus the CTRL key, or by a selection from a pull-down menu. Examples include underscore, center, indent, subscript, or superscript.

3. Less frequent actions might require going to a command mode and typing the command name; for example, MOVE BLOCK or SPELLING CHECK.

4. Still less frequent actions or complex actions might require going through a sequence of menu selections or form fill-ins; for example, to change the printing format or to revise network protocol parameters.

A matrix of users and tasks can help sort out these issues (Figure 2.3). In each box, the designer can put a check mark to indicate that this user carries out this task. A more precise analysis would lead to inclusion of frequencies instead of simple check marks.

FREQUENCY OF TASK BY JOB TITLE

	Task				
	Query by Patient	Update Data	Query across Patients	Add Relations	Evaluate System
Job title					
Nurses	.14	.11			
Physicians	.06	.04			
Supervisors	.01	.01	.04		
Appointments personnel	.26				
Medical record					
maintainers	.07	.04	.04	.01	
Clinical researchers			.08		
Database programmers			.02	.02	.05

Figure 2.3: Hypothetical frequency of use data for a medical clinic information system. Queries by patient from appointments personnel are the highest frequency task.

2.3.3 Interaction styles

When the task analysis is complete and the semantics of the task objects and actions can be identified, the designer can choose from these primary interaction styles (Table 2.1):

- menu selection
- form fill-in
- command language
- natural language
- direct manipulation.

Chapters 3 through 5 explore these styles in detail, but first a comparative overview sets the stage.

INTERACTION STYLE

ADVANTAGES	DISADVANTAGES
Menu selection	
shortens learning	danger of many menus
reduces keystrokes	may slow frequent users
structures decision-making	consumes screen space
permits use of dialog management tools	requires rapid display rate
easy to support error handling	
Form fill-in	
simplifies data entry	consumes screen space
requires modest training	
assistance is convenient	
permits use of form management tools	
Command language	
flexibilty	poor error handling
appeals to "power" users	requires substantial training and
supports user initiative	memorization
convenient for creating user defined macros	
Natural language	
relieves burden of learning syntax	requires clarification dialog
	may require more keystrokes
	may not show context
	unpredictable
Direct Manipulation	
visually presents task concepts	may be hard to program
easy to learn	may require graphics display
easy to retain	and pointing devices
errors can be avoided	
encourages exploration	
high subjective satisfaction	

Table 2.1: Advantages and disadvantages of the five primary interaction styles.

Menu selection: The users read a list of items, select the one most appropriate to their task, apply the syntax to indicate their selection, confirm the choice, initiate the action, and observe the effect. If the terminology and meaning of the items are understandable and distinct, then the users can accomplish their task with little learning or memorization and few keystrokes. The greatest benefit may be that there is a clear structure to decision making since only a few choices are presented at a time. This interaction style is appropriate for novice and intermittent users and can be appealing to frequent users if the display and selection mechanisms are very rapid.

For designers, menu selection systems require careful task analysis to ensure that all functions are supported conveniently and that terminology is chosen carefully and used consistently. Dialog management tools to support menu selection are an enormous benefit in ensuring consistent screen design, validating completeness, and supporting maintenance.

Form fill-in: When data entry is required, menu selection usually becomes cumbersome, and form fill-in (also called fill-in-the-blanks) is appropriate. Users see a display of related fields, move a cursor among the fields, and enter data where desired. With the form fill-in interaction style, the users must understand the field labels, know the permissible values and the data entry method, and be capable of responding to error messages. Since knowledge of the keyboard, the labels, and permissible fields is required, some training may be necessary. This interaction style is most appropriate for knowledgeable intermittent users or frequent users. Chapter 3 provides a thorough treatment of menus and form fill-in.

Command language: For frequent users, command languages provide a strong feeling of locus of control and initiative. The users learn the syntax and can often express complex possibilities rapidly, without having to read distracting prompts. However, error rates are typically high, training is necessary, and retention may be poor. Error messages and online assistance are hard to provide because of the diversity of possibilities plus the complexity of mapping from tasks to computer concepts and syntax. Command languages and lengthier query or programming languages are the domain of the expert frequent users who often derive great satisfaction from mastering a complex set of semantics and syntax. Chapter 4 covers command languages and natural language interaction in depth.

Natural language: The hope that computers will respond properly to arbitrary natural language sentences or phrases engages many researchers and system developers, in spite of limited success thus far. Natural language interaction usually provides little context for issuing the next command, frequently requires "clarification dialog," and may be slower and more cumbersome than the alternatives. Still, where users are knowledgeable about a task domain whose scope is limited and where intermittent use inhibits command language training, there exist opportunities for natural language interfaces.

Direct manipulation: When a clever designer can create a visual representation of the world of action, the users' tasks can be greatly simplified by allowing direct manipulation of the objects of interest. Examples include display editors, LOTUS 1–2–3, air traffic control systems, and video games. By pointing at visual representations of objects and actions, users can rapidly carry out tasks and immediately observe the results. Keyboard entry of commands or menu choices is replaced by cursor motion devices to select from a visible set of objects and actions. Direct manipulation is appealing to novices, easy to remember for intermittent users, and with careful design it can be rapid for frequent users. Chapter 5 describes direct manipulation and its applications.

Blending several interaction styles may be appropriate when the required tasks and users are diverse. Commands may lead the user to a form fill-in where data entry is required or menus may be used to control a direct manipulation environment when a suitable visualization of actions cannot be found.

2.4   EIGHT GOLDEN RULES OF DIALOG DESIGN

Later chapters cover constructive guidance for design of menu selection, command languages, and so on. This section presents underlying principles of design that are applicable in most interactive systems. These underlying principles of interface design include:

1. *Strive for consistency.* This principle is the most frequently violated one, and yet the easiest one to repair and avoid. Consistent sequences of actions should be required in similar situations, identical terminology should be used in prompts, menus, and help screens, and consistent commands should be employed throughout. Exceptions, such as nonprinting of passwords or no abbreviation of the DELETE command, should be comprehensible and limited in number.

2. *Enable frequent users to use shortcuts.* As the frequency of use increases, so does the desire to reduce the number of interactions and increase the pace of interaction. Abbreviations, special keys, hidden commands, and macro facilities are appreciated by frequent knowledgeable users. Shorter response times and faster display rates are other attractions for frequent users.

3. *Offer informative feedback.* For every operator action there should be some system feedback. For frequent and minor actions the response can be very modest, whereas for infrequent and major actions the response should be more substantial. Visual presentation of the objects of interest provides a convenient environment for explicitly showing changes (see direct manipulation in Chapter 5).

4. *Design dialogs to yield closure.* Sequences of actions should be organized into groups with a beginning, middle, and end. The informative feedback at the completion of a group of actions gives the operator the satisfaction of accomplishment, a sense of relief, the signal to drop contingency plans and options from his/her mind, and an indication that the way is clear to prepare for the next group of actions.

5. *Offer simple error handling.* As much as possible, design the system so the user cannot make a serious error. If an error is made, try to have the system detect the error and offer simple, comprehensible mechanisms for handling the error. The user should not have to retype the entire

command, but only need repair the faulty part. Erroneous commands should leave the system state unchanged or give instructions about restoring the system.

6. *Permit easy reversal of actions.* As much as possible, actions should be reversible. This relieves anxiety since the operator knows that errors can be undone, and encourages exploration of unfamiliar options. The units of reversibility may be a single action, a data entry, or a complete group of actions.

7. *Support internal locus of control.* Experienced operators strongly desire the sense that they are in charge of the system and that the system responds to their actions. Surprising system actions, tedious sequences of data entries, incapacity or difficulty in obtaining necessary information, and the inability to produce the action they want all build anxiety and dissatisfaction. Gaines (1981) captured part of this principle with his rule to "avoid acausality" and his encouragement to make users the initiators of actions rather than the responders.

8. *Reduce short-term memory load.* The limitation of human information processing in short-term memory ("seven plus or minus two chunks") requires that displays be kept simple, multiple page displays be consolidated, frequent window motion be reduced, and sufficient training time be permitted for codes, mnemonics, and sequences of actions. Where appropriate, online access to command syntax forms, abbreviations, codes, and other information should be provided.

These underlying principles must be interpreted, refined, and extended for each environment. The principles presented in the ensuing sections focus on increasing the productivity of users by providing simplified data entry procedures, comprehensible displays, and rapid informative feedback that increase feelings of competence, mastery, and control over the system.

2.5 PREVENTING ERRORS

Users of text editors, database query facilities, air traffic control systems, and other interactive systems make mistakes far more frequently than might be expected. Ledgard et al. (1980) found that novice users of a 15-command subset of a text editor made mistakes in 19 percent of their commands. Experienced users made mistakes in 10 percent of their commands. In a more demanding environment, Card et al. (1980) reported that experienced professional users of text editors and operating systems made mistakes or used inefficient strategies in 31 percent of the tasks assigned to them. Barber (1979) found that professional workers in a challenging decision-making job made errors in 7 percent to 46 percent of their transactions, depending on the response time of the computer system. Other studies are beginning to reveal the magnitude of the problem and the loss of productivity due to user errors.

One direction for reducing the loss in productivity due to errors is to improve the error messages provided by the computer system. Shneiderman (1982) reported on five experiments in which changes to error messages led to improved success at repairing the errors, lower error rates, and increased subjective satisfaction. Superior error messages were more specific, positive in tone, and constructive (telling the user what to do, rather than merely reporting the problem). Rather than vague and hostile messages, such as SYNTAX ERROR or ILLEGAL DATA, designers were encouraged to use informative messages, such as UNMATCHED LEFT PARENTHESIS or MENU CHOICES ARE IN THE RANGE OF 1 TO 6.

But improved error messages are only helpful medicine. A more effective approach is to prevent the errors from occurring. This goal is more attainable than it may seem in many systems.

The first step is to understand the nature of errors. One perspective is that people make mistakes or "slips" (Norman, 1983) that can be avoided by organizing screens and menus functionally, designing commands or menu choices to be distinctive, and making it difficult for users to do irreversible actions. Norman offers other guidelines such as "do not have modes," offer feedback about the state of the system, and design for consistency of commands. Norman's analysis provides practical examples and a useful theory. The ensuing sections refine his analysis and describe three specific techniques for reducing errors by ensuring complete and correct actions: correct matching pairs, complete sequences, and correct commands.

2.5.1 Techniques for ensuring correct actions

Correct matching pairs. This is a common problem with many manifestations and several simple prevention strategies. Examples include the failure to provide:

- the right parenthesis to close an open left parenthesis.

  If a bibliographic search system allowed boolean expressions such as

  ```
  COMPUTERS AND (PSYCHOLOGY OR SOCIOLOGY)
  ```

  and the user failed to provide the right parenthesis at the end, the system would produce a SYNTAX ERROR message or hopefully a more meaningful message such as UNMATCHED LEFT PARENTHESES.
- the " to close a string in BASIC. The command 10 PRINT "HELLO" is in error if the rightmost " is missing.
- the @B or other markers to close a boldface, italic, or underscored text in word processors. If the text file contains @BThis is boldface@B then the three words between the @B markers appear in boldface on the printer. If the rightmost @B is missing, then the remainder of the file is printed in boldface.
- the termination of a centering command in a text formatter. Some text formatters have a pair of commands such as .ON CENTER and .OFF CENTER surrounding lines of text to be centered. The omission of the latter command causes the entire file to be centered.

In each of these cases, a matching pair of markers is necessary for operation to be complete and correct. The omission of the closing marker can be prevented by using an editor, preferably screen-oriented, that puts both the beginning and ending components of the pair on the screen in one action. For example, typing a left parenthesis generates a left and right parenthesis and puts the cursor in between to allow creation of the contents. An attempt to delete one of the parentheses will cause the matching parenthesis (and possibly the contents as well) to be deleted. Thus, the text can never be in a syntactically incorrect form.

Some people find this rigid approach to be too restrictive and may prefer a milder form of protection. When the user types a left parenthesis, the screen displays a message in the lower left corner indicating the need for a right parenthesis, until it is typed.

Another approach is to replace the requirement for the ending marker. Many microcomputer versions of BASIC do not require an ending " to terminate a string. They use a carriage return to signal the closing of a string. Variants of this theme occur in line-oriented text editors that allow omission of the final / in a CHANGE /OLD STRING/NEW STRING/ command. Many versions of LISP offer a special character, usually a right square bracket, to terminate all open parentheses.

In each of these cases, the designers have recognized a frequently occurring error and have found a way to eliminate the error situation.

Complete sequences. Sometimes an action requires several steps or commands to reach completion. Since people may forget to complete every step of an action, designers attempt to offer a sequence of steps as a single action. In an automobile, the driver does not have to set two switches to signal a left turn. A single switch causes both turn signal lights on the left side of the car to flash. When a pilot lowers the landing gear, hundreds of steps and checks are invoked automatically.

This same concept can be applied to interactive uses of computers. For example:

- dialing up, setting communication parameters, logging on, and loading files is a frequently executed sequence for many users. Fortunately, most communications software packages enable users to specify these processes once and then execute them by simply selecting the appropriate name.

* programming language loop constructs require a WHILE–DO–BEGIN–END or FOR–NEXT structure, but sometimes users forget to put the complete structure in or delete one component but not the other components. One solution would be for users to indicate that they wanted a loop, and the system could supply the complete and correct syntax, that would be filled in by the user. This approach reduces typing and the possibility of making a typographical error or a slip, such as the omission of one component. Conditional constructs require an IF–THEN–ELSE or CASE–OF–END structure; but again, users may forget a component when creating or deleting. Here again, if users could indicate that they wanted a conditional construct, the system could provide the syntactic template and prompt for the contents to be filled in (Teitelbaum & Reps, 1981).

* programming plans (Soloway et al., 1982) may contain several components that must be created and deleted one component at a time. The counter plan requires a data declaration of the integer variable, initialization to zero, incrementation, and a test. If the user could indicate that a counter plan is desired, then the system could provide the complete template, prompt the user for inclusion of each component, or merely remind the user of the need to complete the plan.

* a user of a text editor should be able to indicate that section titles are to be centered, in upper case, and underlined without having to issue a series of commands each time a section title is entered. Then if a change is made in style, for example, to eliminate underlining, a single command would guarantee that all commands were made correctly.

* air traffic controllers may formulate plans to change the altitude of a plane from 14,000 feet to 18,000 feet in two steps, but after raising the plane to 16,000 feet, the

controller may get distracted and fail to complete the action. The controller should be able to record the plan and then have the computer prompt for completion.

The notion of complete sequences of actions may be difficult to implement because users may need to issue atomic actions as well as complete sequences. In this case, users should be allowed to define sequences of their own—the macro or subroutine concept should be available at every level of usage.

Designers can gather information about potential complete sequences by studying sequences of commands actually issued and the pattern of errors that people actually make.

Correct commands. Industrial designers recognize that successful products must be safe and must prevent the user from making incorrect use of the product. Airplane engines cannot be put into reverse until the landing gear have touched down, and cars cannot be put into reverse while traveling forward at faster than five miles per hour. Cameras prevent double exposures, even though this is sometimes desired, and appliances have interlocks to prevent tampering while the power is on, even though expert users occasionally need to perform diagnoses.

The same principles can be applied to interactive systems. Consider these typical errors made by the users of computer systems: they invoke a command that is not available, make a menu selection choice that is not permitted, request a file that does not exist, or enter a data value that is not acceptable. These errors are often caused by annoying typographic errors, such as using an incorrect command abbreviation, pressing a pair of keys rather than a desired single key, misspelling a file name, or making a minor error such as omitting, inserting, or transposing characters. Error messages range from the annoyingly brief ? or WHAT? to the vague UNRECOGNIZED COMMAND or SYNTAX ERROR to the condemning BAD FILE NAME or ILLEGAL COMMAND. The brief ? is suitable for expert users who have made a trivial error and can recognize it when they see the command line on the screen. But if an expert has ventured to use a new command and has misunderstood its operation, then the brief message is not helpful even for experts.

Whoever made the mistake and whatever were its causes, users must interrupt their planning to deal with the problem and their frustration in not getting what they wanted. As long as a command must be made up of a series of keystrokes on a keyboard, there is a substantial chance of making an error in entering the sequence of keypresses. Some keypressing sequences are more error-prone than others, especially those that require shifting or unfamiliar patterns. Reducing the number of keypresses can help, but it may place a greater burden on learning and memory since an entry with reduced keystrokes; for example, RM may be more difficult to remember than the full command name REMOVE (see Chapter 4).

Some systems offer automatic command completion that allows the users to type just a few letters of a meaningful command. The users may request the computer to complete the command by pressing the space bar or the computer may complete it as soon as the input is sufficient to distinguish the command from others. Automatic command completion can save keystrokes and is appreciated by many users, but it can also be disruptive because the user must consider how much to type for each command and must verify that the computer has made the completion that was intended.

Another approach is to have the computer offer the permissible commands, menu choices, or file names on the screen and let the user select with a pointing device, such as a mouse, lightpen, or arrow keys. This is effective if the screen has ample space, the display rate is rapid, and the pointing device is fast and accurate. When the list grows too long to fit on the available screen space, some approach to hierarchical decomposition must be used.

Imagine that the twenty commands of an operating system were constantly displayed on the screen. After selecting the PRINT command (or icon), the system automatically offers the list of thirty files for selection. Two lightpen, touchscreen, or mouse selections can be done in less time and with higher accuracy than can typing the command PRINT JAN–JUNE–EXPENSES.

In principle, a programmer need type a variable name only once. After it has been typed, the programmer can select it, thus eliminating the chance of a misspelling and an UNDECLARED VARIABLE message.

It is not always easy to convert a complex command into a small number of selections and reduce errors. Pointing devices are often crude, slow, and annoying to use. The Xerox Star and the Apple Macintosh are successful and practical applications of these concepts, but there is still room for further invention and application of this concept.

2.6 GUIDELINES: DATA DISPLAY

Guidelines for display of data are being developed by many organizations. A guidelines document can help by promoting consistency among multiple designers, recording practical experience, incorporating the results of empirical studies, and offering useful rules of thumb. The creation of a guidelines document engages the design community in a lively discussion of input or output formats, command sequences, terminology, and hardware devices (Lockheed, 1981; Gaines & Shaw, 1984; Rubinstein & Hersh, 1984; Brown, 1986).

2.6.1 Organizing the display

Smith and Mosier (1984) offer five high-level objectives for data display (page 93):

1. *Consistency of data display.* This principle is frequently violated, but it is easy to repair. During the design process, the terminology, abbreviations, formats, and so on should all be standardized and controlled by using a written (or computer-managed) dictionary of these items.

2. *Efficient information assimilation by the user.* The format should be familiar to the operator and related to the tasks required to be performed with this data. This objective is served by rules for neat columns of data, left justification for alphanumeric data, right justification of integers, lining up decimal points, proper spacing, comprehensible labels, and appropriate use of coded values.

3. *Minimal memory load on user.* Do not require users to remember information from one screen for use on another screen. Arrange tasks such that completion occurs with few commands, minimizing the chance of forgetting to perform a step. Provide labels and common formats for novice or intermittent users.

4. *Compatibility of data display with data entry.* The format of displayed information should be clearly linked to the format of the data entry.

5. *Flexibility for user control of data display.* Users can get the information in the form most convenient for the task they are working on.

This compact set of high-level objectives is a useful starting point, but each project needs to expand these into application-specific and hardware-dependent standards and practices. For example, these detailed comments for control room design come from a report from the Electric Power Research Institute (Lockheed, 1981):

- be consistent in labeling and graphic conventions
- standardize abbreviations
- use consistent format in all displays (headers, footers, paging, menus, etc.)
- present a page number on each display page and allow actions to call up a page by entering its page number
- present data only if they assist the operator
- present information graphically, where appropriate, using widths of lines, positions of markers on scales, and other techniques that relieve the need to read and interpret alphanumeric data
- present digital values only when knowledge of numerical value is actually necessary and useful
- use high resolution monitors and maintain them to provide maximum display quality
- design a display in monochromatic form, using spacing and

arrangement for organization, and then judiciously add color where it will aid the operator
• involve operators in the development of new displays and procedures.

Chapter 8 further discusses data display issues.

2.6.2 Getting the user's attention

Since substantial information may be presented to users for the normal performance of their work, exceptional conditions or time-dependent information must be presented so as to attract attention. Multiple techniques exist for attention getting:

1. Intensity: use two levels only.
2. Marking: underline, enclose in a box, point to with an arrow, or use an indicator such as an asterisk, bullet, dash, or an X.
3. Size: use up to four sizes.
4. Choice of fonts: use up to three fonts.
5. Inverse video: use normal or inverse.
6. Blinking: use blinking or nonblinking (2–4 hertz).
7. Color: use up to four standard colors, with additional colors reserved for occasional use.
8. Audio: use soft tones for regular positive feedback, harsh sounds for rare emergency conditions.

A few words of caution are necessary. There is a danger in creating cluttered displays by overuse of these techniques. Novices need simple, logically organized, and well-labeled displays that guide their actions. Expert operators do not need extensive labels on fields; subtle highlighting or positional presentation is sufficient. Display formats must be tested with users for comprehensibility.

Similarly highlighted items will be perceived as being related. Color coding is especially powerful in linking related items, but then it becomes more difficult to cluster items across color codes. Operator control over highlighting, for example, allowing the operator in an air traffic control environment to assign orange to aircraft above 18,000 feet, may provide a useful resolution to concerns about personal preferences. Highlighting can be accomplished by intensity, blinking, or other methods.

Audio tones can provide informative feedback about progress, such as the clicks in keyboards or ringing sounds in telephones. Alarms for emergency conditions do rapidly alert operators, but a mechanism to suppress alarms must be provided. Testing is necessary to ensure that operators can distinguish among alarm levels. Prerecorded or synthesized messages are an intriguing alternative, but since they may interfere with communications among operators they should be used cautiously.

2.7   GUIDELINES: DATA ENTRY

Data entry tasks can occupy a substantial fraction of the operator's time and are the source of frustrating and potentially dangerous errors. Smith and Mosier (1984) offer five high-level objectives for data entry (page 19):

1. *Consistency of data entry transactions.* Similar sequences of actions under all conditions; similar delimiters, abbreviations, etc.

2. *Minimal input actions by user.* Fewer input actions mean greater operator productivity and usually less chance for error. Making a choice by a single keystroke, lightpen touch, finger press, etc., rather than by typing in a lengthy string of characters is potentially advantageous. Selecting from a list of choices eliminates the need for memorization, structures the decision-making task, and eliminates the possibility of typographic errors. However, if the operators must move their hands from a keyboard to a separate input device, the advantage is defeated, because home row

position is lost. Experienced operators often prefer to type six to eight characters instead of moving to a lightpen, joystick, or other selection device.

A second aspect of this guideline is that redundant data entry should be avoided. It is annoying for an operator to enter the same information in two locations since it is perceived as a waste of effort and an opportunity for error. When the same information is required in two places, the system should copy the information for the operator, who still has the option of overriding by retyping.

3. *Minimal memory load on user.* Reduce the need for the operator to remember lengthy lists of codes and complex syntactic command strings.

4. *Compatibility of data entry with data display.* The format of data entry information should be closely linked to the format of displayed information.

5. *Flexibility for user control of data entry.* Experienced operators may prefer to enter information in a sequence they can control. On some occasions in an air traffic control environment, the arrival time is the prime field in the controller's mind. On other occasions, the altitude is the prime field. Flexibility should be used cautiously since it goes against the consistency principle.

2.8 PROTOTYPING AND ACCEPTANCE TESTING

A critical component of clear thinking about interactive system design is the replacement of the vague and misleading notion of "user friendliness" with the five measurable quality criteria:

- time to learn

- speed of performance

- rate of errors by users

- subjective satisfaction
- retention over time.

Once the decision about the relative importance of each of the human factors quality criteria has been made, specific measurable objectives should be established to inform customers and users and to guide designers and implementers. The acceptance test plan for a system should be included in the requirements document and should be written before the design is made. Hardware and software test plans are regularly included in requirements documents; extending the principle to human interface development is natural (see Chapter 10).

The requirements document for a word processing system might include this acceptance test:

The subjects will be 35 secretaries hired from an employment agency with no word processing experience, but typing skills in the 35 to 50 words per minute range. They will be given 45 minutes of training on the basic features. At least 30 of the 35 secretaries should be able to complete 80 percent of the typing and editing tasks in the enclosed benchmark test correctly within 30 minutes.

Another testable requirement for the same system might be:

After four half days of regular use of the system, 25 out of these 35 secretaries should be able to carry out the advanced editing tasks in the second benchmark test within 20 minutes while making fewer than six errors.

This second acceptance test captures performance after regular use. The choice of the benchmark tests is critical and highly system dependent. The test materials and procedures must also be refined by pilot testing before use.

A third item in the acceptance test plan might focus on retention:

After two weeks, at least 15 of the test subjects should be recalled and be required to perform the third benchmark test. In 40 minutes, at least 10 of the subjects must be able to complete 75 percent of the tasks correctly.

Such performance tests constitute the definition of "user friendly" for this system. By having an explicit definition, both the managers and the designers will have a clearer understanding of the system goals and whether they have succeeded. The presence of a precise acceptance test plan will force greater attention to human factors issues during the design and ensure that pilot studies are run to determine if the project can meet the test plan goals.

In a programming workstation project, the early requirement for performance helped shape the nature of the interface. That requirement was:

New professional programmer users should be able to sign on, create a short program, and execute it against a stored test data set, without assistance and within 10 minutes.

Specific goals in acceptance tests are useful, but competent test managers will notice and record anecdotal evidence, suggestions from participants, subjective reactions of displeasure or satisfaction, their own comments, and exceptional performance (both good and bad) by individuals. The precision of the acceptance test provides an environment in which unexpected events are most noticeable.

2.9   BALANCE OF AUTOMATION AND HUMAN CONTROL

The principles in the previous sections are in harmony with the goal of simplifying the user's task—eliminating human actions when no judgment is required. The users can then avoid the annoyance of handling routine, tedious, and error-prone tasks and can concentrate on critical decisions, planning, and coping with unexpected situations. The computers should be used to keep track of and retrieve large volumes of data, follow preset patterns, and carry out complex mathematical or logical operations (Table 2.2 has a detailed comparison of human and machine capabilities).

The degree of automation will increase over the years as procedures become more standardized, hardware reliability increases, and software verification and validation improves. With routine tasks, automation is preferred since the potential for error may be reduced. However, I believe that there will always be a critical human role because the real

Humans Generally Better	Machines Generally Better
Sense low level stimuli	Sense stimuli outside human's range
Detect stimuli in noisy background	Count or measure physical quantities
Recognize constant patterns in varying situations	Store quantities of coded information accurately
Sense unusual and unexpected events	Monitor prespecified events, especially infrequent
	Make rapid and consistent responses to
Remember principles and strategies	input signals
	Recall quantities of detailed information accurately
Retrieve pertinent details without a priori connection	Process quantitative data in prespecified ways
Draw upon experience & adapt decisions to situation	
Select alternatives if original approach fails	
Reason inductively: generalize from observations	
Act in unanticipated emergencies & novel situations	Perform repetitive preprogrammed actions reliably
	Exert great, highly controlled physical force
Apply principles to solve varied problems	
Make subjective evaluations	
Develop new solutions	
Concentrate on important tasks when overload occurs	Perform several activities simultaneously
	Maintain operations under heavy information load
Adapt physical response to changes in situation	Maintain performance over extended periods of time

Table 2.2. Relative capabilities of humans and machines. (Compiled from Brown, C. Marlin *Human-Computer Interface Design Guidelines*, New Jersey: Ablex Publishing Company, 1986; McCormick, E.J. *Human factors engineering*. New York: McGraw-Hill, 1970, pp. 20–21; and Estes, W.K. Is human memory obsolete? *American Scientist*, 1980, *68*, pp. 62–69.)

world is an "open system" (there are a nondenumerable number of unpredictable events and system failures). By contrast, computers constitute a "closed system" (there are only a denumerable number of predictable normal and failure situations that can be accommodated in hardware and software). Human judgment is necessary for the unpredictable events in which some action must be taken to preserve safety, avoid expensive failures, or increase product quality.

For example, in air traffic control, common operations include changes to altitude, heading, or speed. These are well understood and potentially automatable by a scheduling and route allocation algorithm, but the operators must be present to deal with the highly variable and unpredictable emergency situations. An automated system might successfully deal with high volumes of traffic, but what would happen if the airport manager changed runways because of turbulent weather? The controller would have to reroute planes quickly. But suppose one pilot called in to request special clearance to land because of a failed engine while a second pilot reported a passenger with a potential heart attack. Human judgment is necessary to decide which plane should land first and how much costly and risky diversion of normal traffic is appropriate. The air traffic controller cannot just jump into the emergency; he or she must be intensely involved in the situation in order to make an informed, rapid, and optimal decision. In short, the real world situation is so complex that it is impossible to anticipate and program for every contingency; human judgment and values are necessary in the decision-making process.

Another example of the complexity of real world situations in air traffic control emerges from an incident in May, 1983. An Air Canada Boeing 727 jet had a fire on board, and the controller cleared away traffic and began to guide the plane in for a landing. The smoke was so bad that the pilot had trouble reading his instruments and then the onboard transponder burned out so that the air traffic controller could no longer read the plane's altitude from the situation display. In spite of these multiple failures, the controller and the pilot managed to bring the plane down quickly enough to save the lives of many, but not all, of the passengers.

The goal of system design in many applications is to give the operator sufficient information about current status and activities so that when intervention is necessary, the operator has the knowledge and the capacity to perform correctly. Increasingly, the human role will be to respond to such anomalies as unanticipated situations, failing equipment, improper human performance, and incomplete or erroneous data (Eason, 1980).

The entire system must be designed and tested, not only for normal situations, but also for as wide a range of anomalous situations as can be anticipated. An extensive set of test conditions might be included as part of the requirements document.

Beyond performance of productive decision-making tasks and handling of failures, the role of the human operator will be to improve the design of the system. In complex systems, an opportunity always exists for improvement, so systems that lend themselves to refinement will evolve under the continual incremental redesign by the operator.

2.10   PRACTITIONER'S SUMMARY

Designing user interfaces is a complex and highly creative process that blends intuition, experience, and careful consideration of numerous technical issues. Designers are urged to begin with a thorough task analysis and specification of the user communities. Explicit recording of task objects and actions based on a task analysis can lead to construction of useful metaphors or system images. Identification of computer objects and actions guides designers to simpler concepts that benefit novice and expert users. Next, designers create consistent and meaningful syntactic forms for input and display. Extensive testing and itcrative refinement are necessary parts of every development project.

Design principles and guidelines are emerging from practical experience and empirical studies. Organizations can benefit by reviewing available guidelines documents and then constructing a local version. A guidelines document records organizational policies, supports consistency, aids the application of dialog management tools, facilitates training of new designers, records results of practice and experimental testing, and stimulates discussion of user interface issues.

2.11   RESEARCHER'S AGENDA

The central problem for psychologists, human factors professionals, and computer scientists is to develop adequate theories and models of human behavior with interactive systems. Traditional psychological theories must be extended and refined to accommodate the complex human learning, memory, and problem-solving required in these applications. Useful goals include descriptive taxonomies, explanatory theories, or predictive models.

A first step might be to investigate thoroughly a limited task for a single community and to develop a formal notation for describing task actions and objects. Then the mapping to computer actions and objects could be made precisely. Finally, the linkage with syntax would follow. This would lead to predictions of learning times, performance speeds, error rates, subjective satisfaction, or human retention over time for competing designs.

Next, the range of tasks and user communities could be expanded to domains of interest such as word processing, information retrieval, or data entry. More limited and applied research problems are connected with each of the hundreds of design principles or guidelines that have been proposed. Each validation of these principles and clarification of the breadth of applicability would be a small and useful contribution to the emerging mosaic of human performance with interactive systems.

REFERENCES

Bailey, Robert W., *Human Performance Engineering: A Guide for System Designers*, Prentice-Hall, Inc., Englewood Cliffs, NJ, (1982).

Barber, Raymond E., Response time, operator productivity and job satisfaction, Ph. D. dissertation, NYU Graduate School of Business Administration (1979).

Brown, C. Marlin, *Human-Computer Interface Design Guidelines*, Ablex Publishing Company, Norwood, NJ (1986).

Card, Stuart, Moran, Thomas P., and Newell, Allen, The keystroke-level model for user performance with interactive systems, *Communications of the ACM 23*, (1980), 396–410.

Card, Stuart, Moran, Thomas P., and Newell, Allen, *The Psychology of Human-Computer Interaction*, Lawrence Erlbaum Associates, Hillsdale, NJ, (1983), 469 pages.

Eason, K. D., Dialogue design implications of task allocation between man and computer, *Ergonomics 23*, 9, (1980), 881–891.

Foley, James D. and Van Dam, Andries, *Fundamentals of Interactive Computer Graphics*, Addison-Wesley Publishing Co., Reading, MA, (1982), 664 pages.

Gaines, Brian R., The technology of interaction— dialogue programming rules, *International Journal of Man-Machine Studies 14*, (1981), 133–150.

Gaines, Brian R. and Shaw, Mildred L. G., *The Art of Computer Conversation*, Prentice-Hall International, Englewood Cliffs, NJ, (1984), 214 pages.

Hansen, Wilfred J., User engineering principles for interactive systems, *Proceedings of the Fall Joint Computer Conference, 39*, AFIPS Press, Montvale, NJ, (1971), 523–532.

Kieras, David, and Polson, Peter G., An approach to the formal analysis of user complexity, *International Journal of Man-Machine Studies 22*, (1985), 365–394.

Ledgard, Henry, Whiteside, John, Singer, Andrew, and Seymour, William, The natural language of interactive systems, *Communications of the ACM 23*, 10, (October 1980), 556–563.

Lockheed Missiles and Space Company, Human Factors Review of Electric Power Dispatch Control Centers: Volume 2: Detailed Survey Results, Prepared for Electric Power Research Institute, 3412 Hillview Avenue, Palo Alto, CA 94304, (1981).

Norman, Donald A., Design rules based on analyses of human error, *Communications of the ACM 26*, 4, (April 1983), 254–258.

Norman, Donald A., Stages and levels in human-machine interaction, *International Journal of Man-Machine Studies 21*, (1984), 365–375.

Robertson, P. J., A guide to using color on alphanumeric displays, IBM, Technical Report G320–6296, IBM, White Plains, NY, (1980).

Rubinstein, Richard, and Hersh, Harry, *The Human Factor: Designing Computer Systems for People*, Digital Press, Burlington, MA, (1984), 249 pages.

Shneiderman, Ben, *Software Psychology: Human Factors in Computer and Information Systems*, Little, Brown and Co., Boston, MA, (1980).

Shneiderman, Ben, A note on the human factors issues of natural language interaction with database systems, *Information Systems 6*, 2, (1981), 125–129.

Shneiderman, Ben, System message design: Guidelines and experimental results, In *Directions in Human-Computer Interaction*, A. Badre and B. Shneiderman (Editors), Ablex Publishing Co., Norwood, NJ, (1982), 55–78.

Shneiderman, Ben, Direct manipulation: A step beyond programming languages, *IEEE Computer 16*, 8, (August 1983), 57–69.

Shneiderman, Ben, and Mayer, Richard, Syntactic/Semantic interactions in programmer behavior: A model and experimental results, *International Journal of Computer and Information Sciences 8*, 3, (1979), 219–239. Reprinted in Curtis, Bill, (Editor), *Human Factors in Software Development*, IEEE Computer Society EHO 185–9, (1981), 9–23.

Smith, Sid L., and Mosier, Jane N., Design Guidelines for the User Interface for Computer-Based Information Systems, The MITRE Corporation, Bedford, MA 01730, Electronic Systems Division, (September 1984), 448 pages. Available from the National Technical Information Service, Springfield, VA.

Soloway, Elliot, Ehrlich, Kate, Bonar, Jeffrey, and Greenspan, Judith, What do novices know about programming?, In *Directions in Human-Computer Interaction*, A. Badre and B. Shneiderman, (Editors), Ablex Publishing Co., Norwood, NJ, (1982), 27–54.

Teitelbaum, T., and Reps, T., The Cornell program synthesizer: A syntax-directed programming environment, *Communications of the ACM 24*, 9, (September 1981), 563–573.

PART II

INTERACTION STYLES

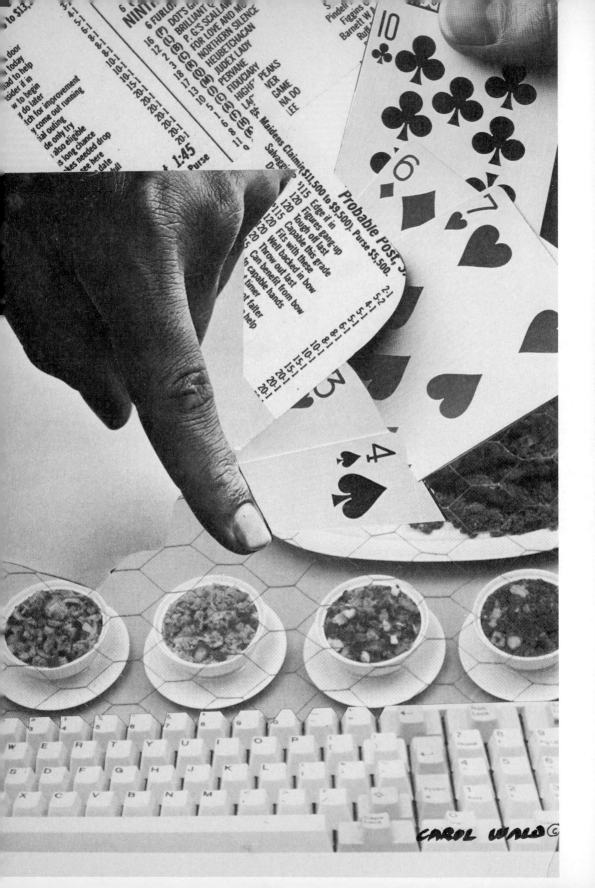

CHAPTER 3

MENU SELECTION SYSTEMS

A man is responsible for his choice
and must accept the consequences,
whatever they may be.

W. H. Auden, *A Certain World*.

3.1   INTRODUCTION

Menu selection systems are attractive because they can eliminate training and memorization of complex command sequences. When the menu items are written using familiar terminology, users can select an item easily and indicate their choice with one or two keypresses or use of a pointing device. This simplified interaction style reduces the possibility of keying errors and structures the task to guide the novice and intermittent user. With careful design and high-speed interaction, menu selection can become appealing to expert frequent users, as well.

Menu selection is often contrasted with command language, but the distinctions are sometimes blurred. Typically, menu selection requires a single keystroke, whereas commands may be lengthy; but how would you classify a menu in which the user has to type a six- or eight-letter item? Typically, menu selection presents the choices on the display, whereas commands must be memorized, but how would you classify a menu that offered four numbered choices and accepted ten more generic choices that are not displayed? How would you classify a system that offers single letter prompts? What about graphical, two-dimensional menus in which selection is made by pointing or voice synthesis/recognition menu interaction?

Rather than debate over terminology, it is more useful to maintain an awareness of how much the system offers on the display at the moment the selection is made, the form and content of item selection, and what task domain knowledge is necessary for users to succeed. Menu selection is especially effective when users have little training, are intermittent in using the system, are unfamiliar with the terminology, and need help in structuring their decision-making process.

However, if a designer uses menu selection, it does not guarantee that the system will be appealing and easy to use. Effective menu selection systems emerge only after careful consideration and testing of numerous design issues, such as semantic organization, menu system structure, the number and sequence of menu items, titling, prompting format, graphic layout and design, phrasing of menu items, display rates, response time, shortcuts through the menus for knowledgeable frequent users, availability of help, and the selection mechanism (keyboard, pointing devices, touchscreen, voice, etc.).

3.2 SEMANTIC ORGANIZATION

The primary goal for menu designers is to create a sensible, comprehensible, memorable, and convenient semantic organization relevant to the user's tasks. Some lessons can be learned by organizing the semantic decomposition of a book into chapters, a program into modules, the animal kingdom into species, or a Sears catalog into sections. Hierarchical decompositions, natural and comprehensible to most people, are appealing because every item belongs to a single category. Unfortunately, in some applications an item may be difficult to classify as belonging to one category, and the temptation to duplicate entries or create a network increases. In spite of some limitations, the elegance of tree structures should be appreciated.

Restaurant menus separate appetizers, soups, main dishes, desserts, and drinks to help customers organize their selections. Menu items should fit logically into categories and have readily understood meanings. Restauranteurs who list dishes with idiosyncratic names such as "Veal Monique," generic terms such as "House dressing," or unfamiliar jargon such as "Wor Shu Op" should expect waiters to spend ample time explaining the alternatives or anticipate customers becoming anxious because of their insecurity in ordering.

Similarly, for computer menu selection systems, the categories should be comprehensible and distinctive so that the users are confident in making their selections. Users should have a clear idea of what will happen when they make a choice. Computer menu selection systems are more difficult to design than restaurant menus because computer screens typically allow less information to be displayed than printed menus. Screen space is a scarce resource. In addition, the number of choices and the complexity is greater in many computer applications, and the computer user may not have a helpful waiter to turn to for an explanation.

The importance of meaningful organization of menu items was demonstrated in a study with 48 novice users (Liebelt et al., 1982). Simple menu trees with 3 levels and 16 target items were constructed in meaningfully organized and disorganized forms. Error rates were nearly halved and user think time (time from menu presentation to user's selection of an item) was reduced for the meaningfully organized form.

In a later menu search study, McDonald, Stone, and Liebelt (1983) found that semantically meaningful categories, such as food, animals, minerals, and cities, lead to shorter response times than do random or alphabetic organizations. This experiment tested 109 novice users who worked through 10 blocks of 26 trials. The authors conclude that "these results demonstrate the superiority of a categorical menu organization over a pure alphabetical organization, particularly when there is some uncertainty about the terms." With larger menu structures the effect is even more dramatic, as has been demonstrated by studies with extensive videotex databases (Lee & Latremouille, 1980; McEwen, 1981).

These results and the syntactic/semantic model suggest that the key to menu structure design is first to consider the semantic organization. The number of items on the screen becomes a secondary issue.

Menu selection applications range from trivial choices between two items to complex videotex systems with 300,000 screens. The simplest applications consist of a single menu, but even with this limitation there are many variations (Figure 3.1). The second group of applications includes a linear sequence of menu selections; the progression of menus is independent of the user's choice. Strict tree structures make up the third group, which is the most common situation. Acyclic (menus which are reachable by more than one path) and cyclic (menus with meaningful paths that allow users to repeat menus) networks constitute the fourth group. These groupings describe the semantic organization; special traversal commands may enable users to jump around the branches of a tree, to go back to the previous menu, or to go to the beginning of a linear sequence.

3.2.1 Single menus

In some situations, a single menu is sufficient to accomplish a task. Single menus may have two or more items, may require two or more screens, or may allow multiple selections. Single menus may pop up on the current work area or may be permanently available (in a separate window or on a data tablet) while the main display is changed. Different guidelines apply for each situation.

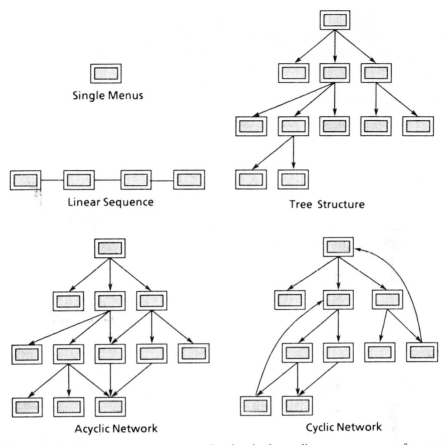

Figure 3.1: Menu systems can use simple single or linear sequences of menus. Tree-structured menus are the most common structure. More elaborate acyclic or cyclic menu structures can become difficult for some users.

Binary menus: The simplest case is a binary menu with yes/no or true/false choices, such as is found in many home computer games:

    DO YOU WANT INSTRUCTIONS (Y,N)?

Even this simple example can be improved. A novice user might not understand the (Y,N) prompt—really an abbreviated form of the menu of choices. Second, this common query leaves the user without a clear sense of what is going to happen next. Typing Y might produce many pages of instructions and the user might not know how to stop a lengthy output. Typing N is also anxiety producing because the user has no idea of what the program will do. Even in writing simple menus, clear and specific choices should be offered that give the user the sense of control:

```
Your choices are:
    1 — Get 12 lines of brief instructions.
    2 — Get 89 lines of complete instructions.
    3 — Go on to playing the game.
Type 1, 2, or 3 and press RETURN:
```

Since this version has three items, it is no longer a binary menu. It offers more specific items so the user knows what to expect, but it still has the problem that users must take instructions now or never. Another strategy might be:

```
At any time, you may type
    ? — Get 12 lines of brief instructions.
   ?? — Get 89 lines of complete instructions.
Be sure to press RETURN after every command
Ready for game playing commands:
```

This example calls attention to the sometimes narrow distinction between commands and menu selection; the menu choices have become more command-like since the user must now recall the ? or ?? syntax.

   Menu items can be identified by single letter mnemonics, as in this photo library retrieval system:

```
Photos are indexed by film type
    B    Black and white
    C    Color
Type the letter of your choice
and press RETURN:
```

The mnemonic letters in this menu are often preferred to the numbered choices (see Section 3.7). The mnemonic letter approach requires additional caution in avoiding collision and increases the effort of translation to foreign langauges, but its clarity and memorability are an advantage in many applications.

These simple examples demonstrate alternative ways to identify menu items and convey instructions to the user. No optimal format for menus has emerged, but consistency across menus in a system is extremely important.

Multiple item menus: Single menus may have more than two items. Examples include online quizzes with a touchscreen:

```
Who invented the telephone?
        Thomas Edison
        Alexander Graham Bell
        Lee De Forest
        George Westinghouse
Touch your answer.
```

or the list of options in a document processing system:

```
EXAMINE, PRINT, DROP, OR HOLD?
```

The quiz example has distinct, comprehensible items, but the document processing example shows an implied menu selection that could be confusing to novice users. There are no explicit instructions and it is not apparent that single letter abbreviations are acceptable. Knowledgeable and frequent users may prefer this short form of a menu selection, usually called a prompt, for its speed and simplicity.

Extended menus: Sometimes the list of menu items may require more than one screen but allow only one meaningful item to be chosen. One resolution is to create a tree structured menu, but sometimes the desire to keep the system to one conceptual menu is very appealing. The first portion of the menu is displayed with an additional menu item that leads to the next screen in the extended menu sequence. A typical application is in word processing systems, where common choices are displayed first, but infrequent or advanced features are kept on the second screen:

```
        SUPERDUPERWRITER MAIN MENU
                PAGE 1
    1   Edit a document
    2   Copy a document
    3   Create a document
    4   Erase a document
    5   Print a document
    6   View the index of documents

Type the number of your choice
    or M for more choices.
    Then Press RETURN
```

```
        SUPERDUPERWRITER MAIN MENU
                PAGE 2
    7   Alter line width
    8   Change character set
    9   Attempt recovery of damaged file
    10   Reconstruct erased file
    11   Set cursor blink rate
    12   Set beep volume
    13   Run diagnostics

Type the number of your choice
    or P to go back to Page 1.
    Then Press RETURN
```

Sometimes the extended screen menu will continue for many screens of command items or data items. More elaborate scrolling capabilities may be needed.

Pop-up menus: Pop-up or pull down menus appear on the screen in response to a click with a pointing device such as a mouse. The Xerox Star, Apple Lisa, and Apple Macintosh (Figure 3.2) made these possibilities widely available. Selection can be made by moving the

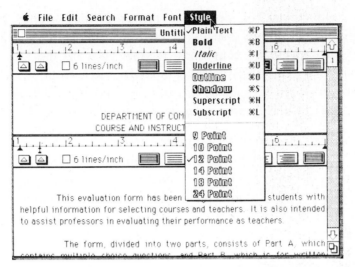

Figure 3.2: The pull-down menu on the Apple Macintosh MacWrite program enables users to select font variations and size. (Photo courtesy of Apple Computer, Inc.)

pointing device over the menu items that respond by highlighting (reverse video, a box surrounding the item, or color have been used).

The contents of the pop-up menu may depend on where the cursor is when the pointing device is clicked. Since the pop-up menu covers a portion of the screen, there is strong motivation to keeping the menu text small. Hierarchical sequences of pop-up menus are also used.

Permanent menus: Single menus can be used for permanently available commands that can be applied to a displayed object. For example, the Bank Street Writer, a word processor designed for children, always shows a fragment of the text and this menu

```
ERASE     MOVE       FIND      TRANSFER
UNERASE  MOVEBACK  REPLACE     MENU
```

Moving the left and right arrow keys causes items to be sequentially highlighted in reverse video. When the desired command is highlighted, pressing the RETURN key initiates the action.

Other applications of permanent menus include Apple Macpaint, computer-assisted design systems, or other graphics systems that display an elaborate menu of commands to the side of the object being manipulated. Price (1982) describes a CAD system with 120 choices in an on-screen menu. Lightpen touches or other cursor action devices allow the user to make selections without using the keyboard.

Multiple selection menus: A further variation on single menus is the capacity to make multiple selections from the choices offered. For example, a political interest survey might allow multiple choice on one screen (Figure 3.3). A multiple selection menu with mouse clicks for selection is a convenient strategy for handling multiple binary choices, since the user gets to scan the full list of items while deciding.

Summary: Even the case of single menus provides a rich domain for designers and human factors researchers. Questions of wording, screen layout, and selection mechanism all emerge even in the simple case of choosing from one set of items. Still more challenging questions emerge from designing sequences and trees of menus.

POLITICAL ISSUES	
	Unemployment
✓	Aid to Elderly
	Nuclear Freeze
	Crime Control
	Abortion
	Minority Rights
✓	Defense Spending

Touch up to three issues

Figure 3.3: This multiple selection touchscreen menu enables users to make up to three selections of political issues.

```
Do you want the document printed at
   1 - your terminal
   2 - the computer center line printer
   3 - the computer center laser printer
Type the number of your choice and press RETURN:
```

```
Do you want
   1 - single spacing
   2 - one and a half spacing
   3 - double spacing
   4 - triple spacing
Type the number of your choice and press RETURN:
```

```
Do you want
   1 - no page numbering
   2 - page numbering on the top, right justified
   3 - page numbering at the bottom, centered
Type the number of your choice and press RETURN:
```

Figure 3.4: A linear sequence of menus allows the user to select three print parameters for a document: printing device, line spacing, and page numbering.

3.2.2 Linear sequence of menus

Often a series of interdependent menus can be used to guide the user through a series of choices in which the user sees the same sequence of menus no matter what choices are made. A document printing package might have a linear sequence of menus to choose print parameters such as device, line spacing, and page numbering (Figure 3.4). Another familiar example is an online examination that has a sequence of multiple choice test items, each made up as a menu.

With high resolution screens and pointing devices, it is possible to include several menus on a single screen, thereby simplifying the user interface and speeding usage (Figure 3.5).

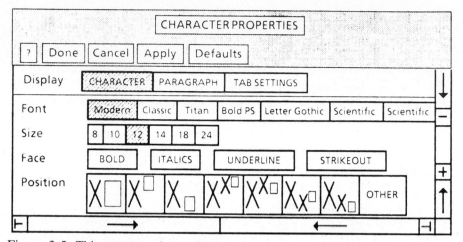

Figure 3.5: This property sheet allows users to select the character properties on the Xerox Star. The user moves the cursor with a mouse and then presses the mouse button to select the item. (Used with permission of Xerox Corporation; Xerox, 8010 Information System, Standard Workstation Software are trademarks of XEROX CORPORATION.)

Movement through the menus: Linear sequences guide the user through a complex decision-making process by presenting one decision at a time. The document printing example could be improved by offering the user several menus on the screen at once. If the menus do not fit on one screen, then there should be a mechanism for going back to previous screens to review or change choices made earlier. A second improvement is to display previous choices, so users can see what decisions have been made. A third improvement might be to let the users know how many and which menus are yet to be seen.

Summary: Linear sequences of menus are a simple and effective means for guiding the user through a decision-making process. The user should be given a clear sense of progress or position within the sequence and the means for going backwards to earlier choices (and possibly to terminating or restarting the sequence).

Choosing the order of menus in a linear sequence is often straightforward, but care must be taken to match user expectations. One strategy is to place the easy decisions first to relieve users of some concerns, enabling them to concentrate on more difficult choices.

3.2.3 Tree structured menus

When a collection of items grows and becomes difficult to maintain under intellectual control, people form categories of similar items, creating a tree structure (Clauer, 1972; Brown, 1982). Some collections can be easily partitioned into mutually exclusive groups with distinctive identifiers. Familiar examples include:

> male, female
> animal, vegetable, mineral
> spring, summer, autumn, winter
> Sunday, Monday, Tuesday, Wednesday, Thursday,
>   Friday, Saturday
> less than 10, between 10 and 25, greater than 25
> percussion, string, woodwind, brass

Even these groupings may occasionally lead to confusion or disagreement. Classification and indexing are complex tasks, and in many situations there is no perfect solution acceptable to everyone. The initial design can be improved as a function of feedback from users. Over time, as the structure is improved and as users gain familiarity with it, success rates will improve.

In spite of their problems, tree structured menu systems have the power to make large collections of data available to novice or intermittent users. If each menu has 8 items, then a menu tree with 4 levels has the capacity to lead an untrained user to the right frame out of a collection of 4,096 frames.

If the groupings at each level are natural and comprehensible to the user, and if the user knows what he or she is looking for, then the menu traversal can be accomplished in a few seconds—more quickly than flipping through a book. On the other hand, if the groupings are unfamiliar and the user has only a vague notion of what he or she is looking for, getting lost in the tree menus for hours is possible (Robertson et al., 1981).

Terminology from the user's task domain can orient the user. Instead of using a title such as MAIN MENU OPTIONS that is vague and

emphasizes the computer domain, use terms such as FRIENDLIBANK
SERVICES or simply GAMES.

Depth versus breadth: The depth (number of levels) of a menu tree
depends, in part, on the breadth (number of items per level). If more
items are put into the main menu, then the tree spreads out and has fewer
levels. This is advantageous, but not if clarity is substantially
compromised or if a slow display rate consumes the user's patience.
Several authors have urged four to eight items per menu, but at the same
time, they urge no more than three to four levels. With large menu
applications, one or both of these guidelines must be compromised.

D. P. Miller (1981) studied user performance in retrieving items from
four versions of a tree structured menu system containing 64 target items.
Menus had 2, 4, 8, or 64 items in each screen, with corresponding depth
of 6, 3, 2, and 1. The 64 items were carefully chosen to "form valid
semantic hierarchies" in each of the four versions. Speed of performance
was fastest with 4 or 8 items per menu, and the lowest error rate occurred
with 8 items per menu. These results are useful, but there were two
special conditions that may limit the applicability of this study: subjects
became very familiar with the menus during the training and the 128
trials, and the 64 items were chosen so that there were meaningful
groupings in all four versions.

Kiger (1984) grouped 64 items in five menu tree forms:

8 - 2	Eight items on each of two levels
4 - 3	Four items on each of three levels
2 - 6	Two items on each of six levels
4 - 1 + 16 - 1	A four item menu followed by a sixteen item menu
16 - 1 + 4 - 1	A sixteen item menu followed by a four item menu

The deep narrow tree, 2 - 6, produced the slowest, least accurate, and
least preferred version; the 8 - 2 was among the best for speed, accuracy,
and preference. The 22 subjects performed 16 searches on each of the
five versions.

Dray et al. (1981) compared a one-level menu having 23 one-word target items arranged on 6 lines with a two-level menu having 6 items in the main menu. Selection was by cursor control arrow keys and an enter key. Subjects had 138 trials in each condition in this counterbalanced within subjects design. Although neither version emerged as superior, there was a significant order effect that the authors interpreted as evidence that the one-level menu was easier to learn. Informal reports from subjects supported the conclusion that seeing the full picture continuously aided decision-making.

When the menu tree contains the numbers 1 to 4,096, time to locate a target number was found to increase with the breadth of the tree (Doughty & Kelso, 1984). Search times were almost twice as long in a 12-level tree having two choices at each level (2-12) as opposed to a three level tree with 16 choices at each level (16-3) (see Figure 3.6). Although the six subjects made choices more rapidly in the shorter menus, the effort to work through the more numerous menus did slow them down substantially. Each subject did twelve trials with each of four widths. Landauer and Nachbar (1985) confirmed the advantage of breadth over depth and developed predictive equations for traversal times.

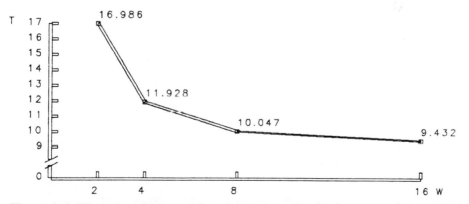

Figure 3.6: Time data for a search to locate a number in the range of 1 to 4,096 by menu selection as a function menu size. As the menu sizes increased from two items to sixteen items, the search time was almost cut in half. (Doughty & Kelso, 1984)

Even though the semantic structure of the items cannot be ignored, these studies suggest that fewer levels aid decision making. Of course, display rates, response time, and screen clutter must be considered in addition to the semantic organization.

Semantic grouping in tree structures: Rules for semantic validity are hard to state, and there is always the danger that some users may not grasp the designer's organizational framework. Young and Hull (1982) examined "cognitive mismatches" in the British Prestel viewdata system (Martin, 1982). Problems included overlapping categories, extraneous items, conflicting classifications in the same menu, unfamiliar jargon, and generic terms. Based on this set of problems, the rules for forming menu trees might be to:

1. *Create groups of logically similar items.* For example, a comprehensible menu would list countries at level one, states or provinces at level two, and cities at level three.

2. *Form groups that cover all possibilities.* For example, a menu with age ranges 0 - 9, 10 - 19, 20 - 29, and older than 30, makes it easy for the user to select an item.

3. *Make sure that items are nonoverlapping.* Lower-level items should be naturally associated with a single higher-level item. Young and Hull offered an example of a poorly designed screen with "Places in Britain" and "Regions of England" as overlapping items on the same menu.

4. *Use familiar terminology, but ensure that items are distinctive from each other.* Choosing the right terminology is a difficult task; feedback from sample users will be helpful during design and testing.

Menu maps: As the depth of a menu tree grows, it becomes increasingly difficult for the user to maintain a sense of position in the tree and a sense of disorientation, or of "getting lost," grows. To overcome this sense of disorientation, some menu systems come with a printed index of terms that is easier to scan than a series of screen displays. The British Prestel system offers a detailed cross-referenced index that in 1982 was 34 pages long and contained thousands of entries.

The CompuServe Information Service's November 1984 index contained almost 1,000 subjects. It included a diagram, or map, of the first three levels of the tree structure that contains 26 menus.

The relative merits of a map and an index were studied in a small menu structure with 18 animals as target items (Billingsley, 1982). In this case, users who had the chance to study an index did somewhat better than a control group that had no special navigation aids. The group with an overall map did substantially better than both the index and control groups:

	Control	Index	Map
Number of subjects	10.0	8.0	8.0
Mean time per search	35.3	30.7	19.2
Mean choices per search	12.3	8.4	4.7

Menu learning for a three-level three-item (3–3) menu was studied with four forms of training (Parton et al., 1985):

Online exploration: subjects could explore the
  menus online.
Command sequences: subjects studied the 27
  paths through the three levels typed on paper, e.g.
  Plan Division, Concepts, Systems Analyst
Frames: subjects studied the 13 menu frames,
  such as

```
Plans Division
    Concepts
    Designs
    Proposals
```

Menu map: subjects studied a tree structured
  layout of the 13 frames.

The 65 undergraduate subjects had a 12-minute training period followed by a 10-minute work period. The results indicate a strong advantage for those who had the menu map (Table 3.1).

	Online exploration	Command sequences	Frames	Menu map	
Targets found	8.2	4.7	6.5	8.5	n.s.
Average number of menus visited	10.6	20.4	19.6	9.4	p<.10
Recall of tree (Max = 27)	10.1	8.4	9.8	16.7	p<.05
Satisfaction (Best = 5)	3.6	3.1	2.8	4.8	p<.01

Table 3.1: Scores for four dependent variables showed improved performance for subjects that had studied a graphical menu map for a three level menu (Parton et al., 1985).

As the tree structure grows, users have greater difficulty in maintaining an overall understanding of the semantic organization. Viewing the structure one menu at a time is like seeing the world through a cardboard tube; it's hard to grasp the overall pattern and see relationships among categories. Offering a spatial map can help overcome this difficulty.

Semantic versus alphabetic organization: Since the creation of a universally acceptable semantic decomposition with several tree levels is a challenge, some designers have attempted an index strategy that provides a tree structure based on simple alphabetic organization of the target items.

Thirty student volunteers were tested in use of a tree structured database of 470 index pages and an alphabetic index of 453 terms (Tombaugh & McEwen, 1982). A typical search in the two forms is shown in Figure 3.7. In this counterbalanced within subjects design, half the subjects began with one method and then tried the second method; the other half of the subjects worked in the opposite order. Subjects performed 20 searches, and no significant differences were found in mean search time, number of keypresses, or number of menus accessed. Under both conditions, subjects "required about twice the minimum number of pages necessary to find the information" and "they made one or more errors on 40 percent of the questions." Users eventually succeeded in

<pre>
                Tree Search for Baseball Scores

User sees: 1. News
                                      2. Sports
                                      3. Entertainment
User selects 2 and sees: SPORTS
                                      1. Hockey
                                      2. Baseball
                                      3. ...
User selects 2 and sees: BASEBALL
                                      1. Scores
                                      2. Standings
                                      3. ...
User selects 1 and sees: BASEBALL SCORES
              Alphabetic Search for Baseball Scores

User sees: 1. A-B-C
                                      2. D-E
                                      3. ...
User selects 1 and sees: 1. A
                                      2. B
                                      3. C
User selects 2 and sees: DIRECTORY FOR B
                                      ...
                                      Banks.......22114
                                      Baseball...221313
                                      Books........2516
User keys 221313 and sees: BASEBALL
                                      1. Scores
                                      2. Standings
                                      3. ...
User selects 1 and sees: BASEBALL SCORES
</pre>

Figure 3.7: Samples from a tree structured database of meaningful terms and an alphabetical index. (J. W. Tombaugh and S. McEwan, Comparison of two information retrieval methods on Videotex: Tree-structure versus alphabetic directory, *Proc. Human Factors in Computer Systems.* Copyright 1982, Association for Computing Machinery, Inc. Reprinted by permission)

98.7 percent of the questions, so that although performance was far from optimal, successful searching was possible with both methods. Subjective evaluations did not favor one method over the other, but when one method required more pages for a specific question, the preference was for the shorter method.

Tombaugh and McEwen conjectured that offering both methods may be the best resolution; subjects can choose the method that is most appealing for each question. If one method leads to difficulty, then the users can try the other.

Summary: There is no perfect menu structure that matches every person's knowledge of the application domain. Designers must use good judgment for the initial implementation but then be receptive to suggested improvements and empirical data. Users will gradually gain familiarity, even with extremely complex tree structures, and will be increasingly successful in locating required items.

3.2.4 Acyclic and cyclic menu networks

Although tree structures are very appealing, sometimes network structures are more appropriate. For example, it might make sense to provide access to banking information from both the financial and consumer parts of a tree structure. A second motivation for networks is that it may be desirable to permit paths between disparate sections of a tree rather than requiring users to begin a new search from the main menu. These and other conditions lead to network structures in the form of acyclic or even cyclic graphs. As users move from trees, to acyclic networks, to cyclic networks, the potential for getting lost increases.

With a tree structure, the user can form a mental model of the structure and the relationship among the menus. Developing this mental model may be more difficult with a network. With a tree structure, there is a single parent menu, so backward traversals toward the main menu are straightforward. In networks, a stack of visited menus must be kept to allow backward traversals.

In a thorough study of seventeen subjects using menu networks of 50 frames, Mantei (1982) concluded that "the structure of the user interface...causes disorientation if this structure is not obvious to the user."

If networks are used, it may be helpful to preserve a notion of "level" or distance from the main menu. Users may feel more comfortable if they have a sense of how far they are from the main menu.

3.3   ITEM PRESENTATION SEQUENCE

Once the items in a menu have been chosen, the designer is still confronted with the problem of presentation sequence. If the items have a natural sequence, such as days of the week, chapters in a book, or sizes of eggs, then the decision is trivial. Typical bases for sequencing items include:

1. *Time*. Chronological ordering.
2. *Numeric ordering*. Ascending or descending ordering.
3. *Physical properties*. Increasing or decreasing length, area, volume, temperature, weight, velocity, etc.

Many cases have no natural ordering, and the designer must choose from such possibilities as:

1. *Alphabetic sequence of terms*.
2. *Grouping of related items*, with blank lines or other demarcation between groups
3. *Most frequently used items first*.
4. *Most important items first*. Importance may be difficult to decide and may vary among users.

Card (1982) experimented with a single 18-item vertical permanent menu of text editing commands such as INSERT, ITALIC, and CENTER. He presented subjects with a command, and they had to locate the command in the list, move a mouse-controlled cursor, and select the command by pressing a button on the mouse. The menu items were sequenced one of three ways: alphabetically, in functional groups, and randomly. Each of four subjects made 86 trials with each sequencing strategy. The mean times were:

alphabetic   0.81 seconds
functional   1.28 seconds
random   3.23 seconds

Since subjects were given the target item, they did best when merely scanning to match the menu items in an alphabetic sequence. The performance with the functional groupings was remarkably good, indicating that subjects began to remember the groupings and could go directly to a group. In menu applications where the users must make a decision about the most suitable menu item, the functional arrangement might become more appealing. Memory for the functionally grouped items would be likely to surpass memory for the alphabetic or random sequences. The poor performance with the random sequence confirms the importance of considering alternative item presentation sequences.

With a 64-item menu, the time for locating a target word was found to increase from just over 2 seconds for an alphabetic menu to above 6 seconds for a random menu (McDonald et al., 1983). When the target word was replaced with a single line definition, the 109 subjects could no longer scan for a simple match and had to consider each menu item carefully. The advantage of alphabetic ordering nearly vanished. User reaction time went up to about 7 seconds for the alphabetic and about 8 seconds for the random organization. Somberg and Picardi (1983) studied user reaction times in finding which category a target word belonged to in a five-item menu. Their three experiments revealed a significant and nearly linear relationship between the user's reaction time and the serial position of the correct category in the menu. Furthermore, there was a significant increase in reaction time if the target word was unfamiliar rather than familiar.

3.4   RESPONSE TIME AND DISPLAY RATE

A critical variable that may determine the attractiveness of menu selection is the speed at which users can move through the menus. The two components of speed are system response time, the time it takes for the system to begin displaying information in response to a user selection, and display rate, the rate in characters per second at which the menus are displayed (see Chapter 7).

Deep menu trees or complex traversals become annoying to the user if system response time is slow, resulting in long and multiple delays. With slow display rates, lengthy menus become annoying because of the volume of text that must be displayed. In positive terms, if the response time is long, then create menus with more items on each menu to reduce the number of menus necessary. If the display rate is slow, create menus with fewer items to reduce the display time. If the response time is long and the display rate is low, menu selection is very unappealing, and command language strategies, in spite of the greater memory demands on the users, become more attractive.

With short response times and rapid display rates, menu selection becomes a lively medium that can be attractive even for frequent and knowledgeable users.

In a study carried out under my direction by Carl Bean and Joel Gallun, twelve psychology undergraduates were given two 5-minute menu selection tasks. Half the subjects went from 300 baud (approximately 30 characters per second) to 1,200 baud (approximately 120 characters per second) display terminals while the other half were tested in the reverse order. The average number of correctly completed searches went from 2.17 to 3.33 as the display rate was increased, a statistically significant difference ($p < 0.01$). Subjective preference scores and anecdotal reports strongly favored the faster display rate.

In five studies with 165 adult users of a videotex system, response time delay pairs (0 vs. 10 seconds, 10 vs. 15 seconds, and 3 vs. 7 seconds) did not yield a statistically significant difference in the preference or performance measures tested (Murray & Abrahamson, 1983). The authors' interpretation was that "inexperienced videotex users are relatively immune to a wide range of constant values of system delay." Other studies have also found that novice users are often pleased with slower response times. However, the large variations in individual performance may have obscured the usual preference for faster response times. Murray and Abrahamson found a significant effect that indicated that large variations in response time led to slower rates of responding.

3.5   MOVING THROUGH MENUS QUICKLY

Even with short response times and high display rates, frequent menu users may become annoyed with making several menu selections to complete a task (Hiltz & Turoff, 1981). There may be some advantage to reducing the number of menus by increasing the number of items per menu, where possible, but this may not be enough. As response times lengthen and display rates decrease, the need for shortcuts through the menus increases.

Instead of creating a command language to accomplish the task with positional or keyword parameters, the menu approach can be refined to accommodate expert and frequent users. Three approaches have been used: allow typeahead for known menu choices, assign names to menus to allow direct access, and create menu macros that assign names to frequently used menu sequences.

3.5.1 Menus with typeahead—the BLT approach

A natural way to permit frequent menu users to speed through the menus is to allow "typeahead." The user does not have to wait to see the menus before choosing the items but can type a string of letters or numbers when presented with the main menu. For example, in the document printing package in Section 3.2, the user could type 131 to get printing at the terminal, double spacing, and no page numbering. The IBM Interactive System Productivity Facility (ISPF) has numbered choices and allows typeahead with a decimal point between choices (e.g., 1.2.1). Full duplex systems such as Control Data Corporation's PLATO Computer-Based Education System naturally permit typeahead, because pressing of a special RETURN or NEXT key is not required—single keystrokes cause an interrupt at the central computer.

If the menu items are identified with single letters, then the concatenation of menu selections in the typeahead scheme generates a command name that acquires mnemonic value. To users of a photo library search system that offered menus with typeahead, a color slide portrait quickly became known as a CSP, and a black and white print of a landscape became known as a BPL. These mnemonics come to be remembered and chunked as a single concept. This strategy quickly became known as the BLT approach after the abbreviation for a bacon, lettuce, and tomato sandwich.

The attraction of the BLT approach is that users can gracefully move from being novice menu users to being knowledgeable command users. There are no new commands to learn, and as soon as users become familiar with one branch of the tree, they can apply that knowledge to speed up their work. Learning can be incremental; users can apply one, two, or three letter typeahead and then explore the less familiar menus. If users forget part of the tree, they simply revert to menu usage.

The BLT approach requires a more elaborate parser for the user input, and handling nonexistent menu choices is a bit more problematic. It is also necessary to ensure distinct first letters for items within each menu, but not across menus. Still, the typeahead or BLT approach is attractive because it is powerful, simple, and allows graceful evolution from novice to expert.

3.5.2 Menu names for direct access

A second approach to support frequent users is to use numbered menu items and assign names to each menu frame. Users can follow the menus or, if they know the name of their destination, they can type it in and go there directly. The CompuServe Information Service has a three-letter identifier for major topics, followed by a dash and a page number. Rather than working their way through three levels of menus at thirty characters per second, users know that they can go directly to TWP–1, the start of the subtree containing today's edition of *The Washington Post*.

This strategy is useful if there are a small number of destinations that each user needs to remember. If users need to access many different portions of the menu tree, it becomes difficult to keep track of the destination names. A list of the current destination names is necessary so that designers are sure to create unique names for new entries.

An empirical comparison of the learnability of the typeahead and direct access strategies demonstrated an advantage for the latter (Laverson, Norman, & Shneiderman, 1985). Thirty-two undergraduates had to learn either path names (typeahead) or destination names (direct access) for a four-level menu tree. The direct access names proved to be significantly faster to learn and were preferred. Different tree structures or menu contents may influence the outcome of similar studies.

3.5.3 Menu macros

A third approach to serving frequent menu users is to allow regularly used paths to be recorded by users as menu macros. In other words, users can define their own commands. A user can invoke the macro facility, traverse the menu structure, and then assign a name. When the name is invoked, the traversal is executed automatically. This mechanism allows individual tailoring of the system and can provide a simplified access mechanism for users with limited needs.

3.6   MENU SCREEN DESIGN

Very little experimental research has been done on menu system screen design. This section contains many subjective judgments that are in need of empirical validation (see Table 3.2).

3.6.1 Titles

Choosing the title for a book is a delicate matter for an author, editor, or publisher. A more descriptive or memorable title can make a big difference in reader responses. Similarly, choosing titles for menus is a complex matter that deserves serious thought.

For single menus, a simple descriptive title that identifies the situation is all that is necessary. With a linear sequence of menus, the titles

MENU SELECTION GUIDELINES

- Use task semantics to organize menu structure
  (single, linear sequence, tree structure, acyclic networks, and cyclic networks)
- Try to give position in organization by graphic design, numbering, and titles
- Items become titles in walking down a tree
- Make meaningful groupings of items in a menu
- Make meaningful sequences of items in a menu
- Items should be brief and consistent in grammatic style
- Permit type-ahead, jump-ahead, or other short-cuts
- Permit jumps to previous and main menu
- Use consistent layout and terminology
- Consider novel selection mechanisms and devices
- Consider response time and display rate impact
- Consider screen size
- Offer help facilities

Table 3.2: Menu selection guidelines distilled from practice, but in need of validation and clarification.

should accurately represent the stages in the linear sequence. For the menus in the document printing package referred to in Section 3.2, the titles might be Printing location, Spacing control, and Page numbering placement. Consistent grammatical style can reduce confusion. If the third menu were titled How do you want page numbering to be done? or Select page numbering placement options, many users would be unsettled. Excess verbiage becomes a distraction. Brief noun phrases are often sufficient.

For tree structured menus, choosing titles is more difficult. Such titles as Main menu or topic descriptions as Bank transactions for the root of the tree clearly indicate that the user is at the beginning of a session. One potentially helpful rule is to use the exact words in the high-level menu items as the titles for the next lower-level menu. It is reassuring to users to see an item such as "Business and Financial Services" and after selecting it, the screen that appears is titled Business and Financial Services. It might be unsettling to get a screen titled Managing your money even though the intent is similar. Imagine looking in the table of contents of a book and seeing a chapter title such as "The American Revolution," but when you turn to the indicated page you find "Our early history"—you might worry about whether you had made a mistake and your confidence might be undermined.

Using menu items as titles may encourage the menu author to choose items more carefully so that they are descriptive in two contexts.

A further concern is consistency in placement of titles and other features in a menu screen. Teitelbaum and Granda (1983) demonstrated that user think time nearly doubled when the position of information, such as titles or prompts, was varied on menu screens.

In networks of menus, titles become even more important as a guidepost because the potential for confusion is greater. If menu items are made to match the title, then several menus in a network may have the same items. It is satisfying to find the item "Electronic mail" in several menus, but unsettling to find menus with variant terms such as "Electronic mail," "Sending a note to another user," and "Communicating with your colleagues."

3.6.2 Phrasing of menu items

Just because a system has menu choices written with English words, phrases, or sentences does not guarantee comprehensibility. Individual words may not be familiar to some users, and often two menu items may appear to satisfy the user's needs. This is an enduring problem with no perfect solution. Designers can gather feedback from colleagues, users, pilot studies, acceptance tests, and user performance monitoring. The following guidelines may seem obvious, but they need to be stated since they are so often violated:

1. *Use familiar and consistent terminology.* Carefully select terminology that is familiar to the designated user community and keep a list of these terms to facilitate consistent use.

2. *Ensure that items are distinct from one another.* Each item should be clearly distinguished from other items. For example, `Slow tours of the countryside`, `Journeys with visits to parks`, and `Leisurely voyages` are less distinctive than `Bike tours`, `Train tours to national parks`, and `Cruise ship tours`.

3. *Use consistent and concise phrasing.* The collection of items should be reviewed to ensure consistency and conciseness. Users are likely to feel more comfortable and be more successful with `Animal, Vegetable`, and `Mineral` than with `Information about animals, Vegetable choices you can make`, and `Viewing mineral categories`.

4. *Bring the keyword to the left.* Try to write menu items so that the first word aids the user in recognizing and discriminating among items. Users scan menu items from left to right, and if the first word indicates that this item is not relevant, they can begin scanning the next item.

3.6.3 Graphic layout and design

The constraints of screen width and length, display rate, character set, and highlighting techniques strongly influence the graphic layout of menus. Presenting 50 states as menu items was natural for the Domestic Information Display System built by NASA on a large screen with rapid display rate. On the other hand, the CompuServe Information Service, which must accommodate microcomputer users with 40 column displays over 30 character per second phone lines, used the main menu page shown in Figure 3.8. An improved menu with greater breadth and more

```
COMPUSERVE                PAGE CIS-1
COMPUSERVE INFORMATION SERVICE
1 HOME SERVICES
2 BUSINESS & FINANCIAL
3 PERSONAL COMPUTING
4 SERVICES FOR PROFESSIONALS
5 USER INFORMATION
6 INDEX
ENTER YOUR SELECTION NUMBER,
OR H FOR MORE INFORMATION.
```

Figure 3.8: Early version of CompuServe main menu. The items are insufficiently distinctive; for example, users would have a hard time deciding where to look for home checkbook management programs. (CompuServe, Incorporated)

```
CompuServe                         TOP
  1 Instructions/User Information
  2 Find a Topic
  3 Communications/Bulletin Bds.
  4 News/Weather/Sports
  5 Travel
  6 The Electronic MALL/Shopping
  7 Money Matters/Markets
  8 Entertainment/Games
  9 Home/Health/Family
 10 Reference/Education
 11 Computers/Technology
 12 Business/Other Interests
Enter choice number !
```

Figure 3.9: Revised CompuServe main menu with more items and more distinctive separation among items. (CompuServe, Incorporated)

distintive terms was introduced in 1985 (Figure 3.9). As users move down the tree, they find the page numbers always displayed at the upper right, a title, numbered choices, and instructions. This consistent pattern puts users at ease and helps them sort out the contents. Menu designers should establish guidelines for consistency of at least these menu components:

1. *Titles*. Some prefer centered titles, but left justification is an acceptable approach, especially with slow display rates.

2. *Item placement*. Typically items are left justified with the item number or letter preceding the item description. Blank lines may be used to separate meaningful groups of items. If multiple columns are used, a consistent pattern of numbering or lettering should be used (e.g., down the columns).

3. *Instructions*. The instructions should be identical in each menu and they should be placed in the same position. This includes instructions about traversals, help, or function key usage.

4. *Error messages*. If the users make an unacceptable choice, the message should appear in a consistent position.

5. *Status reports*. Some systems indicate which portion of the menu structure is currently being searched, which page of the structure is currently being viewed, or which choices must be made to complete a task. This information should appear in a consistent position.

Consistent formats help locate necessary information, focus attention on relevant material, and reduce anxiety by offering predictability.

More on titles: Since disorientation is a potential problem, techniques to indicate position in the menu structure can be useful. In books, different type fonts and type sizes indicate chapter, section, and subsection organization. Similarly, in menu trees, as the user goes down the tree structure, the titles can be designed to indicate the level or distance from the main menu. If different fonts, character sizes, or highlighting techniques are available, they can be beneficially used. But even simple techniques with upper case only can be effective; for example:

```
**************************
*    MAIN  MENU      *
**************************
followed by
        * * * HOME SERVICES * * *
followed by
        - - NEWSPAPERS - -
followed by
        New York Times
```

gives a clear indication of progress down the tree. When traversal back up the tree or to an adjoining menu at the same level are done, the user has a feeling of confidence in the action.

With linear sequences of menus, the users can be given a simple visual presentation of position in the sequence by the use of a "position marker." In a computer-assisted instruction sequence with 12 menu frames, a position marker just below the menu items might show progress. In the first frame, the position marker was +------------, in the second frame it was -+-----------, and in the last frame it was ------------+. The users can gauge their progress and see how much remains to be done. The position marker served to separate the items from the instructions in a natural way and the position was indicated in a nonobtrusive manner.

With rapid high resolution displays, more elegant visual representations are possible. With enough screen space, it is possible to show a large portion of the menu map, and allow users to point at a menu anywhere in the tree. Graphic designers or layout artists may be useful consultants in design projects.

3.7   SELECTION MECHANISMS

At first glance, choosing the menu selection mechanism appears to be a minor design decision that can be made quickly, so that the design team can get on to more important matters. On the other hand, the selection mechanism is the central aspect of the menu system for most users.

This issue might be simplified to: Should the designer use numbers or letters for indicating menu items?

Numbered items: The argument in favor of numbers are that there is a clear sequencing of items and that even nontypists can find the numbers on the keyboard. In some systems, numeric keypads are the only input device. Sequential numbering is satisfying because the user can quickly see how many items there are, and visual scanning is aided by the natural numeric ordering. As the user scans down the items, he or she can use the numbers as a guide to make sure that each choice is reviewed. When menu items have a natural numeric sequence, such as the twelve months of the year, the chapters of a book, or the days of the week, numbered choices are very appealing.

The disadvantages of numbers is that when there are more than ten items, two keypresses are required to make a selection. Another problem with numbers only is that if there are standard menu items such as HELP or BACK TO MAIN MENU, then these items may have a different number on each screen. If there is no natural numbering of menu items, then the numbering may be misleading, somehow indicating preference for number 1. Attaching numbers to a group of colors or of bank loan plans may mislead the user into believing that there is some hidden sequencing or preference.

Lettered items: If letters are used for menu items, then there is the choice between ABCDEF... lettering (sequential) and meaningful letter choices (mnemonic). Sequential lettering is similar to numbering, but twenty-six choices are available before two keypresses are required. There is some evidence that there is less likelihood of a keying error with letters than with numbers because the letters are more spread out on the keyboard. It may be a bit more tricky for someone unfamiliar with a typewriter keyboard to locate the proper letter, but this does not appear to be a serious hindrance. Mnemonic lettering for menu items is appealing because the congruence between the description of the item and the keypress can build user confidence in the task. For example, it makes sense to see that T is for TRANSFER and W is for WITHDRAWAL.

Of course, there are mixed strategies. Some systems, such as CompuServe, use numbers for the primary menu items and letters for generic functions, such as M to get to the previous MENU and H to get to helpful information. This approach solves some problems and helps clarify the grouping of menu items. Other systems, such as PLATO, alternate between numbered and lettered menus to prevent inadvertent menu skipping caused by double keypresses, a problem with early PLATO keyboards.

Perlman (1984) found user think times to be lowest with mnemonic letter items and highest with sequential (and therefore nonmnemonic) letter items. Numbered items produced a middle level of user think time.

3.7.1 Typeahead selections

The design decision cannot be made without looking at the larger issue of tasks that require several menu selections. If a sequence of menus is to be viewed, the mnemonic lettering approach gains substantially because the user can remember sequences such as TCS, for Transfer from Checking to Saving, more easily than 253. If the user can type these selection letters before seeing the full menu, then the mnemonic lettering approach becomes a command language for the frequent user. This typeahead approach (Section 3.5.1) is very powerful since it makes the same system appealing to novices and frequent users. Furthermore, it facilitates the graceful evolution from novice to expert—users type ahead only as much as they can remember and then examine the next menu.

3.7.2 System evolution

Another advantage of mnemonic lettering is that as items are added to menus there is no need to renumber the other choices. Mnemonic lettering does have the problem of collisions, that is, more than one choice with the same first letter. This is a serious concern, but often an acceptable alternate term can be found. If not, then using more than one letter of the term may be necessary.

3.7.3 Data entry

If numeric data entry is to be made on some menu/data entry screens, then the lettered item approach will be advantageous since the typeahead command string will be more comprehensible. For example, Depositing $40.00 in Savings account 38847 might be entered as D40.00S38847, which is more appealing than 340.00638847. On the other hand, if the data entry is for alphabetic strings, then the numbered approach might yield a more comprehensible command string. The alternation of letters and numbers helps break a string into more meaningful chunks.

3.7.4 Alternate strategies

Instead of typing a choice, users can move a cursor to the intended item. The cursor could be moved by arrow keys, mouse, joysticks, tab key, or by a touch screen. This approach is appealing to novice users for single screen selections, even though there may be more keystrokes and the RETURN key must be pressed. There is a great sense of satisfaction in being able to move the cursor around the screen. The menu item is highlighted clearly on the screen and in the user's mind, and screen space is conserved since item numbers are not needed. In fact, highlighting, underscoring, drawing a box, moving a pointer, color, or reverse video can be used to indicate visually the item that has been selected. Of course, this approach does not lend itself to typeahead schemes.

Dunsmore reported on a 1981 study at Purdue University in an unpublished memo. Thirty-six high school students used three forms of menu selection. Item-RETURN called for typing the number of the item followed by the RETURN key. Immediate response eliminated the need to type RETURN. Highlight-RETURN called for typing the item, which was then highlighted by reverse video until the RETURN key was pressed. Each subject worked for three minutes with each form. The results were:

	Mean tasks completed	Total errors	Preferred form
Item-RETURN	14.8	4	0 subjects
Immediate response	15.5	7	7 subjects
Highlight-RETURN	15.3	3	29 subjects

Subjects worked slightly faster with the immediate response form, but the error rate was highest. The subjective preference strongly favored the highlighting, which looks very impressive to novice users.

3.8 EMBEDDED MENUS

All the menus discussed thus far might be characterized as explicit menus in that there is an orderly enumeration of the menu items with little extraneous information. However, in many situations the menu items might be embedded in text or graphics and still be selectable.

In designing a textual database about people, events, and places for a museum application, it seemed natural to allow users to retrieve detailed information by selecting a name in context. Selectable names were highlighted and the user could move a reverse video bar among highlighted names by pressing the four arrow keys (Figure 3.10). Selection was made by pressing ENTER and the user obtained a new article plus the option of returning to the previous article. The names, places, phrases, or foreign language words were menu items embedded in meaningful text that informed the user and helped clarify the meaning of the items. Subsequent implementations used mouse selection or touchscreens, leading to the generic term *touchtext* for this application of embedded menus.

Touchtext was also used in an implementation of online maintenance manuals that provided diagnostic information in textual form on one

```
┌─────────────────────────────────────────────────────────────────────┐
│ INTRODUCTION: STAMP UNION                                 PAGE 1 of 2 │
│                                                                       │
│                                                                       │
│        The Adele H. Stamp Union, formerly known as the Student Union, is the │
│                                                                       │
│    cultural and social center for the University. The Union provides a variety of │
│                                                                       │
│    services to the faculty, staff, and students. A plethora of restaurants are │
│                                                                       │
│    available providing a wide choice of atmosphere and a variety of menus. The Union │
│                                                                       │
│    is also center for entertainment. Several shops and many special services │
│                                                                       │
│    are available, too. Union programs include concerts, exhibitions, and craft │
│                                                                       │
│    classes. The Union is open all week from 7 A.M. to 1 A.M. Monday through Friday, │
│                                                                       │
│    and until 2 A.M. on weekends.                                      │
│                        [Select option then press RETURN]              │
│ NEXT PAGE                                                        END   │
└─────────────────────────────────────────────────────────────────────┘
```

Figure 3.10: Display from the database on the Adele H. Stamp Student Union at the University of Maryland showing the embedded menu style of TIES. A reverse video selector box initially covers the NEXT PAGE command. Users move the selector box over highlighted references or commands and then select by pressing RETURN. A touch screen version allows selection by merely touching the highlighted reference or command.

monitor and graphics assistance on a second monitor (Koved & Shneiderman, 1986).

Embedded menus have emerged in other applications. Air traffic control systems allow selection of airplanes in the spatial layout of flight paths to provide more detailed information for controllers. Geographic display systems allow selection of cities or zooming in on specific regions to obtain more information (Herot, 1984). In these applications, the items are icons, text, or regions in a two-dimensional layout.

Language-directed editors permit users to select programming language constructs for expansion during the program composition process (Teitelbaum & Reps, 1981). In a program browser at the University of Maryland, Phil Shafer offered programmers the capability of moving the cursor onto a variable name or procedure invocation, pressing a function key, and receiving the data declaration or procedure definition in a separate window. The variable and procedure names were menu items embedded in the context of a Pascal program.

Many spelling checkers use the embedded menu concept by highlighting the possibly misspelled words in the context of their use. The author of the text can move a cursor to a highlighted word and request possible words or type in the correctly spelled word.

Embedded menus permit items to be viewed in context and they eliminate the need for a distracting and screen-wasting enumeration of items. Contextual display helps keep the users focused on their tasks and the objects of interest. Items rewritten in list form may require longer descriptions (of the items) and increase the difficulty of making selections because of confusion arising from cross-referencing between the menu and the context.

3.9   FORM FILL-IN

Menu selection is effective in choosing an item from a list, but some tasks are cumbersome with menus. If data entry of personal names or numeric values is required, then keyboard typing becomes more attractive. The keyboard may be viewed as a continuous single menu from which multiple selections are made rapidly. When many fields of data are necessary, the appropriate interaction style might be called form fill-in. For example, the user might be presented with a purchase order form for ordering from a catalog, as in Figure 3.11. Another example of a form using color coding is in Color Plate 1.

The form fill-in approach is attractive because the full complement of information is visible, giving the users a feeling of being in control of the dialog. Few instructions are necessary since this approach resembles familiar paper forms. On the other hand, users must be familiar with keyboards, use of the TAB key to move the cursor, error correction by backspacing, field label meanings, permissible field contents, and use of the ENTER key. Form fill-in must be done on displays, not hardcopy devices, and the display device must support cursor movement.

```
Type in the information below,
pressing TAB to move the cursor, and
press ENTER when done.

Name: _____  Phone: (___) ___-___

Address: _____

       : _____

City: _____  State: __  Zip Code: ____


Charge Number:  ____  ____  ____  ____

Catalog                          Catalog
Number         Quantity          Number          Quantity

_____         _____            _____          _____

_____         _____            _____          _____

_____         _____            _____          _____

_____         _____            _____          _____
```

Figure 3.11: A form fill-in design for a department store.

An experimental comparison of database update by form fill-in and a command language strategy demonstrated a significant speed advantage for the form fill-in style (Ogden & Boyle, 1982). Eleven of the twelve subjects expressed a preference for the form fill-in approach.

3.9.1 Form fill-in design guidelines

There is a paucity of empirical work on form fill-in, but a number of design guidelines have emerged from practitioners (Galitz, 1980; Pakin & Wray, 1982; Brown, 1986). Many companies offer form fill-in creation

FORM FILL-IN GUIDELINES

- Meaningful title
- Comprehensible instructions
- Logical grouping and sequencing of fields
- Visually appealing layout
- Familiar field labels
- Consistent terminology and abbreviations
- Error correction for characters and fields
- Visual templates for common fields
- Help facilities

Table 3.3: Form fill-in guidelines based on practical experience, but in need of validation and clarification.

tools, such as Hewlett-Packard's Forms 3000, IBM's ISPF, Digital Equipment Corporation's FORM, Ashton-Tate's dBASE and Lotus Development Corporation's Symphony. Software tools simplify design, help ensure consistency, ease maintenance, and speed implementation. But even with excellent tools, the designer must still make many complex decisions (Table 3.3).

The elements of form fill-in design include:

- *Meaningful title*: Identify the topic and avoid computer terminology

- *Comprehensible instructions*: Describe the user's tasks in familiar terminology. Try to be brief; but if more information is needed, make a set of help screens available to the novice user. In support of brevity, just decribe the necessary action ("Type the address" or simply "address:") and avoid pronouns ("You should type the address") or references to the user "The user of the form should type the address." Another useful rule is to use the word *type* for entering information and *press* for special keys such as the TAB, ENTER, cursor movement, or Programmed Function (PFK, PF, or F) keys. Since ENTER often refers to the special key, avoid using it in the instructions (for example, do not use "Enter the address," but stick to "Type the address.") Once a grammatic style for instructions is developed, be careful to apply that style consistently.

- *Logical grouping and sequencing of fields*: Related fields should be adjacent and aligned with blank space for separation between groups. The sequencing should reflect common patterns; for example, city followed by state followed by zip code.

- *Visually appealing layout of the form*: A uniform distribution of fields is preferable to crowding one part of the screen and leaving other parts blank. Alignment creates a feeling of order and comprehensibility. For example, the field labels, Name, Address, and City, were right justified so that the data entry fields would be vertically aligned. This allows the frequent user to concentrate on the entry fields and ignore the labels. If working from hard copy, the screen should match the paper form.

- *Familiar field labels*: Common terms should be used. If Address were replaced by Domicile, many users would be uncertain or anxious about what to do.

- *Consistent terminology and abbreviations*: Prepare a list of terms and acceptable abbreviations and diligently use the list, making additions only after careful consideration. Instead of varying such terms as Address, Employee Address, ADDR., and Addr., stick to one term, such as Address.

- *Visible space and boundaries for data entry fields*: Underscores or other markers indicate the number of characters available, so users will know when abbreviations or other trimming strategies are needed.

- *Convenient cursor movement*: A simple and visible mechanism is needed for moving the cursor, such as a TAB key or cursor movement arrows.

- *Error correction for individual characters and entire fields*: A backspace key and overtyping should be allowed to enable easy repairs or changes to entire fields.

- *Error messages for unacceptable values*: If users enter an unacceptable value, the error message should appear on completion of the field. The message should indicate permissible values of the field, for example, if the zip code is entered as 28K21 or 2380, the message might indicate that "Zip codes should have 5 digits."

- *Optional fields should be marked*: The word optional or other indicators should be visible. Optional fields should follow required fields, whenever possible.

- *Explanatory messages for fields*: If possible, explanatory information about a field or its values should appear in a standard position, such as in a window on the bottom, whenever the cursor is in the field.

- *Completion signal*: It should be clear to the users what to do when they are finished filling in the fields. Generally, designers should avoid automatic completion when the last field is filled, because users may wish to go back and review or alter field entries.

These considerations may seem obvious, but often forms designers omit the title or have unnecessary computer file names, strange codes, unintelligible instructions, unintuitive groupings of fields, cluttered layouts, obscure field labels, inconsistent abbreviations or field formats, awkward cursor movement, confusing error correction procedures, hostile error messages, and no obvious way to signal completion.

Detailed design rules should reflect local terminology and abbreviations; field sequences familiar to the users; the width and height of the display device; highlighting features such as reverse video, underscoring, intensity levels, color, and fonts; the cursor movement keys; and coding of fields.

3.9.2 Coded fields

Columns of information require special treatment for data entry and for display. Alphabetic fields are customarily left justified on entry and on display. Numeric fields may be left justified on entry but then become right justified on display. When possible, avoid entry and display of leftmost zeroes in numeric fields. Numeric fields with decimal points should line up on the decimal points.

Special attention should be paid to such common fields as:

- *Telephone numbers*: Offer a form to indicate the subfields:

```
Phone: (_ _ _) _ _ _-_ _ _ _
```

Be alert to such special cases as addition of extensions or the need for nonstandard formats for foreign numbers.

- *Social Security numbers*: The pattern for Social Security numbers should appear on the screen as:

```
Social Security Number: _ _ _-_ _-_ _ _ _
```

When the user has typed the first three digits, the cursor should jump to the leftmost position of the two-digit field.

- *Times*: Even though the twenty-four hour clock is convenient, many people find it confusing and prefer A.M. or P.M. designations. The form might appear as:

```
_ _:_ _   _ _   (9:45   AM or PM)
```

    Seconds may or may not be included, adding to the variety of necessary formats.

- *Dates*: This is one of the nastiest problems for which no good solution exists. Different formats for dates are

appropriate for different tasks, and European rules differ
from American rules. It may take a generation until an
acceptable standard emerges.

When presenting coded fields, the instructions might
show an example of correct entry, for example:

```
Date: _ _/_ _/_ _   (04/22/86 indicates April 22, 1986)
```

For many people, examples are more comprehensible than
an abstract description, such as MM/DD/YY.

 * *Dollar amounts (or other currency):* The dollar sign should
   appear on the screen, and users then type only the amount.
   If a large volume of whole dollar amounts are to be
   entered, the user might be presented with a field such as:

```
        Deposit amount: $_ _ _ _ _.00
```

with the cursor to the left of the decimal point. As the user
types numbers, they shift left. To enter an occasional cents
amount, the user must type the decimal point to reach the
00 field for overtyping.

Other considerations in form fill-in design include dealing with
multiscreen forms, mixing menus with forms, the role of graphics,
relationship to paper forms, use of pointing devices, use of color,
handling of special cases, and integration of a word processor to allow
remarks.

3.10   PRACTITIONER'S SUMMARY

Begin by understanding the semantic structure of your application
within the vast range of menu selection situations. Concentrate on
organizing the sequence of menus to match the user's tasks, ensure that

each menu is a meaningful semantic unit, and create items that are distinctive and comprehensible. If some users make frequent use of the system, then typeahead, shortcut, or macro strategies should be allowed. Permit simple traversals to the previously displayed menu and to the main menu. Finally, be sure to conduct human factors tests and involve human factors specialists in the design process (Savage et al., 1982). When the system is implemented, collect usage data, error statistics, and subjective reactions to guide refinement.

Whenever possible, use a menu builder/driver system to produce and display the menus. Commercial menu creation systems are available and should be used to reduce implementation time, ensure consistent layout and instructions, and simplify maintenance.

3.11   RESEARCHER'S AGENDA

Experimental research could help refine the design guidelines concerning semantic organization and sequencing in single and linear sequences of menus. How can differing communities of users be satisfied with a common semantic organization when their information needs are very different? Should users be allowed to tailor the structure of the menus or is the advantage greater in compelling everyone to use the same structure and terminology?

Should a tree structure be preserved even if some redundancy is introduced? How can networks be made safe?

Research opportunities abound. Depth versus breadth tradeoffs under differing conditions need to be studied to provide guidance for designers. Layout strategies, wording of instructions, phrasing of menu items, use of color, response time, and display rate are all excellent candidates for experimentation. Exciting possibilities are becoming available with larger screens, multiple displays, and novel selection devices.

Implementers would benefit from the development of software tools to support menu system creation, management, usage statistics gathering, and evolutionary refinement. Portability of "menu-ware" could be enhanced to facilitate transfer across systems.

REFERENCES

Billingsley, P. A., Navigation through hierarchical menu structures: Does it help to have a map? *Proc. Human Factors Society, 26th Annual Meeting*, (1982), 103–107.

Brown, C. Marlin, *Human-Computer Interface Design Guidelines*, Ablex Publishing Company, Norwood, NJ, (1986).

Brown, James W., Controlling the complexity of menu networks, *Communications of the ACM 25*, 7, (July 1982), 412–418

Card, Stuart K., User perceptual mechanisms in the search of computer command menus, *Proc. Human Factors in Computer Systems*, (March 1982), 190–196.

Clauer, Calvin Kingsley, An experimental evaluation of hierarchical decision-making for information retrieval, IBM Research Report RJ 1093, (September 15, 1972), 83 pages.

Doughty, Roger K., and Kelso, John, An evaluation of menu width and depth on user performance, Unpublished project paper done with Prof. James Foley, George Washington University, Washington, DC (1984).

Dray, S. M., Ogden, W. G., and Vestewig, R. E., Measuring performance with a menu-selection human-computer interface, *Proc. Human Factors Society, 25th Annual Meeting*, (1981), 746–748.

Galitz, Wilbert O., *Human Factors in Office Automation*, Life Office Managment Assn., Atlanta, GA, (1980).

Herot, Christopher F., Graphical user interfaces, in Vassiliou, Y. (Editor), *Human Factors and Interactive Computer Systems*, Ablex Publishers, Norwood, NJ, (1984), 83–103.

Hiltz, Starr Roxanne, and Turoff, Murray, The evolution of user behavior in a computerized conferencing system, *Communications of the ACM 24*, 11, (November 1981), 739–751.

Kiger, John I., The depth/breadth trade-off in the design of menu-driven user interfaces, *International Journal of Man-Machine Studies 20*, (1984), 201–213.

Koved, Lawrence, and Shneiderman, Ben, Embedded menus: Menu selection in context, *Communications of the ACM 29*, (1986) , 312–318.

Landauer, T. K., and Nachbar, D. W., Selection from alphabetic and numeric menu trees using a touch screen: Breadth, depth, and width, *Proc. Human Factors in Computing Systems* (April 1985), ACM SIGCHI, New York, 73–78.

Laverson, Alan, Norman, Kent, and Shneiderman, Ben, An evaluation of jump-ahead techniques for frequent menu users, University of Maryland Computer Science Technical Report 1591, (December 1985).

Lee, E., and Latremouille, S., Evaluation of tree structured organization of information on Telidon, *Telidon Behavioral Research I*, Department of Communications, Ottawa, Canada, (1980).

Liebelt, Linda S., McDonald, James E., Stone, Jim D., and Karat, John, The effect of organization on learning menu access, *Proc. Human Factors Society, 26th Annual Meeting*, (1982), 546–550.

McDonald, James E., Stone, Jim D., and Liebelt, Linda S., Searching for items in menus: The effects of organization and type of target, *Proc. Human Factors Society, 27th Annual Meeting*, (1983), 834–837.

McEwen, S. A., An investigation of user search performance on a Telidon information retrieval system, *Telidon Behavioral Research 2*, Ottawa, Canada, (May 1981).

Mantei, Marilyn, Disorientation behavior in person-computer interaction, Ph. D. Dissertation, University of Southern California (August 1982).

Martin, James, *Viewdata and the Information Society*, Prentice-Hall, Inc., Englewood Cliffs, NJ, (1982), 293 pages.

Miller, Dwight, P., The depth/breadth tradeoff in hierarchical computer menus, *Proc. Human Factors Society, 25th Annual Meeting*, (1981), 296–300.

Murray, Robert P., and Abrahamson, David S., The effect of system response delay and delay variability on inexperienced videotex users, *Behaviour and Information Technology 2*, 3, (1983), 237–251.

Ogden, William C., and Boyle, James M., Evaluating human-computer dialog styles: Command vs. form/fill-in for report modification, *Proc. Human Factors Society, 26th Annual Meeting*, Human Factors Society, Santa Monica, CA, (1982), 542–545.

Pakin, Sherwin E., and Wray, Paul, Designing screens for people to use easily, *Data Management*, (July 1982), 36–41.

Parton, Diana, Huffman, Keith, Pridgen, Patty, Norman, Kent, and Shneiderman, Ben, Learning a menu selection tree: Training methods compared, *Behaviour and Information Technology 4*, 2, (1985), 81–91.

Perlman, Gary, Making the right choices with menus, *INTERACT '84*, First IFIP International Conference on Human-Computer Interaction, North-Holland, Amsterdam (September 1984), 291–295.

Price, Lynne A., Design of command menus for CAD systems, *Proc. ACM-IEEE 19th Design Automation Conference*, (June 1982), 453–459.

Robertson, G., McCracken, D., and Newell, A., The ZOG approach to man-machine communication, *International Journal of Man-Machine Studies 14*, (1981), 461–488.

Savage, Ricky E., Habinek, James K., and Barnhart, Thomas W., The design, simulation, and evaluation of a menu driven user interface, *Proc. Human Factors in Computer Systems*, (1982), 36–40.

Shneiderman, Ben, Direct manipulation: A step beyond programming languages, *IEEE Computer 16*, 8, (August 1983).

Somberg, Benjamin, and Picardi, Maria C., Locus of information familiarity effect in the search of computer menus, *Proc. Human Factors Society, 27th Annual Meeting*, (1983), 826–830.

Teitelbaum, Richard C., and Granda, Richard, The effects of positional constancy on searching menus for information, *Proc. CHI '83, Human Factors in Computing Systems*, Available from ACM, Baltimore, MD (1983), 150–153.

Teitelbaum, T., and Reps, T., The Cornell program synthesizer: A syntax-directed programming environment, *Communications of the ACM 24*, 9, (September 1981), 563–573.

Tombaugh, Jo W., and McEwen, Scott A., Comparison of two information retrieval methods on Videotex: Tree-structure versus alphabetic directory, *Proc. Human Factors in Computer Systems*, (1982), 106–110.

Young, R. M., and Hull, A., Cognitive aspects of the selection of Viewdata options by casual users, *Pathways to the Information Society, Proc. 6th International Conference on Computer Communication*, London, (September 1982), 571–576.

16	EXPENSES						
17							
18	MATERIALS	6000	7000	8000	7800	7200	6000	80
19	SUPPLIES	3000	3500	3800	2700	2900	3000	40
20	PAYROLL	10000	10000	11000	9500	8800	12000	120
21	RENT	2000	2000	2000	2000	2000	2200	22
22	UTILITIES	1000	1100	1200	1100	1000	1200	13
23	ADVERTISING	1000	1000	1200	1300	1300	1500	20
24	LEGAL	300	400	500	500	100	150	2
25	ACCOUNTING	250	250	250	250	250	250	2
26	TAXES	3000	3200	3600	2100	2000	4000	44
27		1200	1200	1200	1200	1200	1200	12
28								
29	TOTAL EXPENSES	27750	29650	32750	23450	26750	31500	35
30								

CHAPTER 4

COMMAND LANGUAGES

I soon felt that the forms of ordinary language were far too diffuse....I was not long in deciding that the most favorable path to pursue was to have recourse to the language of signs. It then became necessary to contrive a notation which ought, if possible, to be at once simple and expressive, easily understood at the commencement, and capable of being readily retained in the memory.

Charles Babbage, "On a method of expressing by signs the action of machinery," 1826

4.1 INTRODUCTION

The history of written language is rich and varied. Early tally marks
and pictographs on cave walls existed for millenia before precise
notations for numbers or other concepts appeared. The Egyptian
hieroglyphs of 5,000 years ago were a tremendous advance because
standard notations facilitated communication across space and time.
Eventually, languages with a small alphabet and rules of word and
sentence formation dominated because of the relative ease of learning,
writing, and reading. In addition to these natural languages, special
languages for mathematics, music, and chemistry emerged because they
facilitated communication and problem solving. In the twentieth century,
novel notations were created for such diverse domains as dance, knitting,
higher forms of mathematics, logic, and DNA molecules.

The basic goals of language design are:

- precision
- compactness
- ease in writing and reading
- speed in learning
- simplicity to reduce errors
- ease of retention over time.

Higher level goals include:

- a close correspondence between reality and the notation
- convenience in carrying out manipulations relevant to the users' tasks
- compatibility with existing notations
- flexibility to accommodate novice and expert users
- expressiveness to encourage creativity
- visual appeal.

Constraints on a language include:

- the capacity for human beings to record the notation
- a good match with the recording and the display media (e.g., clay tablets, paper, printing presses)
- the convenience in speaking (vocalizing).

Successful languages evolve to serve the goals within the constraints.

The printing press was a remarkable stimulus to language development because it made widespread dissemination of written work possible. The computer is another remarkable stimulus to language development, not only because widespread dissemination through networks is possible, but also because the computer is a tool to manipulate languages and because languages are a tool for manipulating computers.

The computer has had only a modest influence on spoken natural languages, compared to its enormous impact as a stimulus to the development of numerous new formal written languages. Early computers were meant to do mathematical computations, so the first programming languages had a strong mathematical flavor. But computers were quickly found to be effective manipulators of logical expressions, business data, graphics, and text. Increasingly, computers are used to operate on the real world: directing robots, issuing dollar bills at bank terminals, controlling manufacturing, and guiding spacecraft. These newer applications encourage language designers to find convenient notations to direct the computer while preserving the needs of people to use the language for communication and problem solving.

Therefore, effective computer languages must not only represent the users' tasks and satisfy the human needs for communication but must also be in harmony with mechanisms for recording, manipulating, and displaying these languages in a computer.

Computer programming languages that were developed in the 1960s and early 1970s, such as FORTRAN, COBOL, ALGOL, PL/I, or Pascal, were designed for use in a noninteractive computer environment. Programmers would compose hundreds or thousands of lines of code, carefully check them over, and then compile or interpret by computer to produce a desired result. Incremental programming was one of the design considerations in BASIC and such advanced languages as LISP,

APL, or PROLOG. Programmers in these languages were expected to build smaller pieces online and interactively execute and test them. Still the common goal was to create a large program that was preserved, studied, extended, and modified.

Database query languages developed in the mid to late 1970s, such as SQL or QUEL, emphasized shorter segments of code (three to twenty lines) that could be written at a terminal and immediately executed. The goal of the user was more to create a result than a program.

Command languages, which originated with operating systems commands, are distinguished by their immediacy and by their impact on devices or information. Users issue a command and watch what happens. If the result is correct, the next command is issued; if not, some other strategy is adopted. The commands are brief and their existence is transitory. Of course, command histories are sometimes kept and macros are created in some command languages, but the essence of command languages is their ephemeral nature and the fact that they produce an immediate result on some object of interest.

Command languages are distinguished from menu selection systems by the fact that the users of command languages must recall notation and initiate action. Menu selection users receive instructions and must only recognize and choose among a limited set of visible alternatives; they respond more than initiate. Command language users are often called on to accomplish remarkable feats of memorization and typing. For example, does it make sense to type the UNIX command:

```
GREP -V ^$ FILEA > FILEB
```

in order to delete blank lines from a file? Similarly, to get printout on unlined paper with the IBM 3800 laser printer, a user at one installation was instructed to type

```
CP TAG DEV E VTSO LOCAL 2 OPTCD=J F=3871 X=GB12
```

The puzzled user was greeted with a shrug of the shoulders and the equally cryptic comment that "sometimes logic doesn't come into play, it's just getting the job done." This style of work may have been acceptable in the past, but user communities and their expectations are changing. The empirical studies described in this chapter are beginning to clarify guidelines for many command language design issues.

Command languages may consist of single commands or have complex syntax (Section 4.2). The language may have only a few operations or thousands. Commands may have a hierarchical structure or permit concatentation to form variations (Section 4.3). A typical form is a verb followed by a noun object with qualifiers or arguments for the verb or noun. Abbreviations may be permitted (Section 4.5). Feedback may be generated for acceptable commands and error messages (see Section 8.1) may result from unacceptable forms or typos. Command language systems may offer the user brief prompts or they may be close to menu selection systems (Section 4.6). Finally, natural language interaction can be considered as a complex form of command language (Section 4.7).

4.2   FUNCTIONALITY TO SUPPORT USERS' TASKS

People use computers and command language systems to accomplish tasks. The most common application of command languages is for text editing; other applications include operating systems control, bibliographic retrieval, database manipulation, electronic mail, financial management, airline or hotel reservations, inventory, manufacturing process control, and adventure games.

The critical determinant of success is the functionality of the system. People will use a computer system if it gives them powers not otherwise available. If the power is attractive enough, people will use a system despite its poor user interface. Therefore, the first step for the designer is to determine the functionality of the system by assessing the user task domain.

A common design error is excess functionality. In a misguided effort to add features, options, and commands, the designer can overwhelm the user. Excess functionality means more code to maintain, potentially more bugs, possibly slower execution, and more help screens, error messages, and user manuals (see Chapter 9). For the user, excess functionality slows learning, increases the chance of error, and adds the confusion of longer manuals, more help screens, and less specific error messages. On the other hand, insufficient functionality leaves the user frustrated because an apparent function is not supported. For instance, the system might require the user to copy the contents of the screen by hand because there is no simple print command or to reorder the output because there is no sort command.

Evidence of excessive functionality comes from a study of 17 secretaries at a scientific research center who used IBM's XEDIT editor for a median of 18 months for 50 to 360 minutes per day (Rosson, 1983). Their usage of XEDIT commands was monitored for five days. The average number of commands used was 26 per user with a maximum of 34; the number of commands was correlated with experience (r=.49). XEDIT has 141 commands, so even the most experienced user dealt with less than a quarter of the commands. Users did not appear to employ idiosyncratic subsets of the language but added commands to their repertoire in an orderly and similar pattern.

Careful task analysis might result in a table of user communities and tasks with each entry indicating expected frequency of use. The high volume tasks should be made easy to carry out, and then the designer must decide which communities of users are the prime audience for the system. Users may differ in their position in an organization, their knowledge of computers, or their frequency of system usage. One difficulty in carrying out such a task analysis is predicting who the users might be and what tasks they need to accomplish.

Inventing and supplying new functions are the major goals of many designers. They know that marketplace acceptance is often determined by the availability of functions that the competition does not provide. Word processor designers continue to add such functions as boldface, footnotes, dual windows, mail merge, or spelling checks to entice customers. A feature analysis list (Figure 4.1) can be very helpful in comparing designs and in discovering novel functions (Roberts, 1980).

At an early stage, the destructive operations such as deleting objects or changing formats should be carefully evaluated to ensure that they are reversible or at least protected from accidental invocation. Designers should also identify error conditions and prepare error messages. A transition diagram showing how each command takes the user to another state is a highly beneficial aid to design, as well as to eventual training of

TEXT EDITOR FEATURE LIST

Estimated time to install
(15 minutes to two hours)

Number of diskettes provided
(1 to 7)

Right to make copies

On-screen tutorial

Textbook tutorial

Textbook reference guide

Online help

Meaningful error messages

Spelling checker built in
to word processor

Thesaurus built in to word
processor

Mail merge

Automatic table of contents
generation

Automatic index generation

Menu, command, or function
key driven

Save block

Block defined by highlight
or markers

Maximum size for block
operation

Document size limit

Capacity to edit more
than one file

Can rename disk files

Can copy disk files

Can show disk directory

What you see is what you get

Preview print format

Editing allowed during
printing

Print part of file

Can chain documents
for printing

Can queue documents
for printing

Automatic page numbering

Print multiple copies

Automatic file save

Save file without exiting

Automatic backup file

Can create file without
embedded codes

Subscript/superscript

Italics

Underscoring

Boldface

Multiple fonts

Multiple font sizes

Left and right justification

Centering

Tabbing

Proportional spacing

Multiple column output

Footnotes

Endnotes

Line spacing options

Number of printers supported

Characters per line range
(78–455)

Lines per screen

Can change screen colors

Can redefine key functions

Can specify macros

Automatic hyphenization

Can switch from insert to
overwrite modes

Automatic indentation

Multiple indents/outdents

Change case command

Ruler line can be displayed
to show tabs

Display column, line,
and page number

Headers and footers

Math functions

Sort functions

Move cursor by character,
word, sentence, paragraph

Move cursor by screen

Move cursor to left or
right ends of line

Move cursor to top or
bottom of screen

Move cursor to top or
bottom of document

Delete by character, word,
line, sentence, or
paragraph

Delete to end of document

Undelete

Search forward and backward

Search by patterns

Can ignore case in searching

Leave and locate markers

Copy/move

Copy/move by columns

Figure 4.1: Feature list for word processors distilled from Roberts (1980) and Wiswell, Phil, Word processing: The latest word, *PC Magazine*, (August 20, 1985), 110–134.

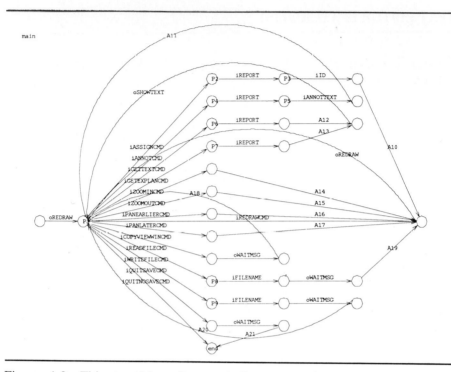

Figure 4.2: This transition diagram indicates user inputs with an "i" and computer outputs with an "o". This is a relatively simple diagram showing only a portion of the system. Complete transition diagrams may take many pages. (Courtesy of Robert J. K. Jacob, Naval Research Laboratory, Washington, DC)

users (Figure 4.2). If the diagram gets too complicated, it may signal the need to redesign the system.

Major considerations for expert users are the possibilities of tailoring the language to suit personal work styles and creating named macros to permit several operations to be carried out with a single command. Macro facilities allow extensions that the designers could not foresee or that are beneficial to only a small fragment of the user community. A macro facility can be a full programming language that might include specification of arguments, conditionals, iteration, integers, strings, and screen manipulation primitives, plus library and editing tools. Well-developed macro facilities are one of the strong attractions of command languages.

4.3   COMMAND ORGANIZATION STRATEGIES

Several strategies for command organization have emerged, but guidelines for choosing among these are only beginning to be discussed. A unifying concept, model, or metaphor is an aid to learning, problem solving, and retention (Carroll & Thomas, 1982). In electronic mail circles, lively discussions can be started over the metaphoric merits of such task-related objects as file drawers, folders, documents, memos, notes, letters, or messages. The debates continue about the appropriate task domain actions (CREATE, EDIT, COPY, MOVE, DELETE) and the choice of an action pair LOAD/SAVE (too much in the computer domain), READ/WRITE (acceptable for letters but awkward for file drawers), or OPEN/CLOSE (acceptable for folders but awkward for notes).

Similarly, debate continues over whether the commands should manipulate lines, as in program editors and older line-oriented editors, or words, sentences, and paragraphs, as in new word processors. Choosing one strategy over another is helpful. Designers who fail to choose and attempt to support every possibility risk overwhelming the users while missing the opportunity to optimize for one strategy. Designers often err by choosing a metaphor closer to the computer domain rather than the user's task domain. Of course, metaphors can mislead the user, but careful design can reap the benefits while reducing the detriments.

Having adopted a concept, model, or metaphor for operations, the designer must now choose a strategy for the command structure. Mixed strategies are possible, but learning, problem solving, and retention may be aided by limiting the complexity.

4.3.1 Simple command list

Each command is chosen to carry out a single task, and the number of commands matches the number of tasks. With a small number of tasks, this approach can produce a system that is simple to learn and use. With a large number of commands, there is danger of confusion. The VI editor on UNIX systems offers many commands while attempting to keep

VI COMMANDS TO MOVE THE CURSOR

Moving within a window

H	go to home position (upper left)
L	go to last line
M	go to middle line
(CR)	next line (carriage return)
+	next line
−	previous line
CTRL−P	previous line in same column
CTRL−N	next line in same column
(LF)	next line in same column (line feed)

Moving within a line

0	go to start of line
$	go to end of line
(space)	go right one space
CRTL−H	go left one space
h	go left one space
w	forward one word
b	backward one word
e	end (rightmost) character of a word
)	forward one sentence
(	backward one sentence
}	forward one paragraph
{	backward one paragraph
W	blank out a delimited word
B	backwards blank out a delimited word
E	go to the end of a delimited word

Finding a character

fx	find the character x going forward
Fx	find the character x going backward
tx	go up to x going forward
Tx	go up to x going backward

Scrolling the window

CTRL-F	go forward one screen
CTRL-B	go backward one screen
CTRL-D	go forward one half screen
CTRL-U	go backward one half screen
G	go to line
/pat	go to line with pattern forward
pat	go to line with pattern backward

Figure 4.3: The profusion of commands in vi may enable expert users to get tasks done with just a few actions, but the number of commands can be overwhelming to novice and intermittent users.

thc number of keystrokes low. This results in complex strategies employing single letters, shifted single letters, and CTRL key plus single letters (Figure 4.3). Furthermore, some commands stand alone, whereas others must be combined in often irregular patterns.

4.3.2 Command plus arguments

Each command (COPY, DELETE, PRINT,...) is followed by one or more arguments (FILEA, FILEB, FILEC,...) that indicate objects to be manipulated.

```
COPY FILEA,FILEB
DELETE FILEA
PRINT FILEA,FILEB,FILEC
```

Commands may be separated from the arguments by a blank or other delimiter, and the arguments may have blanks or delimiters between them (Schneider et al., 1984). Keyword labels for arguments may be helpful to some users; for example;

```
COPY FROM=FILEA TO=FILEB
```

The labels require extra typing and increase chances of a typo, but readability is improved and order dependence is eliminated.

4.3.3 Command plus options and arguments

Commands may have options (3, HQ, ...) to indicate special cases. For example

```
PRINT/3,HQ FILEA
PRINT (3,HQ) FILEA
PRINT FILEA −3,HQ
```

may produce three copies of FILEA at the printer in the headquarters building. As the number of options grows, the complexity can become overwhelming and the error messages less specific. The arguments may also have options, such as version numbers, privacy keys, or disk addresses.

The number of arguments, number of options, and the permissible syntactic forms can grow very rapidly. One airline reservations system uses the following command to locate availability of flight on August 21, from Washington's National Airport (DCA) to New York's La Guardia Airport (LGA) around 3:00 P.M.:

```
A0821DCALGA0300P
```

Even with substantial training, error rates can be high with this approach, but frequent users seem to manage and even appreciate the compact form of this type of command.

UNIX is a widely used command language system in spite of the complexity of the command formats (see Figure 4.4) that have been severely criticized (Norman, 1981). Here again, users will master complexity to benefit from the rich functionality in a system. Error rates with actual use of UNIX commands ranged from 3 percent to 53 percent (Kraut et al., 1983; Hanson et al., 1984). Even common commands generated high syntactic error rates: mv (18 percent), cp (30 percent), and awk (34 percent). Still, there is a certain attraction to the complexity

at 2A Friday timehog
at 2:00 a.m. Friday, run program
awk '{print $1 + $2}' file1
print sum of first two fields of each line
cat −n file1
print specified file to terminal, number output lines
cat file1 >> file2
*append **file1** to end of **file2***
cc file.c
*compile C program, executable in **a.out***
cd /usr/lib
change working directory to specified one
chmod g + rw file1 file2
change mode of files, adding group read and write access
chmod 600 file
change mode of file, allow only read and write by owner
cp file1 file2
*make a copy of **file1** named **file2***
cp −r dir /tmp
*recursively copy **dir** and its subdirectories to **/tmp***
diff −l dir1 dir2
*summarize differences between files in **dir1** and **dir2***
f77 file.f
*compile Fortran program, executable in **a.out***
f77 −o file file.f file.o
*compile Fortran program, link with **file.o**, executable in **file***
find $HOME −name '#•' −exec rm { } \;
remove files with names beginning with a pound sign
finger name
look up information on user's login or real name
grep '[Pp]hone' file
*print all lines in file containing **Phone** or **phone***
grep −l main •
*print names of files in current directory containing **main***
head −6 file
print first six lines of file
kill −9 0
send a KILL signal to processes started since login
ln −s file1 file2 /tmp
make symbolic links to files in specified directory
lpq job user
report print spooler status of user's job
lpr −p file
paginate file and spool it to the line printer

ls
print a list of the files in the current directory
ls −R /bin
list files in specified directory and its subdirectories
mail molly tracey < file
send a file to specified users as mail
man spell
print Unix user's manual page for a command
mkdir /tmp/myjunk
make a new directory
more +50 file
view file by screenful, starting at line 50
mv file1 file2 /tmp
move files to specified directory
nroff file ¦ more
preview formatted file on terminal
pc file.p
*compile Pascal program, executable in **a.out***
pr file ¦ lpr
paginate a file with default header, spool output
ps l
print long listing of current processes, PID's and status
pwd
print current working directory
rlogin puter2
login on remote computer
rm file
remove (delete) a file
rm −i junk[0 − 9]
*remove files **junk0** ... **junk9**, confirming first*
sort +3 −4 file
print file sorted only on fourth field
stty everything
print all stty option settings
stty raw; prog; stty −raw
*set terminal to **raw** mode, run a program, and restore mode*
style −p file
print sentences in file containing a passive verb
vi file
edit file using full screen editor
w
list who's logged in, and what they're doing

Figure 4.4: Examples of common UNIX commands with brief explanations. (Courtesy of Specialized Systems Consultants, Inc., Seattle WA)

among a portion of the potential user community. There is satisfaction in overcoming the difficulties and becoming one of the inner circle ("gurus" and "wizards") who are knowledgeable about system features—command language macho.

4.3.4 Hierarchical command structure

The full set of commands is organized into a tree structure, like a menu tree. The first level might be the command action, the second might be an object argument, and the third might be a destination argument:

Action	Object	Destination
CREATE	File	File
DISPLAY	Process	Local printer
REMOVE	Directory	Screen
COPY		Laser printer
MOVE		

If a hierarchical structure can be found for a set of tasks, it offers a meaningful structure to a large number of commands. In this case, 5 x 3 x 4 = 60 tasks can be carried out with only five command names and one rule of formation. Another advantage is that a command menu approach can be developed to aid the novice or intermittent user, as was done in VisiCalc and Lotus 1–2–3.

Several help systems allow a hierarchical command to retrieve text about subsystems and their commands. For example, to get help on the editor command for deleting lines in a document, the user might type:

        HELP EDIT DELETE LINES

Of course, the difficulty comes in knowing what keywords are available. Users can type the first few elements of the command and then receive a menu of items.

Many word processors use a hierarchical command structure for the numerous commands that they support. For example, Figure 4.5 shows the command structure for FinalWord.

4.4   THE BENEFITS OF STRUCTURE

Human learning, problem solving, and memory are greatly facilitated by meaningful structure. If command languages are well-designed, users

```
                          Buffers_Menu
                            Delete buffer          Switch buffer
                            List buffers           Z - exit menu
                            Previous buffer

                          Capitalization_Menu
                            Clear highlighting     Set highlighting
                            Flip highlighting      Uppercase
                            Lowercase              Z - exit menu

                          Files_Menu
  Menus_-_CTRL-X            Backup and save file   Save file
    Buffers                 Directory edit         Write file
    Capitalization          Find file             Z - exit menu
    Files                   Read file
    Help
    Layout                 Help_Menu
    Miscellaneous           Explain key            Remove help buffer
    Regions                 Help about             Z - exit menu
    Set
    Windows                Layout_Menu
    Z - exit menu           Advanced print         Print
                            Center line            Right flush line
                            Fill paragraph         Unjustify paragraph
                            Justify paragraph      Verify advanced print
                            Left flush line        Z - exit menu

                          Miscellaneous_Menu
                            Abort printing         Line count
                            Center point           Query replace
                            Display refresh        Report position
                            Exit editor            Z - exit menu
                            Global replace

                          Regions_Menu
                            Append to KILLS        Outdent
                            Copy to marker         Set marker
                            Delete to marker       Undelete
                            Indent

                          Set_Menu
                            Fill mode on/off       Overwrite mode on/off
                            Highlight on/off       Report values
                            Indent column          Tab interval
                            Line length            Z - exit menu

                          Windows_Menu
                            Grow window            Switch windows
                            Move other             Two windows
                            One window             Z - exit menu
```

Figure 4.5: The tree structure of menus in the FinalWord word processor (Mark of the Unicorn). For example, by typing CTRL-X F W, the user can write the file out to the disk. The menus are shown if the user pauses for more than three seconds between the three keypresses.

can recognize the structure and easily encode it in their semantic knowledge storage. For example, if users can uniformly edit such objects as characters, words, sentences, paragraphs, chapters, and documents, this meaningful pattern is easy to learn, apply, and recall. On the other hand, if they must overtype a character, change a word, revise a sentence, replace a paragraph, substitute a chapter, and alter a document, then the challenge grows substantially, no matter how elegant the syntax (Scapin, 1982).

Meaningful structure is beneficial for task concepts, computer concepts, and syntactic details of command languages. Yet, many sytems fail to provide a meaningful structure. One widely used operating system displays various information as a result of forms of the LIST, QUERY, HELP, and TYPE commands, and moves objects as a result of the PRINT, TYPE, SPOOL, PUNCH, SEND, COPY, or MOVE commands. Defaults are inconsistent for different features, four different abbreviations for PRINT and LINECOUNT are required, binary choices vary between YES/NO and ON/OFF, and function key usage is inconsistent. These flaws emerge from multiple uncoordinated design groups and insufficient attention by the managers, especially as features are added over time.

An explicit list of design conventions can be an aid to designers and managers. Exceptions may be permitted, but only after thoughtful discussions. Users can learn systems with inconsistencies, but more slowly and with greater chance of making mistakes. One difficulty is that there may be conflicting design conventions.

4.4.1 Consistent argument ordering

Choices among conventions can sometimes be resolved by experimentation with alternatives (Barnard et al., 1981). A command language with six functions, each requiring two arguments, was developed for decoding messages. One argument was always a message identification number and the other argument was a file number, code number, digit, and so on. In normal English usage, the message identification would sometimes be the direct object of an explanatory sentence, such as SAVE the MESSAGE ID with this REFERENCE NUMBER. So, one rule of consistent command formation was to follow English usage. The second consistency rule was to have the message identification always as the first or always as the second argument. This resulted in four possible command groups:

```
DIRECT OBJECT ARGUMENT FIRST        DIRECT OBJECT ARGUMENT SECOND

SEARCH   file no,message id         SEARCH   message id,file no
TRIM     message id,segment size    TRIM     segment size,message id
REPLACE  message id,code no         REPLACE  code no,message id
INVERT   group size,message id      INVERT   message id,group size
DELETE   digit,message id           DELETE   message id,digit
SAVE     message id,reference no     SAVE     reference no,message id


CONSISTENT ARGUMENT FIRST           CONSISTENT ARGUMENT SECOND

SEARCH   message id,file no         SEARCH   file no,message id
TRIM     message id,segment size    TRIM     segment size,message id
REPLACE  message id,code no         REPLACE  code no,message id
INVERT   message id,group size      INVERT   group size,message id
DELETE   message id,digit           DELETE   digit,message id
SAVE     message id,reference no     SAVE     reference no,message id
```

Forty-eight female subjects used one of these systems for an hour to decode messages. Actually, half the subjects had variant command names, such as SELECT instead of SEARCH, but this manipulation was a minor effect. Time to perform tasks decreased during the ten trials, but the speed-up was consistent across command styles. The results strongly favored using consistent argument positions rather than the consistent direct object position, suggesting that English language rules of formation were not as effective as the simpler positional rule. The shortest task times, fewest help requests, and fewest errors occurred with the consistent argument first. These results lead to the conjecture that command languages should allow users to express the simple, familiar, or well-understood features first, and then allow users to consider the more varying aspects.

Follow-up studies by the same group (Barnard et al., 1981; Barnard et al., 1982) replicated the results about positional consistency and pursued several related issues. One frequent design consideration is whether the command verb or the object of interest should come first. Command first form would be DISPLAY FILE or INSERT LIST; the object first form would be FILE DISPLAY or LIST INSERT. The evidence supports the command first strategy used in most languages and the principle that there is a fixed order. Allowing users the freedom to put the command and object in either order generated more requests for help than fixing the order. Subjects pressed PF keys to initiate commands and select objects, so a further replication is necessary to validate the result if they had to remember and type commands. Mitigating factors may be the relative number of commands and objects and the familiarity the user has with each.

Finally, pilot studies by Jim Foley at George Washington University suggest that object first may be more appropriate when using selection by pointing on graphic displays. Different thinking patterns may be engaged in using visually oriented (right brain) interfaces than in using syntax-oriented command notations (left brain). The object first approach also fits conveniently with the strategy of leaving an object selected (and highlighted) after an action is complete, so that if the same object is used in the next action, it is already selected.

4.4.2 Symbols versus keywords

Further evidence that command structure affects performance comes from a comparison of fifteen commands in a commercially used symbol-oriented text editor and revised commands that had a more keyword-oriented style (Ledgard et al., 1980). Here are three sample commands:

```
Symbol editor                Keyword editor

FIND:/TOOTH/;-1              BACKWARD TO "TOOTH"
LIST;10                      LIST 10 LINES
RS:/KO/,/OK/;*               CHANGE ALL "KO" TO "OK"
```

The revised commands performed the same functions. Single letter abbreviations (L;10 or L 10 L) were permitted in both editors so the number of keystrokes was approximately the same. The difference in the revised commands was that keywords were used in an intuitively meaningful way, but there were no standard rules of formation. Eight subjects at three levels of text editor experience used both versions in this counterbalanced order within-subjects design.

	Percentage of Task Completed		Percentage of Erroneous Commands	
	Symbol	Keyword	Symbol	Keyword
Inexperienced users	28	42	19	11
Familiar users	43	62	18	6.4
Experienced users	74	84	9.9	5.6

Table 4.1: Impact of revised text editor commands on three levels of users (Ledgard et al., 1980)

The results (Table 4.1) clearly favored the keyword editor, indicating that command formation rules do make a difference. Unfortunately, no specific guidelines emerge except to avoid using unfamiliar symbols for new users of text editors, even if they are experienced with other text editors. It is interesting that the difference in percentage of task completed between the symbol and keyword editor was small for the experienced users. One conjecture, supported in other studies, is that experienced computer users develop skill in dealing with strange notations and therefore are less effected by syntactic variations.

4.4.3 Hierarchicalness and congruence

Carroll (1982) altered two design variables to produce four versions of a sixteen-command language for controlling a robot (Table 4.2). Commands could be hierarchical (verb-object-qualifer) or nonhierarchical (verb only) and congruent (for example, ADVANCE/RETREAT or RIGHT/LEFT) or non-congruent (GO/BACK or TURN/LEFT). Carroll uses congruent to refer to meaningful paris of opposites. Hierarchical structure and congruence (symmetry might be a better term) have been shown to be advantageous in psycholinguistic experiments. Thirty-two undergraduate subjects studied one of the four command sets in a written manual, gave subjective ratings, and then carried out paper and pencil tasks.

CONGRUENT		NONCONGRUENT	
Hierachical	Nonhierarchical	Hierarchical	Nonhierarchical
MOVE ROBOT FORWARD	ADVANCE	MOVE ROBOT FORWARD	GO
MOVE ROBOT BACKWARD	RETREAT	CHANGE ROBOT BACKWARD	BACK
MOVE ROBOT RIGHT	RIGHT	CHANGE ROBOT RIGHT	TURN
MOVE ROBOT LEFT	LEFT	MOVE ROBOT LEFT	LEFT
MOVE ROBOT UP	STRAIGHTEN	CHANGE ROBOT UP	UP
MOVE ROBOT DOWN	BEND	MOVE ROBOT DOWN	BEND
MOVE ARM FORWARD	PUSH	CHANGE ARM FORWARD	POKE
MOVE ARM BACKWARD	PULL	MOVE ARM BACKWARD	PULL
MOVE ARM RIGHT	SWING OUT	CHANGE ARM RIGHT	PIVOT
MOVE ARM LEFT	SWING IN	MOVE ARM LEFT	SWEEP
MOVE ARM UP	RAISE	MOVE ARM UP	REACH
MOVE ARM DOWN	LOWER	CHANGE ARM DOWN	DOWN
CHANGE ARM OPEN	RELEASE	CHANGE ARM OPEN	UNHOOK
CHANGE ARM CLOSE	TAKE	MOVE ARM CLOSE	GRAB
CHANGE ARM RIGHT	SCREW	MOVE ARM RIGHT	SCREW
CHANGE ARM LEFT	UNSCREW	CHANGE ARM LEFT	TWIST

Subjective Ratings (1 = Best, 5 = Worst)

1.86	1.63	1.81	2.73

Test 1

14.88	14.63	7.25	11.00

Problem 1 Errors

0.50	2.13	4.25	1.63

Problem 1 Omissions

2.00	2.50	4.75	4.15

Table 4.2: Command sets and partial results from Carroll (1982).

Subjective ratings prior to performing tasks showed disapproval of the nonhierarchical noncongruent form with the highest rating for the nonhierarchical congruent form. Memory and problem-solving tasks showed that congruent forms were clearly superior and the hierarchical forms were superior for several dependent measures. Error rates were dramatically lower for the congruent hierarchical forms.

This study assessed performance of new users of a small command language. Congruence helped subjects remember the natural pairs of concepts and terms. The hierarchical structure enabled subjects to master 16 commands with only one rule of formation and 12 keywords. With a larger command set, say 60 or 160 commands, the advantage of hierarchical structure should increase, assuming that a hierarchical structure could be found to accommodate the full set of commands. Another conjecture is that retention will be facilitated by the hierarchical structure and congruence.

Carroll's study was conducted during a half-day period; with a week of regular use, it is probable that differences would be substantially reduced. However, with intermittent use or under stress, the hierarchical congruent form might again prove superior. An online experiment might have been more realistic and would have brought out differences in command length that would have been a disadvantage to the hierarchical forms because of the greater number of keystrokes required. However, the hierarchical forms could all be replaced with three first-letter abbreviations (for example, MAL for MOVE ARM LEFT), thereby providing an advantage even in keystroke counts.

4.4.4 Consistency, congruence, and mnemonicity

An elegant demonstration of the importance of structuring principles comes from a study of four command languages for text editing (Green & Payne, 1984). Language L4 (Figure 4.6) is a subset of the commercial word processor based on EMACS, but it uses several conflicting organizing principles. Language L3 is simplified by using only the CTRL key, and it uses congruence and mnemonic naming where possible. Language L2 uses CTRL to mean forward and META for backwards, but mnemonicity is sacrificed. Language L1 uses the same meaningful structure for CTRL and META, congruent pairs, and mnemonicity.

Forty undergraduate subjects with no word processing experience were given twelve minutes to study one of the four languages (Figure 4.6). Then they were asked to recall and write on paper as many of the

	L1	L2	L3	L4
move pointer forward a paragraph	CTRL-[	CTRL-A	CTRL-]	META-]
move pointer backward a paragraph	META-[	META-A	CTRL-[	META-[
move pointer forward a sentence	CTRL-S	CTRL-B	CTRL-)	META-E
move pointer backward a sentence	META-S	META-B	CTRL-(	META-A
view next screen	CTRL-V	CTRL-C	CTRL-V	CTRL-V
view previous screen	META-V	META-C	CTRL-∧	META-V
move pointer to next line	CTRL-<	CTRL-D	CTRL-N	CTRL-N
move pointer to previous line	META-<	META-D	CTRL-P	CTRL-P
move pointer forward a word	CTRL-W	CTRL-E	CTRL-}	META-F
move pointer backward a word	META-W	META-E	CTRL-{	META-B
redisplay screen	CTRL-R	CTRL-F	CTRL-Y	CTRL-L
undo last command	META-G	META-G	CTRL-U	CTRL-G
kill sentence forward	CTRL-Z	CTRL-H	CTRL-S	META-K
kill line	CTRL-K	CTRL-I	CTRL-K	CTRL-K
delete character forward	CTRL-D	CTRL-J	CTRL-D	CTRL-D
delete character backward	META-D	META-J	CTRL-DEL	CTRL-DEL
delete word forward	CTRL-DEL	CTRL-K	CTRL-X	META-D
delete word backward	META-D	META-K	CTRL-W	META-DEL
move pointer forward a character	CTRL-C	CTRL-L	CTRL-F	CTRL-F
move pointer backward a character	META-C	META-L	CTRL-B	CTRL-B
move pointer to end of file	CTRL-F	CTRL-M	CTRL->	META->
move pointer to beginning of file	META-F	META-M	CTRL-<	META-<
move pointer to end of line	CTRL-L	CTRL-N	CTRL-Z	CTRL-E
move pointer to beginning of line	META-L	META-N	CTRL-A	CTRL-A
forward string search	CTRL-X	CTRL-O	CTRL-S	CTRL-S
reverse string search	META-X	META-O	CTRL-R	CTRL-R

Figure 4.6: The four languages used in the study. (Green and Payne, "Organization and learnability in computer languages," *International Journal of Man-Machine Studies [1984] 21*, 7–18. Used by permission of Academic Press Inc. [London] Limited.)

commands as possible. This was followed by presentation of the command descriptions with the request to write down the associated command syntax. The free recall and prompted recall tasks were both repeated. The results showed a statistically significant difference (p < .001) for languages, with L4 having the worst performance. The best performance was attained with L1 having the most structure. An online test would have been a useful follow-up to demonstrate the advantage in practice and over a longer period of time.

In summary, sources of structure that have proven advantageous include:

- positional consistency
- grammatical consistency
- congruent pairing
- hierarchical form.

In addition, as discussed in the next section, a mixture of meaningfulness, mnemonicity, and distinctiveness is helpful.

One remaining form of structure is visual or perceptual form. Up-arrow or down-arrow are highly suggestive of function, as are characters such as right- and left-angle-bracket, the plus sign, or ampersand. WORDSTAR takes advantage of a perceptual clue embedded in the QWERTY keyboard layout:

```
        E
   A  S  D  F
        X
```

CTRL-E moves the cursor up one line, CTRL-X moves the cursor down one line, CTRL-S moves the cursor one character left, CTRL-D moves the cursor one character right, CTRL-A moves the cursor one word left, and CTRL-F moves the cursor one word right. Other word processors use a similar principle with the CTRL-W, A, S, and Z keys or the CTRL-I, J, K, and M keys.

4.5   NAMING AND ABBREVIATIONS

In discussing command language names, Michael L. Schneider (1984) takes a delightful quote from Shakespeare's *Romeo and Juliet*: "A rose by any other name would smell as sweet." As Schneider points out, the lively debates in design circles suggest that this concept does not apply to command language names. Indeed, the command names are the most visible part of a system and are likely to provoke complaints from disgruntled users.

Critics (Norman, 1981, for example) focus on the strange names in UNIX, such as MKDIR (make directory), CD (change directory), LS (list directory), RM (remove file), and PWD (print working directory); or in IBM's CMS, such as SO (temporarily suspend recording of trace information), LKED (link edit), NUCXMAP (identify nucleus extensions), and GENDIRT (generate directory). Part of the concern is the inconsistent abbreviation strategies that sometimes take the first few letters, first few consonants, first and last letter, or first letter of each word in a phrase. Worse still are abbreviations with no perceivable pattern.

4.5.1 Specificity versus generality

Names are important for learning, problem solving, and retention over time. With only a few names, a command set is relatively easy to master; but with hundreds of names the choice of meaningful, organized sets of names becomes more important. Similar results were found for programming tasks in which variable name choices were less important in small modules with from ten to twenty names than in longer modules with dozens or hundreds of names.

In a word processing training session (Landauer et al., 1983), 121 students learned one of three command sets containing only three commands: Old (delete, append, substitute), a new supposedly improved set (omit, add, change), and a random set designed to be confusing (allege, cipher, and deliberate). Task performance times were essentially the same across the three command sets, although subjective ratings indicated a preference for the old set. The random names were highly distinctive and the mismatch with function may have been so disconcerting as to become memorable. These results apply only to small command sets.

With larger command sets, the names do make a difference, especially if they support congruence or some other meaningful structure. One naming rule debate revolves around the question of specificity versus generality (Rosenberg, 1982). Specific terms can be more descriptive, and if they are more distinctive, they may be more memorable. General terms may be more familiar and therefore easier to accept. Two weeks after a training session with twelve commands, subjects were more likely to recall and recognize the meaning of specific commands than general commands (Barnard et al., 1982).

In a paper-and-pencil test, 84 subjects studied one of seven sets of eight commands (Black & Moran, 1982). Two of the eight commands— the commands for inserting and deleting text—are shown here in all seven versions:

```
Infrequent, discriminating              insert     delete
Frequent, discriminating                add        remove
Infrequent, nondiscriminating           amble      perceive
Frequent, nondiscriminating words       walk       view
General (frequent, nondiscri-
  minating) words                       alter      correct
Nondiscriminating nonwords
  (nonsense)                            GAC        MIK
Discriminating nonwords (icons)         abc-adbc   abc-ac
```

The "infrequent, discriminating" command set resulted in faster learning and superior recall than did other command sets. The general words performed worst on all three measures. The nonsense words did surprisingly well, supporting the possibility that with small command sets, distinctive names are helpful even if they are not meaningful.

4.5.2 Abbreviation strategies

Even though command names should be meaningful for human learning, problem-solving, and retention, they must satisfy another important criterion. They must be in harmony with the mechanism for expressing the commands to the computer. The traditional and widely used command entry mechanism is the keyboard. This means that commands should use brief and kinesthetically easy codes. Commands requiring shifted keys or CTRL keys, special characters, or difficult sequences are likely to have higher error rates. For text editing, when many commands are applied and speed is appreciated, single-letter approaches are very attractive. Overall, brevity is a worthy goal since it can speed entry and possibly reduce error rates. Many word processor designers have pursued this approach even when mnemonicity was sacrificed, thereby making it difficult for novice and intermittent users.

In less demanding applications, designers have used longer command abbreviations, hoping that the gains in recognizability were appreciated over the reduction in key strokes. Novice users may actually prefer typing the full name of a command because they have a greater confidence in its success (Landauer et al., 1983). Novices who were required to use full command names before being taught two-letter abbreviations made fewer errors with the abbreviations than those who were taught the abbreviations from the start and than those who could create their own abbreviations (Grudin & Barnard, 1985).

The phenomenon of preferring the full name at first appeared in our study of bibliographic retrieval with the Library of Congress's SCORPIO system. Novices preferred typing the full name, such as BROWSE or SELECT, rather than the traditional four letter abbreviations BRWS or SLCT, or the single letter abbreviations B or S. After five to seven uses of the command, their confidence increased and they attempted the single-letter abbreviations. A designer of a text adventure game recognized this principle and instructs novice users to type EAST, WEST, NORTH, or SOUTH; after five full-length commands, the system informs the user about the single-letter abbreviations. A related report comes from some users of IBM's CMS, who find that the minimal length abbreviations are too difficult to learn and they stick with the full form of the command.

With experience and frequent use, abbreviations become attractive and even necessary to satisfy the "power" user. Efforts have been made to find optimal abbreviation strategies. Several studies support the notion that abbreviation should be made by a consistent strategy (Ehrenreich & Porcu, 1982; Benbasat & Wand, 1984; Schneider, 1984). Potential strategies are:

1. Simple truncation: use the first, second, third, etc. letters of each command. This strategy requires that each command

be distinguishable by the leading string of characters. Abbreviations can be all of the same length or of different lengths.

2. Vowel drop with simple truncation: eliminate vowels and use some of what remains. If the first letter is a vowel it may or may not be retained. H, Y, and W may or may not be considered as vowels.

3. First and last letter: since the first and last letters are highly visible, use them; for example ST for SORT.

4. First letter of each word in a phrase: this popular technique often fits with a hierarchical design plan.

5. Standard abbreviations from other contexts: familiar abbreviations such as QTY for QUANTITY, XTALK for CROSSTALK (a software package), PRT for PRINT, or BAK for BACKUP.

6. Phonics: focus attention on the sound; for example XQT for execute.

Truncation appears to be the most effective mechanism overall, but it has its problems. Conflicting abbreviations appear often, and decoding of an unfamiliar abbreviation is not as good as with vowel dropping (Schneider, 1984).

4.5.3 Guidelines for using abbreviations

Ehrenreich and Porcu (1982) offer this compromise set of guidelines:

1. A *simple*, primary rule should be used to generate abbreviations for most items and a *simple* secondary rule used for those items where there is a conflict.

2. Abbreviations generated by the secondary rule should have a marker (e.g., an asterisk) incorporated in them.

3. The number of words abbreviated by the secondary rule should be kept to a minimum.

4. Users should be familiar with the rules used to generate abbreviations.

5. Truncation is an easy rule for users to work with, but it may also produce a large number of identical abbreviations for different words.

6. Fixed length abbreviations are preferable to variable length ones.

7. Abbreviations should not be designed to incorporate endings (e.g., ING, ED, S).

8. Unless there is a critical space problem, abbreviations should not be used in messages generated by the computer and read by the user.

Abbreviations are an important part of system design and they are appreciated by experienced users. Abbreviations are more likely to be used if users are confident in their knowledge of the abbreviations and if the benefit is more than a savings of one to two characters (Benbasat & Wand, 1984). The appearance of new input devices and strategies (for example, selecting by pointing) will change the criteria for abbreviations. Each situation has its idiosyncrasies and should be carefully evaluated by the designer, applying empirical tests where necessary.

4.6 COMMAND MENUS

To relieve the burden of memorization of commands, some designers offer users brief prompts of available commands. The online version of the Official Airline Guide uses such prompts as:

```
ENTER +,L#,X#,S#,R#,M,RF(#=LINE NUMBER)
```

This prompt is to remind users of the commands related to fares that have been displayed and the related flight schedules

```
+     move forward one screen
L#    limitations on airfares
```

```
X#    detailed information on a listed flight
S#    schedule information for the listed fare
R#    return flight information for this route
M     main menu
RF    return fares
```

Experienced users come to know the commands and do not need to read the prompt or the help screens. Intermittent users know the concepts and refer to the prompt to jog their memory and help them retain the syntax for future uses. Novice users do not benefit as much from the prompt and must take a training course or consult the online help.

The prompting approach emphasizes syntax and serves more frequent users. It is closer to but more compact than a standard numbered menu and preserves screen space for task-related information. WORDSTAR offers the novice and intermittent user help menus containing commands with one or two word descriptions (Figure 4.7). Frequent users can turn off the display of help menus, thereby gaining screen space for additional text.

```
        A:GETTYS  PAGE 1 LINE 9 COL 62            INSERT ON
                     < < <     M A I N   M E N U      > > >
       --Cursor Movement--     : -Delete- :    -Miscellaneous-  :   -Other   Menus-
    ^S char left ^D char right :^G   char  : ^I Tab    ^B Reform : (from Main only)
    ^A word left ^F word right :DEL chr lf: ^V INSERT ON/OFF    :^J Help  ^K Block
    ^E line  up   ^X line down :^T word rt:^L Find/Replce again:^Q Quick ^P Print
          --Scrolling--        :^Y  line  :RETURN End paragraph:^O Onscreen
    ^Z line down ^W line up     :         : ^N Insert a RETURN :
    ^C screen up ^R screen down:          : ^U Stop a command  :
    L----!----!----!----!----!----!----!----!----!----!----!--------R
         Fourscore  and seven years ago our fathers brought forth on
    this continent a new nation conceived in liberty and dedicated to
    the  proposition  that   all  men  are created equal.    Now   we   are
    engaged in a great civil war testing whether that nation,   or  any
    nation so conceived and so dedicated, can long endure.

         We are met on a great battlefield of that war.  We have come
    to dedicate a portion of that field as a final resting-place   for
    those  who here gave their lives that that nation might live.
```

Figure 4.7: WordStar offers the user the option of bringing a help menu to a portion of the screen while the task is in process.

Several interactive systems on personal computers have another still more attractive form of prompts called command menus. Users are shown a list of descriptive words and make a selection by pressing the left and right arrow keys to move a light bar. When the desired command word is highlighted, the user presses the return key to carry out the command. Often, the command menu is a hierarchical structure that branches to a second- or third-level menu.

Even though arrow key movement is relatively slow and less preferred by frequent users, command menu items can be selected by single-letter keypresses. This strategy becomes a hierarchical command language, but it is identical to the typeahead (BLT) approach of menu selection. Novice users can use the arrow keys to highlight their choice or type single letter choices, but frequent users don't even look at the menus as they type 2, 3, 4, or longer sequences of single letters that come to be thought of as a command (see FinalWord commands in Figure 4.5).

The Lotus 1–2–3 (Figure 4.8) implementation is especially fast and elegant. As command words are selected, a brief description appears on the line below, providing further assistance for novice users without distracting experts from their concentration on the task. Experienced users appear to work as fast as touch typists, making three to six keystrokes per second.

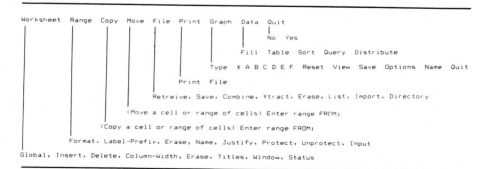

Figure 4.8: The first two levels of command menus from LOTUS 1–2–3 reveal the rich function available to users. At the third level, users may receive another menu or enter values.

Pop-up or pull-down menus that use mouse selection are another form of command menu. Frequent users can be extremely fast, and novices can take the time to read the choices before selecting a command. With a fast display, command menus blur the boundaries between what is thought of as commands and menus.

4.7   NATURAL LANGUAGE INTERACTION

Even before there were computers, people dreamed about creating machines that would accept natural language. It is a wonderful fantasy, and the success of word manipulation devices such as tape recorders, word processors, printing presses, and telephones may give encouragement to some people. A recurring hope is that computers will respond to commands issued by typing or speaking in natural language.

Natural language interaction (NLI) might be defined as the operation of computers by people using a familiar natural langauge (such as English) to give instructions. They do not have to learn a command syntax nor select from menus.

The problem with NLI is not only implementation on the computer, but also desirability for large numbers of users for a wide variety of tasks. People are different from computers, and human-human interaction is not necessarily an appropriate model for human operation of computers. Since computers can display information 1,000 times faster than people can enter commands, it seems advantageous to use the computer to display large amounts of information and allow novice and intermittent users simply to choose among the items. Selection helps guide the user by making clear what functions are available. For knowledgeable and frequent users, who are thoroughly aware of the available functions, a concise command language is usually preferred.

The syntactic/semantic model helps sort out the issues. NLI does not provide information about actions and objects in the task domain; users are usually presented with a simple prompt that invites a natural language query. But assume that the user is knowledgeable about the task domain; for example, the meaning of database objects and permissible actions.

Neither does NLI necessarily convey knowledge of the computer concepts; for example, tree-structuring of information, implications of a deletion, boolean operations, or query strategies. NLI does relieve the user of learning new syntactic rules, since it presumably will accept familiar English language requests. Therefore, NLI can be effective for the user who is knowledgeable about some task domain and computer concepts but who is an intermittent user who cannot retain the syntactic details.

NLI might apply to checkbook maintenance (Shneiderman, 1980) where the users recognize that there is an ascending sequence of integer numbered checks, and that each check has a single payee field, single amount, single date, and one or more signatures. Checks can be issued, voided, searched, and printed. In fact, following this suggestion, Ford (1981) created and tested an NLI system for this purpose. Subjects were paid to maintain their checkbook registers by computer using an APL-based program that was incrementally refined to account for unanticipated entries. The final system successfully handled 91 percent of users' requests, such as:

```
Pay to Safeway on 3/24/86 $29.77.
June 10 $33.00 to Cindy Lauper.
Show me all the checks paid to Ronald Reagan.
Which checks were written on October 29?
```

Users reported satisfaction with the system and were eager to use the system even when the several months of experimentation were completed. This can be seen as a success for NLI, but alternatives might be even more attractive. Showing a full screen of checkbook entries with a blank line for new entries might accomplish most tasks without any commands and minimal typing. Searches could be accomplished by entering partial information (for example, Ronald Reagan in the payee field) and then pressing a query key.

There have been numerous informal tests of NLI systems, but only a few have been experimental comparisons against some other design. A simulated query system was used to compare a subset of the structured SQL database facility to a natural language system (Small & Weldon, 1983). The SQL simulation resulted in faster performance on a benchmark set of tasks. Similarly, a field trial with a real system, users, and queries pointed to the advantages of SQL over the natural language alternative (Jarke et al., 1985). Researchers seeking to demonstrate the advantage of NLI over command language and menu approaches for creating business graphics were surprised to find no significant differences for time, errors, or attitude (Hauptmann & Green, 1983).

Believers in NLI may claim that more research and system development is needed before excluding NLI, but improvements in menus, command languages, and direct manipulation seem equally likely. Supporters of NLI can point with some pride at the modest success of the commercially available INTELLECT system that has approximately 300 installations on large mainframe computers (Figure 4.9).

Business executives, salespeople, and others use INTELLECT to search databases on a regular basis. Several innovative implementation ideas help to make INTELLECT successful. The parser uses the contents of the database to parse queries; for example, the parser can determine that a query containing Cleveland refers to city locations because Cleveland is an instance in the database. Next, the system administrator can conveniently include guidance for handling domain-specific requests, by indicating fields related to who, what, where, when, how, etc. queries. Third, INTELLECT rephrases the user's query and displays a response such as: PRINT THE CHECK NUMBERS WITH PAYEE = RONALD REAGAN. This structured response serves as an educational aid, and users gravitate toward expressions that mimic the style. Eventually, as users become more frequent, they often use concise commandlike expressions that they believe will be successfully parsed. Even the promoters of INTELLECT recognize that novice users who are unfamiliar with the task domain will have a difficult time, and that the ideal user is a knowledgeable intermittent user.

There is some portion of the user spectrum that can benefit from NLI, but it may not be as large as promoters believe. Computer users usually seek predictable responses and are discouraged if they must frequently engage in clarification dialog. Since NLI has such varied forms, the users must constantly be aware of what the computer's response is to verify that the users' intentions were recognized. Finally, visually oriented interactions, embracing the notions of direct manipulation (see Chapter 5), make more effective use of the computer's capacity for rapid

```
PLEASE ENTER YOUR FIRST REQUEST

WHAT'S IN THE DATABASE?
FIELDS IN THE FILE OF EMPLOYEES

NAME                    JOB          SALARY        SEX
AGE                     FAMILY       CITY          STATE
EMPLOYEE NUMBER

WHO WORKS IN NEW YORK CITY
PRINT THE JOB AND NAME OF ALL EMPLOYEES WITH CITY = NEW YORK

PROFESSIONAL                        NAME
OCCUPATION

MACHINIST                           ANGELIN
PHYSICIAN                           ANGUS

WHAT IS THE NUMBER OF ANGUS
COUNT THE EMPLOYEES WITH NAME = ANGUS

ANSWER:  1

WHAT IS THE EMPLOYEE NUMBER OF ALL EMPLOYEES WITH NAME = ANGUS
EMPLOYEE
NUMBER

0034

WHICH WOMEN WORK IN NEW YORK CITY
PRINT THE JOB OF ALL EMPLOYEES WITH SEX = FEMALE & CITY = NEW YORK

PROFESSIONAL
OCCUPATION

MACHINIST
ADMINISTRATOR
ELECTRICIAN

FEMALE EMPLOYEES IN NEW YORK CITY
PRINT THE NAME OF ALL EMPLOYEES WITH SEX = FEMALE & CITY = NEW YORK

NAME

ANGELIN
CANTEBURY
EDWARDS

HOW MANY NEW YORK CITY MEN ARE OVER 30 YEARS OLD
COUNT THE EMPLOYEES WITH CITY = NEW YORK & SEX = MALE & AGE>30

ANSWER:  9

PRINT THEM
PRINT THE NAME AND AGE OF ALL EMPLOYEES WITH CITY = NEW YORK &
       SEX = MALE & AGE>30

               YEARS
NAME             OF
               AGE

ANGUS           43
ELEY            69
HILTON          44
```

Figure 4.9: Demonstration session with Intellect from Artificial Intelligence Corp., Cambridge, MA. User input is underscored. Intellect rephrases user input into a structured query language, which users often mimic as they become more frequent users.

display. In short, pointing and selecting in context is often more attractive than typing or even speaking an English sentence.

It is surprising that designers of expert systems have attempted to embed NLI. Expert systems already tax the user with complexity, lack of visibility of the underlying processes, and confusion about what functions the system can and cannot handle. A precise, concise notation or selection in context from a list of alternatives seems far more suitable in providing users with predictable and comprehensible behavior (Hayes-Roth, 1984) (Figure 4.10).

An innovative blend of NLI and menus was developed under the name NLMENU (Tennant et al., 1983) and is now distributed by Texas

SAMPLE SESSION FROM AN EXPERT SYSTEM FOR OIL DRILLING ADVISOR

What is the name of WELL–159?
  AGF7–93E

What is the profile of AGF7–93E?
  DEVIATED

Please enter information about FORMATION–1:

upper-limit meters	lower-limit meters	main-rock- type	homogeneous/ interbedded
747	806	SHALE	HOMOGENEOUS

Please enter information on PROBLEM–1:

problem-type	prior-action	total-depth	casing-shoe depth
STICKING	REAMING	1111 METERS	747 METERS

Please enter the composition of the drill-string starting from the bit (type ? for assistance):
  BIT 9"5/8 STAPB"5/8 SHORTDC7"3/4STAB9"5/8...NDP5

What was the drilling method employed when the problem occurred:
  ROTARY

What is the depth of the freepoint?
  UNKNOWN

Figure 4.10: This extract demonstrates one designers attempt at an expert system dialog. User input is shown in all upper case letters. Users must type in values even when selection from a menu would be more meaningful, rapid, and error-free. Furthermore, there does not appear to be any way to go back and change values, view values, or reuse values from previous sessions (F. Hayes-Roth, The knowledge-based expert system: A tutorial, *IEEE Computer 17*, 9 (Sept. 1984), 11–28. © 1984 IEEE)

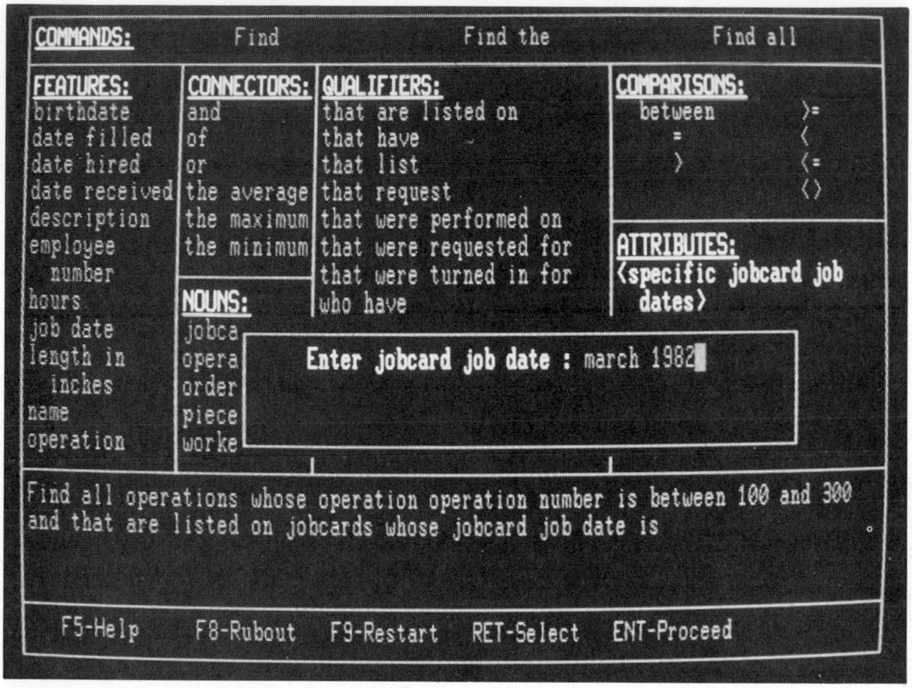

```
COMMANDS:          Find                 Find the              Find all

FEATURES:       CONNECTORS: QUALIFIERS:                    COMPARISONS:
birthdate       and         that are listed on                 between        >=
date filled     of          that have                             =           <
date hired      or          that list                             >           <=
date received   the average that request                                      <>
description     the maximum that were performed on
employee        the minimum that were requested for   ATTRIBUTES:
  number                    that were turned in for   <specific jobcard job
hours           NOUNS:      who have                      dates>
job date        jobca
length in       opera         Enter jobcard job date : march 1982
  inches        order
name            piece
operation       worke


Find all operations whose operation operation number is between 100 and 300
and that are listed on jobcards whose jobcard job date is                        °


   F5-Help       F8-Rubout     F9-Restart    RET-Select   ENT-Proceed
```

Figure 4.11: The NaturalLink (TM) allows users to specify natural langauge English queries against a database by choosing phrases from a set of menus. The content of the menus is determined by the contents of the database. (Courtesy of Texas Instruments, Dallas, TX)

Instruments under the name NaturalLink (Figure 4.11). Natural language phrases are shown as a series of menus. As phrases (for example, FIND / COLOR / AND / NAME OF PARTS / WHOSE COLOR IS) are chosen by a pointing strategy, a query is formed in a command window. Users receive information from the menus, obviating the need for a query. For example, if the parts and suppliers database contains only red, green, and blue parts, only these choices appear in the window containing the PART COLOR menu. Users can see the full range of possible queries and thereby avoid the frustration of probing the boundaries of system functionality. With this strategy, typing is eliminated and the user is guaranteed a semantically and syntactically correct query.

A notable and widespread success of NLI techniques is in the variety of adventure games (Figure 4.12). Users may indicate directions of

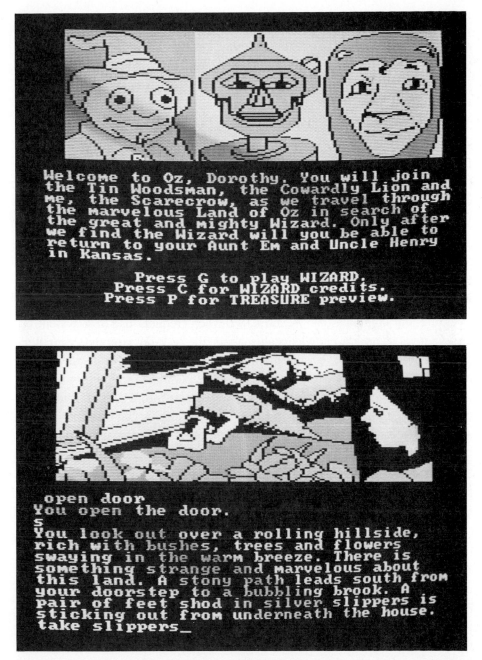

Figure 4.12: This adventure game is modelled on the Wizard of Oz story. The user types phrases such as "open the door" or "take slippers" or abbreviations such as "s" to move south. More complex phrases such as "put the hat on the scarecrow" are possible. (Courtesy of Spinnaker Software, Cambridge, MA)

movement or type commands, such as TAKE ALL OF THE KEYS, OPEN THE GATE, or DROP THE CAGE AND PICK UP THE SWORD. Part of the attraction of NLI in this situation is that the system is unpredictable and some exploration is necessary to discover the proper incantation.

So much research has been invested in NLI systems that undoubtedly some successes will emerge, but widespread use may not develop because the alternatives may be more appealing. More rapid progress can be made if carefully controlled experimental tests are used to discover the designs, users, and tasks for which NLI is most beneficial.

4.8   PRACTITIONER'S SUMMARY

Command languages can be attractive when frequent use of a system is anticipated, users are knowledgeable about the task domain and computer concepts, screen space is at a premium, response time and display rates are slow, and numerous functions that can be combined in many ways are supported. Users will have to learn the semantics and syntax, but they can initiate rather than respond, rapidly specifying actions involving several objects and options. Finally, complex sequences of commands can be easily specified and stored for future use as a macro.

Designers should begin with a careful task analysis to determine what functions should be provided. Hierarchical strategies and congruent structures facilitate learning, problem solving, and human retention over time. Laying out the full set of commands on a single sheet of paper helps show the structure to the designer and to the learner. Meaningful specific names aid learning and retention. Compact abbreviations constructed according to a consistent rule facilitate retention and rapid performance for frequent users.

Innovative strategies, such as command menus, can be effective if rapid response to screen actions can be provided. Natural language interaction can be implemented, but its advantage for widespread application is yet to be demonstrated.

4.9 RESEARCHER'S AGENDA

Designers could be helped by development of strategies for task analysis, taxonomies of command language designs, and criteria for using commands or other techniques. The benefits of structuring such concepts as hierarchicalness, congruence, consistency, and mnemonicity have been demonstrated in specific cases, but replication in varied situations is important. Experimental testing should lead to a more comprehensive cognitive model of command language learning and use. (See Table 4.3.)

A command language system generator would be a useful tool for research and development of new command languages. The designer

---

COMMAND LANGUAGE GUIDELINES

- Create explicit model of objects and actions

- Choose meaningful, specific, distinctive names

- Try for hierarichical structure

- Provide consistent structure
  (hierarchy, argument order, action-object)

- Support consistent abbreviation rules
  (prefer truncation to one letter)

- Offer frequent users the capability to create macros

- Consider command menus on high-speed displays

- Limit number of commands and ways of accomplishing a task

Table 4.3: High-level design guidelines based on empirical studies and practical experience.

could provide a formal specification of the command language, and the system would generate an interpreter. With experience in using such a tool, design analyzers might be built to critique the design, detect ambiguity, check for consistency, verify completeness, predict error rates, or suggest improvements. Even a simple but thorough checklist for command language designers would be a useful contribution.

Novel input devices and high-speed, high-resolution displays offer new opportunities, such as command and pop-up menus, for breaking free from the traditional syntax of command languages. Natural language interaction still holds promise in certain applications, and empirical tests offer a good chance to identify rapidly the appropriate niches and design strategies.

REFERENCES

Barnard, P. J., and Hammond, N. V., Cognitive contexts and interactive communication, IBM Hursley (U.K.) Human Factors Laboratory Report HF070, (December 1982), 18 pages.

Barnard, P., Hammond, N., MacLean, A., and Morton, J., Learning and remembering interactive commands, *Proc. Conference on Human Factors in Computer Systems*, Available from ACM DC., (1982), 2–7.

Barnard, P. J., Hammond, N. V., Morton, J., Long, J. B., and Clark, I. A., Consistency and compatibility in human-computer dialogue, *International Journal of Man-Machine Studies 15*, (1981), 87–134.

Benbasat, Izak, and Wand, Yair, Command abbreviation behavior in human-computer interaction, *Communications of the ACM 27*, 4, (April 1984), 376–383.

Black, J., and Moran, T., Learning and remembering command names, *Proc. Conference on Human Factors in Computer Systems*, Available from ACM DC., (1982), 8–11.

Carroll, John M., Learning, using and designing command paradigms, *Human Learning 1*, 1, (1982), 31–62.

Carroll, J. M., and Thomas, J., Metaphor and the cognitive representation of computing systems, *IEEE Transactions on Systems, Man, and Cybernetics, SMC–12*, 2, (March/April 1982), 107–115.

Ehrenreich, S. L., and Porcu, Theodora, Abbreivations for automated systems: Teaching operators and rules, In Badre, Al, and Shneiderman, Ben, (Editors), *Directions in Human-Computer Interaction*, Ablex Publishers, Norwood, NJ, (1982), 111–136.

Ford, W. Randolph, Natural Language Processing by Computer —A New Approach, Ph. D. Dissertation, The Johns Hopkins University Department of Psychology, Baltimore, MD, (1981), 88 pages.

Green, T. R. G., and Payne, S. J., Organization and learnability in computer languages, *International Journal of Man-Machine Studies 21*, (1984), 7–18.

Grudin, Jonathan, and Barnard, Phil, When does an abbreviation become a word and related questions, *Proc. CHI '85 Conference on Human Factors in Computer Systems*, Available from ACM Order Dept., P. O. Box 64145, Baltimore, MD 21264, (1985), 121–126.

Hanson, Stephen J., Kraut, Robert E., and Farber, James M., Interface design and multivariate analysis of UNIX command use, *ACM Transactions on Office Information Systems 2*, 1, (January 1984), 42–57.

Hauptmann, Alexander G., and Green, Bert F., A comparison of command, menu-selection and natural language computer programs, *Behaviour and Information Technology 2*, 2, (1983), 163–178.

Hayes-Roth, Frederick, The knowledge-based expert system: a tutorial, *IEEE Computer 17, 9*, (September 1984), 11–28.

Jarke, Matthias, Turner, Jon A., Stohr, Edward A., Vassiliou, Yannis, White, Norman H., and Michielsen, Ken, A field evaluation of natural language for data retrieval, *IEEE Transactions on Software Engineering SE–11*, 1, (January 1985), 97–113.

Kraut, Robert E., Hanson, Stephen J., and Farber, James, M., Command use and interface design, *Proc. CHI '83 Conference on Human Factors in Computing Systems*, Available from ACM Order Dept., P. O. Box 64145, Baltimore, MD 21264, (1983), 120–123.

Landauer, T. K., Calotti, K. M., and Hartwell, S., Natural command names and initial learning, *Communications of the ACM 26*, 7, (July 1983), 495–503.

Ledgard, H., Whiteside, J. A., Singer, A., and Seymour, W., The natural language of interactive systems, *Communications of the ACM 23*, (1980), 556–563.

Norman, Donald, The trouble with UNIX, *Datamation 27*, (1981), 556–563.

Roberts, Terry, Evaluation of computer text editors, Ph. D. dissertation, Stanford University. Available from University Microfilms, Ann Arbor, MI, order number AAD 80–11699, (1980).

Rosenberg, Jarrett, Evaluating the suggestiveness of command names, *Behaviour and Information Technology 1*, (19822), 371–400.

Rosson, Mary Beth, Patterns of experience in text editing, *Proc. CHI '83 Conference on Human Factors in Computing Systems*, Available from ACM Order Dept., P. O. Box 64145, Baltimore, MD 21264, (1983), 171–175.

Scapin, Dominique L., Computer commands labelled by users versus imposed commands and the effect of structuring rules on recall, *Proc. Conference on Human Factors in Computer Systems*, Available from ACM DC, (1982), 17–19.

Schneider, M. L., Ergonomic considerations in the design of text editors, In Vassiliou, Y. (Editor), *Human Factors and Interactive Computer Systems*, Ablex Publishers, Norwood, NJ, (1984), 141–161.

Schneider, M. L., Hirsh-Pasek, K., and Nudelman, S., An experimental evaluation of delimiters in a command language syntax, *International Journal of Man-Machine Studies 20*, 6, (June 1984), 521–536.

Shneiderman, Ben, *Software Psychology: Human Factors in Computer and Information Systems*, Little, Brown and Co., Boston, MA, (1980), 320 pages.

Small, Duane, and Weldon, Linda, An experimental comparison of natural and structured query languages, *Human Factors 25*, (1983), 253–263.

Tennant, Harry R., Ross, Kenneth M., and Thompson, Craig W., Usable natural language interfaces through menu-based natural language understanding, *Proc. CHI '83 Conference on Human Factors in Computing Systems*, available from ACM Order Dept., P. O. Box 64145, Baltimore, MD 21264 (1983), 154–160.

CHAPTER 5

DIRECT MANIPULATION

Leibniz sought to make the form of a symbol reflect its content. "In signs," he wrote, "one sees an advantage for discovery that is greatest when they express the exact nature of a thing briefly and, as it were, picture it; then, indeed, the labor of thought is wonderfully diminished."

Frederick Kreiling, "Leibniz," *Scientific American,* May 1968.

5.1. INTRODUCTION

Certain interactive systems generate a glowing enthusiasm among users that is in marked contrast with the more common reaction of grudging acceptance or outright hostility. The enthusiastic users' reports are filled with the positive feelings of:

- mastery of the system
- competence in performance of their task
- ease in learning the system originally and in assimilating advanced features
- confidence in their capacity to retain mastery over time
- enjoyment in using the system
- eagerness to show it off to novices
- desire to explore more powerful aspects of the system

These feelings are not universal, but this amalgam is meant to convey an image of the truly pleased user. The central ideas seem to be visibility of the objects and actions of interest, rapid reversible incremental actions, and replacement of complex command language syntax by direct manipulation of the object of interest—hence, the term *direct manipulation*.

5.2 EXAMPLES OF DIRECT MANIPULATION SYSTEMS

No single system has all the admirable attributes or design features— that may be impossible; but each of the following examples has enough to win the enthusiastic support of many users.

My favorite example of direct manipulation is driving an automobile. The scene is directly visible through the front window, and actions such as braking or steering have become common knowledge in our culture. To turn left, the driver simply rotates the steering wheel to the left. The response is immmediate and the scene changes, providing feedback to refine the turn. Imagine trying to turn by issuing a command LEFT 30 DEGREES and then having to issue another command to see the new scene; but this is the level of operation of many office automation tools of today.

5.2.1 Display editors

Users of full-page display editors are great advocates of their systems as compared with line-oriented text editors (Figure 5.1). A typical comment was, "Once you've used a display editor you will never want to go back to a line editor—you'll be spoiled." Similar comments came from users of stand-alone word processors such as the WANG system, personal computer word processors such as WORDSTAR 2000,

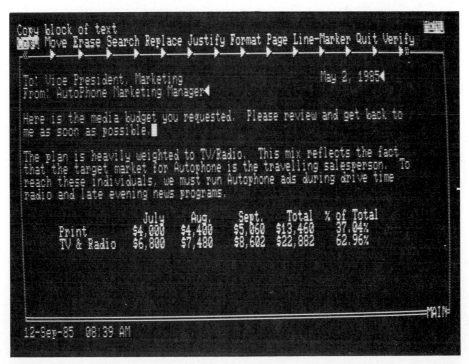

Figure 5.1: Word processor from Symphony. (Courtesy of © Lotus Development Corporation 1985. Used with permission.)

FINALWORD, XYWRITE, and Microsoft WORD, or display editors such as EMACS on the MIT/Honeywell MULTICS system or "vi" (for visual editor) on the UNIX system. A beaming advocate called EMACS "the one true editor."

Roberts (1980) found overall performance times with line-oriented editors were twice as long as with display editors. Training time with display editors is also reduced, so there is evidence to support the enthusiasm of display editor devotees. Furthermore, office automation evaluations consistently favor full-page display editors for secretarial and executive use.

The advantages of display editors include:

- *display of a full 24 to 66 lines of text.*
  This gives the reader a clearer sense of context for each sentence while permitting simpler reading and scanning of the document. By contrast, the one-line-at-a-time view offered by some line editors is like seeing the world through a narrow cardboard tube.

- *display of the document in the form that it will appear when the final printing is done.*
  Eliminating the clutter of formatting commands also simplifies reading and scanning of the document. Tables, lists, page breaks, skipped lines, section headings, centered text, and figures can be viewed in their final form. This style has come to be known as WYSIWYG (what you see is what you get). The annoyance and delay of debugging the format commands are eliminated because the errors are immediately apparent.

- *cursor action that is visible to the user.*
  Seeing an arrow, underscore, or blinking box on the screen gives the operator a clear sense of where to focus attention and apply action.

- *cursor motion through physically obvious and intuitively natural means.*
  Arrow keys or cursor motion devices such as a mouse, joystick, or graphic tablet provide natural physical

mechanisms for moving the cursor. This is in marked contrast to commands such as UP 6 that require an operator to convert the physical action into a correct syntactic form that may be difficult to learn, hard to recall, and a source of frustrating errors.

* *labeled buttons for actions.*
Many workstations designed for use with display editors have buttons with actions etched onto them, such as INSERT, DELETE, CENTER, UNDERLINE, SUPERSCRIPT, BOLD, or LOCATE. These buttons act as a permanent menu selection display to remind the operator of the features and to avoid the need to memorize a complex command language syntax. On some editors, only ten or fifteen labeled buttons provide the basic functionality. A specially marked button may be the gateway to the world of advanced or infrequently used features that are offered on the screen in menu form.

* *immediate display of the results of an action.*
When a button is pressed to move the cursor or center text, the results are shown immediately on the screen. Deletions are immediately apparent since the character, word, or line is erased and the remaining text is rearranged. Similarly, insertions or text movements are shown after each keystroke or function button press. This is in contrast to line editors in which print or display commands must be issued to see the results of changes.

* *rapid action and display.*
Most display editors operate at high speed; a full page of text appears in a fraction of a second. This high display rate coupled with short response time produces a thrilling sense of power and speed. Cursors can be moved quickly, large amounts of text can be scanned rapidly, and the results of commands can be shown almost instantaneously. Rapid action also reduces the need for additional commands and thereby simplifies design and learning. Line editors operating at thirty characters per second with three to eight

second response times seem bogged down in the mud. Speeding up line editors adds to their attractiveness, but they would still lack such features as direct overtyping, deletion, and insertion.

- *easily reversible actions.* When entering text, an incorrect keystroke is repaired by merely backspacing and overstriking. Simple changes can be made moving the cursor to the problem area and overstriking, inserting, or deleting characters, words, or lines. A useful design strategy is to include natural inverse operations for each operation. Carroll (1982a) has shown that congruent pairs of operations are easy to learn (see Section 4.4.3). An alternative offered by many display editors is a simple UNDO command to return the text to its state before the previous action or action sequence. The easy reversibility reduces user anxiety about making a mistake or fear of destroying the file.

Display editors are worth studying because the large market demand generates an active competition that propels the rapid evolutionary refinement of design.

5.2.2 VISICALC and its descendents

The first electronic spreadsheet, VISICALC, was the product of a Harvard MBA student who was frustrated when trying to carry out the multiple calculations in a graduate business course. He built an "instantly calculating electronic worksheet" (as the user manual describes it) that permits computation and display of results across 254 rows and 63 columns. The worksheet can be programmed so that column 4 displays the sum of columns 1 through 3; then, every time a value in the first three columns changes, the fourth column changes as well. Complex dependencies among manufacturing costs, distribution costs, sales revenue, commissions, and profits can be stored for several sales districts and months so that the impact of changes on profits can be immediately seen.

By simulating an accountant's spreadsheet or worksheet, VISICALC made it easy for novices to comprehend the objects and permissible actions. The display of twenty rows and up to nine columns, with the provision for multiple windows, gave the user sufficient visibility for easy scanning of information and comprehension of relationships among entries. The command language for setting up the worksheet can be tricky for novices to learn and infrequent users to remember, but most users need learn only the basic commands. The distributor of VISICALC attributed its appeal to the fact that "it jumps," referring to the user's delight in watching the propagation of changes across the screen.

VISICALC users can easily try out many alternate plans and rapidly see the impact on sales or profit. Changes to commissions or economic slowdowns can be quickly added to the worksheet. The current status of the worksheet can be saved for later review.

Competitors to VISICALC emerged quickly and made attractive improvements to the user interface and expanded the tasks that were supported. Among these, LOTUS 1–2–3 has come to dominate the market (Figure 5.2a). It offers integration with graphics and database

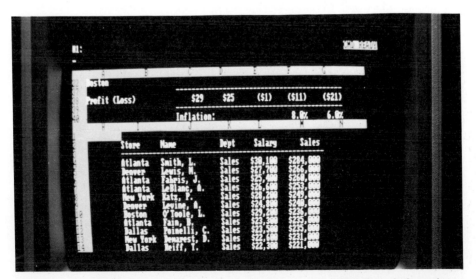

Figure 5.2a: Spreadsheet showing split window in the LOTUS 1–2–3 package. (Courtesy of © Lotus Development Corporation 1985. Used with permission.)

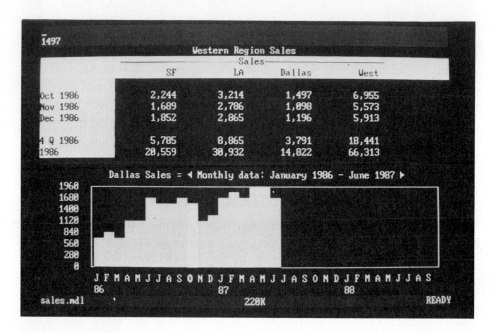

Figure 5.2b: The worksheet in Javelin has row and column labels created by the user. The top half of the screen shows sales data in a tabular format; the bottom half shows a bar chart. Changes to the data are immediately reflected in the bar chart and vice versa. (Used with permission of Javelin Software Corporation, Cambridge, MA)

features. The actions are easily invoked with command menus. Advanced systems such as Javelin (Figure 5.2b) are attempting to win users with novel ways of showing and manipulating data items and graphs.

5.2.3 Spatial data management

In geographic applications, it seems natural to give a spatial representation in the form of a map that provides a familiar model of reality. The developers of the prototype spatial data management system (Herot, 1980; Herot, 1984), attribute the basic idea to Nicholas Negroponte of MIT. In one scenario, the user is seated before a color graphics display of the world and can zoom in on the Pacific Ocean to see markers for military ship convoys (Figure 5.3). By moving a

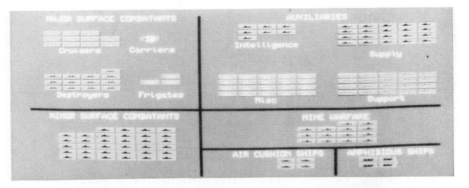

Figure 5.3: The Spatial Data Management System has three displays to show multiple levels of detail or related information. The user moves a joystick to traverse information spaces or zoom in on a map and see more details about ship convoys. (Courtesy of the Computer Corporation of America, Cambridge, MA)

joystick, the screen becomes filled with silhouettes of individual ships that can be zoomed in on to display detailed data or ultimately a full-color picture of the captain.

In another scenario, icons representing such different aspects of a corporation as personnel, an organizational chart, travel information, production data, or schedules are shown on a screen. By moving the joystick and zooming in on objects of interest, the user is taken through complex "information spaces" or "I-spaces" to locate the item of interest. A building floor plan showing departments might be shown, and when a department is chosen, individual offices become visible. On moving the cursor into a room, details about its occupant appear on the screen. If you choose the wrong room, merely back out and try another. The lost effort is minimal and there is no stigma of error.

The Filevision software for the Macintosh enables designers to perform database retrievals visually. For example, if a map of the United States is shown on the screen, the user can retrieve facts about each state by pointing and clicking.

The success of a spatial data management system depends on the skill of the designers in choosing icons, graphical representations, and data layouts that are natural and comprehensible to the user. The joy of zooming in and out, or of gliding over data with a joystick, entices even anxious users, who quickly demand additional power and data.

5.2.4 Video games

For many people, the most exciting, well-engineered, and commercially successful application of these concepts is in the world of video games. The early but simple and popular game called PONG required the user to rotate a knob that moved a white rectangle on the screen. A white spot acted as a ping pong ball that ricocheted off the wall and had to be hit back by the movable white rectangle. The user developed skill involving speed and accuracy in placing the "paddle" to keep the increasingly speedy ball from getting by, while the speaker emitted a ponging sound when the ball bounced. Watching someone else play for thirty seconds is all the training needed to become a competent novice, but many hours of practice are required to become a skilled expert.

Contemporary games, such as Missile Command, Donkey Kong, Pac Man, Tempest, TRON, Centipede, or Space Invaders, are much more sophisticated in their rules, color graphics, and sound effects. The designers of these games provide stimulating entertainment, a challenge for novices and experts, and many intriguing lessons in the human factors of interface design—somehow they have found a way to get people to put quarters in the sides of computers (Figure 5.4). The strong attraction of these games is in marked contrast to the anxiety and resistance many users have for office automation equipment.

These games provide a field of action that is simple to understand since it is an abstraction of reality—learning is by analogy. The commands are physical actions, such as button presses, joystick motions, or knob rotations, whose results are shown immediately on the screen. There is no syntax to remember and therefore no syntax error messages. If users move their spaceships too far left, then they merely use the natural inverse operation of moving back to the right. Error messages are

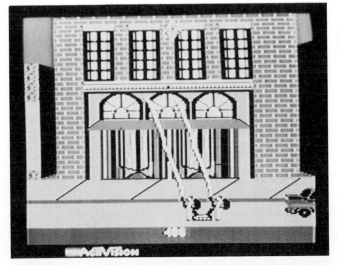

Figure 5.4: Videogames employ direct manipulation principles to create a world of action and fantasy. (*Ghostbusters: The Computer Game* art work courtesy of Activision, Inc.)

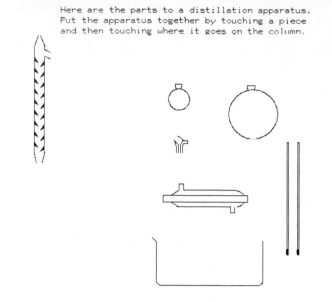

For help press HELP

Figure 5.5: Computer-based instruction can become more appealing with direct manipulation, instead of drill and practice. This CDC PLATO lesson, written by Stan Smith of the Department of Chemistry at the University of Illinois, allows students to construct a distillation aparatus by proper finger actions on a touch-sensitive screen. Once the student has assembled the apparatus and begun

unnecessary because the results of actions are obvious and can be easily reversed. These principles can be applied to office automation, personal computing, or other interactive environments.

Most games continuously display a numeric score so that users can measure their progress and compete with their previous performance, with friends, or with the highest scorers. Typically, the ten highest scorers get to store their initials in the game for regular display. This is one form of positive reinforcement that encourages mastery. Malone (1981) and our studies with elementary school children have shown that continuous display of scores is extremely valuable. Machine-generated value judgments, such as "Very Good" or "You're doing great!" are not as effective, since the same score means different things to different people.

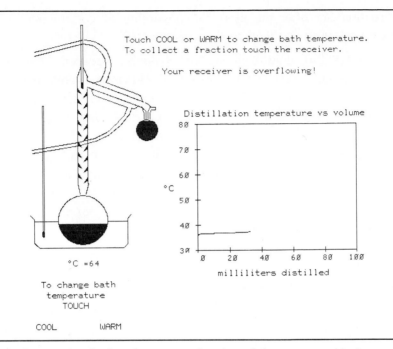

Touch COOL or WARM to change bath temperature.
To collect a fraction touch the receiver.

Your receiver is overflowing!

Distillation temperature vs volume

°C =64

To change bath
temperature
TOUCH

COOL   WARM

the experiment, the display shows an animation of the process with the graph of distillation temperature versus volume. The second figure shows that the student experimenter has gotten into trouble. (Courtesy of Stan Smith, University of Illinois.)

Users prefer to make their own subjective judgments and perceive the machine-generated messages as an annoyance and a deception.

Many educational games use direct manipulation effectively. Elementary or high school students can learn about logic by using Rocky Boots, which shows logic circuits visually and lets students progress to more complex tasks by going through doors to enter a series of rooms. Stan Smith's chemistry lessons on the PLATO system often enabled college students to conduct lab experiments by touching beakers, pipettes, or burners in order to assemble and operate equipment (Figure 5.5). A Navy training simulator shows gauges, dials, and knobs that can be directly manipulated to gain experience with boilers, valves, and so on (Hollan, Hutchins, & Weitzman, 1984). Several versions of the Music

Construction Set offer the users the possibility of constructing musical scores by selecting and moving notes onto a staff.

Carroll (1982b) draws productive analogies between game-playing environments and applications systems. However, game players are seeking entertainment and focus on the challenge of mastery, whereas applications systems users focus on their task and may resent the intrusion of forced learning of system constraints. Furthermore, the random events that occur in most games are meant to challenge the user; but in nongame designs, however, predictable system behavior is preferred. Game players are engaged in competition with the system, whereas applications systems users apparently prefer strong internal locus of control that gives them the sense of being in charge.

5.2.5 Computer-aided design/manufacturing

Many computer-aided design systems for automobiles, electronic circuitry, architecture, aircraft, or newspaper layout use principles of direct manipulation. The operator may see a circuit schematic on the screen and with lightpen touches can move resistors or capacitors into or out of the proposed circuit. When the design is complete, the computer can provide information about current, voltage drops, fabrication costs, and warnings about inconsistencies or manufacturing problems. Similarly, newspaper layout artists or automobile body designers can easily try multiple designs in minutes and record promising approaches until a better one is found. A playful application is Bill Budge's Pinball Construction Set that allows users to select bumpers, flippers, or flashers, drag them onto a pinball table, and then shoot the ball to see how the game plays (Figure 5.6).

The pleasures in using these systems stem from the capacity to manipulate the object of interest directly and to generate multiple alternatives rapidly. Some systems have complex command languages, but others have moved to using cursor action and graphics-oriented commands.

Another related direction is the world of computer-aided manufacturing and process control. Honeywell's process control system provides an oil

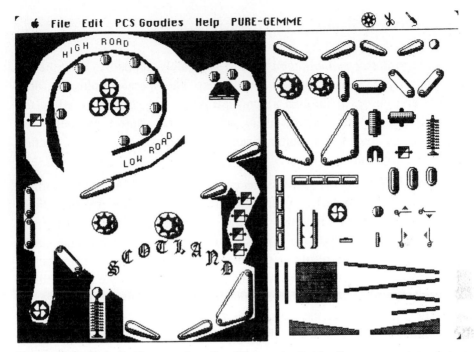

Figure 5.6: Pinball Construction Set (Electronic Arts) allows users to point at pinball components on the right and move them to the board on the left. When the user is satisfied, he or she can shoot the ball and work the flippers. (Courtesy of Electronic Arts, San Mateo, CA)

refinery, paper mill, or power utility plant manager with a colored schematic view of the plant. The schematic may be on eight displays, with red lines indicating a sensor value that is out of normal range. By pressing a single numbered button (there are no commands to learn or remember), the operator can get a more detailed view of the troubling component; and with a second press, the operator moves down the tree structure to examine individual sensors or to reset valves and circuits.

A basic strategy for this design is to eliminate the need for complex commands that need only be recalled in once-a-year emergency conditions. The schematic of the plant facilitates problem-solving by analogy since the linkage between real world high temperatures or low pressures and screen representations is so close.

5.2.6 Further examples

The term *direct manipulation* is most accurately applied to describe the programming of some industrial robot tools. The operator holds the robot "hand" and guides it through a spray painting or welding task while the controlling computer records every action. The control computer can then operate the robot automatically and repeat the precise action whenever necessary.

A large part of the success and appeal of the Query-by-Example (Zloof, 1975) approach to data manipulation is due to the direct representation of the relations on the screen (Figure 5.7). The user moves a cursor through the columns of the relational table and enters examples of what the result should look like. There are just a few single letter keywords to supplement the direct manipulation style. Of course, complex booleans or mathematical operations require knowledge of syntactic forms. Still, the basic ideas and facilities in this language can be learned within a half hour by many nonprogrammers.

```
Query:
SKI-RESORTS :   NAME    :  CITY   :   STATE   :  LIFTS   :   VERTICAL
----------------------------------------------------------------------
                :   P.    :  P.     :   NY      :          :   P. >1200
                :         :         :           :          :
```

```
Response:

SKI-RESORTS :   NAME           :  CITY         :   VERTICAL
----------------------------------------------------------------
                :  BELLEAYRE     :  HIGHMOUNT     :   1340
                :  GORE          :  NORTH CREEK  :   2100
                :  HUNTER        :  HUNTER        :   1600
                :  SKI WINDHAM  :  WINDHAM       :   1550
                :  WHITEFACE     :  WILMINGTON    :   3216
```

Figure 5.7: The Query-by-Example facility shows users a relational table skeleton and enables users to fill in literals (such as NY or 1200) and specify fields to be printed (P.). Users can also specify variables to link between relations. In this example, the query produces the NAMEs of ski resorts in NY state that have a vertical drop of more than 1200 feet.

Query-by-Example succeeds because novices can begin working with just a little training, yet there is ample power for the expert. Directly manipulating the cursor across the relation skeleton is simple, and showing the linking variable by giving an example is intuitively clear to someone who understands tabular data. Zloof (1982) expands his ideas into Office-by-Example, which elegantly integrates database search with word processing, electronic mail, business graphics, and menu creation.

Designers of advanced office automation systems have made use of direct manipulation principles. The Xerox Star (Smith et al., 1982) offers sophisticated text formatting options, graphics, multiple fonts, and a high resolution, cursor-based user interface (Figure 5.8). Users can move a document icon to a printer icon to generate a hardcopy printout. The Apple Lisa system elegantly applied many of the principles of direct manipulation and, although it was not a commercial success, it laid the groundwork for the successful Macintosh. The Macintosh designers drew from the Star and Lisa experience but made many simplifying decisions while preserving adequate power for users (Figure 5.9). The hardware and software designs supported rapid graphical interaction for pull-down menus, window manipulation, graphics and text editing, and dragging of icons. Imitations of the Macintosh appeared soon afterward for popular personal computers, such as the IBM PC (Figure 5.10 and Color Plate 2).

Researchers at IBM's Yorktown Heights Labs (Schild et al., 1980) propose a future office system, called PICTUREWORLD, in which graphic icons represent file cabinets, mailboxes, notebooks, phone messages, and so on. The user could compose a memo with a display editor and then indicate distribution and filing operations by selecting from the menu of icons. Yedwab et al. (1981) describe a generalized office system with a visual representation under the term *automated desk*.

5.3   EXPLANATIONS OF DIRECT MANIPULATION

Several authors have attempted to describe the component principles of direct manipulation. Don Hatfield (1981), who is applying many of these principles in an advanced office automation system, describes the general

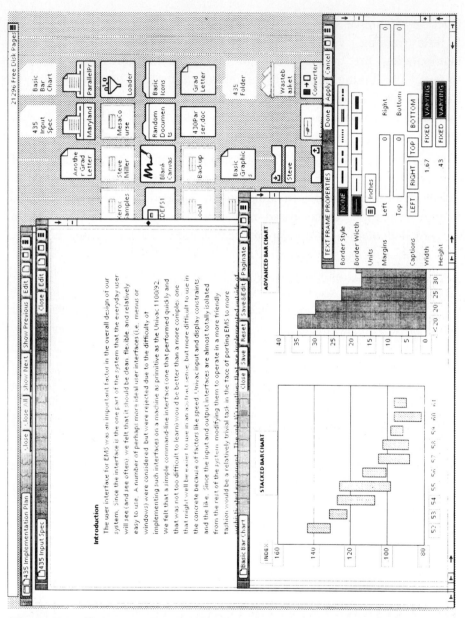

Figure 5.8: The Xerox Star 8010 with the ViewPoint system enables users to create documents with multiple fonts and graphics. This session shows the Text Frame Properties sheet over sample bar charts, with a document in the background and many desktop icons available for selection. (Prepared by Steve Miller, University of Maryland)

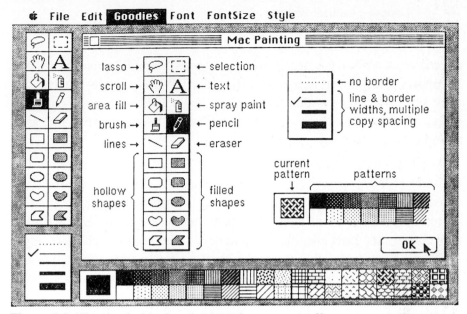

Figure 5.9: The Apple Macintosh Macpaint program offers a command menu on the top, a menu of action icons on the left, a choice of line thicknesses on the lower left, and a palette of texture on the bottom. All actions can be accomplished with only the mouse. (Photo courtesy of Apple Computer, Inc.)

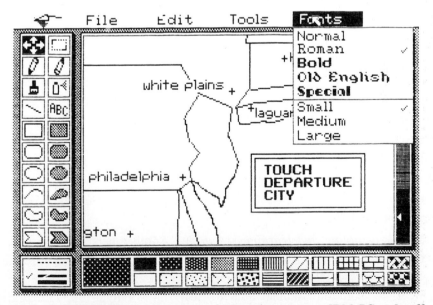

Figure 5.10: PCPAINT, a descendent of Macpaint, runs on IBM PCs. It offers similar features, but adds color. (Courtesy of Mouse Systems Corporation, Santa Clara, CA)

approach as "What you see is what you get." Harold Thimbleby (1982) expands in this direction by suggesting that "What you see is what you have got." He suggests that the display should indicate a more complete image of what the current status is, what errors have occurred, and what actions are appropriate.

Another imaginative observer of interactive system designs, Ted Nelson (1980), perceives user excitement when the interface is constructed by what he calls the principle of virtuality—a representation of reality that can be manipulated. Rutkowski (1982) conveys a similar concept in his principle of transparency: "The user is able to apply intellect directly to the task; the tool itself seems to disappear." MacDonald (1982) emphasizes the term *visual programming* as a solution to the shortage of application programmers. He feels that visual programming speeds system construction and allows end users to generate or modify applications systems to suit their needs.

Heckel (1984) laments that "Our instincts and training as engineers encourage us to think logically instead of visually, and this is counterproductive to friendly design." He suggests that thinking like a filmmaker can be helpful for interactive systems designers: "When I design a product, I think of my program as giving a performance for its user."

Hutchins et al. (1986) review the concepts of direct manipulation and offer a thoughtful decomposition of concerns. They describe the "feeling of involvement directly with a world of objects rather than of communicating with an intermediary."

Each of these writers supports the growing recognition that a new form of interactive systems is emerging. Much credit also goes to the individual designers who have created systems that exemplify aspects of direct manipulation.

Problem-solving and learning research. Another perspective on direct manipulation comes from the problem-solving psychology literature. Suitable representations of problems have been clearly shown to be critical to solution finding and to learning. Polya (1957) suggests drawing a picture to represent mathematical problems. This is in harmony with Maria Montessori's teaching methods for children (1964). She proposed use of physical objects such as beads or wooden sticks to convey such mathematical principles as addition, multiplication, or size comparison. Bruner (1966) extended the physical representation idea to cover polynomial factoring and other mathematical principles. Carroll, Thomas, and Malhotra (1980) found that subjects given spatial representation were faster and more successful in problem-solving than subjects given an isomorphic problem with a temporal representation. Deeper understanding of the relationship between problem-solving and visual perception can be obtained from Arnheim (1972) and McKim (1972).

Physical, spatial, or visual representations also appear to be easier to retain and manipulate than do textual or numeric representations. Wertheimer (1959) found that subjects who memorized the formula for the area of a parallelogram, A = h x b, rapidly succeeded in doing such calculations. On the other hand, subjects who were given the structural understanding of cutting off a triangle from one end and placing it on the other end could more effectively retain the knowledge and generalize it to solve related problems. In plane geometry theorem proving, spatial representation facilitates discovery of proof procedures over a strictly axiomatic representation of Euclidean geometry. The diagram provides heuristics that are difficult to extract from the axioms. Similarly, students of algebra word problems are often encouraged to draw a picture to represent the problem.

Papert's (1980) LOGO language creates a mathematical microworld in which the principles of geometry are visible. Based on the Swiss psychologist Jean Piaget's theory of child development, LOGO offers students the opportunity to create line drawings easily with an electronic turtle displayed on a screen. In this environment, users derive rapid feedback about their programs, can easily determine what has happened, can quickly spot and repair errors, and gain satisfaction from creative production of drawings. These features are all characteristic of a direct manipulation environment.

5.3.1 Problems with direct manipulation

In professional programming, use of high-level flowcharts, record structures, and database schema diagrams can be helpful for some tasks, but there is an additional effort in absorbing the rules of the representation. Visual representations can be helpful when there are multiple relationships among objects and when the representation is more compact than the detailed object. Selectively screening out detail and presenting an abstraction suitable for a given task can facilitate performance.

Use of spatial or visual representations is not necessarily an improvement. In one study, subjects given a detailed flowchart did no better in comprehension, debugging, or modification than subjects given the code only (Shneiderman et al., 1977). In another study, subjects given a graphic representation of control flow or data structure did no better than subjects given textual descriptions of control flow or data structure in a program comprehension task (Shneiderman, 1982). On the other hand, subjects given the data structure documentation consistently did better than subjects given the control flow documentation. This study suggests that the content of graphic representations is a critical determinant of utility. The wrong information, or a too cluttered presentation, can lead to greater confusion.

A second problem is that users must learn the meaning of components of the graphic representation. A graphic icon may be meaningful to the designer but may require as much or more learning time than a word. Some airports that serve multilingual communities use graphic icons extensively, but their meaning may not be obvious. Similarly, some computer terminals designed for international use have icons in place of names, but the meaning is not always clear.

A third problem is that the graphic representation may be misleading. The user may rapidly grasp the analogical representation but then make incorrect conclusions about permissible actions. Ample testing must be carried out to refine the displayed objects and actions and minimize negative side effects.

A fourth problem is that graphic representations may take excessive screen display space. For experienced users, a tabular textual display of fifty document names may be more appealing than only ten document graphic icons with the names abbreviated to fit the icon size.

A fifth problem is that for experienced typists, moving a mouse or raising a finger to point may sometimes be slower than typing. This is true especially if the user is familiar with a compact notation, such as arithmetic expressions, that is easy to enter from a keyboard, but may be more difficult with screen selection. The keyboard remains the most effective direct manipulation device for some tasks.

Choosing the right objects and actions is not an easy task. Simple metaphors, analogies, or models with a minimal set of concepts seem most appropriate to start. Mixing metaphors from two sources may add complexity that contributes to confusion. The emotional tone of the metaphor should be inviting rather than distasteful or inappropriate (Carroll & Thomas, 1982)—sewage disposal systems are an inappropriate metaphor for electronic message systems. Since the users may not share the metaphor, analogy, or conceptual model with the designer, ample testing is required. For help in training, an explicit statement of the model, the assumptions, and the limitations is necessary.

5.3.2 The syntactic/semantic model

The attraction of systems that use principles of direct manipulation is apparent in the enthusiasm of the users. The designers of the examples in Section 5.2 had an innovative inspiration and an intuitive grasp of what users would want. Each example has features that could be criticized, but it seems more productive to construct an integrated portrait of direct manipulation:

- continuous representation of the objects and actions of interest
- physical actions or labeled button presses instead of complex syntax
- rapid incremental reversible operations whose impact on the object of interest is immediately visible.

Using these three principles, it is possible to design systems that have these beneficial attributes:

- novices can learn basic functionality quickly, usually through a demonstration by a more experienced user

- experts can work rapidly to carry out a wide range of tasks, even defining new functions and features
- knowledgeable intermittent users can retain operational concepts
- error messages are rarely needed
- users can immediately see if their actions are furthering their goals, and, if not, they can simply change the direction of their activity
- users experience less anxiety because the system is comprehensible and because actions are so easily reversible
- users gain confidence and mastery because they are the initiators of action, they feel in control, and the system responses are predictable.

The success of direct manipulation is understandable in the context of the syntactic/semantic model. The object of interest is displayed so that actions are directly in the high level task domain. There is little need for the mental decomposition of tasks into multiple commands with a complex syntactic form. On the contrary, each action produces a comprehensible result in the task domain that is immediately visible. The closeness of the task to the action syntax reduces operator problem-solving load and stress. This principle is related to the principle of stimulus-response compatibility in the human factors literature.

The task semantics dominate the users' concerns, and the distraction of dealing with the computer semantics and the syntax is reduced (Figure 5.11).

Dealing with representations of objects may be more "natural" and closer to innate human capabilities: action and visual skills emerged well before language in human evolution. Psychologists have long known that spatial relationships and actions are grasped more quickly with visual rather than linguistic representations. Furthermore, intuition and discovery are often promoted by suitable visual representations of formal mathematical systems.

The Swiss psychologist Jean Piaget described four stages of growth: sensorimotor (from birth to approximately two years), preoperational (two

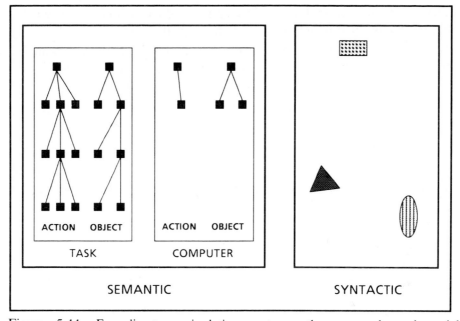

Figure 5.11: For direct manipulation systems, there may be substantial task-domain semantic knowledge. However, users must acquire only a modest amount of computer-related semantic knowledge and syntacctc knowledge.

to seven years), concrete operational (seven to eleven years), and formal operations (begins at approximately 11 years) (Copeland, 1979). According to this theory, physical actions on an object are comprehensible during the concrete operational stage, and children acquire the concept of conservation or invariance. At around age eleven, children enter the formal operations stage of symbol manipulation to represent actions on objects. Since mathematics and programming require abstract thinking, it is more difficult for children, and a greater effort must be made to link the symbolic representation to the actual object. Direct manipulation is an attempt to bring activity to the concrete operational stage, thus making some tasks easier for children and adults.

It is easy to envision direct manipulation in cases where the task is confined to a small number of objects and simple actions. In complex applications, it may be more difficult to design a direct manipulation approach. On the other hand, display editors provide impressive functionality in a natural way. The limits of direct manipulation will be determined by the imagination and skill of the designer. With more examples and experience, researchers should be able to test competing theories about the most effective metaphor or analogy. Familiar visual analogies may be more appealing in the early stages of learning to use the system; more specific abstract models may be more useful during regular use.

The syntactic/semantic model provides a simple model of human cognitive activity. It must be refined and extended to enhance its explanatory and predictive power. Empirical tests and careful measurements of human performance with a variety of systems are needed to develop and validate an improved model. Cognitive models of user behavior and mental models or system images of computer supplied functions are rapidly expanding areas of research in computer science and psychology.

5.4   POTENTIAL APPLICATIONS OF DIRECT MANIPULATION

The trick in creating a direct manipulation system is to come up with an appropriate representation or model of reality. Some designers may find it difficult to think about information problems in a visual form, but with practice it can become more natural. With many applications, the jump to visual language may be difficult, but later users and designers can hardly imagine why anyone would want to use a complex syntactic notation to describe an essentially visual process.

One application that we explored was a personal address list program that displays a Rolodex-like device (Figure 5.12). The most recently retrieved address card appears on the screen and the top line of the next two appear behind, followed by the image of a pack of remaining cards. As the joystick is pushed forward the Rolodex appears to rotate and successive cards appear in front. As the joystick is pushed further, the cards pass by more quickly; as the joystick is reversed, the direction of

Figure 5.12: This electronic Rolodex or phone number card file gives users rapid control over the card motion by a forward or backward joystick press. Commands are displayed by moving the joystick left or right. The lively motion of the cards appeals to many users.

movement reverses. To change an entry, the user need only move the cursor over the field to be updated and type the correction. To delete an entry, the user just blanks out the fields. Blank cards might be left at the top of the file, but when the fields are filled in, proper alphabetic placement is provided. To find all entries with a specific zip code, the user types the zip code in the proper field and enters a question mark.

Checkbook maintenance and searching might be done in a similar fashion. Display a checkbook register with labeled columns for check number, date, payee, and amount. The joystick might be used to scan earlier entries, changes could be made in place, new entries would be made at the first blank line, and a check mark could be made to indicate verification against a monthly report or bank statement. Searches for a particular payee could be made by filling in a blank payee field and then typing a question mark.

Bibliographic searching has more elaborate requirements, but a basic system could be built by first showing the user a wall of labeled catalog index drawers. A cursor in the shape of a human hand might be moved over to the section labeled "Author Index" and to the drawer labeled "F-L." Depressing the button on the joystick or mouse would cause the drawer to open, revealing an array of index cards with tabs offering a finer index. By moving the cursor-finger and depressing the selection button, the actual index cards could be made to appear. Depressing the button while holding a card would cause a copy of the card to be made in the user's notebook, also represented on the screen. Entries in the notebook might be edited to create a printed bibliography or combined with other entries to perform set intersections or unions. Copies of entries could be stored on user files or transmitted to colleagues by electronic mail. It is easy to visualize many alternate approaches, so careful design and experimental testing would be necessary to sort out the successful comprehensible approaches from the idiosyncratic ones.

Why not do airline reservations by showing the user a map and prompting for cursor motion to the departing and arriving cities? Then, use a calendar to select the date and a clock to indicate the time. Seat selection is done by showing the seating plan of the plane on the screen, with a diagonal line to indicate an already reserved seat.

Why not do inventory by showing the aisles of the warehouse with the appropriate number of boxes on each shelf? McDonald (1983) deals with medical supply inventory with a visual warehouse display by combining videodisc and computer graphics technology.

Why not teach students about polynomial equations by letting them bend the curves and watch how the coefficients change or where the X-axis intercept occurs or how the derivative equation reacts (Shneiderman, 1974)?

These ideas are sketches for real systems. Competent designers and implementers must complete the sketches and fill in the details. Direct manipulation has the power to attract users because it is comprehensible, natural, rapid, and even enjoyable. If actions are simple, reversibility ensured, and retention easy, then anxiety recedes and satisfaction flows in.

5.5 DIRECT MANIPULATION DISK OPERATING SYSTEM (DMDOS)

This section gives a detailed description of one design project whose goal was to develop a direct manipulation user interface for a widely used command language. The difficulty of designing a direct manipulation system was explored in a visual design for the commands in the Microsoft Disk Operating System (MS-DOS) for IBM and compatible computers (detailed design and implemention by Osamu Iseki). The motivations were to avoid the:

1. Error-prone, difficult-to-remember, and difficult-to-type commands, such as:

   ```
   dir/w c:level2
   copy a:filel.pas b:filel.bak
   erase c:level2 filel
   ```

2. Need for many commands, such as: VERsion, VOLume DATE, TIME, CD, MKDIR, RMDIR, CHDIR, TYPE, PRINT, DELETE, and RENAME.

3. Frustration of watching the directory listings scroll off of the screen too quickly.

4. Uncertainty of not seeing the source and destination directories while copying, comparing, or deleting files. After issuing a file command, many users issue a directory display command to verify that the command was carried out correctly.

5. Need to type file and directory names, except when they are created. Once created, file and directory names can be selected from the display. When the number of files is in

the hundreds, it may be more convenient to type the file name, but with only tens of files, selection by pointing is often more rapid and accurate.

5.5.1 Design goals

In a positive way, we sought to provide a world in which the:

1. Task-related objects (files) and the actions (commands) were always visible.
2. Users could select objects and actions by pointing instead of typing.
3. Results of actions were immediately visible.

We hoped that such a design would be easy to learn and retain, rapid in performing tasks, low in errors, and high in user satisfaction. After many revisions and tests with hundreds of knowledgeable observers and novices, the screen layout was determined (Figure 5.13).

5.5.2 Screen organization

The largest parts of the screen are the right and the left drive information areas. Each area has the:

1. Drive name (A, B, or C).
2. Volume name of the disk.
3. [SUB–DIR/FILE], the toggle switch for changing the listing from/to file names or subdirectory names.
4. [SORT] switch that allows users to set the sort condition of the file listing to sort by file name, extension, size, or date.
5. [WIDE/FULL], toggle switch for changing the format of the file listing from a single to a double column listing.

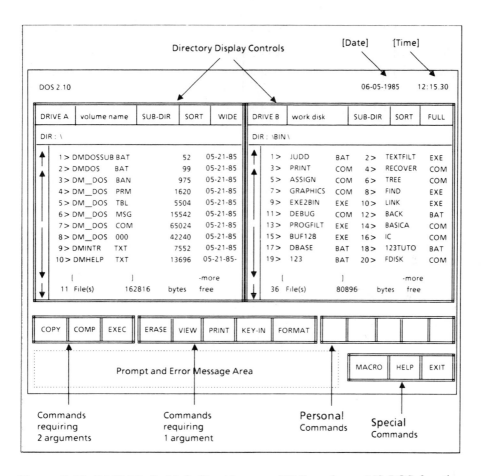

Figure 5.13: DMDOS (Iseki & Shneiderman, 1986) performs MS-DOS functions by arrow key or mouse movements instead of typing commands. The display shows the source and destination directory displays that are scrollable under user control.

6. Current directory name.

7. The listing of file names or subdirectory names in the current directory. Each listing has a maximum of twenty file names or ten subdirectory names.

8. Icons for scrolling up and down the listing. The short arrows serve for one-line scrolling and the long arrows for five-line.

These two large areas are independent from each other.

Below these drive information areas are command areas that are categorized into four groups:

1. Commands requiring two arguments: COPY, COMPare, EXECute.
2. Commands requiring one argument: ERASE, VIEW, PRINT, KEY-IN, and FORMAT.
3. Definable personal commands (space is provided for only five).
4. Special commands: MACRO, HELP, and EXIT.

The screen format contains most items users need, and it remains visible unless a program file is executed or the contents of a file are seen by using the [VIEW] command. Therefore, users may have less anxiety about the correct execution of a command than working in a line-by-line mode.

5.5.3 Functions

DMDOS functions are categorized into seven groups:

1. Functions automatically executed. For example, the directory listing is always displayed on the screen. This eliminates the need for the DIR command.
2. Functions executed by single object or switch selection. Selecting an object causes some functions.
3. Functions executed by overtyping the selected object. These are mainly for renaming files and changing the date or time.
4. Functions executed by commands with one argument. These commands need only a source object.
5. Functions executed by commands with two arguments. These commands need source and destination objects.

6. Functions executed by personal commands. These commands can be defined by the user and include a sequence of operations.

7. Functions executed by special commands.

Table 5.1 shows functions in each category. These are described with the equivalent MS-DOS commands for comparison. Since we tried to

DMDOS command category	PC-DOS internal commands		PC-DOS external commands	
Automatically Executed or Executed by Single Selection	DIR DATE(display) TIME (display) VERsion VOLume name (CHDIR)		SORT(only for filename)	
Executed by Overtyping the Object	RENAME MKDIR CHDIR DATE(set) TIME (set)			
1-object Command	ERASE RMDIR TYPE	[ERASE] [ERASE] [VIEW]	FORMAT PRINT	[FORMAT] [PRINT]
2-object Command	COPY	[COPY]	COMP DISKCOMP DISKCOPY	[COMP] [COMP] [COPY]
Additional Command	[EXEC] [KEY-IN] [HELP] [MACRO]			
not necessary in DMDOS	CLS			
not implemented in DMDOS	(Batch command), BREAK, PATH , VERIFY		ASSIGN, BACKUP, CHKDISK, GRAPHICS, MODE, RECOVER, RESTORE, SYS	

Table 5.1: A comparison of DMDOS (Iseki & Shneiderman, 1986) and MS-DOS commands showing how selection of visible objects and actions replaces typed commands.

to reduce the number of commands to the minimum, some MS-DOS functions used infrequently have not been implemented. The most important commands not implemented are batch processing commands that allow users to make their own command sequences in an executable batch file. However, DMDOS has a special command [MACRO] to make user-definable commands (see Section 5.5.5).

5.5.4 Operational principles

Operation in DMDOS is mainly based on movement of the cursor and selection of an object or a command of interest. Cursor movement and selection can be done by using either keyboard or mouse.

Using a keyboard. Users can use four arrow keys to move the cursor. The cursor is moved from item to item instead of from character to character except if it is in a selected object. Selection is done by placing the cursor in the object of interest and pressing the RETURN key.

Using a mouse. The cursor moves character by character according to the mouse movement. Selection is made by pressing one mouse button. The keyboard can also be used at the same time.

The mouse is a more 'direct' tool to locate the cursor on the item of interest quickly. However, two sets of special keys may help users move the cursor effectively by the keyboard. First, four corner keys adjacent to four arrow keys allow users to make a shortcut by jumping the cursor to the four corners of the screen. Second, the ten function keys (F1-F10) are dedicated to moving the cursor onto the drive field or scrolling icons of each drive and making a selection. Figure 5.14 shows the keys used for cursor movement.

The item visited by the cursor is reverse-displayed partly or fully. Once the item is selected, it remains highlighted until it is unselected or a function is executed.

As a special case of selection, multiselection of file names is permitted. The operation of multiselection is to hold down the CTRL key while pressing the RETURN key when selecting some file names. The

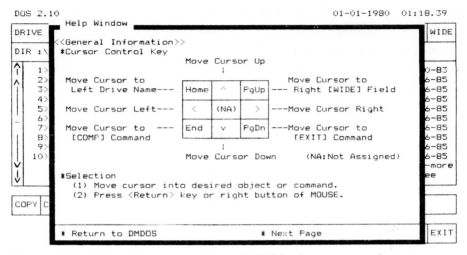

Figure 5.14: This help screen from DMDOS shows cursor key movement possibilities.

maximum number of multiselection files is ten. This function may be used for copying several files to another drive or erasing several files at one time. In MS-DOS, it is necessary to use such wild-card characters as "*" and "?" to indicate the multiple files. Though this mechanism is also allowed in DMDOS, multiselection is sometimes an easier way to indicate a set of files.

The general principle of operation is to select an object first, called the source object. After that, overtyping or selecting a command is effective. Three typical operational sequences are:

1. Overtyping
    a. Select an object of interest
    b. Overtype the new name
    c. Select the object again to install the new name
2. Command with one argument
    a. Select an object of interest
    b. Select a command

  c. Users might be prompted by some messages.
    Answer these prompts, if any.
    Then the command will be executed.
 3. Command with two arguments
  a. Select a source object
  b. Select a command
  c. Select a destination object
  d. Users might be prompted by some messages.
    Answer these prompts, if any.
    Then the command function will be executed.

  This object-first strategy is different from the order of MS-DOS's command syntax. After executing a command function, the most recently selected object is still selected. Therefore, if users need to execute any other command on this object, they can simply select a new command just after the execution of the previous command.

5.5.5 Programming with the macro command

  One major objective of DMDOS development was to try to implement a programming capability based on direct manipulation. This macro definition function corresponds to the batch command in MS-DOS. A command defined by this function is called a personal command and can be regarded as a small program. To maintain consistency, a personal command can be programmed by showing an example of a sequence of ordinary operations. Users can enter the macrodefining stage by selecting the MACRO special command. A sequence of selections will be recorded as a replayable operational sequence during this stage.

  Each personal command can have one or two arguments like other commands for source and destination objects. By modifying the example of the operational sequence, these arguments can be implemented in the personal command.

For example, making a personal command called "MOVE," whose function is to move a file (source argument) from one drive to another (destination argument), requires these steps:

1. Select [MACRO] special command.

2. Select [Define...] macro subcommand.

3. Type the name of MOVE and press RETURN. The macrodefining stage begins.

4. Show an operational example.

    a. Select a file named FILE1.

    b. Select [COPY] command.

    c. Select a drive name B:.

    d. Select FILE1 again.

    e. Select [ERASE] command.

    f. Select [Yes] for confirmation.

5. Select [Macro] command again to indicate the end of the macrodefining stage. Then the recorded operational sequence and edit-parameter will be displayed.

6. Select [Source Argument] parameter for the first object FILE1. Then the FILE1 selected at 4.d will also be changed to the source argument automatically.

7. Select [Destination Argument] parameter for the second object B:.

8. Select [Return to DMDOS] to indicate the end of the modification.

This MOVE command will copy a source file to the destination drive and erase the source file.

5.6 CONCLUSION

Novice and knowledgeable users have expressed a strong interest in DMDOS, but field trials with real users are just beginning. There are some performance problems that may limit use of the current version. DMDOS takes almost 20 seconds to load on a standard PC, requires use of one of the floppy disk drives, and consumes more than 52,000 bytes. These problems are reduced when a hard drive is available. Since DMDOS invokes MS-DOS functions, hardware failures produce error messages that sometimes destroy the DMDOS screen.

On the user interface side, there is some annoyance in having to do so much arrow key pressing, and therefore some further shortcuts should be explored. The mouse version reduces this problem. Single-letter alternates for some commands might further speed the work of some frequent users. The KEY-IN feature that uses the MS-DOS console input mechanism might be replaced by a small text editor.

Knowledgeable users often remark that they would prefer to type commands and believe that they can work more rapidly by just typing the commands. A field trial over several weeks would be helpful in ascertaining actual performance.

We feel that we succeeded in our goal to create a direct manipulation interface for MS-DOS commands. Whether these ideas can become successfully integrated into commercial software remains to be seen. The 6,000 lines of Turbo Pascal were written in a seven-month period by one person (Osamu Iseki). Re-implementation should be easier and would permit inclusion of additional features.

Several competing software products accomplish some of the goals of DMDOS. File Command from IBM reduces the memorization and keystroking burden by showing commands on the screen and allowing users to press function keys to produce commands. The 1DIR package from Bourbaki provides some features of DMDOS but shows only one directory at a time. The Apple Macintosh desktop and the GEM Desktop for IBM PCs offer visual representations of directories and convenient icon movement or copying.

5.7   DIRECT MANIPULATION PROGRAMMING

Performing tasks by direct manipulation is not the only goal. It should be possible to do programming by direct manipulation as well, for at least some problems. The MACRO command of DMDOS supports a limited form of programming, but more complex forms of programming seem possible with direct manipulation ideas.

Robot programming is sometimes done by moving the robot arm through a sequence of steps that are later replayed, possibly at higher speed. This example seems to be a good candidate for generalization. How about moving a drill press or a surgical tool through a complex series of motions that are then repeated exactly? How about programming a car by driving it once through a maze and then having the car repeat the path? In fact, these direct manipulation programming ideas are implemented in modest ways with automobile radios that are preset by turning the frequency control knob and then pulling out a button. When the button is depressed, the radio tunes to the frequency. Some professional television camera supports allow the operator to program a sequence of pans or zooms and then replay them smoothly when required.

Programming of physical devices seems quite natural by direct manipulation, but an adequate visual representation of information may make direct manipulation programming possible in other domains. Several word processors allow creation of macros by simply performing a sequence of commands that are stored away for later reuse. The Wang Decision Processing system enables the creation of "glossary" items that can be lengthy sequences of text, special function keys such as TAB, and control structures (Figure 5.15). The control structures can test for user input and cursor location. Glossary items can invoke each other, leading to complex programming possibilities. LOTUS 1–2–3, Symphony, and Framework have rich programming languages and allow portions of programs to be created by carrying out standard spreadsheet operations. The result of the operations is stored in another part of the spreadsheet and can be edited, printed, and stored in a textual form.

A delightful children's program, Delta Drawing from Spinnaker, enables children to move a cursor and draw on the screen by typing D to draw one unit, R to rotate right 30 degrees, and so on. The forty commands provide rich possibilities for drawing some kinds of screen images. In addition, Delta Drawing allows users to save, edit, and then invoke programs. For example, a circle can be drawn by saving the

(g)

(-TAB-) (-TAB-) Very truly yours, (-RETURN-)
(-RETURN-) (-RETURN-)
(-TAB-) (-TAB-) J. S. Bach
(-RETURN-) (-TAB-) (-TAB-)
President (-RETURN-)

(-PROMPT-)
    Printout? y or n
(-EXECUTIVE-)
(–1-KEY-)

(-BACKSPACE-)

(-IF-) "y"
    (-GO-TO-GL-)y
(-END-)
(-GO-TO-GL-)n

Figure 5.15: Direct manipulation programming in the Wang Decision Processing System. Users press labelled function keys for each token to create the program which is stored in the glossary.

program consisting of a D and a R. Invoking the program with the argument, 12, then produces a rough twelve-sided circle.

A number of research projects have attempted to create direct manipulation programming systems. Halbert's Smallstar (1984) was a programming-by-example system to enable programming of Xerox Star actions. PICT-D (Glinert & Tanimoto, 1984) and ThinkPad (Rubin, Golin, & Reiss, 1985) both tried to make graphical icons into a programming language. This strategy has many of the elements of direct manipulation.

5.8   PRACTITIONER'S SUMMARY

Among interactive systems that provide equivalent functionality and reliability, some systems emerge to dominate the competition. Often the most appealing systems have an enjoyable user interface that offers a natural representation of the task and commands, hence the term *direct manipulation*. These systems are easy to learn, use, and retain over time. Novices can acquire a simple subset of the commands and then progress to more elaborate operations. Actions are rapid, incremental, reversible, and often performed with physical actions instead of complex syntactic forms. The results of operations are immediately visible, and error messages are needed less often.

Just because direct manipulation principles have been used in a system does not ensure its success. A poor design, slow implementation, or inadequate functionality can undermine acceptance. For some applications, menu selection, form fill-in, or command languages may be more appropriate. Iterative design (see Section 10.2) is especially important in testing direct manipulation systems because the novelty of this approach may lead to problems for designers and users.

5.9   RESEARCHER'S AGENDA

Research needs to be done to refine our understanding of the contribution of each feature of direct manipulation: analogical representation, incremental operation, reversibility, physical action instead of syntax, immediate visibility of results, graceful evolution, and graphic form. The relative merits of competing analogical representations could be better understood through experimental comparisons (Bewley et al., 1983). Reversibility is easily accomplished by a generic UNDO command, but designing natural inverses for each operation may be more attractive. Can complex actions always be represented with direct manipulation, or is there a point at which command syntax becomes appealing?

If researchers and designers can free themselves to think visually, then the future of direct manipulation is promising. Tasks that could have been performed only with tedious command or programming languages may soon be accessible through lively, enjoyable interactive systems that reduce learning time, speed performance, and increase satisfaction.

REFERENCES

Arnheim, Rudolf, *Visual Thinking*, University of California Press, Berkeley, CA, (1972).

Bewley, William L., Roberts, Teresa L., Schroit, David, and Verplank, William L., Human factors testing in the design of Xerox's 8010 "Star" Office Workstation, *Proc. CHI '83 Conference - Human Factors in Computing Systems*, Available from ACM Order Dept., P. O. Box 64145, Baltimore, MD 21264, (1983), 72–77.

Bruner, James, *Toward a Theory of Instruction*, Harvard University Press, Cambridge, MA, (1966).

Carroll, J. M., Learning, using and designing command paradigms, *Human Learning 1*, (1982a), 31–62.

Carroll, J. M., The adventure of getting to know a computer, *IEEE Computer 15*, (1982b), 49–58.

Carroll, John M., and Thomas, John C., Metaphor and the cognitive representation of computing systems, *IEEE Transactions on Systems, Man, and Cybernetics, SMC–12*, 2, (March/April 1982), 107–116.

Carroll, J. M., Thomas, J. C., and Malhotra, A., Presentation and representation in design problem-solving, *British Journal of Psychology 71*, (1980), 143–153.

Copeland, Richard W., *How Children Learn Mathematics*, Third Edition, MacMillan, New York, (1979).

Glinert, Emphraim, and Tanimoto, Steven L., Pict: An interactive graphical programming environment, *IEEE Computer 17*, 11, (November 1984), 7–25.

Halbert, Daniel, Programming by Example, Ph. D. dissertation, Department of Electrical Engineering and Computer Systems, University of California, Berkeley, CA, Available as Xerox Report OSD-T8402, Palo Alto, CA, (1984).

Hatfield, Don, Personal communication and lecture at Conference on Easier and More Productive Use of Computer Systems, Ann Arbor, MI (1981).

Heckel, Paul, *The Elements of Friendly Software Design*, Warner Books, New York, NY, (1984), 205 pages.

Herot, Christopher F., Spatial management of data, *ACM Transactions on Database Systems*, Vol. 5, No. 4, (December 1980), 493–513.

Herot, Christopher, Graphical user interfaces, In Vassiliou, Yannis (Editor), *Human Factors and Interactive Computer Systems*, Ablex Publishing Co., Norwood, NJ, (1984), 83–104.

Hollan, J. D., Hutchins, E. L., and Weitzman, L., STEAMER: An interactive inspectable simulation-based training system, *AI Magazine*, (Summer 1984), 15–27.

Hutchins, Edwin L., Hollan, James D., and Norman, Don A., Direct manipulation interfaces, In Norman, Don A., and Draper, Stephen W. (Editors), *User Centered System Design: New Perspectives on Human-Computer Interaction*, Lawrence Erlbaum Associates, Hillsdale, NJ, (1986).

Iseki, Osamu and Shneiderman, Ben, Applying direct manipulation concepts: Direct Manipulation Disk Operating System (DMDOS), *Software Engineering Notes 11*, 2, (March 1986).

MacDonald, Alan, Visual Programming, *Datamation 28*, 11, (October 1982), 132–140.

McDonald, Nancy, Multi-media approach to user interface, In Vassiliou, Yannis (Editor), *Human Factors in Interactive Computer Systems*, Ablex Publishing Co., Norwood, NJ, (1983).

McKim, Robert H., *Experiences in Visual Thinking*, Brooks/Cole Publishing Company, Monterey, CA, (1972).

Malone, Thomas W., What makes computer games fun?, *BYTE 6*, 12, (December 1981), 258–277.

Montessori, Maria, *The Montessori Method*, Schocken, New York, (1964).

Nelson, Ted, Interactive systems and the design of virtuality, *Creative Computing* Vol. 6, No. 11, (November 1980), 56 ff., and Vol. 6, No. 12, (December 1980), 94 ff.

Papert, Seymour, *Mindstorms: Children, Computers, and Powerful Ideas*, Basic Books, Inc., New York, NY, (1980).

Polya, G., *How to Solve It*, Doubleday, New York, (1957).

Roberts, Teresa L., Evaluation of Computer Text Editors, Ph. D. dissertation, Stanford University, Available from University Microfilms, Ann Arbor, MI, Order Number AAD 80–11699, (1980).

Rubin, Robert V., Golin, Eric J., and Reiss, Steven P., Thinkpad: a graphics system for programming by demonstrations, *IEEE Software* Vol. 2, No. 2, (March 1985), 73–79.

Rutkowski, Chris, An introduction to the Human Applications Standard Computer Interface, Part 1: Theory and principles, *BYTE* 7, 11, (October 1982), 291–310.

Schild, W., Power, L. R., and Karnaugh, M., PICTUREWORLD: A concept for future office systems, IBM Research Report RC 8384, Yorktown Heights, NY, (July 30, 1980).

Shneiderman, Ben, A computer graphics system for polynomials, *The Mathematics Teacher*, Vol. 67, No. 2, (1974), 111–113.

Shneiderman, Ben, Control flow and data structure documentation: Two Experiments, *Communications of the ACM*, Vol. 25, No. 1, (January 1982), 55–63.

Shneiderman, Ben, Mayer, R., McKay, D., and Heller, P., Experimental investigations of the utility of detailed flowcharts in programming, *Communications of the ACM*, Vol. 20, (1977), 373–381.

Smith, Cranfield, Irby, Charles, Kimball, Ralph, Verplank, Bill, and Harslem, Eric, Designing the Star user interface, *BYTE*, Vol. 7, No. 4, (April 1982), 242–282.

Thimbleby, Harold, What you see is what you have got? Unpublished paper, University of York, England, (1982).

Wertheimer, M., *Productive Thinking*, Harper and Row, New York, (1959).

Yedwab, Laura, Herot, Christopher F., and Rosenberg, Ronni L., The automated desk, *Sigsmall Newsletter* 7, 2, (October 1981), 102–108.

Zloof, M. M., Office-by-Example: A business language that unifies data and word processing and electronic mail, *IBM Systems Journal 21*, 3, (1982), 272–304.

Zloof, M. M., Query-by-Example, *Proceedings of the National Computer Conference*, AFIPS Press, Montvale, NJ (1975).

PART III

CONSIDERATIONS AND AUGMENTATIONS

CHAPTER 6

INTERACTION DEVICES

The wheel is an extension of the foot, the book is an extension of the eye, clothing, an extension of the skin, electric circuitry an extension of the central nervous system.

Marshall McLuhan and Quentin Fiore, *The Medium is the Message*, 1967

6.1 INTRODUCTION

The remarkable progress in computer processor speeds and storage capabilities has been matched only partially by improvements in input/output devices. Ten-character-per-second teletypes have been replaced by high-speed displays for output, but the 100-year-old keyboard remains the primary input mechanism. Improvements have been modest in part because human abilities are slow to change and breaking away from previous strategies has proven to be more difficult than anticipated. For example, improvements to the common Sholes keyboard layout, such as the Dvorak layout, have been demonstrated to reduce time and errors, but few users are willing to make the transition.

The increased concern for human factors has led to hundreds of new devices and variants on the old devices: novel keyboards, refinements of the Sholes keyboard, function keypads; such pointing devices as the lightpen, joystick, mouse, touchscreen, graphics pad, and trackball; the use of speech recognition and generation; color displays; and varieties of monochrome displays (Dunsmore, 1983). The lively controversy surrounding these devices is healthy, and empirical studies are now beginning to yield comparative evaluations as well as insights that lead to further innovations (Foley & Van Dam, 1982; Brown, 1986).

6.2 KEYBOARDS AND FUNCTION KEYS

The primary mode of data entry is still by keyboards. These often-criticized devices are quite impressive in their success. Hundreds of millions of people have managed to use these devices with speeds of up to 15 keystrokes per second (approximately 150 words per minute), although rates for beginners are less than 1 keystroke per second and rates for average office workers are 5 keystrokes per second (approximately 50 words per minute). Contemporary keyboards generally permit only one keypress at a time, although dual keypresses (SHIFT plus a letter) are used to produce capitals and special functions (CTRL plus a letter).

More rapid data entry can be accomplished by chord keyboards that allow several keys to be pressed simultaneously to represent several characters or a word. Courtroom recorders regularly use chord keyboards serenely to enter the full text of spoken arguments, reaching rates of up to 300 words per minute. This feat requires months of training and frequent use to retain the complex pattern of chord presses. The piano keyboard is an impressive data entry device that allows several finger presses at once and is responsive to different pressures and durations. It seems that there is potential for higher rates of data entry than with the current keyboards.

Keyboard size and packaging also influence user satisfaction and usability. Large keyboards with many keys leave an impression of professionalism and complexity but may threaten novice users. Small keyboards seem lacking in power to some users, but their compact size is an attraction to others. A thin profile (30 to 45 millimeters thick) allows users to rest the keyboard on their laps easily and permits a comfortable hand position when the keyboard is on a desk. A moderate keyboard slope (10 to 25 degrees) is thought to provide greater comfort (Emmons & Hirsch, 1982).

6.2.1 Keyboard layouts

The Smithsonian Institution's National Museum of American History in Washington, D. C., has a remarkable exhibit on the development of the typewriter. During the middle of the nineteenth century, hundreds of attempts were made to build typewriters, with a stunning variety of positions for the paper, mechanisms for producing a character, and layouts for the keys. By the 1870s, Christopher Latham Sholes's design was becoming successful because of a good mechanical design and a clever placement of the letters that slowed the users down enough so that key jamming was infrequent. This QWERTY layout put frequently used letter pairs far apart, thereby increasing finger travel distances.

Sholes's success led to such widespread standardization that a century later almost all English language keyboards use the QWERTY layout

Figure 6.1: QWERTY keyboard from IBM 3290 with 24 function keys, numeric keypad, separate cursor control keys, and special functions.

(Figure 6.1). The development of electronic keyboards eliminated the mechanical problems and led many twentieth century inventors to propose alternative layouts to reduce finger travel distances (Montgomery, 1982). The Dvorak layout (Figure 6.2), developed in the 1920s, supposedly

Figure 6.2: Dvorak keyboard from IBM 3290 with 24 function keys, separate cursor control keys, and special functions. The keycaps also show the APL character set.

reduces finger travel distances by at least one order of magnitude, thereby increasing the typing rate of expert typists from about 150 words per minute to more than 200 words per minute, while reducing errors (Kroemer, 1972; Martin, 1972).

Acceptance of the Dvorak design has been slow despite the dedicated efforts of some devotees. They hope that the ease of switching keyboards on some machines may entice some users. Those who have tried report that it takes about one week of regular typing to make the switch, but most users have been unwilling to invest the effort. We are confronted with an interesting example of how even documented improvements are hard to disseminate because the perceived benefit of change does not appear to outweigh the effort.

A third keyboard layout of some interest is the ABCDE style that has the twenty-six letters of the alphabet laid out in alphabetical order. The rationale here is that nontypists will find it easier to locate the keys. Some data entry terminals for numeric and alphabetic codes use this style (Figure 6.3). The widespread availability of QWERTY keyboards has

Figure 6.3: One approach to an ABCDE layout on the Texas Instruments Speak & Spell educational toy. The vowels are highlighted and special functions are included to fill the 4 by 10 array of membrane keys.

made typing a more common skill and has reduced the importance of the ABCDE style.

Beyond the letters, many debates rage about the placement of additional keys. The IBM PC keyboard was widely criticized because of the placement of a few keys, such as a back-slash key where most typists expected to find the SHIFT key, and the placement of several special characters near the ENTER key (Figure 6.4). Later versions eliminated the offending keys, to the acclaim of critics. Other improvements included a larger ENTER key and LEDs to signal the status of the CapsLock, NumLock, and ScrollLock keys.

Number pads are another source of controversy. Telephones have the 1–2–3 keys on the top row, but calculators place the 7–8–9 keys on the top row. Studies have shown a slight advantage for the telephone layout, but most computer keyboards use the calculator layout.

Some researchers have recognized that the wrist and hand placement for standard keyboards is awkward. Redesigned keyboards that separated the keys for the left and right hands by 9.5 centimeters, had an opening angle of 25 degrees with an inclination of 10 degrees, and offered large areas for forearm-wrist support led to lower reported tension, better posture, and higher preference scores (Nakaseko et al., 1985).

Figure 6.4: Standard IBM PC keyboard with ten function keys on the left, a numeric keypad on the right, and cursor control keys embedded in the numeric keypad.

6.2.2 Keys

Modern electronic keyboards use half-inch square keys with about a quarter-inch space between keys. The design has been carefully refined and thoroughly tested in research labs and the marketplace. The keys have a slightly concave surface for good contact with fingertips and a matte finish to reduce reflective glare while reducing the chance of finger slips. The keypresses require a 40 to 125 gram force and a displacement of 3 to 5 millimeters (IBM, 1984). The force and displacement have been shown to produce rapid typing with low error rates while providing suitable feedback to users. As user experience grows and the chance of a misplaced finger is reduced, the force and displacement can be lowered.

An important element in key design is the profile of force displacement. When the key has been depressed far enough to send a signal, the key gives way and emits a click. The tactile and audible feedback is extremely important in touch typing (Figure 6.5) (Brunner et al., 1984). For these reasons, membrane keyboards that use a nonmoving touch-sensitive surface are unacceptable for touch typing. However, they are durable and therefore effective for public installations at museums or amusement parks.

Certain keys, such as the space bar, ENTER key, SHIFT key, or CTRL key, should be larger to allow easy, reliable access. Other keys, such as the CapsLock or NumLock should have a clear indication of what position they are in. This is done by a physical locking in a lowered position or by an embedded light. Key labels should be large enough to read, meaningful, and permanent. Discrete color coding of keys helps make a pleasing, informative layout. A further design principle is that some of the home keys, F and J in the QWERTY layout, may have a deeper concavity or a small raised dot to reassure users that their fingers are properly placed.

6.2.3 Function keys

Many keyboards contain a set of additional keys for special functions or programmed functions. These keys are often labeled F1...F10 or

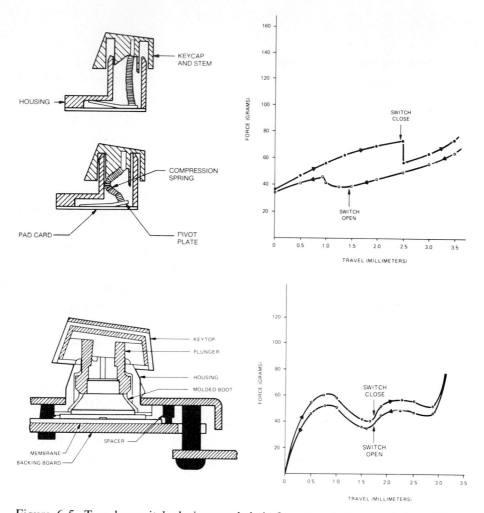

Figure 6.5: Two keyswitch designs and their force/travel characteristics. (From Effects of keyboard design and typing skill on user performance, Honeywell Microswitch Technical Report, June 1984. Used with permission.)

PF1...PF24. Users must remember the functions, learn about them from the screen, or consult an attachable plastic template. This strategy attempts to reduce user keystrokes by replacing a command name with a single keystroke. Most function key strategies do not require pressing the ENTER key to invoke the function.

On the positive side, the function keys can reduce keystrokes and errors, thereby speeding work for novice users who are poor typists and for expert users who readily recall the purpose of each function key. On the negative side, the purpose of each function key may not be apparent to some users and they must remove their fingers from the home position.

For function keys, there are several design decisions that impact users. The association of a function with a key is vital. Novices need a screen display or a template to remind them of the function. Many systems confuse users by having inconsistent key use. For example, the HELP key varies from F1 to F9 to F12 on some systems. Consistent use is important.

The placement of function keys is very important if the task requires users to go from typing to using function keys. The greater the distance of the function keys from the home position on the keyboard, the worse the problem. Some users would rather type six or eight characters than remove their fingers from the home position. The layout of the keys also influences ease of use. A 3-by-4 layout of twelve keys is helpful because users quickly learn functions by their placement on the upper-left or lower-right. A 1-by-12 layout only has two anchors and leads to slower and more error-prone selection of middle keys. A small gap between the sixth and seventh keys could aid users by grouping keys. A 2-by-5 layout is a reasonable intermediate style.

Function keys are sometimes built in the display screen bezel so that they are close to displayed labels. This position supports novices who need labels, but it still requires hands to stray from the home position. Lights can be built into and next to function keys to indicate availability or on/off status.

If all work can be done with labeled function keys, as on some computer-aided design systems, then they can be a benefit. If movement between the home position on the keyboard and the function keys is frequent, then function keys can be disruptive. An alternative strategy is to use CTRL plus a letter to invoke a function. This approach has some mnemonic value, keeps hands on the home keys, and reduces the need for extra keys.

6.2.4 Cursor movement keys

A special category of function keys is the cursor movement keys. There are usually four keys—pointing up, down, left, and right. Some keyboards have eight keys to simplify diagonal movements. The placement of the cursor movement keys is important in facilitating rapid and error-free use. The best layouts place the keys in their natural positions (Figure 6.6a, b, c), but designers have attempted at least two major variations (Figure 6.6d, e). The cross arrangement in Figure 6.6a was found to be faster for novice users than the linear arrangement in Figure 6.6d (Foley, 1983). The cross arrangement was also found to be faster for novices, but not for frequent users, than the box arrangement in Figure 6.6e (Emmons, 1984).

Cursor movement keys often have a typamatic (auto-repeat) feature; that is, repetition is automatic with continued depression. This is widely

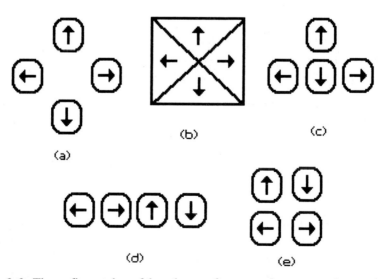

(a)   (b)   (c)   (d)   (e)

Figure 6.6: These five styles of key layout for arrow keys are only a subset of what is commercially available. Figures 6.6a b, and c have key layouts that are compatible with the arrow directions. Figures 6.6d and e have incompatible layouts that may result in slower performance and higher error rates.

appreciated and probably improves productivity. The speed of typamatic cursor movement is controllable on some systems. Varying the cursor speed from ten to fourteen to thirty-three characters per second did not improve productivity in a text-editing task (Gould et al., 1985).

Cursor movement keys have become more important with the increased use of form fill-in strategies, widespread word processing, and the appeal of direct manipulation. Cursor movement keys can be used to select items in a menu or on a display, but more rapid pointing at displays than can be provided by cursor movement keys is often desired.

6.3   POINTING DEVICES

When a screen is used to display information, such as in air traffic control, text editing, and computer-aided design, it is often convenient to point at and select an item. This direct manipulation approach is attractive because the users can avoid learning commands, reduce the chance of typographic errors on a keyboard, and keep their attention on the display. The results are often faster performance, fewer errors, easier learning, and higher satisfaction (Foley et al., 1984; Buxton, 1985).

6.3.1 Pointing tasks

Pointing devices are applicable in six types of interaction tasks (Foley et al., 1984):

1. *Select*: the user chooses from a set of items. This may be traditional menu selection, identification of a file in a directory, or marking of a part in an automobile design.

2. *Position*: the user chooses a point in a one, two, three, or higher dimensional space. Positioning may be used to create a drawing, place a new window, or drag a block of text in a figure.

3. *Orient*: the user chooses a direction in a two, three, or higher dimensional space. The direction may simply rotate a symbol on the screen, indicate a direction of motion for a space ship, or control the operation of a robot arm.

4. *Path*: the user rapidly performs a series of position and orient operations. The path may be realized as a curving line in a drawing program, the instructions for a cloth cutting machine, or the route on a map.

5. *Quantify*: the user specifies a numeric value. The quantify task is usually a one-dimensional selection of integer or real values to set parameters, such as the page number in a document, velocity of a ship, or amplitude of a sound.

6. *Text*: the user enters, moves, and edits text in a two-dimensional space. The pointing device indicates the location of an insertion, deletion, or change. Beyond the simple manipulation of the text there are more elaborate tasks, such as centering; margin setting; font sizes; highlighting, such as boldface or underscore; and page layout.

It is possible to perform all these tasks with a keyboard by typing: numbers or letters to select, integer coordinates to position, a number representing an angle to point, a number to quantify, and cursor control commands to move about text. In the past, the keyboard was used to perform all these tasks, but novel devices have been created that permit performing these tasks r. ore rapidly and with fewer errors.

These devices can be grouped into those that offer:

- direct control on the screen surface
  lightpens
  touchscreens
- indirect control away from the screen surface
  mouse
  trackball
  joystick
  graphics tablet.

Within each category are many variations, and novel designs emerge frequently (Pearson & Weiser, 1986).

6.3.2 Direct pointing devices

The lightpen was an early device that enabled users to point to a spot on a screen and perform a select, position, or other task (Figure 6.7). In fact, the lightpen could also be used to perform all six tasks. The lightpen was attractive because it allowed direct control by pointing to a spot on the display, as opposed to the indirect control provided by a

Figure 6.7: The light pen allows direct control in pointing to a spot on the display. (Courtesy of Koala Technologies Corporation, San Jose, CA)

graphics tablet, joystick, or mouse. Most lightpens incorporate a button for the user to press when the cursor is resting on the desired spot on the screen. Lightpens vary in thickness, length, weight, shape (the lightgun with a trigger is a one variation), and position of buttons. Unfortunately, direct control on an upright screen can be fatiguing for the arms of some users. The lightpen has three further disadvantages: the user's hand obscures part of the screen, users must remove their hands from the keyboard, and users must reach to pick up the lightpen.

Some of these disadvantages are overcome by the touchscreen (Tyler, 1984) that does not require picking up some device, but allows direct control touches on the screen using a finger (Figure 6.8). The fatigue, hand-obscuring-the-screen, and hand-off-keyboard problems remain, accompanied by imprecise pointing (due to thick fingers and parallax) and the eventual smudging of the screen. Most touchscreen implementations have a further problem: the software accepts the touch immediately, denying the user the opportunity to verify the correctness of the selected spot, as is done with lightpens. A two-touch strategy (touch once to produce a highlighted spot and touch again to execute the operation) or a touch-in-touch-out pattern (the user's finger breaks the infrared light-beams above the screen to produce a cursor that is dragged on the screen, then when the finger is pulled out, the operation is executed) may prove to be more appealing. In addition to infrared beams, touchscreens have been built that operate on resistive, capacitive, and acoustic principles.

Refinements to each form of touchscreen can be expected since they are in high demand for applications directed at novice users in which the keyboard can be eliminated and touch is the only interface mechanism. Touchscreens are valued by system designers because there are no moving parts, durability in high use environments is good (touchscreens are the only input devices that have survived at EPCOT), and the price is relatively low.

6.3.3 Indirect pointing devices

Indirect pointing devices eliminate the hand-fatigue and hand-obscuring-the-screen problems but must overcome the problem of

Figure 6.8: With a touchscreen, the user needs only to point with a finger. (Courtesy of Personal Touch Corporation, San Jose, CA)

indirection. As with the lightpen, the hand-off-keyboard and picking-up problems remain. Finally, indirect control devices require more cognitive processing and hand-eye coordination to bring the on-screen cursor to the desired target.

Figure 6.9: Three versions of the mouse with one (Apple Macintosh), two (Xerox Star), and three (PC Mouse for IBM PCs) buttons.

The mouse concept (Lu, 1984) is appealing because the hand rests in a comfortable position, buttons on the mouse are easily pressed, even long motions can be rapid, and positioning can be very precise (Figure 6.9). However, the mouse must be picked up to begin work, desk space is consumed, the mouse wire can be distracting, pickup and replace actions are necessary for long motions, and some practice is required to develop skill. The variety of mouse technologies (physical, optical, or acoustic), varying number of buttons, placement of the sensor, weight, and size indicate that designers and users have yet to settle on alternatives. Personal preferences and the variety of tasks leave room for lively competition.

The trackball concept has sometimes been described as an upside down mouse (Figure 6.10). It is usually implemented as a rotating ball two to six inches in diameter that moves a cursor on the screen as the ball is moved. The trackball is firmly mounted in a desk or a solid box to allow the operators to hit the ball vigorously and make it spin. The trackball has been the preferred device in the high-stress world of air traffic control and in some videogames.

The joystick concept has a long history that begins in automobile and aircraft control devices (Figure 6.11). There are dozens of computer

Figure 6.10: The trackball moves the cursor through the rotating motion of the ball. (Courtesy of WICO Corporation)

Figure 6.11: The joystick makes it easy to move around on the screen. (Courtesy of WICO Corporation)

Figure 6.12: The graphics tablet enlarges the working surface and accommodates user needs at several levels. Photograph courtesy of Apollo Computer, Inc., Chelmsford, Massachusetts) MA)

versions with varying stick lengths and thicknesses, displacement forces and distances, buttons or triggers, anchoring strategies for bases, and placement relative to the keyboard and screen. Joysticks are appealing for tracking purposes, that is, to follow a moving object on a screen, in part because of the relatively small displacements necessary to move a cursor and the ease of direction changes.

The graphics tablet concept is to have a touch-sensitive surface separate from the screen, usually flat on the table or in the user's lap (Figure 6.12). This allows for a comfortable hand position and keeps the users' hands off the screen. Furthermore, the graphics tablet concept permits a surface even larger than the screen to be covered with printing to indicate available choices, thereby providing guidance to novice users and preserving valuable screen space. Limited data entry can be done with the graphics tablet. The graphics tablet can be operated by placement of a finger, pencil, puck, or stylus, using acoustic, electronic, or contact position sensing.

6.3.4 Comparisons of pointing devices

Each pointing concept has its enthusiasts and detractors, motivated by commercial interests, personal preference, and increasingly by empirical evidence. Human factors variables of interest include speed of motion for short and long distances, accuracy of positioning, error rates, learning time, and user satisfaction. Other variables include cost, durability, space requirements, weight, left/right hand use, and compatibility with other systems.

Direct pointing devices such as the lightpen or touchscreen are often the fastest but the least accurate devices (Stammers & Bird, 1980; Albert, 1982; Haller et al., 1984). The speed appears to accrue from the directness of pointing and the inaccuracy from problems with obscuring the screen. Therefore, when the targets are large and spread out on a large screen, the direct devices are strongly recommended. Differences between the lightpen and touchscreen were found to be small.

Indirect pointing devices have been the cause of much controversy. The graphics tablet is appealing when the user can remain with the device for long periods without switching to a keyboard. The mouse was found to be faster than the joystick (English et al., 1967; Card et al., 1978). A trackball was found to be faster and more accurate than a joystick, and a graphics tablet was found to be slightly faster but slightly less accurate than the trackball (Figure 6.13) (Albert, 1982).

The usual wisdom is that pointing devices are faster than keyboard controls such as cursor movement keys (Goodwin, 1975; Card et al., 1978; Albert, 1982), but this result depends on the task. When a few targets are on the screen (two to ten) and the cursor can be made to jump from one target to the next, then the cursor jump keys can become faster

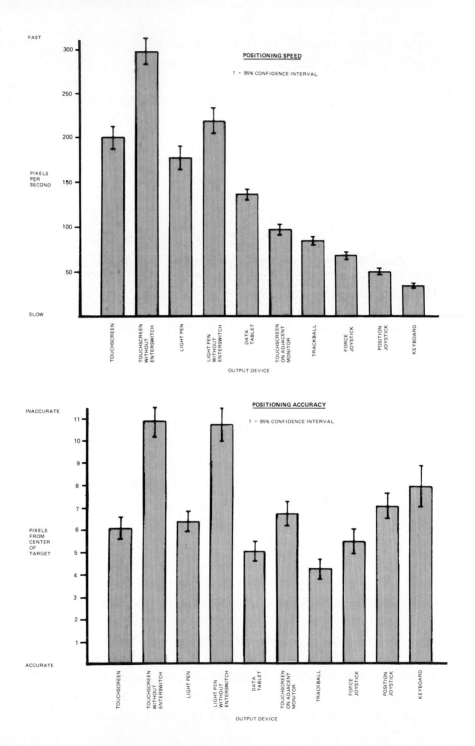

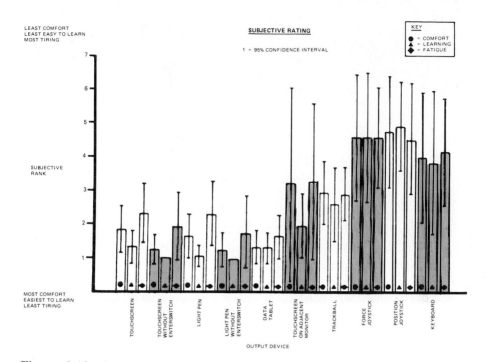

Figure 6.13: A study by The Foxboro Company compared many devices for positioning speed (a), positioning accuracy (b), and subjective ratings (c). (Used with permission of The Foxboro Company, Foxboro, MA. These charts are a revised version of the charts that appeared in Albert, Alan E., The effect of graphic input devices on performance in a cursor positioning task, *Proc. Human Factors Society —26th Annual Meeting*, Santa Monica, CA, [1982], 54–58)

than pointing devices (Figure 6.14) (Ewing et al., 1986). For tasks that mix typing and pointing, cursor keys have also been shown to be faster and more preferred than the mouse (Karat et al., 1984). Since muscular strain is low for cursor keys (Haider et al., 1982), they should be considered for this special case. This result is supported by Card et al. (1978), who reported that for short distances, the cursor keys were faster than the mouse (Figure 6.15). The positioning time increases rapidly with distance for cursor keys but only slightly for the mouse or trackball.

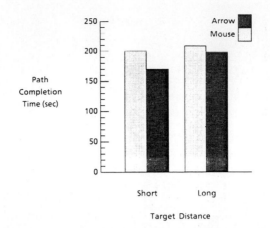

Figure 6.14: Path completion time for arrow-jump and mouse as a function of average target distance of the traversed path (Ewing et al., 1986). Long distance targets were further away from the start point than short distance targets. The arrow-jump strategy was faster since a single keypress produced a jump to the target, whereas mouse users had to move the cursor across the screen.

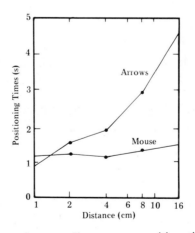

Figure 6.15: The effect of target distance on position time for arrow keys and mouse (Card et al., 1978). The positioning time for arrow keys increased dramatically with distance because many keypresses were necessary to move the cursor to the target. The mouse time is quite independent of time over these distances. With very short distances and a few character positions, the arrow keys had a shorter mean time. (Adapted from S. K. Card, W. K. English, and B. J. Burr, Evaluation of mouse, rate-controlled isometric joystick, step keys, and task keys for text selection on a CRT, *Ergonomics 17* 6 [1965])

In summary, much work remains to sort out the task and individual differences with respect to pointing devices. However, some practical recommendations can be made until precise evidence emerges (Reinhart & Marken, 1985; Shinar et al., 1985). The touchscreen seems attractive when accurate positioning is not required. The mouse and trackball are attractive when accurate pixel level pointing is needed. Cursor jump keys are attractive when there is a small number of targets.

There is little evidence about use of graphics tablets, but the additional space they provide for options not listed on the screen is appealing, although the physical space requirements are a serious limitation in many applications.

Lightpens show no advantage over touchscreens, and the requirement to pick up the lightpen is a serious disadvantage. Joysticks are attractive to game or aircraft cockpit designers, apparently because of the firm grip and easy movement, but they are slow and inaccurate in guiding a cursor to a fixed destination in office automation and personal computing.

6.4   SPEECH RECOGNITION, DIGITIZATION, AND GENERATION

The dream of speaking to computers and having computers speak has lured many researchers and visionaries. Arthur C. Clarke's fantasy of the HAL 9000 computer in the book and movie *2001* has set the standard for future performance of computers in science fiction and for some advanced developers. The reality is more complex and sometimes more surprising than the dream. Hardware designers have made dramatic progress with speech and voice manipulation devices, and current directions are diverging from the science fiction fantasy (McCauley, 1984; Schmandt, 1985).

The vision of a computer that chats leisurely with the user seems more of a fantasy than a desired or believable reality. Instead, practical applications for specific tasks with specific devices are being designed to be more effective in serving the user's need to work rapidly with low error rates. The benefits to people with certain physical handicaps are rewarding to see, but the general users of office or personal computing are not rushing toward speech input/output. However, speech store and forward systems, speech-assisted instructional systems, and speech help systems are growing in popularity.

Speech technology has four components: discrete word recognition, continuous speech recognition, speech store and forward, and speech generation.

6.4.1 Discrete word recognition

Devices to recognize individual words spoken by a specific person work with 90 percent to 98 percent reliability for vocabularies of from 50 to 150 words. Speaker-dependent training, in which the user repeats the full vocabulary once or twice, is a part of most systems. Speaker-independent systems are under development but are not yet reliable enough for commercial applications.

Applications for the physically handicapped have been successful in enabling bedridden patients, paralyzed workers, or amputees to broaden the horizons of their life. They can control wheel chairs, operate equipment, or use personal computers for a variety of tasks.

Other applications have been successful when at least one of these conditions exist:

- speaker's hands are busy
- mobility is required
- speakers eyes are occupied
- harsh (underwater or battlefield) or cramped (airplane cockpit) conditions preclude use of a keyboard.

Example applications include aircraft engine inspectors who wear a wireless microphone as they walk around the engine opening coverplates or adjusting components. They can issue orders, read serial numbers, or retrieve previous maintenance records by using a thirty-five-word vocabulary. Baggage handlers for a major airline speak the destination city names as they place bags on a moving conveyor belt, thereby routing the bag to the proper airplane loading gate. For this application, the speaker-dependent training produced higher recognition rates when done in the noisy environment of the conveyor belt, rather than in the quiet conditions of a recording studio. Implementers should consider conducting the speaker-dependent training in the same environment as the task.

Many advanced development efforts have tested speech recognition in military aircraft, medical operating rooms, training laboratories, and office automation. The results reveal problems with recognition rates, even for speaker-dependent training systems, when background sounds change, when the user is ill or under stress, and when words in the vocabulary are similar (dime–time or Houston–Austin).

For common computing applications when a screen is used, the speech input mechanism has not been found to be beneficial. Studies of cursor movement by voice (Murray et al., 1983) found that cursor movement keys were twice as fast and more preferred. In a study with four one-hour sessions, ten typists and ten nontypists used typed and spoken commands to correct online documents using the UNIX ed editor (Morrison et al., 1984). For both typed and spoken commands, the user still had to type parameter strings. Typists preferred to use the keyboard. Nontypists began with a preference for spoken commands but switched to favor using the keyboard by the end of the four sessions. No significant differences were found for task completion time or error rates.

In a study of twenty-four knowledgeable programmers, a voice editor led to a lower task completion rate than a keyboard editor. However, the keyboard entry produced a higher error rate (Leggett & Williams, 1984) (see Table 6.1). The authors suggest that further experience with voice systems, beyond the ninety minutes of this study, might lead to better performance. A speed advantage for voice entry over a menu selection strategy was found in a study of two beginners and three advanced users of a computer-assisted design system (Shutoh et al., 1984).

Current research efforts are devoted to improving the recognition rates in difficult conditions, eliminating the need for speaker-dependent training, and increasing the vocabularies handled to 5,000 and even 10,000 words.

	Key editor	Voice editor
Input task		
Input task completed	70.6	50.7
Erroneous input	11.0	3.8
Edit Task		
Edit task completed	70.3	55.3
Erroneous commands	2.4	1.5
Erroneous input	14.3	1.2

Table 6.1: Average percentage scores for input and editing tasks using keyboard and voice editors. (Data from Leggett, John, and Williams, Glen, An empirical investigation of voice as an input modality for computer programming, *International Journal Man-Machine Studies 21*, [1984], 493–520.)

Speech recognition for discrete words shows much promise for special purpose applications, but not as a general interaction medium. Keyboards with function keys or pointing devices are more rapid and the commands can be made visible for easy editing; error handling is difficult and slow by voice, and the audio channel is reserved for human-human communication.

6.4.2 Continuous speech recognition

HAL's ability to understand the astronauts' spoken words and even to read their lips was an appealing fantasy, but the reality is more sobering. Although many research projects have pursued continuous speech recognition, most observers feel that a commercially successful product will not be forthcoming in the next decade or longer. The difficulty revolves around recognizing the boundaries between spoken words. Normal speech patterns slur the boundaries.

The hope is that with a continuous speech recognition system, users could dictate letters, compose reports verbally for automatic transcription, and enable computers to scan long audio tapes, radio programs, or phone calls for specific words or topics.

In 1985, Kurzweil Computer Products announced an experimental system that could handle a 3,000-word vocabulary for continuous speech. Testing is necessary to determine how effective this device is in realistic situations.

6.4.3 Speech store and forward

Less exciting, but probably more immediately useful, are the systems that enable the storing and forwarding of spoken messages. After registering with the service, users can touch commands on a twelve-key telephone to store spoken messages and have them sent to one or more people who are also registered with the service. Users can receive messages, replay messages, reply to the caller, forward the message to others, delete messages, or archive messages. The messages are converted from the analog voice input to a digitized and usually compressed form for storage on magnetic media. Conversion from digital to analog for output is a standard technique, preserving the original tone quality quite well. Automatic elimination of silences and speedup by sound clipping are available.

This technology works reliably, is fairly low cost, and is generally liked by users. Problems focus mainly on the awkwardness of using the twelve-key phone pad for commands, the need to dial-in to check if messages have been left, and the potential for too many "junk" telephone messages because of the ease of broadcasting a message to many people.

Other applications of digitized speech are for instructional systems and online help. Educational psychologists conjecture that if several senses (sight, touch, hearing) are engaged, then learning can be facilitated. Adding a spoken voice to a computer-assisted instructional system or an online help system may improve the learning process.

6.4.4 Speech generation

Speech generation is an example of a successful technology that is used, but its applicability was overestimated by some developers. Inexpensive, compact, reliable speech generation (also called synthesis)

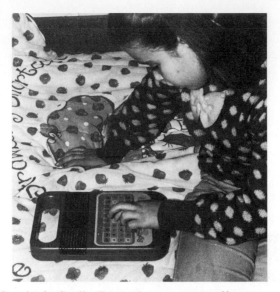

Figure 6.16: Speak & Spell (Texas Instruments) offers several word games, including a version of hangman and spelling drill. See Figure 6.3 for a close-up. Instructions are given by synthesized voice, and the user presses on the membrane keyboard.

devices have been used in cameras ("too dark—use flash"), soft-drink vending machines ("insert correct change and make your selection," "thank you"), automobiles ("your door is ajar"), children's games (Figure 6.16), and utility control rooms to warn of danger.

In some cases, the novelty wears off quickly and the application needs become dominant, leading to removal of the speech generation. Talking supermarket checkout machines that read products and prices were found to violate a sense of privacy about purchases and to be too noisy. Automobile speech generation devices are now less widely used; a few tones and red light indicators were found to be more acceptable. Spoken warnings in cockpits or control rooms were sometimes missed or were in competition with human-human communication.

Applications for the blind are an important success story (Songco et al., 1980). The Kurzweil Reader is used in hundreds of libraries. Patrons can place a book on a copier-like device that scans the text and does an acceptable job of reading the text one word at a time.

The quality of the sound can be very good when the words and pronunciation or digitized human speech can be stored in a dictionary. When algorithms are used to generate the sound, the quality is sometimes degraded. Digitized human speech for phrases or sentences is often a useful strategy since human intonation provides more authentic sound. For some applications, a computer-like sound may be preferred. Apparently, the robot-like sound in the Atlanta airport subway drew more attention than a tape recording of a human giving directions.

Michaelis and Wiggins (1982) suggest that speech generation is "frequently preferable" under these circumstances:

1. The message is simple.
2. The message is short.
3. The message will not be referred to later.
4. The message deals with events in time.
5. The message requires an immediate response.
6. The visual channels of communication are overloaded.
7. The environment may be too brightly lit, too poorly lit (possibly to preserve dark adaptation), subject to severe vibration, or otherwise unsuitable for transmission of visual information.
8. The user must be free to move around.
9. The user may be subjected to high G forces or anoxia (lack of oxygen, typically at high altitudes). The magnitude of G forces or anoxia at which eyesight begins to be impaired is well below that needed to affect hearing.

These criteria apply to digitized human speech and to simple playbacks of tape recordings.

In summary, speech generation is technologically feasible. Now, clever designers must find the situations in which it is superior to competing technologies. Novel applications may be by way of the telephone, as a supplement to the CRT, or through embedding in small consumer products.

6.5   DISPLAYS

The visual display unit (VDU) has become the primary source of feedback to the user from the computer (Cakir et al., 1980; Grandjean, 1980; Helander et al., 1984). The VDU has many important features, including:

- rapid operation: thousands of characters per second or a full image in a few milliseconds
- reasonable size: typically 24 lines of 80 characters, but devices of at least 66 lines of 166 characters are available
- reasonable resolution: typically 320 by 400 pixels, but 1,000–by–1,000 are common
- quiet operation
- no paper waste
- relatively low cost: displays can cost as little as $100
- reliability
- highlighting, such as overwriting, windowing, blinking
- graphics and animation.

The widespread use of VDUs has led designers to develop a variety of technologies with hundreds of special purpose features. International standards are beginning to appear and costs continue to decrease, even as quality increases. Such health concerns as visual fatigue, stress, and radiation levels are being addressed by manufacturers and government agencies, but some concerns remain (Kleiner, 1985).

6.5.1 Monochrome displays

For many applications, monochrome displays are adequate, and even preferred, especially if the monochrome display has a higher resolution than the color display. Monochrome displays are produced by several technologies (Foley & Van Dam, 1982; IBM, 1984):

- raster scan cathode ray tube (CRT): This popular device is similar to a television monitor with an electron beam sweeping out lines of dots to form letters. The refresh rates (the reciprocal of the time required to produce a full screen image) vary from 30 to 65 per second. Higher rates are preferred because they reduce flicker. CRT displays are often green because the P39 green phosphor has a long decay time, permitting relatively stable images. The P38 orange-amber phosphor has an even longer decay time and is preferred by many users. Another important property of a phosphor is its low bloom level, allowing sharp images because the small granules of the phosphor do not spread the glow to nearby points. The maximum resolution of a CRT is about 100 lines per inch. Displays can have light letters against a dark background or dark letters against a light background. CRT sizes (measured diagonally) range from less than two inches to almost thirty inches, but popular models are in the nine to fifteen inch range.

• stroke character CRT: Instead of a line of dots, characters are formed by movement of the electron beam to paint the character. This approach is effective when line-drawn images are the main display items, as in air traffic control or computer-assisted design.

• storage tube CRT: The interior surface of the display contains special phosphors that maintain the image created by the electron beam sweep. This approach eliminates the need for rapid refreshing and the distraction of flicker, but the contrast is usually poorer.

• plasma panels: Rows of horizontal wires are slightly separated from vertical wires by a small glass-enclosed capsule of neon-based gases. When the horizontal and vertical wires on either side of the capsule receive a high voltage, the gas glows. Plasma displays are usually orange and flicker-free, but the size of the capsules limits the resolution. Plasma computer displays have been built to display up to 62 lines of 166 characters.

• liquid crystal displays (LCDs): Voltage changes influence the reflectivity of tiny capsules of liquid crystals, turning some spots darker when viewed by reflected light. LCDs are flicker-free; but again, the size of the capsules limits the resolution. Watches and calculators often use LCDs because of their small size, light weight, and low power consumption. Portable computers have been built with LCD displays having up to 24 lines by 80 characters.

- light-emitting diodes (LEDs): Certain diodes emit light when a voltage is applied. Arrays of these small diodes can be assembled to display characters. Here again, the resolution is limited by manufacturing techniques.

- electroluminescent displays: Instead of striking a phosphor by an electron beam, the electroluminescent displays operate with phosphors that emit light when a voltage is applied directly. The front panel conductor must be transparent to allow the user to see the phosphor. The manufacturing technology enables these displays to be of high resolution, in addition to their attractive properties of thinness and light weight. Electroluminescent displays have been used for pocket-sized televisions but have yet to be widely used for computer displays because of the high cost of producing a large display.

The technology employed has an impact on these variables:

- size
- refresh rate
- capacity to show animation
- resolution
- surface flatness
- surface glare from reflected light
- contrast between characters and background
- brightness
- flicker
- line sharpness
- character formation
- tolerance for vibration.

Each display technology has advantages and disadvantages with respect to these variables. Further consideration should be given to the availability of these features:

- user control of contrast and brightness
- software highlighting of characters by brightness
- underscoring
- reverse video
- character set (alphabetic, numeric, special and foreign characters)
- multiple fonts (for example, italic, bold)
- multiple font sizes
- shape, size, and blinking rate of the cursor
- user control of cursor variables
- blinking (possibly at several rates)
- scrolling mechanism (smooth scrolling is preferred)
- user control of number of lines or characters per line displayed
- support of negative and positive polarity (light on dark or dark on light characters).

Some frequent users place contrast enhancement filters or masks in front of displays. Filters reduce reflected glare by using polarizers or thin film antireflection coatings. Masks may be made of nylon mesh or simple matte surfaces. These devices are helpful to some users, but they can reduce resolution and are subject to smudging from fingerprints.

6.5.2 Color displays

Color displays can make videogames, educational simulations, computer-assisted design, and many other applications programs more attractive and effective for users, but there are real dangers in misusing color.

Color images are produced by having several phosphors on the display surface. The RGB shadow-mask displays have small dots of red, green, and blue phosphors closely packed so that a full range of colors can be created by combining these dots. With all three dots illuminated, the users see white. This approach reduces the resolution when monochrome images or text are displayed. A second, but increasingly rare strategy is to have translucent layers of phosphors that glow in response to different electron beam frequencies. In this beam-penetration strategy, combinations of beams cause several layers to glow, producing a range of colors while preserving high resolution.

Color images are attractive to the eye, and color coding of screen objects can lead to rapid recognition and identification (Christ, 1975; Robertson, 1980; IBM, 1984). Of course, excessive or inappropriate use of color can inhibit performance and confuse users (Durrett & Trezona, 1982). See Chapter 8 for a discussion of color use in screen design.

Software for creating color graphics images is rapidly becoming more effective. Still, it may take several hours or weeks to generate a satisfactory image. Simple shapes, such as boxes, circles, or lines, are done conveniently, but designing an automobile engine part, creating a map, or laying out a building floor plan may take weeks. The great gift of computer graphics is that small changes to existing images can usually be made rapidly. Effective computer graphics systems are often application specific.

Dramatic progress in computer graphics has led to increasing use in motion pictures and television. Startling images have been created for movies, such as the Star Wars series (George Lucas's Industrial Light and Magic) or TRON (Walt Disney Studios). Many television commercials, station identification segments, and news-related graphics have been constructed by computer animation. Finally, videogames are another source of impressive computer graphics images. The ACM's SIGGRAPH (Special Interest Group on Graphics) has an exciting annual conference with exhibitions of novel graphics devices and applications. The conference proceedings and videotape digest are rich sources of information.

6.5.3 Television images, videodisks, and compact disks

Another approach to graphics is to use television technology to capture an image from an existing photo, drawing, or map, or from the real world. This strategy provides a detailed image rapidly and allows modifications to be made relatively easily. These images can be stored in digitized form on magnetic media, sent electronically, edited, and printed. Several computer-based videoconferencing systems allow users to send an image over normal telephone lines in compressed data formats in from fifteen to thirty seconds. About sixty images can be stored on a single 320K floppy disk. Printers for television images are beginning to appear commercially. Kodak offers an attachment that enables consumers to print images taken with home video recording equipment.

In addition to video cameras as input devices, there are many digitizing packages that support input of maps or line drawings by having users mark coordinates for line beginnings and endings. An automatic scanner is available that turns a printer into a cheap input device for paper images. The paper image is placed in the printer and the printer ribbon is replaced by a photoelectric scanner. As the printer head moves back and forth, the image is digitized and entered into the computer's storage.

Another emerging blend of image display and computers is the computer-controlled videodisk. Videodisks can store more than 100,000 images on a single 12-inch diameter platter. Each image is directly addressable, and retrieval time is a maximum of eight seconds. The Library of Congress uses videodisks to store 100,000 publicity photos from 6,000 commercial films. After selecting a film from the menu-based index, successive images from that film appear within a fraction of a second after a single keypress. Another Library of Congress project provides online access to more than 1,000,000 images of frequently used current magazines and old deteriorating books. The optical disk jukebox rotates to deliver the proper disk to the reading device within 15 seconds. Users perform searches using the standard SCORPIO system and then receive the image on a high resolution monitor (200 pixels/inch) or in hardcopy from a laser printer.

Art, photo, travel, consumer goods, and historical videodisks are appearing regularly. The videodisk technology is read-only, and the cost of producing a videodisk is still a limitation to more widespread use.

Compact disks (often called CD-ROMs, for compact disk with read-only memory) with sound, text, or images have a promising future. Electronic encyclopedias, numerical databases, and maps are appearing with increasing frequency. A compact disk player and a small display

will enable automobile drivers to view highway or street maps. The
potential for rapid access to indexed databases of images and text will
attract many designers and users.

6.5.4 Multiple display workstations

A single small screen often limits what the user can accomplish. One
remedy is a larger screen, possibly with multiple windows; but another,
sometimes easier and 'less expensive approach is to have two or more
screens. A computer graphics display and a videodisk display side by
side can display computer-generated text and a television image
simultaneously. The Spatial Data Management System installed on the
aircraft carrier USS *Carl Vinson* by Computer Corporation of America
has three displays for graphics, maps, reconnaissance photos, and text.

Air traffic controllers, satellite controllers at NASA, pilots, power plant
operators, stock market traders, and computer or telephone network
control room workers may view three or more displays to perform their
tasks. Screens may show related data from different sources or in
different formats (graphics, text, or images).

6.6   PRINTERS

Even with good quality and high-speed displays, there is still a great
desire for hardcopy printouts. Paper documents can be easily copied,
mailed, marked, and stored. Important criteria for printers are:

- speed
- print quality
- cost
- compactness
- quiet operation
- use of ordinary paper (fanfolded or single sheet)
- character set
- variety of fonts and font sizes
- highlighting techniques (bold face, underscore, etc.)

- support for special forms (printed forms, different lengths, etc.)
- reliability.

Early computer printers worked at 10 characters per second and did not support graphics. Modern personal computer dot matrix printers print more than 200 characters per second, have multiple fonts, boldface, variable width and size, and graphics capabilities. Daisy wheel printers generate 30 to 65 letter-quality characters per second. Inkjet printers offer quiet operation and high quality output. Thermal printers offer quiet, compact, and inexpensive output on specially coated papers. This technology has led to cheap portable typewriters with storage for a few thousand characters of text and the capability to act as a terminal.

Printing systems on mainframe computers have impact line printers that operate at 1,200 lines per minute and laser printers that operate at 30,000 lines per minute. The laser printers, now widely available for microcomputer systems, support graphics and produce high quality images. Software to permit publication-quality typesetting has opened the door to desktop publishing ventures. Compact laser printers offer users the satisfaction of producing elegant business documents, scientific reports, novels, or personal correspondence. Users should consider output quality, speed, choice of fonts, graphics capabilities, and special paper requirements.

Color printers allow users to produce hardcopy output of color graphics, usually by a dot matrix or inkjet approach with three-color print heads or inks. The printed image is often of lower quality than the screen image and may not be faithful to the screen colors.

Plotters enable output of graphs, bar charts, line drawings, and maps on rolls of paper or sheets up to 36 by 50 inches. Plotters may have single pens or multiple pens for color output. Other design factors are the precision of small movements, the accuracy in placement of the pens, the speed of pen motion, the repeatability of drawings, and the software support.

Photographic printers allow the creation of 35mm or larger slides and photographic prints. These printers are often designed as add-on devices in front of a display, but high quality printing systems are independent devices. Computer output to microfilm devices are effective with high volume applications. Newspaper or magazine layout systems allow electronic editing of images and text before generation of production quality output for printing presses.

6.7   PRACTITIONER'S SUMMARY

Choosing hardware is always a compromise between the ideal and the practical. The designer's vision of what an input or output device should be must be tempered by the realities of what is commercially available within the project budget. Devices should be tested in the application domain to verify the manufacturer's claims, and testimonials or suggestions from other users should be obtained.

Attention to current trends for specific devices, such as the mouse or voice recognition, should be paid, and service to the user's real needs should also be adequately considered. Since new devices and refinements to old devices appear regularly, an attempt at device-independent architecture and software will permit easy integration of novel devices. In short, don't get locked in to one device; the hardware is often the softest part of the system. Also, remember that a successful idea can become even more successful if re-implementation on other devices is easy.

Keyboard entry is here to stay for a long time, but consider other forms of input when text entry is limited. Selecting rather than typing has many benefits for both novice and frequent users. Direct pointing devices are faster and more convenient for novices than are indirect pointing devices, but direct devices are less accurate. Beware of the hand-off-the-keyboard problem for all pointing devices and strive to reduce the number of shifts between the keyboard and the pointing device.

Speech input/output is commercially viable and should be applied where appropriate, but take care to ensure that performance is genuinely improved over other interaction strategies. Display technology is moving rapidly and user expectations are increasing. Higher resolution, color, larger screens, and multiple screens will be sought by users. Even with beautiful displays, users have a strong desire to have high quality hardcopy output.

6.8   RESEARCHER'S AGENDA

Novel text-entry keyboards to speed input and reduce error rates will have to provide significant benefits to displace the well-entrenched QWERTY design. For numerous applications not requiring extensive text entry, opportunities exist to create special-purpose devices or to redesign the task to permit direct manipulation selection instead. Increasingly, input can be accomplished by copying data from other online sources; for example, instead of keying in economic research data, they may be obtained from a commercial database system. Another input source is from optical character recognition of bar codes printed in magazines, on bank statements, in books, or on record albums.

Pointing devices will certainly play an increasing role. A clearer understanding of pointing tasks and the refinement of pointing devices to suit each task seem inevitable. Improvements can be made not only to the devices but also to the software with which they are used. The same mouse hardware can be used in many ways to speed up movement, provide better feedback to the user, and reduce errors.

Research on speech systems can also be directed at improving the device and at redesigning the application to make more effective use of the speech input and output technology. Complete and accurate continuous speech recognition does not seem attainable, but if users will modify their speaking style in specific applications, then more progress is possible. Another worthy direction is to increase continuous recognition rates for such tasks as finding a given phrase in a large body of recorded speech. Speech output to support training or offer additional information to users is attractive.

Larger, higher resolution displays seem attainable. Techniques such as anti-aliasing do improve text readability and graphics clarity. Thin, lightweight, durable, and inexpensive displays will spawn many applications not only in portable computers but also for embedding in briefcases, appliances, telephones, and automobiles. A battery-powered book-sized computer ought to contain the information from thousands of books and make it rapidly available by simple finger touches on indexes or embedded menus. Small data cards or a built-in modem would expand the information without limitation.

Among the most exciting developments will be the increased facility for manipulating images. Improved graphics editors, faster image processing hardware and algorithms, and cheaper image input, storage, and output devices will open up many possibilities. How will people search for images, integrate them with text, or modify them? What level of increased visual literacy will be expected? Can animation become a more common part of computer applications? Will computer displays become more like movies? Can the hardware/software evoke more emotional responses and broaden the spectrum of computer devotees?

REFERENCES

Albert, Alan E., The effect of graphic input devices on performance in a cursor positioning task, *Proc. Human Factors Society—26th Annual Meeting*, (1982), 54–58.

Brown, C. Marlin, *Human-Computer Interface Design Guidelines*, Ablex Publishing Company, Norwood, NJ, (1986).

Brunner, Hans, Marken, Richard, and Briggs, Amy, Effects of key action design on keyboard preference and throughput performance, MICRO SWITCH, A Honeywell Division, Technology Strategy Center, 1700 West Highway 36, Roseville, MN 55113, (1984), 41 pages.

Buxton, William, There's more to interaction than meets the eye: Some issues in manual input, In Norman, D. A., and Draper, S. W. (Editors), *User Centered System Design: New Perspectives on Human-Computer Interaction*, Lawrence Erlbaum Associates, Hillsdale, NJ, (1985) 319–337.

Cakir, A., Hart, D. J., and Stewart, T. F. M., *The VDT Manual*, John Wiley and Sons, New York, (1980).

Card, S. K., English, W. K., and Burr, B. J., Evaluation of mouse, rate-controlled isometric joystick, step keys, and task keys for text selection on a CRT, *Ergonomics 21*, 8, (August 1978), 601–613.

Christ, Richard E., Review and analysis of color coding research for visual displays, *Human Factors 17*, 6, (1975), 542–570.

Dunsmore, H. E., Data entry, In Kantowitz, Barry H., and Sorkin, Robert D., *Human Factors: Understanding People-Systems Relationships*, John Wiley and Sons, New York, (1983), 335–366.

Durrett, John, and Trezona, Judi, How to use color displays effectively, *BYTE*, (April 1982), 50–53.

Emmons, W. H., A comparison of cursor-key arrangements (box versus cross) for VDUs, In Grandjean, Etienne (Editor), *Ergonomics and Health in Modern Offices*, Taylor and Francis, London and Philadelphia, (1984), 214–219.

Emmons, William H., and Hirsch, Richard, Thirty millimeter keyboards: How good are they?, *Proc. Human Factors Society—26th Annual Meeting*, (1982), 425–429.

English, William K., Engelbart, Douglas C., and Berman, Melvyn L., Display-selection techniques for text manipulation, *IEEE Transactions on Human Factors in Electronics, HFE–8*, 1, (March 1967), 5–15.

Ewing, John, Mehrabanzad, Simin, Sheck, Scott, Ostroff, Dan, and Shneiderman, Ben, An experimental comparison of a mouse and arrow-jump keys for an interactive encyclopedia, *International Journal of Man-Machine Studies 23*, (1986).

Foley, James D., Unpublished report of a student project, George Washington University, Washington, DC, (1983).

Foley, James D., and Van Dam, Andries, *Fundamentals of Interactive Computer Graphics*, Addison-Wesley Publishing Co., Reading, MA, (1982), 664 pages.

Foley, James D., Wallace, Victor L., and Chan, Peggy, The human factors of computer graphics interaction techniques, *IEEE Computer Graphics and Applications*, (November 1984), 13–48.

Goodwin, N. C., Cursor positioning on an electronic display using lightpen, lightgun, or keyboard for three basic tasks, *Human Factors 17*, 3, (June 1975), 289–295.

Gould, John D., Lewis, Clayton, and Barnes, Vincent, Effects of cursor speed on text-editing, *Proc. ACM CHI '85 Conference*, (1985), 7–10.

Grandjean, E., Ergonomics of VDUs: Review of present knowledge, In Grandjean, E., and Vigliani, E., *Ergonomic Aspects of Visual Display Terminals*, Taylor and Francis, London, (1980).

Haider, E., Luczak, H., and Rohmert, W., Ergonomics investigations of workplaces in a police command-control centre equipped with TV displays, *Applied Ergonomics 13*, 3, (1982), 163–170.

Haller, R., Mutschler, H., and Voss, M., Comparison of input devices for correction of typing errors in office systems, *INTERACT 84*, (1984), 218–223.

Helander, Martin G., Billingsley, Patricia A., and Schurick, Jayne M., An evaluation of human factors research on visual display terminals in the workplace, In Muckler, Frederick A., *Human Factors Review: 1984*, Human Factors Society, Santa Monica, CA, (1984), 55–129.

IBM Corporation, Human factors of workstations with visual displays, San Jose, CA, (April 1984), 64 pages.

Karat, John, McDonald, James, and Anderson, Matt, A comparison of selection techniques: Touch panel, mouse and keyboard, *INTERACT 84*, (September 1984), 149–153.

Kleiner, Art (Editor), The health hazards of computers: A guide to worrying intelligently, *Whole Earth Review 48*, (Fall 1985), 80–93.

Kroemer, K. H. E., Human engineering the keyboard, *Human Factors 14*, 1, (February 1972), 51–63.

Leggett, John, and Williams, Glen, An empirical investigation of voice as an input modality for computer programming, *International Journal of Man-Machine Studies 21*, (1984), 493–520.

Lu, Cary, Computer pointing devices: Living with mice, *High Technology*, (January 1984), 61–65.

McCauley, Michael E., Human factors in voice technology, In Muckler, Frederick A. (Editor), *Human Factors Review: 1984*, Human Factors Society, Santa Monica, CA (1984), 131–166.

Martin, A., A new keyboard layout, *Applied Ergonomics 3*, 1, (1972).

Mehr, M. H., and Mehr, E., Manual digital positioning in 2 axes: A comparison of joystick and trackball controls, *Proc. Human Factors Society—16th Annual Meeting*, (1972).

Michaelis, Paul Roller, and Wiggins, Richard H., A human factors engineer's introduction to speech synthesizers, In Badre, A., and Shneiderman, B., *Directions in Human-Computer Interaction*, Ablex Publishing Co., Norwood, NJ, (1982), 149–178.

Montgomery, Edward B., Bringing manual input into the 20th century, *IEEE Computer 15*, 3, (March 1982), 11–18.

Morrison, D. L., Green, T. R. G., Shaw, A. C., and Payne, S. J., Speech-controlled text-editing: effects of input modality and of command structure, *International Journal of Man-Machine Studies 21*, 1, (1984), 49–63.

Murray, J. Thomas, Van Praag, John, and Gilfoil, David, Voice versus keyboard control of cursor motion, *Proc. Human Factors Society—27th Annual Meeting*, (1983), 103.

Nakaseko, M., Grandjean, E., Hunting, W., and Gierer, R., Studies of ergonomically designed alphanumeric keyboards, *Human Factors 27*, 2, (1985), 175–187.

Pearson, Glenn, and Weiser, Mark, Of moles and men: The design of foot controls for workstations, *Proc. ACM CHI '86: Human Factors in Computing Systems*, ACM, New York, (1986).

Reinhart, William, and Marken, Richard, Control systems analysis of computer pointing devices, *Proc. Human Factors Society—29th Annual Meeting*, (1985), 119–121.

Robertson, P. J., A Guide to Using Color on Alphanumeric Displays, IBM Technical Report G320–6296–0, White Plains, NY, (June 1980), 35 pages.

Schmandt, Christopher, Voice communication with computers, In Hartson, H. Rex (Editor), *Advances in Human-Computer Interaction: Volume 1*, Ablex Publishing Co., Norwood, NJ, (1985), 133–159.

Shinar, David, Stern, Helman, I., Bubis, Gad, and Ingram, David, The relative effectiveness of alternate selection strategies in menu driven computer programs, *Proc. Human Factors Society—29th Annual Meeting*, (1985), 645–649.

Shutoh, Tomoki, Tsuruta, Shichiro, Kawai, Ryuichi, and Shutoh, Masamichi, Voice operation in CAD system, In Hendrick, H. W., and Brown, O., Jr., (Editors), *Human Factors in Organizational Design and Management*, Elsevier Science Publishers B. V. (North-Holland), Amsterdam, (1984), 205–209.

Songco, D. C., Allen, S. I., Plexico, P. S., and Morford, R. A., How computers talk to the blind, *IEEE Spectrum*, (May 1980), 34–38.

Stammers, R. B., and Bird, J. M., Controller evaluation of a touch input air traffic data system: An indelicate experiment, *Human Factors 22*, 5, (1980), 581–589.

Tyler, Michael, Touchscreens: Big deal or no deal?, *Datamation 30*, 1, (January 1984), 146–154.

CAROL WAID

CHAPTER 7

RESPONSE TIME AND DISPLAY RATE

Stimulation is the indispensable requisite for pleasure in an experience, and the feeling of bare time is the least stimulating experience we can have.

William James, *Principles of Psychology,* Volume I, 1890

Nothing can be more useful to a man than a determination not to be hurried.

Henry David Thoreau, *Journal*

7.1   INTRODUCTION

Time is precious. When unexpected delays impede the progress of a task, many people become frustrated, annoyed, and eventually angry. Lengthy system response times and slow display rates produce these reactions from computer users, leading to more frequent errors and lower satisfaction. Even if they simply accept the situation with a shrug of their shoulders, most users would prefer to work more quickly than the computer allows.

But there is also a danger in working too quickly. As users pick up the pace of a rapid interaction sequence, they may learn less, read with lower comprehension, make ill-considered decisions, and commit more data entry errors. Stress can build in this situation if errors are hard to recover from or if they destroy data, damage equipment, or imperil human life (for example, in air traffic or medical systems).

7.1.1 Definitions

The computer system's response time is the number of seconds it takes from the moment a user initiates an activity (usually by pressing an ENTER, RETURN, or a mouse button) until the computer begins to present results on the screen or printer (Figure 7.1). When the response is completely displayed, the user begins formulating the next command. The user think time is the number of seconds the user thinks before entering the next command. In the simple model, the user initiates, waits for the computer to respond, watches while the results appear, thinks for a while, and initiates again.

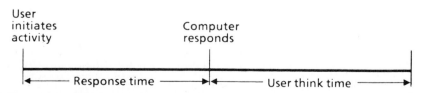

Figure 7.1: Simple model of system response time and user think time.

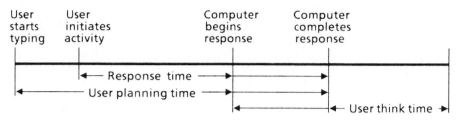

Figure 7.2: More realistic model of system response time, user planning time, and user think time.

In a more realistic model (Figure 7.2), the user plans while reading results, while typing, and while the computer is generating a display of the results. Most people will use whatever time they have to plan ahead; thus, precise measurements of user think time are difficult to obtain. The computer's response is usually more precisely defined and measurable, but there are problems here as well. Some systems respond with distracting messages, informative feedback, or a simple prompt immediately after a command is initiated, but actual results may not appear for a few seconds. Measurement of computer response time can also be difficult because network delays arc not captured by hardware or software monitors in the central processor.

7.1.2 Raising the issues

Designers who specify response times and display rates in human-computer interactions have to consider the complex interaction of technical feasibility, costs, task complexity, user expectations, speed of task performance, error rates and error-handling procedures. These decisions are further complicated by the impact of personality differences, time of day, fatigue, familiarity with computers, experience with the task, and motivation (Carbonell et al., 1968; Shneiderman, 1980).

Although some people are content with a slower system for some tasks, the overwhelming majority prefer rapid interactions. Overall productivity depends not only on the speed of the system but also on the rate of human error and the ease of recovery from those errors. It seems clear that lengthy response times (longer than fifteen seconds) are generally detrimental to productivity, increasing error rates and decreasing satisfaction. More rapid interactions (less than one second) are generally preferred and can increase productivity but may increase errors. The high cost of providing rapid response time or display rate and the loss from increased errors must be evaluated in choosing an optimum pace.

This review begins with a model of short-term human memory and the sources of human error (Section 7.2). Section 7.3 isolates the issue of display rate from response time. Section 7.4 focuses on the role of users' expectations and attitudes in shaping their subjective reactions to the computer system response time. Section 7.5 concentrates on productivity as a function of response time, and Section 7.6 reviews the research on the impact of variable response times.

7.2   THEORETICAL FOUNDATIONS

A cognitive model of human performance that accounts for the substantive experimental results in response time and display rates would be useful in making predictions, designing systems, and formulating management policies. A complete, predictive model that accounts for all the variables is currently inaccessible, but we are able to realize useful fragments of such a model.

Robert B. Miller's review (1968) presented a lucid analysis of response-time issues and a list of seventeen situations in which preferred response times might differ. Much has changed since his paper was written, but the principles of closure, short-term memory limitations, and chunking still apply.

7.2.1 Short-term and working memory limitations

Any cognitive model must emerge from an understanding of human problem-solving abilities and information-processing capabilities. A central issue is the limitation of our short-term memory capacity.

George Miller's classic 1956 paper, "The magical number seven —plus or minus two," identified the limited capacities people have for absorbing information (Miller, 1956). People can rapidly recognize approximately seven (this value was contested by later researchers, but serves as a good estimate) "chunks" of information at a time and hold them in short-term memory for fifteen to thirty seconds. The size of a chunk of information depends on the person's familiarity with the material.

For example, most people could look at seven binary digits for a few seconds and then recall the digits correctly from memory within fifteen seconds. A distracting task, such as reciting a poem, would erase the binary digits. Of course, if they concentrate on remembering the binary digits and succeed in transferring them to long-term memory, then the binary digits can be maintained for much longer periods. Most Americans could also probably remember seven decimal digits, seven alphabetic characters, seven English words, or even seven familiar advertising slogans. Although these items have increasing complexity, they are still treated as single chunks. However, an American might not succeed in remembering seven Russian letters, Chinese pictograms, or Polish sayings. Knowledge and experience govern the size of a chunk for each individual.

The short-term memory is used in conjunction with working memory for processing information and for problem solving. Short-term memory processes perceptual input whereas working memory is used to generate and implement solutions. If many facts and decisions are necessary to solve a problem, then short-term and working memory may become overloaded. People learn to cope with complex problems by developing higher-level concepts that bring together several lower-level concepts into a single chunk. Novices at any task tend to work with smaller chunks until they can cluster concepts into larger chunks. Novices will break a complex task into a sequence of smaller tasks that they feel confident about accomplishing.

This chunking phenomenon was demonstrated by Neal (1977), who required 15 experienced keypunch operators to type data records organized into numeric, alphanumeric, and English word fields. The median interkeystroke time was .2 seconds but rose to more than .3 seconds at field boundaries and .9 seconds at record boundaries.

Short-term and working memory are highly volatile; disruptions cause loss of memory, and delays can require that the memory be refreshed. Visual distractions or noisy environments also interfere with cognitive processing. Furthermore, anxiety apparently reduces the size of the available memory since the person's attention is partially absorbed in concerns that are beyond the problem-solving task.

7.2.2 Sources of errors

If people are able to construct a solution to a problem in spite of possible interference, they must still record or implement the solution. If they can implement the solution immediately, they can proceed very quickly through their work. On the other hand, if they must record the solution in long-term memory, on paper, or on a complex device, the chances for error increase and the pace of work slows.

Multiplying two four-digit numbers in your head is difficult because the intermediate results cannot be maintained in working memory and must be transferred to long-term memory. Controlling a nuclear reactor or air traffic is a challenge, in part because the task often requires integration of information (in short-term and working memory) from several sources while maintaining an awareness of the complete situation. In attending to newly arriving information, operators may be distracted and lose the contents of their short-term or working memory.

When using an interactive computer system, users may formulate plans and then have to wait while they execute each step in the plan. If a step produces an unexpected result or if the delays are long, then the user may forget part of the plan or be forced to review it continually.

Long (1976) studied delays of approximately .1 to .5 seconds in the time for a keystroke to produce a character on an impact printer. He found that unskilled and skilled typists worked more slowly and made more errors with longer response times. Even these brief delays were distracting in the rapid process of typing.

On the other hand, if users try to work too quickly, they may not allow sufficient time to formulate a solution plan correctly and error rates may increase. As familiarity with the task increases, the user's capacity to work more quickly and correctly should increase.

This model leads to the conjecture that for a given user and task there is a preferred response time. Long response times lead to wasted effort and more errors when a solution plan is continually reviewed. Shorter response times may generate a faster pace in which solution plans are hastily and incompletely prepared. More data from a variety of situations and users would help clarify these conjectures.

7.2.3 Conditions for optimum problem-solving

As response times grow longer, users may become more anxious because the penalty for an error increases and they often slow down in their work. As the difficulty in handling an error increases, the anxiety level increases, further slowing performance and increasing errors. As response times grow shorter and display rates increase, users pick up the pace of the system and may fail to comprehend the presented material, generate incorrect solution plans, and make more execution errors. Wickelgren (1977) reviews speed-accuracy tradeoffs.

Car driving may offer a useful analogy. Although higher speed limits are attractive to many drivers and do produce faster completion of trips, they also lead to higher accident rates. Since automobile accidents have dreadful consequences, we accept speed limits. When incorrect use of computer systems can lead to damage to life, property, or data, shouldn't speed limits be provided?

Rapid task performance, low error rates, and high satisfaction can occur if:

- the user has adequate knowledge of the objects and actions necessary for the problem-solving task
- the solution plan can be carried out without delays
- distractions are eliminated
- anxiety is low
- there is feedback about progress toward solution

- errors can be avoided or, if they occur, can be handled easily.

These conditions for optimum problem-solving, along with cost and technical feasibility, are the basic constraints on design. However, other conjectures may play a role in choosing the optimum interaction speed:

- novices to a task exhibit bcttcr pcrformance and prefer to work at slower speeds than knowledgeable frequent users.
- when there is little penalty for an error, users will prefer to work more quickly.
- when the task is familiar and easily comprehended, users will prefer more rapid action.
- if users have had rapid performance in previous experiences, they will expect it in future situations.

These informal conjectures need to be qualified and verified. Then, a more rigorous cognitive model needs to be developed to accommodate the great diversity in human work styles and in computer use situations. Practitioners can conduct field tests to measure productivity, error rates, and satisfaction as a function of response times in their application areas.

The experiments described in the following sections are tiles in the mosaic of human performance with computers, but many more tiles are necessary before the fragments form a complete image. Some guidelines have emerged for designers and computer center managers, but local testing and continuous monitoring of performance and satisfaction are useful. The remarkable adaptability of computer users means that researchers and practitioners will have to be alert to novel conditions that require revisions to these guidelines.

7.3 DISPLAY RATE AND VARIABILITY

For alphanumeric hardcopy or display terminals, the display rate is the speed, in characters per second (cps), at which characters appear for the user to read. On hardcopy terminals, typical rates vary from 10 to 160 characters per second; faster rates are possible with line printer devices. On display terminals, the rate may be limited by inexpensive modems to 30 characters per second or may be 1,000 characters per second with special cables. At very high rates, the screen appears to fill in a single instant.

If a lot of data are to be displayed, and the text is only scanned, then fast display rates may produce a powerful advantage in task completion times and satisfaction. On the other hand, if the full text must be read and comprehended, then speeds above the user's reading rate may be useless or even counterproductive.

7.3.1 Reading from display screens

Bevan (1981) divided twenty-four subjects into low and high reading ability groups. Each subject worked on a computer-assisted instruction (CAI) lesson at four display rates: 10 cps, 15 cps, 60 cps, and word–15 cps (each word appeared instantaneously but the average rate was 15 cps). When the text filled the screen, the subject could issue a command to clear it and continue the display process. The total lesson time decreased as the display rate increased, but the number of errors increased. The mean number of errors was highest at 60 cps, with little difference among the other three treatments. Surprisingly, the 60 cps treatment was liked least by both high and low ability subjects. Low ability subjects preferred the 10 cps speed, and the high ability subjects preferred the 15 cps or word–15 cps treatments. As the display rate increased, subjects attempted to keep up with the display of characters; and at 60 cps, they were working beyond their accustomed reading rate. As comprehension deteriorated, errors during the CAI lesson and during the post-test increased, and satisfaction decreased.

Bevan's second experiment was run with treatments of 10, 18, 25, and 480 cps. At 480 cps, the screen was filled within two to three seconds, far faster than human reading rate. As the display rate increased, the total lesson time decreased as before, but in this experiment the error rate peaked at 18 cps. Errors were still lowest at 10 cps, but the very high display rate of 480 cps produced an intermediate level of errors. The preference scores showed wide diversity, with no treatment showing dominance. Five subjects rated 10 cps as best since they preferred to read the text as it appeared, but seven subjects found the slow pace to be irritating. Eight subjects rated 480 as best since they preferred to read at their own pace and could look at the questions at the bottom of the screen before reading the text; but eight subjects found the fast display worst since "they felt rushed, although they knew there was no reason to be."

A related study (Tombaugh et al., 1985) tested reading comprehension at 150, 300, 1200, 9600 baud and in an instantaneous condition. These correspond to 15, 30, 133, and 860 characters per second, and instantaneous presentation. Ninety undergraduate psychology students read standard passages and answered comprehension questions (Figure 7.3). The best performances occurred with 30 characters per second and with the instantaneous condition. We can conjecture that 15 characters per second was distractingly slow, and that 133 or 860 characters per second led to futile attempts to keep up with the display.

In summary, for many people, the slower display rate is appealing because they can keep up with the output and comprehend the full text. As the display rate increases beyond human reading rates, comprehension and satisfaction probably deteriorate. If the display rate can be made so fast that the screen appears to fill instantly (beyond the speed at which

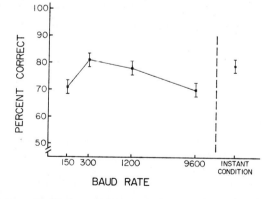

Figure 7.3: Comprehension scores (percent correct out of 28 questions) by presentation rate. (J. Tombaugh, M. D. Arkin, and R. F. Dillon, The effects of VDU text-presentation rate on reading comprehension and reading speed, *Proc. CHI'85—Human Factors in Computing Systems*. Copyright 1985, Association for Computer Machinery, Inc., Reprinted by permission.)

someone might feel compelled to keep up), subjects seem to pace themselves and work productively. These conclusions apply to situations in which the users must read the full text presented on the screen.

7.3.2 Time-sharing usage

Cotton (1978) reports on a study of 105 randomly selected days when usage was monitored on the National Bureau of Standards's UNIVAC 1108. After culling irregular sessions, 283 sessions with operating system and editing commands were analyzed in detail. Users had different equipment operating at 10 cps (33 sessions, 2,638 interactions), 15 cps (7 sessions, 361 interactions), and 30 cps (243 sessions, 19,706 interactions).

The amount of statistical evidence is impressive, and despite the relatively small number of interactions at slower rates, many significant differences were found. As the display rate rose from 10 to 30 cps, the user's median think time declined from 2.3 to 1.4 seconds. The user's rate of keystroking commands also increased as the display rate increased.

Cotton found another example of how users change their work habits as the speed of a system changes. As the display rate increased, users requested longer outputs.

Many contemporary systems offer much higher display rates; this is an attraction to most users. If the screen can fill in a few tenths of a second, then users may learn to scan for what they want and control their pace of interaction.

7.3.3 Variability in display rates

L. H. Miller (1977) investigated changes from 120 cps to 240 cps in an information retrieval task with thirty-six knowledgeable users. Half the subjects at each display rate received "high output variability" by an algorithm "such that the total time to display N characters on the screen would be approximately double the amount of time to display the same N characters without variability." For the eleven retrieval tasks, there was no significant difference in performance time as the display rate was changed from 120 to 240 cps. Apparently, the task performance time was limited by human reading speed, not by machine display rate. However, there was a statistically significant difference performance times that favored the low output variability group. In other words, an increased display rate made no difference, but increased variability in output did slow performance.

7.3.4 Summary

Reading textual information from a screen or printer is a challenging cognitive and perceptual task—more difficult than reading from a book. The pacing provided by the emergence of characters on the screen may be too rapid for many users, who, in their effort to keep up, have lower comprehension of what they are reading. One possible approach is to allow users to control the display rate. Another possibility is to fill the screen rapidly (in a fraction of a second) and hope users learn to accept this working style, scanning down the screen as desired and reading at their own pace.

If users only scan a display to pick out relevant material, then faster display rates may speed performance. Since many computer-related tasks do not require careful reading of the full screen, rapid filling of the screen seems preferable; it is pleasing and relieves the anxiety about delays in paging back and forth through multiple screens.

If the task is largely data entry, then rapid display of brief prompts is of little benefit to overall productivity. Variability in the display rate should be limited. Optimal display rates should be determined from performance and error data from subjects working on the specific task.

7.4   RESPONSE TIME: EXPECTATIONS AND ATTITUDES

How long will users wait for the computer to respond before they become annoyed? This apparently simple question has provoked much discussion and a few experiments. There is no simple answer to the question; more important, it may be the wrong question to ask.

Related design issues may clarify the question of acceptable response time. For example, how long should users have to wait before they hear a dial tone on a telephone or see a picture on their television? If the cost is not excessive, the frequently mentioned two-second limit (Miller, 1968) seems appropriate for many tasks. However, in some situations, users expect responses within a tenth of a second, such as turning the wheel of a car; pressing a key on a typewriter, piano, or telephone; or changing channels on a television. Two-second delays in these cases might be unsettling because users have adapted a working style and expectation based on responses within a fraction of a second. In other situations, users are accustomed to longer response times, such as waiting thirty seconds for a red traffic light, two days for a letter to arrive, or a month or more for flowers to grow.

7.4.1 Factors influencing response time expectations

The first factor influencing acceptable response time is that people have established expectations based on their past experiences of the time required to complete a given task. If a task is completed more quickly than expected, people will be pleased; but if the task is completed much more quickly than expected, they may become concerned that something is wrong. Similarly, if a task is completed much more slowly than expected, users become concerned or frustrated. Even though people can detect 8 percent changes in a 2- or 4-second response time (Miller, 1968), users apparently do not become concerned until the change from experience is much greater.

Two installers of time-shared computer systems have reported a problem concerning user expectations with new systems. The first users are delighted because the response is short with a light load. As the load builds, these first users become unhappy as the response time deteriorates. The users who have come on later may be satisfied with what they perceive as normal response times. Both installers devised a *response time choke* by which they could slow down the system when the load was light, thus making the response time uniform over time and across users.

Computer center managers have similar problems with varying response times as new equipment is added or as large projects begin or complete their work. The variation in response time can be disruptive to users who have developed expectations and working styles based on a specific response time. There are also periods within each day when the response time is short, such as at lunch time, or long, such as midmorning or late afternoon. Some users rush to complete a task when response times are short, and as a result they may make more errors. Some workers refuse to work when the response time is poor relative to their expectations.

There has also been a change in expectations during the past years as people in general are becoming more accustomed to using computers. The widespread dissemination of microcomputers will further raise expectations about how quickly computers should respond.

A second factor influencing response time expectations is the individual's tolerance for delays. Novice computer users may be willing to wait much longer than experienced users.

In short, there are large variations in what individuals consider acceptable waiting time. These variations are influenced by many factors, such as the nature of the task, familiarity with the task, experience in performing the task, personality, costs, age, mood, cultural context, time of day, and by such environmental issues as noise and perceived pressure to complete work.

A third factor influencing response time expectations is that people are highly adaptive and can change their working style to accommodate different response times. This factor, discussed in detail in Section 7.5, was found in early studies of batch programming environments and in more recent studies of interactive system usage. Briefly, if delays are long, users will seek alternate strategies that reduce the number of interactions, whenever possible. They will fill in the long delays with other tasks, daydreaming, or planning ahead in their work. These long delays may or may not increase error rates in the range of three to fifteen seconds, but they will probably increase error rates above fifteen seconds if people must remain at the keyboard waiting for a response. Even if diversions are available, dissatisfaction grows with longer response times.

The three factors influencing response time expectation can be summarized as:

1. Previous experiences are critical in shaping expectations.
2. There is enormous variation in response time expectations across individuals and tasks.
3. People are highly adaptive. However, although they may be able to accommodate long and variable delays, their performance and satisfaction are likely to suffer.

7.4.2 Experimental results

Experimental results do show interesting patterns of behavior for specific tasks, individuals, times of day, and so on, but it is difficult to distill a simple set of conclusions. Several experiments focused on acceptable waiting times by allowing subjects to press a key if they felt the waiting time was too long. In some cases, the subjects received immediate response for that interaction; in other cases, subjects could shorten the response time in future interactions.

Youmans (1983) publicly reports on an IBM confidential study done in 1979 by Hogan and Youmans in which eight subjects were tested for two days while they performed text entry and editing tasks at a display station. The system response time was varied, and subjective satisfaction questionnaires were filled out after each of the sixteen sessions. Results indicated that "subjective operator reaction to system response time changed from predominantly acceptable to predominantly unacceptable as the overall mean response time of the system increased from 1.8 to 2.5 seconds." Such findings support the conjecture of a two-second limit for response time to simple commands.

7.4.3 Forcing immediate responses

C. M. Williams (1973) had twenty-four subjects working for four hours a day for five consecutive days on a 15-cps printing terminal. Subjects were divided into three groups that worked with 2, 4, or 8 second response times on four types of data entry tasks. Each subject worked on all four tasks but stayed at the same response time. Subjects could get immediate response from the system if they pressed the "attention" key. The main results are summarized as follows:

Standard Response Time	Total number of trials	Average delay (seconds)	Standard deviation (seconds)	Percent of trials attention key pressed
2 seconds	11,634	1.98	0.53	1.42
4 seconds	9,754	3.50	2.08	17.44
8 seconds	10,103	2.27	5.63	82.92

The results for this task indicate that two seconds was generally an acceptable response time since the attention key was pressed only 1.42 percent of the time. Eight seconds was generally unacceptable, since the attention key was pressed almost 83 percent of the time. A closer look at the data shows enormous individual differences, especially among the eight subjects in the eight-second group. One subject occasionally pressed the attention key, all others pressed it almost every time.

The four tasks required brief and long requests for either an information retrieval or a calculation. Subjects tolerated longer response times only for the long calculation when the standard response time was 8 seconds.

Half the subjects received instructions that emphasized speed and half received instructions that emphasized accuracy, but there was no difference in the toleration of delay.

This study provides detailed and intriguing results, but the author makes too general a summary statement: "An absolute maximum response time interval of four seconds appears acceptable for a transaction-oriented system."

7.4.4 Shortening response times

In another extensive study, Youmans (1981) allowed subjects to reduce the response time for each type of command by one-eighth by pressing a red button. Five subjects performed a variety of office automation tasks over four days using a specially prepared keyboard and a display with 55 lines of 112 characters. Subjects were tolerant of longer delays during training, but as they became proficient, they pressed the red button more frequently, driving the response time lower and lower. Subjects would remain at a certain response time for many invocations of a command and then return to pressing the red button to reduce the response time further. There were clear differences across subjects, commands, and times of day.

The data from the two least tolerant subjects were reported in a summary table. They forced the response time to below one second for all commands (except one command that the system could not perform in less than one second). Such editing commands as inserting a line, deleting a line, or turning a page were forced into the 0.3- to 0.5-second range, and display and copy commands were forced into the 0.6- to 0.8-second range.

These results suggest that, given the chance to choose a shorter response time, many users will take advantage of that feature as they become more experienced users. It seems appealing to offer users the choice of the pace of the interaction.

7.4.5 Is the computer down?

If users are working with a response time of from 3 to 5 seconds and suddenly the computer does not respond within the expected period, how much time will elapse before users take some action? This question was the subject of a study (Farivari & Levy, 1983) in which students were required to play tic-tac-toe against the computer with 1-, 2-, 4-, or 8-second response times. The screen displayed the board and the message, "If you believe the computer did not receive your response, please retype it." Play proceeded normally until the machine did not respond during the second game. There were six subjects per response time treatment.

The results for mean waiting times were almost linear with respect to response time. The results suggest that people will wait approximately seven to nine times the customary response time before they take action. This interpretation should be limited to similar situations and to one-time interruptions. With regular interruptions of service, users are likely to take action more quickly.

Different findings emerge from a study of ten teenagers who regularly played video games and ten adults with little video game experience (Liverman, 1983). They were asked to play a computer version of the Othello board game at 3-second and 6-second response times in this counterbalanced-orderings within-subjects design. Subjects were told that the experimenters were still developing the game and that it might go into an infinite loop, but that the subjects could get the machine to work again by simply pressing any one of the keys. No significant differences emerged across age groups, order groups, and response time groups. The mean values in the eight cells ranged from 6.16 to 13.28 seconds, with an overall mean of 10.19 seconds. The means for the 3- second and 6-second groups were close to the overall mean.

As with any study, results with game programs need to be replicated before they can be applied to frequent users in professional settings.

7.4.6 User-defined response times

Twelve university students with minimal computing experience were told of three tasks that the computer would carry out for them (Dunsmore, 1981). The subjects were asked "to specify their perceived complexity of each and the time units they expected each to require." The *proportional* system delivered the expected time, the *constant* system offered the same time for all three tasks (the mean of the three times in the proportional system), and the *inverse proportional* system gave response times inversely proportional to the subjects expectations.

Dunsmore anticipated that either the proportional or constant system would yield the shortest performance times, the lowest error rates, and the highest subjective preference. However, the inversely proportional system produced a statistically significant advantage in performance time ($p < 0.05$), which a majority of the subjects preferred. The lowest error rate did occur with the proportional system, as this summary table indicates:

	Mean performance time	Mean errors	Preferred system
System			
Proportional	16.4 minutes	0.5	2 subjects
Constant	16.4 minutes	1.1	3 subjects
Inversely proportional	13.8 minutes	1.3	7 subjects

Dunsmore reported that he could not explain this result. The performance time differences are only about 15 percent, but the inversely proportional system was preferred by seven out of twelve subjects (not significant by chi-squared test). This result seems to indicate that users are more pleased by an unanticipated rapid response than they are distressed by an unanticipated slow response. This study should be repeated with a larger number of subjects.

7.4.7 Summary

There appear to be so many variables governing response time expectations and attitudes that it is difficult to arrange adequate experimental controls. Even if that were possible, the generalizability of the results would be in question.

In spite of these unsatisfying observations, three conjectures do arise:

1. People will work faster as they gain experience with a command, so it may be useful to allow people to set their own pace of interaction.
2. In the absence of such constraints as cost or technical feasibility, people will eventually force response time to well under a second.
3. Although people can adapt to working with slower response times, they are generally dissatisfied with it.

7.5   RESPONSE TIME: USER PRODUCTIVITY

Shorter system response times may lead to higher productivity, but it is possible that users who receive long system response times can find clever shortcuts to reduce the effort necessary to accomplish a task. Working too quickly may lead to errors that reduce productivity.

In computing, just as in driving, there is no general rule about whether the high-speed highway or the slower, clever shortcut is better. Each situation has to be surveyed carefully to make the optimal choice. The choice is not critical for the occasional excursion but becomes worthy of investigation when the frequency is great. When computers are used in high volume situations, more effort can be expended in discovering the proper response time for a given task and set of users. It should not be surprising that a new study must be conducted when the tasks and users change, just as a new evaluation must be done in each choice of highways.

Some tasks have been studied in controlled experimental conditions, with the general conclusion that response times do impact performance times, error rates, and user satisfaction. In general, with shorter response times, performance times are reduced, error rates are increased, and user satisfaction is increased. The frequent exceptions to these results depend on the nature of the task, the difficulty in repairing an error, the feedback from the system, the possibility of using different methods to solve the given problem, and the expectations of the users. Careful design of computer systems and highways can reduce errors so that higher speeds can be safely permitted.

7.5.1 Repetitive control tasks

The nature of the task has a strong influence on whether changes in response time alter user productivity. A repetitive control task involves monitoring a display and issuing commands in response to changes in the display. Although the operator may be trying to understand the underlying process, the basic activities are to respond to a change in the display, to issue commands, and then to see if the commands produce the desired effect. When there is a choice among commands, the problem becomes more interesting and the operator tries to pick the optimal command in each situation. With shorter system response times, the operator picks up the pace of the system and works more quickly, but decisions on commands may be less than optimal. On the other hand, with short response times, the penalty for a poor choice may be small because it is easy to try another command. In fact, operators may learn to use the system more quickly with short system response times because they can more easily explore alternatives.

Response times of 0.16, 0.72, and 1.49 seconds. Goodman and Spence (1978) studied a control task involving multiparameter optimization. The goal was to force "a displayed graph to lie wholly within a defined acceptance region." Operators could adjust five parameters by using lightpen touches, altering the shape of the graph. There were response times of 0.16, 0.72, or 1.49 seconds.

Each of the thirty subjects worked at each of the three response times in this repeated measures experiment. The total times to solution (just over 500 seconds) and the total user think time (around 300 seconds) was the same for the 0.16 and 0.72 second treatments. The 1.49 second treatment led to a 50 percent increase in solution time and a modest increase in user think time. In this case, reducing the response time to less than one second was beneficial in terms of human productivity. A pilot study of this task with six subjects provided further support for short response time, since a response time of three seconds drove the solution time up to more than 1,200 seconds.

Response times of 2, 6, and 10 seconds. A related experiment (Weiss et al., 1982) involved twenty subjects who worked at each of the five treatments in random order: 2 second, 6 second, 6 second with variability, 10 second, and 10 second with variability. The variability treatments, conducted with a normal distribution around the mean and a variance of 0.33 seconds, showed no significant effect.

The task required subjects to press an increase, null, or decrease button to keep a visual display within a given range. The time-varying display "was formed by the addition of five sine waves, differing in frequency, phase, and amplitude." If the display got out of range, the operators heard a beep and the word *error* was shown. The number of errors was lowest with a 2-second response time (approximately 19.2), highest at six seconds (approximately 23.5), and intermediate at ten seconds (approximately 21.5). The range was modest, but the difference was significant at the 5 percent level. Individual differences were substantial and accounted for a large proportion of the variance. Heart rates and blood pressure were monitored and varied significantly among subjects but not across response times. The authors conclude that "perhaps a greater range of system response delay and variance values would indicate a more pronounced trend" for the physiological measures.

In summary, a response time of 2 seconds led to better performance in this specialized task—subjects were more capable of keeping the visual display in the acceptable range. The poorest performance occurred at 6-second response time, but the intermediate performance at 10-second response time suggests that with more time to think carefully, subjects made better decisions than at 6 seconds.

7.5.2 Problem-solving tasks

Response times of 1, 4, 16, and 64 seconds. When complex problem-solving is required and many approaches to the solution are possible, users will adapt their work style to the response time. A demonstration of this effect emerged from studies done in the late 1960s (Grossberg et al., 1976) using four experienced subjects in a complex computational problem-solving situation. The response times were variable, but the means were set at 1, 4, 16, and 64 seconds for commands that generated output or an error message. Nonoutput commands were simply accepted by the system. Each subject peformed a total of 48 tasks of approximately 15-minutes duration each, distributed across the four response time treatments.

The remarkable outcome of this study was that the time to solution was invariant with respect to response time! When working with 64-second delays, subjects used substantially fewer output commands and also fewer total commands. Apparently, with long response times, subjects thought carefully about the problem solution, since there were also longer intervals between commands. There were differences across subjects, but each subject stayed within a limited range of solution times across the four system response times they worked on.

Although the number of subjects was small, the results are very strong in support of the notion that, if possible, users will change their work habits as the response time changes. When the cost, in time, of an error or an unnecessary output command became great, subjects made fewer errors and commands. These results are closely tied to this complex, intellectually demanding task in which there were several ways to solve the problem.

Response times of 0.33 and 1.25 seconds. Similar (but less dramatic) results appeared in a study of computer-based instruction in chemistry distillation (Weinberg, 1981). In a question-answering situation, 120 students worked at either 0.33 or 1.25 second response times. If they guessed wrong, the students received a hint about the correct answer. With 0.33 second response times, subjects averaged 11.11 errors; but when working at 1.25 seconds, the subjects considered their guesses more carefully and averaged only 4.73 errors. This performance result contrasted with another part of the study in which subjects used repetitive control to keep the distillation running within prescribed bounds. The subjects violated the bounds only 28.40 times with the 0.33 delay, but 35.04 times with the longer delay. Shorter response times allowed more interventions in the fixed time of the lesson. Overall, subjects working at the shorter response time completed their lessons more quickly and had a more favorable attitude toward the system. There were clear indications that subjects tried to work more carefully and made fewer errors with the longer response time.

Response times of 0 and 10 seconds. Another problem-solving study (Bergman et al., 1981) offered subjects a game in which they had to guess at permissible patterns of Xs and Os. They could offer a test pattern or the formation rule about which of the six slots contains an X. A sample session was as follows:

Trial	User	System	Comments
	XXXXXX	HIT	Printed out at the beginning
	000000	MISS	of each problem
1	XXX000	HIT	Subject inquires about
			pattern
2	1 AND 2	WRONG	Subject states hypothesis
3	X0X000	HIT	
4	X00000	MISS	
5	0000XX	MISS	Three tenable hypotheses
			1 AND 3, 2 OR 3, 3 OR 4
6	00000X	MISS	Uninformative trial
7	1 OR 4	IMPOSSIBLE	Would make trial 4 a HIT
8	2 OR 3	WRONG	One hypothesis left
9	3 OR 4	CORRECT	

Subjects worked with 0-second delay (instantaneous feedback), 10-second delay, and 10-second mean delay with variations around the mean. The two tested variations around the 10-second mean delay were generated from a Gamma distribution with standard deviations of 2.5 and 7.5 seconds. One hundred and five male psychology students were assigned to one of the four treatments for training and three trial sessions. Subjects working at zero delay took a mean of 10.61 trials to solve the problems, but subjects with the 10-second delays took between 9.19 and 9.47 trials, depending on the variability treatment. The variability in response times did not seem to affect users in this task.

The modest but statistically significant ($p = .032$) reduction in trials as the response time increased agrees with results from other experiments. People work more carefully with longer response times. With short response times and no serious cost of an additional interaction, subjects often feel freer to try things out on the machine rather than to think through the solution.

7.5.3 Programming tasks

Since programmers often use interactive systems, it is not surprising that several studies have been conducted to measure the impact of response time changes on programmer productivity (Boies, 1974; Doherty & Kelisky, 1979; Smith, 1983). These studies tend to focus on the number of interactions per hour as measured by the system, rather than on specific task completion times. The programmers performed a mixture of program and text editing, compilations, program testing, and debugging. These studies also tend to be field studies of actual work rather than controlled experiments.

A preliminary study by Dannenbring (1983) focused on novices and experienced programmers debugging a 25-line BASIC program. Changing the response time from 0 to 5 to 10 seconds did not affect performance time or satisfaction for novices or experienced programmers, although there were significant differences between the scores of novices and experienced programmers. By contrast, knowledgeable programmers generally benefit from shorter response times. Programmers often have a sequence of commands they are ready to apply, but they must maintain these plans in their short-term memory while they wait for the computer to complete the previous command. This additional burden prevents swift completion and may lead to higher error rates. The danger of shorter response time is that programmers may make hasty decisions as they keep up the rapid pace of interaction. Can programmers learn the discipline of working carefully, even with short response times?

Interaction rate. Thadhani (1981) found that on one IBM MVS/TSO system, users went from 106 interactions per hour at 3.0 second response time up to 222 interactions per hour at 0.5 seconds response time. On another system, the users went from approximately 200 to 340 interactions per hour as the response time was reduced from 3.0 to 0.5 seconds. Similar results were reported with IBM programmers in England (Lambert, 1984), where the rate of interactions per hour went from 161 for the control group to 258 for the study group. The control group was given a mean response time of 2.22 seconds, and the study group was given a mean response time of 0.84 seconds.

These results are strong, but they only measure interactions per hour, not productivity, and they do not reveal how work habits changed as the response time was changed. Thadhani (1984) offers further evidence that programmer interaction rates increase with short response times. He also refers to a study of engineers that showed no significant change in number of interactions to complete a task when the response time was varied from 0.25 to 2.0 seconds, but a doubling in the total task time. The task was not described, but Thadhani suggests that these results have relevance for programming tasks.

Several studies demonstrate that as the system response time increases, so does the user think time. Boies (1974) found that as the response time increased from 1 to 10 seconds, the user think time increased from about 15 to 24 seconds. Thadhani (1981) found somewhat higher times on one system and somewhat lower times on another system (see Figure 7.4).

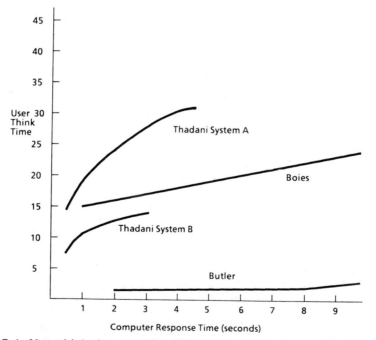

Figure 7.4: User think time as a function of computer response time from Boies (1974), Thadhani (1981), and Butler (1983).

We may conjecture that knowledgeable programmers build a plan and then seek to carry it out as rapidly as possible. They pick up the pace of the system, being more cautious with long response times and moving quickly with short response times. They are not afraid of making errors when working rapidly because their knowledge of the system allows rapid error recovery.

Session length. The length of each work session is another aspect of working style. Boies (1974) found that sessions ranged from 0 to 600 minutes, with the median session length of less than 10 minutes, but made no effort to link session length with response time. Thadhani (1981) found that the work session increased from 27 to 57 minutes as the mean response time went from 0.5 up to 3.0 seconds. On a second system with different users, Thadhani found the session increased from 20 to 32 minutes. A National Institute of Health study found that the mean session length increased from 32 to 48 minutes as the mean response time lengthened from 0.5 to 4.0 seconds.

These results were not supported by Lambert's work (1984), which found study group members (at 0.84 seconds) spent 72 minutes per session whereas the control subjects (at 2.22 seconds) spent only 54 minutes per session. An important factor in these results is that the study group subjects each had individual terminals, whereas the control subjects had 1.8 people per terminal. There is some evidence that the study group members did more documentation and other work online that contributed to their longer session length.

These results are provocative, but more controlled experimentation is necessary to ascertain what happens as response times decrease.

7.5.4 Professionals at work

Programmers are a special community of users because of their familiarity with computers, but other professional users are also affected by response time issues. Users of computer-assisted design systems tend to work at a rapid rate in making changes to a displayed object. An IBM study (Smith, 1983) of circuit designers using lightpens at a graphics workstation found dramatic improvements in interaction rates as the response time was reduced. The most skilled user went from 800 interactions per hour with a 1.5 second response time up to 4,300 interactions per hour with 0.4 second response time. A novice designer went from 60 to 650 interactions per hour as the response time was reduced from 1.5 to 0.25 seconds. Error rates and user satisfaction were not presented in this report.

Very few tasks have the high interaction rate of this graphics system. Barber and Lucas (1983) studied 100 professional circuit layout clerks who assigned phone equipment in response to service requests. Ten or more interactions were needed to complete these complex tasks. Data were collected for twelve days about normal performance, with an average response time of 6 seconds. Then, 29 clerks were given response times averaging 14 seconds for four days. When the response time was as short as 4 seconds, there were 49 errors out of 287 transactions. As the response time increased to 12 seconds, the errors dropped to 16 of 222 transactions; and as the response time increased further to 24 seconds, the errors increased to 70 of 151 transactions (Figure 7.5). The volume of transactions was recorded with an "active

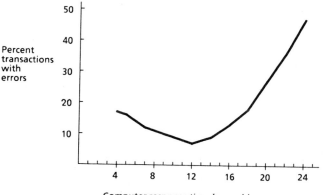

Figure 7.5: Error rates as a function of reponse time for complex telephone circuit layout task by Barber and Lucas (1983). Although error rates were lowest with long response times (12 seconds), the productivity increased with shorter response times because the system could detect errors and users could rapidly correct them.

time" (session length) of 200 minutes. For this complex task, the data reveal that the lowest error rate was with a 12-second response time. With shorter response times, the workers made hasty decisions; and with longer response times, the frustration of waiting burdened short-term memory. It is important to recognize that the number of productive transactions (total minus errors) increased almost linearly with reductions in response time.

Apparently, reduced error rates were not sufficient to increase satisfaction, since subjective preference was consistently in favor of the shorter response time.

In a Bell Labs study with low complexity data entry tasks, J. D. Williams (1975) found no differences in error rates with 5-, 15-, 30-, or 45-second response times. With higher complexity tasks such as data retrieval and correction, the 30- and 45-second conditions resulted in higher error rates. Typing speed during data entry deteriorated steadily as the response time increased.

Butler (1983), also at Bell Labs, studied simple data entry tasks with computer-displayed prompts. The response times were 2, 4, 8, 16, and 32 seconds. Error rates remained unchanged over this range, but the user think time increased, contributing to an overall decrease in productivity.

7.5.5 Summary

It is clear that users pick up the pace of the system to work more quickly with shorter response times, and that they consistently prefer the faster pace. The profile of error rates at shorter response times varies across tasks. Not surprisingly, there appears to be an optimal pace for each user/task situation—response times that are shorter or longer than this pace lead to increased errors. The ease of error recovery and the damage caused by an error must be evaluated carefully when managers are choosing the optimal pace of interaction. If higher throughput of work is desired, then attention must be paid to minimizing the cost and delay of error recovery. In short, the optimal response time may be longer than the minimum possible response time.

7.6   RESPONSE TIME: VARIABILITY

People are willing to pay substantial amounts of money to reduce the variability in their life. The entire insurance industry is based on the reduction of present pleasures, through the payment of premiums, in order to reduce the severity of a loss. Most people appreciate predictable behavior that lessens the anxiety of unpleasant surprises.

7.6.1 Range of variation

In using computers, the operator cannot see into the machine to gain reassurance that the commands are being executed properly, but the response time can provide some clue. If users come to expect a response time of three seconds for a common operation, they may become apprehensive if this operation takes a half a second or fifteen seconds. Such extreme variation is unsettling and should be prevented or acknowledged by the system, with a message for unusually fast response and progress reports for unusually slow response.

The more difficult issue is the impact of modest variations in response time. As discussed earlier, Miller (1968) raised this issue and reported that 75 percent of subjects tested could perceive 8 percent variations in time for time periods in the interval of 2 to 4 seconds. These results prompted some designers to suggest restrictive rules for variability of response time. For example, Gallaway (1981) proposed a variability of plus or minus 5 percent for response times in the 0- to 2-second range, and 10 percent for the 2- to 4-second range.

Since it may not be technically feasible to provide a fixed short response time (such as 1 second) for all commands, several authors have suggested that the time be fixed for classes of commands. Many commands could have a fixed response time of less than 1 second, other commands could take 4 seconds, and still other commands could take 12 seconds. Experimental results on all these conjectures would help clarify the impact of variations in response time.

7.6.2 Experimental results

Goodman and Spence (1981) attempted to measure performance changes in a problem-solving situation (a similar situation was used in their earlier experiment described in Section 7.5.1). Subjects used lightpen touches to manipulate a displayed graph. The mean response time was set at 1.0 second with three levels of variation: quasi-normal distributions with standard deviations of 0.2, 0.4, and 0.8 seconds. The minimum response time was 0.2 seconds, and the maximum response time was 1.8 seconds. Goodman and Spence found no significant performance changes as the variability was increased. The time to solution and the profile of command use were unchanged. As the variability increased, they did note that subjects took more advantage of fast responses by making their subsequent commands immediately. This balanced the time lost in waiting for slower responses. In summary, this study found that as the percentage of responses deviating from the mean grew, performance remained largely unchanged, within the range specified (0.2 to 1.8 seconds).

A closely related experiment (Goodman & Spence, 1982) found "no significant direct effect of response variability. But a large and nearly significant $F(2,96) = 3.04$, $p < 0.10$" interaction was found with time of day for the number of lightpen touches. Increased response time variability led to slower performance in the morning and faster performance in the afternoon. The main effect of time to solution "just failed to reach the 10 percent level." The "mean response interval and its variability tended to increase with increasing (variability), with significance approaching the 10 percent and 5 percent level, respectively."

Similar results were found using a mean response time of 10 seconds and three variations: standard deviations of 0.0, 2.5, and 7.5 seconds (Bergman et al., 1981, described in Section 7.5.2). The authors conclude that an increase in variability of response time "does not have any negative influence on the subject's performance on a rather complicated problem-solving task."

A third failure to find variability effects emerged from a study of a repetitive control task (Weiss et al., 1982, described in Section 7.5.1). Variances of 0 and 0.33 seconds were applied to mean response times of 6 and 10 seconds. No significant main effects were found for the response time or the response time variability. A significant two-way interaction of response time and response time variability was intriguing. With a 10-second response time and high variability, errors, heart rate, and blood pressure were reduced. The authors conjecture that the occasional short response time was perceived as a positive opportunity. This conjecture fits with Dunsmore's results (1981, described in Section 7.4.6) that surprising short response times were very much appreciated, even if the penalty was occasional unanticipated long response times.

Two studies detected modest increases in user think time as variability increased. Butler (1983) studied six subjects who worked for two hours at each of ten response time conditions: means of 2, 4, 8, 16, and 32 seconds each with low and high variability. Subjects performed simple data entry tasks but had to wait for the system response before they could proceed. The accuracy and typing rate were unaffected by the duration or variability of response time. The user think time increased with the duration and variability of the computer's response time (Figure 7.4). Butler describes a second experiment with a more complex task whose results are quite similar.

Four videotex studies (Murray & Abrahamson, 1983) with novice users examined response time and response time variability. No significant effects were found for response time changes. The authors interpret this result as "a strong indication that inexperienced videotex users are relatively immune to a wide range of constant values of system delay." Of the three experiments that tested response time variability, two had significant effects that indicated that subjects who had higher variability took longer in responding.

7.6.3 Summary

In summary, modest variations in response time (plus or minus 50 percent of the mean) appear to be tolerable and to have little impact on performance. As the variability grows, there may be some decrease in performance speed. Frustration may emerge only if delays are unusually long —at least twice the anticipated time. Similarly, anxiety about an erroneous command may emerge only if the response time is unusually short —say, less than one quarter of the anticipated time. But even with extreme changes, users appear to be adaptable enough to complete their tasks. Of course, the conjectures are task dependent and need further validation.

It may be useful to slow down unexpected fast responses to avoid surprising the user. This is a controversial proposal, but it should affect only a small fraction of user interactions. Certainly, a serious effort should be made to avoid extremely slow responses, or, if they must occur, the user should be given information to indicate progress toward the goal. One graphics system displays a large clock ticking backwards, and the output appears only when the clock has ticked down to zero. A document formatting system displays the section numbers to indicate progress and confirm that the computer is productively at work on the appropriate document.

7.7 PRACTITIONER'S SUMMARY

Computer system response time and display rate are important determinants of user productivity, error rates, working style, and satisfaction. In most situations, shorter response times (less than a second) lead to higher productivity. For typed data entry, mouse actions, direct manipulation, and animation, even faster performance is necessary for each individual step. Satisfaction generally increases as the response time shortens, but there may be a danger from stress induced by a rapid pace. As users pick up the pace of the system, they may make more errors; if these errors are easily detected and corrected, then productivity will generally increase. If errors are hard to detect or very costly, then a moderate pace may be the most beneficial.

The optimal response time for a specific application and user community can be determined by measuring the productivity, cost of errors, and cost of providing short response times. Managers must be alert to changes in work style as the pace quickens; productivity is measured by correctly completed tasks, not by interactions per hour. Novices may prefer a slower pace of interaction. When technical feasibility or costs prevent response times of less than a second, each class of commands can be assigned to a response time category: for example, 2 to 4 seconds, 4 to 8 seconds, 8 to 12 seconds, and more than 12 seconds. Modest variations around the mean response time are acceptable, but large variations (less than a quarter of the mean or more than twice the mean) should be accompanied by an informative message. An alternative approach is to slow down overly rapid responses and avoid the message.

Display rates that are faster than human reading speed (15 to 30 cps) may be counterproductive when the full text must be read and comprehended unless the screen can be filled instantaneously. For other tasks that do not require full text reading, faster display rates will speed performance but may lead to more errors. Keeping these important exceptions in mind, faster display rates are preferable.

7.8 RESEARCHER'S AGENDA

In spite of the many experiments described here, many unanswered questions remain. The taxonomy of issues provides some framework for research, but a finer taxonomy of tasks, relevant cognitive style differences, and work situations is necessary to specify adequate experimental controls. Next, a sound theory of problem-solving behavior with computers is necessary to generate useful hypotheses.

Doherty and Kelisky (1979) suggest that longer response times lead to slower work, emotional upset, and more errors. This statement appears to be true with very long response times of more than 15 seconds, but there is little evidence to support the claim that fewer errors are made with very short response times (less than 1 second). Barber and Lucas (1983) found a U-shaped error curve with the lowest error rate at a 12-second response time. It would be very productive to study error rates as a function of response time for a range of tasks and users.

It is understandable that error rates vary with response times, but how else is the work style impacted? Do users issue more commands as

response times shorten? Grossberg et al. (1976) found this result for a complex task with very long response times of up to 64 seconds, but there is little evidence with more common tasks and speeds. Does the profile of commands shift to a smaller set of more familiar commands as the response time shortens? Does the session length increase or decrease with response time increases? Are workers more willing to pursue higher quality when they are given shorter response times that enable multiple quick changes?

Many other questions are worthy of investigation. When technical feasibility prevents short responses, can users be satisfied by diversionary tasks or are progress reports sufficient? Do warnings of long responses relieve anxiety or further frustrate users?

Operating systems designers can also contribute by providing better control over response time. It should be possible for a designer to specify upper and lower limits for response time for each command. It is still difficult on large time-shared computers to specify a response time, even on an experimental basis. With better control of response time, new approaches could be tried. For example, imagine that the response time is always 1.0 second but that keyboard lockout time is a function of command type. After a quick simple command, you could immediately enter the next command; but after a longer, more complex command, you would be forced to review your work and consider the next step because your terminal was locked out for 12 seconds. Boehm et al. (1971) and others suggest that keyboard lockout may be less disruptive than anticipated and that lockout has several beneficial effects.

Program designers can contribute by actively pursuing algorithms that reduce response time, designing software to reduce the impact of long response times, and simplifying error recovery to reduce the problems of higher error rates with short response times.

REFERENCES

Barber, Raymond E., and Lucas, H. C., System response time, operator productivity and job satisfaction, *Communications of the ACM 26*, 11, (November 1983), 972–986.

Bergman, Hans, Brinkman, Albert, and Koelega, Harry S., System response time and problem solving behavior, *Proc. of the Human Factors Society, 25th Annual Meeting,* (October 12–16, 1981), Rochester, NY, 749–753.

Bevan, Nigel, Is there an optimum speed for presenting text on a VDU?, *International of Journal Man-Machine Studies,* 14, (1981), 59–76.

Boehm, Barry W., Seven, M. J., and Watson, R. A., Interactive problem solving—An experimental study of "lockout" effects, *Proc. Spring Joint Computer Conference Volume 38,* (1971), 205–210.

Boies, S. J., User behavior on an interactive computer system, *IBM Systems Journal 13,* 1, (1974), 1–18.

Butler, T. W., Computer response time and user performance, *ACM SIGCHI'83 Proceedings: Human Factors in Computer Systems,* (December 1983), 56–62.

Carbonell, J. R., Elkind, J. I., and Nickerson, R. S., On the psychological importance of time in a timesharing system, *Human Factors 10,* 2, (1968), 135–142.

Cotton, Ira W., Measurement of interactive computing: Methodology and application, National Bureau of Standards Special Publication 500–548, (1978), 101 pages.

Dannenbring, Gary L., The effect of computer response time on user preference and satisfaction: A preliminary investigation, *Behavioral Research Methods and Instrumentation 15,* (1983), 213–216.

Doherty, W. J., and Kelisky, R. P., Managing VM/CMS systems for user effectiveness, *IBM Systems Journal 18,* 1, (1979), 143–163.

Dunsmore, H. E., A report on research, unpublished manuscript, Purdue University, (1981).

Farivari, Reza, and Levy, Irving, A test of patience, unpublished manuscript, research project report to James Foley, George Washington University, (1983).

Gallaway, Glen R., Response times to user activities in interactive man/machine computer systems, National Cash Register Corporation HFP 81–25, (August 25, 1981).

Goodman, T. J., and Spence, Robert, The effect of computer system response time on interactive computer aided problem solving, *ACM*

SIGGRAPH 1978 Conference Proceedings, (1978), 100–104.

Goodman, T. J., and Spence, R., The effect of computer system response time variability on interactive graphical problem solving, *IEEE Transactions on Systems, Man and Cybernetics, Vol. 11*, 3 (March 1981), 207–216.

Goodman, Tom, and Spence, Robert, The effects of potentiometer dimensionality, system response time, and time of day on interactive graphical problem solving, *Human Factors 24*, 4 (1982), 437–456.

Grossberg, Mitchell, Wiesen, Raymond A., and Yntema, Douwe B., An experiment on problem solving with delayed computer responses, *IEEE Transactions on Systems, Man, and Cybernetics*, (March 1976), 219–222.

IBM, The economic value of rapid response time, IBM Department 824, 1133 Westchester Avenue, White Plains, NY, GE20–0752–0, (November 1982), 11 pages.

Lambert, G. N., A comparative study of system response time on program developer productivity, *IBM System Journal 23*, 1, (1984), 36–43.

Liverman, R., Unpublished manuscript, research project report to James Foley, Dept. of Electrical Engineering and Computer Science, George Washington University, Washington, DC, (1983).

Long, John, Effects of delayed irregular feedback on unskilled and skilled keying performance, *Ergonomics 19*, 2, (1976), 183–202.

Miller, G. A., The magical number seven, plus or minus two: Some limits on our capability for processing information, *Psychological Science 63*, (1956), 81–97.

Miller, L. H., A study in man-machine interaction, *Proceedings of the National Computer Conference*, 46, AFIPS Press, Montvale, NJ, (1977), 409–421.

Miller, Robert B., Response time in man-computer conversational transactions, *Proceedings Spring Joint Computer Conference 1968*, 33, AFIPS Press, Montvale, NJ, (1968), 267–277.

Murray, Robert P., and Abrahamson, David, The effect of system response time delay variability on inexperienced videotex users, *Behaviour and Information Technology 2*, 3, (1983), 237–251.

Neal, Alan S., Time interval between keystrokes, records, and fields in data entry with skilled operators, *Human Factors 19*, 2, (1977), 163–170.

Shneiderman, Ben, *Software Psychology: Human Factors in Computer and Information Systems*, Little, Brown and Co., Boston, MA, (1980).

Smith, Dick, Faster is better: A business case for subsecond response time, *Computerworld*, (April 18, 1983), in depth pages 1–11.

Thadhani, A. J., Interactive user productivity, *IBM Systems Journal 20*, 4, (1981), 407–423.

Thadhani, A. J., Factors affecting programmer productivity during application development, *IBM Systems Journal 23*, 1, (1984), 19–35.

Tombaugh, Jo W., Arkin, Michael D., and Dillon, Richard F., The effects of VDU text-presentation rate on reading comprehension and reading speed, *Proc. CHI'85—Human Factors in Computing Systems*, Available from ACM, P. O. Box 64145, Baltimore, MD 21264, (1985), 1–6.

Weinberg, Sherry, Learning effectiveness: The impact of response time, Slides for presentation at May 1981 Conference, Control Data Corporation, Minneapolis, MN, (May 1981).

Weiss, Stuart Martin, Boggs, George, Lehto, Mark, Shodja, Sogand, and Martin, David J., Computer system response time and psychophysiological stress II, *Proc. Human Factors Society —26th Annual Meeting*, (1982), 698–702.

Wickelgren, Wayne A., Speed-accuracy tradeoff and information processing dynamics, *Acta Psychologica 41*, (1977), 67–85.

Williams, C. M., System response time: A study of users' tolerance, IBM Advanced Systems Development Division Technical Report, 17–272, Yorktown Heights, NY, (July 1973).

Williams, J. D., The effects of computer subsystem response time and response time variance on operator performance in an interactive computer system, unpublished manuscript, Bell Telephone Laboratories, Memorandum 75–9131–3, Human Performance Technology Center, (1975).

Youmans, D. M., User requirements for future office workstations with emphasis on preferred response times, IBM United Kingdom Laboratories, Hursley Park, (September 1981).

Youmans, D. M., The effects of system response time on users of interactive computer systems, IBM United Kingdom Laboratories, Hursley Park, (January 1983).

CHAPTER 8

SYSTEM MESSAGES, SCREEN DESIGN, COLOR, AND WINDOWS

Words are sometimes sensitive instruments of precision with which delicate operations may be performed and swift, elusive truths may be touched.

Helen Merrell Lynd, *On Shame and the Search for Identity.*

8.1   INTRODUCTION

User experiences with computer system prompts, explanations, error diagnostics, and warnings play a critical role in influencing acceptance of software systems. The wording of messages is especially important in systems designed for novice users; experts also benefit from improved messages.

Another opportunity for design improvements is in the layout of information on a screen. Densely packed screens may overwhelm even knowledgeable users; but with only modest effort, screen formats can be substantially improved to reduce search time and increase subjective satisfaction. Large, rapid, multicolor, high resolution displays offer new possibilities and challenges for designers. Multiple windows become an attraction, but cluttered displays and numerous window commands are a distraction. Designers and users are developing strategies to make good use of these opportunities.

8.2   ERROR MESSAGES

Normal prompts, advisory messages, and system responses to commands may influence user perceptions, but the phrasing of error messages or diagnostic warnings is critical. Since errors occur because of lack of knowledge, incorrect understanding, or inadvertent slips, the user is likely to be confused, feel inadequate, and be anxious. Error messages with an imperious tone that condemns the user can heighten anxiety, making it more difficult to correct the error and increasing the chances of further errors. Messages that are too generic, such as WHAT? or SYNTAX   ERROR,   or   too   obscure,   such   as   FAC   RJCT 004004400400 or 0C7, offer little assistance to the novice user.

These concerns are especially important with respect to the novice user whose lack of knowledge and confidence amplify the stress-related feedback that can lead to a sequence of failures. The discouraging effects of a bad experience in using a computer are not easily overcome by a few good experiences. In some cases, systems are remembered more for what happens when things go wrong than when things go right. Although these effects are most prominent with novice computer users, experienced users also suffer. Experts in one system or part of a system are still novices in many situations.

Awareness of the difficulties that novice programmers encounter has prompted the development of some student-oriented language compilers that emphasize good diagnostic messages and even limited error correction. The early DITRAN effort (Moulton & Muller, 1967) and CORC (Conway & Maxwell, 1963) were followed by the WATFOR/WATFIV compilers (Cress, Dirksen, & Graham, 1970) and the PL/C compiler (Conway & Wilcox, 1973). These efforts demonstrate what can be accomplished if the developers are sincere about their concern for ease of use. PL/C and WATFIV are widely used in academic environments not only because of their diagnostic messages but also because of their rapid compilation speeds. These systems demonstrate that although there may be a greater development cost for good diagnostics, the production costs can be kept low. There is no published evidence that proves that students using these compilers learn faster, make fewer errors, or have a more positive attitude toward computers, but these hypotheses are shared by many people. Rigorous human factors studies would be useful in evaluating the improvement brought about by these systems and would be helpful in convincing skeptics about the importance of designing good system messages.

Producing a set of guidelines for writing system messages is not an easy task because of differences of opinion and the impossibility of being complete (Golden, 1980; Dwyer, 1981a, 1981b). Explicit guidelines may generate discussions and help less experienced designers produce better systems. Input parsing strategies, message generation techniques, and message phrasing can be changed without affecting system functionality. More attention to the impact of system messages on users might lead to instrumentation of systems to capture data on error frequency distributions. Such data would enable system designers and maintainers to revise error handling procedures, improve documentation and training manuals, alter instructional materials, or even change the programming or command language syntax. The complete set of messages should be reviewed by peers and managers, tested empirically, and included in user manuals.

Specificity, constructive guidance, positive tone, user-centered style, and appropriate physical format are recommended (see Section 8.2.1) as the bases for preparing system messages. These guidelines are especially important when the users are novices, but they can benefit experts as well. The phrasing and contents of system messages can significantly impact user performance and satisfaction.

8.2.1 Specificity

Messages that are too general make it difficult for the novice to know what has gone wrong. Simple and condemning messages such as SYNTAX ERROR or ILLEGAL ENTRY or INVALID DATA are frustrating because they do not provide enough information about what has gone wrong. Improved versions might be Unmatched left parenthesis, Type first letter: *Send*, *Read*, *File*, or *Drop*, or Days range from 1 to 31.

Even such widely appreciated systems as WATFIV have room for improvement. Messages such as INVALID TYPE OF ARGUMENT IN REFERENCE TO A SUBPROGRAM or WRONG NUMBER OF ARGUMENTS IN A REFERENCE TO A SUBPROGRAM might be improved if the name of the subprogram were included and the correct type or number of arguments were provided. The APL system that has many admirable features comes out poorly when evaluated for system messages. The extremely brief SIZE ERROR, RANK ERROR, or DOMAIN ERROR comments are too cryptic for novices and fail to provide information about which variables were involved. On the plus side, the standardization (most systems use the APL360 messages) of messages makes it easier for users to move from one system to another. Language standardization efforts should include standardization of at least the fundamental messages.

Execution time messages in programming languages should provide the user with specific information about where the problem arose, what variables were involved, and what values were improper. When division by zero occurs, some processors will terminate with a crude message, such as DOMAIN ERROR in APL, or SIZE ERROR in some COBOL compilers. PASCAL specifies "division by zero" but may not include the line number or variables that the PLUM compiler offers (Zelkowitz, 1976). Maintaining symbol table and line number information at execution time so that better messages can be generated is usually well worth the modest resource expenditure.

One hotel check-in system required the desk clerk to enter a 40 to 45 character string containing the name, room number, credit card information, and so on. If a data entry error was committed, the only message was INVALID INPUT. YOU MUST RETYPE THE ENTIRE RECORD. This led to frustration for users and delays for irritated guests. Interactive systems should be designed to minimize input errors by proper form fill-in strategies (see Chapter 3); and when an error occurs, the users should only have to repair the incorrect part.

Systems that offer an error code number leading to a paragraph-long explanation in a manual are also annoying because the manual may not be available or consulting it may be disruptive and time consuming. In most cases, system developers can no longer hide behind the claim that printing complete messages consumes too many system resources (Hahn & Athey, 1972; Heaps & Radhakrishnan, 1977).

8.2.2 Constructive guidance and positive tone

Rather than condemning novice users for what they have done wrong, messages should, where possible, indicate what they need to do to set things right. Messages such as DISASTROUS STRING OVERFLOW. JOB ABANDONED. (from a well-known compiler-compiler), UNDEFINED LABELS, or ILLEGAL STA. WRN. (both from a major manufacturer's FORTRAN compiler) can be replaced by more constructive phrases, such as String space consumed. Revise program to use shorter strings or expand string space; Define statement labels before use; or RETURN statement cannot be used in a FUNCTION subprogram.

Unnecessarily hostile messages using violent terminology can disturb nontechnical users. An interactive legal citation searching system uses this message: FATAL ERROR, RUN ABORTED. A popular operating system threatens many users with CATASTROPHIC ERROR; LOGGED WITH OPERATOR. There is no excuse for these hostile messages; they can easily be rewritten to provide more information about what happened and what must be done to set things right. Such negative tone words as ILLEGAL, ERROR, INVALID, or BAD should be eliminated or used infrequently.

It may be difficult for the software writer to create a code that accurately determines what the user's intention was, so the advice to be constructive is often difficult to apply. Some designers argue for automatic error correction, but the disadvantage is that the user may fail to learn proper syntax and become dependent on unpredictable alterations that the system makes. Another approach is to inform the user of the possible alternatives and let the user decide. A preferred strategy is to prevent errors from occurring (see Section 2.5).

8.2.3 User-centered phrasing

The term *user-centered* suggests that the user controls the system — initiating more than responding. This is partially accomplished by avoiding the negative and condemning tone in messages and by being courteous to the user. Prompting messages should avoid such imperative forms as ENTER DATA and focus on such user control as READY FOR COMMAND or simply READY.

Brevity is a virtue, but the user should be allowed to control the kind of information provided. Possibly, the standard system message should be less than one line; but by keying a "?" the user should be able to obtain a few lines of explanation. Two question marks might yield a set of examples, and three question marks might produce explanations of the examples and a complete description. CONFER from the University of Michigan and EIES from the New Jersey Institute of Technology are two teleconferencing systems that provide appealing assistance similar to this.

Many word processing systems offer a special HELP button to provide explanations when the user needs assistance.

The designers of the Library of Congress's SCORPIO system (Woody et al., 1977) for bibliographic retrieval understood the importance of making the users feel they are in control. In addition to using the properly subservient READY FOR NEXT COMMAND, the designers avoid the use of the words *error* or *invalid* in the text of system messages. Blame is never assigned to the user; instead, the system displays SCORPIO COULD NOT INTERPRET THE FOURTH PART OF THE COMMAND CONTENTS, WHICH IS SUPPOSED TO BE A 4–CHARACTER OPTION CODE. The message then goes on to define the proper format and present an example of its use.

The phone company, long used to dealing with nontechnical users, offers this tolerant message: "We're sorry, but we were unable to complete your call as dialed. Please hang up, check your number or consult the operator for assistance." They take the blame and offer constructive guidance for what to do. A thoughtless programmer might have generated: Illegal phone number. Call aborted. Error number 583–2R6.9. Consult your user manual for further information.

8.2.4 Appropriate physical format

Although professional programmers have learned to read upper-case-only text, most users prefer and find it easier to read upper- and lower-case messages (see Section 8.4 and Chapter 9). Upper-case-only messages should be reserved for serious conditions. Messages that begin with a lengthy and mysterious code number only serve to remind the user that the designers were insensitive to the user's real needs. If code numbers are needed at all, they might be enclosed in parentheses at the end of a message.

There is some disagreement about the placement of messages in a program display. One school of thought argues that the messages should be placed at the point in the program where the problem has arisen. The second opinion is that the messages clutter the program; also, it is easier for the compiler-writer to place them all at the end! This is a good subject for experimental study, but a reasonable strategy is to place messages in the program body, assuming that a blank line is left above and below the message to minimize interference with reading. Of course, certain messages must come at the end and execution-time messages must appear in the output display.

Some application systems ring a bell or sound a tone when an error has occurred. This can be useful if the operator could miss the error, but it is extremely embarrassing if other people are in the room and potentially annoying even if the operator is alone. The use of audio signals should be under the control of the operator.

The early high-level language MAD (Michigan Algorithmic Decoder) printed out a full-page picture of Alfred E. Neuman if there were syntactic errors in the program. Novices enjoyed this playful approach, but after they had accumulated a drawer full of pictures, the portrait became an annoying embarrassment. Highlighting errors with rows of asterisks is a common but questionable approach. Designers must walk a narrow path between calling attention to a problem and avoiding embarrassment to the operator. Considering the wide range of experience and temperament in users, maybe the best solution is to offer the user control over the alternatives—this coordinates with the user-centered principle.

8.2.5 Developing effective messages

The designer's intuition can be supplemented by simple, fast, and inexpensive design studies with actual users and several alternative messages. If the project goal is to serve novice users, then ample effort must be dedicated to designing, testing, and implementing the user interface. This commitment must extend to the earliest design stages so that programming language, command language, or menu selection approaches can be modified in a way that contributes to the production of specific error messages. Messages should be evaluated by several people and tested with suitable subjects (Isa et al., 1983). Messages should appear in user manuals and be given greater visibility. Records should be kept on the frequency of occurrence of each error. Frequent errors should lead to software modifications that provide better error handling, to improved training, and to revisions in user manuals.

Users may remember the one time when they had difficulties with a computer system rather than the twenty times when everything went well. The strong reaction to problems in using computer systems comes in part from the anxiety and lack of knowledge that novice users have. This reaction may be exacerbated by a poorly designed, excessively complex system; a poor manual or training experience; or from the hostile, vague, and irritating system messages they receive. Improving the messages will not turn a bad system into a good one, but it can play a significant role in improving the user's performance and attitude.

To explore the impact of error messages on users, we conducted five controlled experiments (Shneiderman, 1982). In one experiment, COBOL compiler syntactic error messages were modified, and undergraduate novice users were asked to repair the COBOL statement. Messages with increased specificity generated 28 percent better repair scores.

Subjects using a text editor with only a question mark for an error message made an average of 10.7 errors but only 6.1 errors when they switched to an editor offering brief explanatory messages. In another experiment, students corrected 4.1 out of 10 erroneous text editor commands using the standard system messages. Using improved messages, the experimental group could correct 7.5 out of the 10 commands.

In a study of the comprehensibility of job control language error messages from two popular contemporary systems, students scored 2.9 and 3.8 out of 6, while students receiving improved messages scored 4.8. Subjective preferences also favored the improved messages.

Mosteller (1981) studied error patterns in IBM's MVS Job Entry Control Language by capturing actual runs in a commercial environment. Analysis of the 2,073 errors resulted in specific suggestions for revisions to the error messages, parser, or command language. Remarkably, 513 of the errors were exact retries of the previous runs, confirming concerns over the persistence of errors when messages are poor. As improvements were made to the messages, Mosteller found evidence of lower error rates.

These initial experiments support the contentions that improving messages can upgrade performance and result in greater job satisfaction. They have led us to make the following recommendations for system developers (Table 8.1):

ERROR MESSAGE GUIDELINES

Product

- Be as specific and precise as possible
- Be constructive: indicate what needs to be done
- Use a positive tone: avoid condemnation
- Choose user-centered phrasing
- Consider multiple levels of messages
- Keep consistent grammatical form, terminology, and abbreviations
- Keep consistent visual format and placement

Process

- Establish a message quality control group
- Include messages in the design phase
- Place all messages in a file
- Review messages during development
- Attempt to eliminate the need for messages
- Carry out acceptance tests
- Collect frequency data for each message
- Review and revise messages over time

Table 8.1: Error message guidelines for the end product and the development process. These guidelines come from practical experience and some empirical data.

1. *Increase attention to message design*: The wording of messages displayed by a computer system should be more carefully considered. Technical writers or copy editors should be consulted about the choice of words and phrasing to improve both clarity and consistency.

2. *Establish quality control*: Messages should be approved by an appropriate quality control committee consisting of programmers, users, and human factors specialists. Changes or additions should be monitored and recorded.

3. *Develop guidelines*: Error messages should meet these criteria:

    *   have a positive tone, indicating what must be done, rather than condemning the user for the error. Reduce or eliminate the use of such terms as `ILLEGAL`, `INVALID`, `ERROR`, or `ILLEGAL PASSWORD`. Try: `Your password did not match the stored password.  Please try again.`

    *   be specific and address the problem in the user's terms. Avoid the vague `SYNTAX ERROR` or obscure internal codes. Use variable names and concepts known to the user. Instead of `INVALID DATA` in an inventory application, try: `Dress sizes range from 5 to 16.`

    *   place the users in control of the situation and provide them with enough information to take action. Instead of `INCORRECT COMMAND,` try: `Permissible commands are: SAVE, LOAD, or EXPLAIN.`

    *   have a neat, consistent, and comprehensible format. Avoid lengthy numeric codes, obscure mnemonics, and cluttered displays.

        Writing good messages, like writing poems, essays, or advertisements, requires experience, practice, and a sensitivity to how the reader will react. It is a skill that can be acquired and refined by programmers/designers who are intent on serving the user. However, perfection is impossible and humility is the mark of the true professional.

4. *Carry out acceptance test*: System messages should be subjected to an acceptance test with an appropriate user community to determine if they are comprehensible. The test could range from a rigorous experiment with realistic situations (for life-critical or high reliability systems) to an informal reading and review by interested users (for personal computing or low-threat applications).

    Complex interactive systems that involve thousands of users are never really complete until they are obsolete. Under these conditions, the most effective designs facilitate evolutionary refinement (see Chapter 10). If designers, maintainers, and operators of interactive systems are genuinely interested in building "user-friendly" systems, they must understand users' problems.

5. *Collect user performance data*: Frequency counts should be collected for each error condition on a regular basis. If possible, the user's command should be captured for a more detailed study. If you know where users run into difficulties, you can then revise the message, improve the training, modify the manual, or change the system. The error rate per thousand commands should be used as a metric of system quality and a gauge of how improvements affect performance. An error-counting option is useful for internal systems and can be a marketing feature for software products.

Improved messages will be of the greatest benefit to novice users, but regular users and experienced professionals will also profit. As examples of excellence proliferate, complex, obscure, and harsh systems will seem more and more out of place. The crude programming environments of the past will gradually be replaced by systems designed with the user in mind. Resistance to such a transition should not be allowed to impede progress toward the goal of serving the growing user community.

8.3 NONANTHROPOMORPHIC INSTRUCTIONS

There is a great temptation to have computers "talk" as if they were people. It is a primitive urge that designers often follow, and children and many adults accept without hesitation. Children accept humanlike references and qualities for almost any object from Humpty Dumpty to Tootle the Train. Adults reserve the anthropomorphic references for objects of special attraction, such as cars, ships, or computers.

Unfortunately, the words and phrases used in designing computer dialogs can make important differences in people's perceptions, emotional reactions, and motivations. Attributions of intelligence, independent activity, free will, or knowledge to computers can deceive, confuse, and mislead users. The suggestion that computers can think, know, or understand may give users an erroneous model of how computers work and what their capacities are. Ultimately, the deception becomes apparent and users may feel poorly treated.

A second reason for nonanthropomorphic phrasing stems from a personal belief that everyone benefits from a clear sense of how people are different from computers. Relationships with people are different from relationships with computers. Users learn to control computers, but they must respect the unique desires of individuals. Furthermore, users and designers must accept responsibility for misuse of computers rather than blaming the machine for errors.

A third motivation is that although an anthropomorphic machine may be attractive to some people, it can be anxiety-producing for others. A large proportion of the population expresses anxiety about using computers and believes that computers "make you feel dumb." Presenting the computer through the specific functions it offers may be a stronger stimulus to user acceptance than the fantasy that the computer is a friend, parent, or partner. As users become engaged, the computer becomes transparent and they can concentrate on their writing, problem-solving, or exploration.

Although children and some adults may be attracted by the anthropomorphized computer, they eventually prefer the sense of mastery, internal locus of control, competence, and accomplishment that can come from using a computer as a tool.

In an experimental test with twenty-six college students, the anthropomorphic design (HI THERE, JOHN! IT'S NICE TO MEET YOU, I SEE YOU ARE READY NOW) was seen as less honest than a mechanistic dialog (PRESS THE ENTER KEY TO BEGIN

SESSION) (Quintanar et al., 1982). In this computer-assisted instruction task, subjects took longer with the anthropomorphic design, possibly contributing to the observed improved scores on a quiz, but they felt less responsible for their performance.

In a study of thirty-six junior high school students conducted by Lori Gay and Diane Lindwarm under my direction, the style of interaction was varied. Students received a computer-assisted instruction session in one of three forms:

I: (HI! I AM THE COMPUTER. I AM GOING TO ASK YOU SOME QUESTIONS);

YOU: (YOU WILL BE ANSWERING SOME QUESTIONS. YOU SHOULD...); or

NEUTRAL: (THIS IS A MULTIPLE CHOICE EXERCISE.).

Before and after the three sessions at the computer, subjects were asked to describe whether using a computer was easy or hard. Most subjects thought using a computer was hard and did not change their opinion. Of the seven who changed their minds, the five who moved toward hard-to-use were all in the I or NEUTRAL groups. Both subjects who moved toward easy-to-use were in the YOU group. Performance measures on the tasks were not significantly different, but anecdotal evidence and the positive shift for YOU group members warrant further study.

Software designers and evaluators should be alert to phrasing and choice of words. The anthropomorphic computer that uses first-person pronouns may be counterproductive because it deceives, misleads, and confuses. It may seem cute on first encounter to be greeted by I AM SOPHIE, THE SOPHISTICATED TEACHER, AND I WILL TEACH YOU TO SPELL CORRECTLY; but by the second session, this approach feels uselessly repetitive; and by the third session, it is an exaggeration and an annoying distraction from the task.

The alternative for the software designer is to focus on the user and use third-person singular pronouns or to avoid pronouns altogether; for example:

POOR: I will begin the lesson when you press RETURN

BETTER: You can begin the lesson by pressing RETURN

BETTER: To begin the lesson, press RETURN

The YOU form seems preferable for introductory screens, but once the session is underway, a reduced number of pronouns avoids distractions from the task.

An alternative for children is to have a fantasy character such as a teddy bear or busy beaver as a guide through a lesson. A cartoon character can be drawn on the screen and possibily animated, adding visual appeal. Another approach is to identify the human author of a lesson or other software package and allow that person to speak to the reader, much as Carl Sagan or Jacob Bronowski speaks to the television viewer.

Similar arguments apply to the use of value judgments as reinforcement for correct answers. Our study with twenty-four third-grade students found that positive reinforcement with value judgment phrases (EXCELLENT, THAT'S GOOD!, YOU'RE DOING GREAT, etc.) did not improve performance or satisfaction in an arithmetic drill and practice lesson. On the other hand, the presence of a simple numerical counter (6 CORRECT 2 INCORRECT) improved learning.

A study of fifty-four users of a medical history-taking program indicated higher preference for moderate use of encouraging and "chatty" phrases (Spiliotopoulos & Shackel, 1981). A high level of these nonfunctional phrases led to increased scores for such terms as *boring* or *awkward*.

Male and female styles of wording for instructions were tested on male and female undergraduates with varying levels of computer experience (Fulton, 1985). Potency ratings of the computer varied with gender and experience. Further research is indicated to determine the acceptability and performance with differing wordings of instructions and feedback.

Instead of making the computer into a person, software designers may put their names on a title or credits page, just as authors do in a book. The credits are an acknowledgement for the work done, and they identify the people responsible for the contents if there are complaints. In software, there is the additional motivation of making it clear that people created the software and that the computer is merely the medium. Credits may encourage designers to work a bit harder since they know their names will appear.

8.4   SCREEN DESIGN

For most interactive systems, the screen displays are a key component to successful designs and the source of many lively arguments. Dense or cluttered displays can provoke anger, and inconsistent formats can inhibit performance. The complexity of this issue is suggested by the 162 guidelines for data display offered by Smith and Mosier (1984). This diligent effort (see Table 8.2 for some examples) is progress over the many useful but sometimes vague guidelines from earlier reviews (for example, Jones, 1978; Galitz, 1980; Pakin & Wray, 1982). Hopes for an expert system to perform screen layout seem dim because the demands of each task and user community are so varied and difficult to measure. Screen design will always have elements of art and require invention, but some principles are becoming clearer.

Designers should begin, as always, with a thorough knowledge of the users' tasks, free from the constraints of screen size, response time, or available fonts. Effective screen designs must provide all the necessary data in the proper sequence to carry out the task. To account for limited screen sizes, the displays can then be organized into pages. Meaningful groupings of items (with labels suitable to the user's knowledge), consistent sequences of groups, and orderly formats all support task performance. Groups can be surrounded by blank spaces or a marker, such as a box. Alternatively, related items can be indicated by highlighting, reverse video, color, or special fonts. Within a group, orderly formats can be accomplished by left or right justification, alignment on decimal points for numbers, or markers to decompose lengthy fields.

8.4.1 Field layout

Exporation with a variety of layouts can be a helpful process. The design alternatives on pages 328 and 329 should be developed directly on a display screen. An employee record with information about a spouse and children could be displayed crudely as:

At any step in a transaction sequence, ensure that whatever data a user needs will be available for display.

Display data to users in directly usable form; do not make users convert displayed data.

For any particular type of data display, maintain consistent format from one display to another.

Use short, simple sentences.

Use affirmative statements rather than negative statements.

Adopt some logical principle by which to order lists; where no other principle applies, order lists alphabetically.

Ensure that labels are sufficiently close to be associated with their data fields but are separated from their data fields by at least one space.

Left-justify columns of alphabetic data to permit rapid scanning.

In multipaged displays, label each page to show its relation to the others.

Begin every display with a title or header, describing briefly the contents or purpose of the display; leave at least one blank line between the title and the body of the display.

For size coding, a larger symbol should be at least 1.5 times the height of the next smaller symbol.

Consider color coding for applications in which users must rapidly distinguish among several categories of data, particularly when the data items are dispersed on the display.

When blink coding is used, the blink rate should be 2 to 5 Hz, with a minimum duty cycle (ON interval) of 50 percent.

For a large table that exceeds the capacity of one display frame, ensure that users can see column headings and row labels in all displayed sections of the table.

When data display requirements may change, which is often the case, provide some means for users (or a system administrator) to make necessary changes to display functions.

Table 8.2: Samples of the 162 data display guidelines from Smith and Mosier (1984).

```
TAYLOR,SUSAN034787331WILLIAM TAYLOR
THOMAS102974
ANN082177
ALEXANDRA090872
```

This record may contain the necessary information for a task, but extracting the information will be slow and error prone. As a first step at improving the format, blanks can separate fields:

```
TAYLOR, SUSAN  034787331      WILLIAM TAYLOR
THOMAS 102974
ANN 082177
ALEXANDRA 090872
```

The children's names can be listed in chronological order, with alignment of the dates. Familiar separators for the dates and the employee's social security number also aid recognition:

```
TAYLOR, SUSAN  034-78-7331      WILLIAM TAYLOR
ALEXANDRA 09-08-72
THOMAS    10-29-74
ANN       08-21-77
```

The reversed order of last name, first name for the employee may be desired to highlight the lexicographic ordering in a long file. However the first name, last name order for the spouse is usually more readable. Consistency seems important so a compromise might be made to produce:

```
SUSAN TAYLOR  034-78-7331      WILLIAM TAYLOR
ALEXANDRA 09-08-72
THOMAS    10-29-74
ANN       08-21-77
```

For frequent users, this format may be acceptable since labels have a cluttering effect; but for most users, labels will be helpful:

```
Employee: SUSAN TAYLOR  Social Security Number: 034-78-7331
Spouse: WILLIAM TAYLOR
```

```
Children:
Names       Birthdates
ALEXANDRA 09—08—72
THOMAS      10—29—74
ANN         08—21—77
```

Lower case has been used for labels, but the coding might be switched. The lengthy label for social security number might be abbreviated if the users are knowledgeable. Indenting the information about children might help convey the grouping of these repeating fields:

```
EMPLOYEE: Susan Taylor    SSN: 034—78—7331
SPOUSE: William Taylor
CHILDREN:
    NAMES        BIRTHDATES
    Alexandra 09—08—72
    Thomas       10—29—74
    Ann          08—21—77
```

Even in this simple example, the possibilities are numerous. In more realistic situations, a variety of designs should be explored. Further improvements could be made by using other coding strategies, such as highlighting, underscoring, color, and reverse video. An experienced graphic designer can be a great benefit. Pilot testing with actual users can yield subjective satisfaction scores and objective times to complete tasks plus error rates for a variety of proposed formats.

8.4.2 Empirical results

Empirical tests of alternative screen designs have been conducted in some cases. A narrative form (Figure 8.1a), taken from a telephone line testing program, was replaced with a structured form (Figure 8.1b) (Tullis, 1981). The structured form eliminated unnecessary information, grouped related information, and emphasized the information relevant to

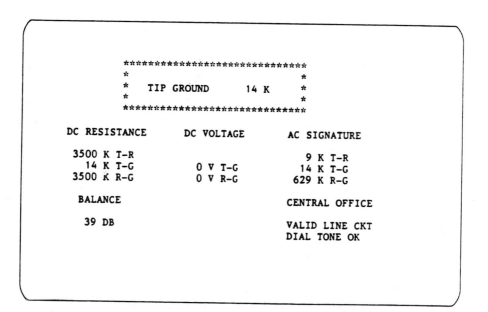

```
TEST RESULTS    SUMMARY: GROUND

GROUND, FAULT T-G
3 TERMINAL DC RESISTANCE
  >  3500.00 K OHMS T-R
  ■     14.21 K OHMS T-G
  >  3500.00 K OHMS R-G
3 TERMINAL DC VOLTAGE
  ■      0.00 VOLTS  T-G
  ■      0.00 VOLTS  R-G
VALID AC SIGNATURE
3 TERMINAL AC RESISTANCE
  ■      8.82 K OHMS T-R
  ■     14.17 K OHMS T-G
  ■    628.52 K OHMS R-G
LONGITUDINAL BALANCE POOR
  ■      39    DB
COULD NOT COUNT RINGERS DUE TO
  LOW RESISTANCE
VALID LINE CKT CONFIGURATION
CAN DRAW AND BREAK DIAL TONE
```

```
        ********************************
        *                              *
        *    TIP GROUND       14 K     *
        *                              *
        ********************************

DC RESISTANCE        DC VOLTAGE         AC SIGNATURE

3500 K T-R                                 9 K T-R
  14 K T-G           0 V T-G              14 K T-G
3500 K R-G           0 V R-G             629 K R-G

  BALANCE                                CENTRAL OFFICE

  39 DB                                  VALID LINE CKT
                                         DIAL TONE OK
```

Figure 8.1: Two versions of screens in Bell Labs study (Tullis, 1981). Version (a) was the narrative format and version (b) was the structured format.

the required tasks. After practice in reading these displays, Bell System employees were required to carry out typical tasks. The narrative form required an average of 8.3 seconds, whereas the structured form took only 5.0 seconds, resulting in an estimated saving of 79 person-years over the life of the system.

Central issues in displaying complex information are: How much information should be placed on a display and when are multiple displays preferred? If data fields can be grouped so that tasks can be accomplished using only one display, this approach seems preferable. Crowded screens are more difficult to scan, especially for novice users. In a NASA study of space shuttle displays, sparsely filled screens with approximately 70 percent blanks were searched in an average of 3.4 seconds (Figure 8.2), but more densely packed screens with approximately 30 percent blanks took an average of 5.0 seconds (Dodson & Shields, 1978). This study also demonstrated that functionally grouped displays yielded shorter search times.

Frequent expert users can deal with more dense screens and may prefer them because they are familiar with the format and they must initiate fewer operations. Stock market data, air traffic control, and airline reservation systems are examples of successful applications that have dense packing, limited labels, and highly coded fields.

8.4.3 Screen complexity metrics

Although a thorough knowledge of the users' tasks and abilities is the key to designing effective screen displays, an objective automatable metric of screen complexity is an attractive aid. After a thorough review of the literature, Tullis (1984) developed four metrics for alphanumeric screens:

1. Overall density: Number of filled character spaces as a percentage of total spaces available.
2. Local density: Average number of filled character spaces in a 5-degree visual angle around each character, expressed as

```
AEPI COMMANDS                    70 PERCENT DSPLY
1 EMERGENCY PARK=YES/NO          6 START=YES/NO
2 MOUNT CHECK=YES/NO             7 EDIT=YES/NO
3 SW CHECK=YES/NO                8 SELF DUMP=YES/NO
4 RUN=YES/NO            43:4     9 SW RELOAD=YES/NO
5 HALT=YES/NO                   10 CALIBRATE=YES/NO
                  126:26:48        XRAY=ON
FO SEQUENCE 11 1A-774:12:36      15 2C-445:35:43
            12 1B-785:48:50      16 03-451:19:42
63 XLG2     13 2A-930:15:28      17 04-287:23:51
            14 2B-300:56:41      18 05-515:21:20
08-288:28:26        432:48:56 DELAYED
19 FWO=73      23 FOCUS=15       27 TRACK=YES/NO
20 FW1=83      24 CAM HV=2       28 RAY=90
21 FW2=61      25 PCA HV=9       29 MPD DELAY 80
22 FOV=14      26 EXP TIME=1     30 RESET=703



WHAT IS THE TIME VALUE OF 1A >
```

```
CMDS
1 FAULT CK=YES/NO                5 SRT=YES/NO
2 VAL CK=YES/NO                  7 FC=YES/NO
3 START=YES/NO                   8 TEST SELF=YES/NO
4 CAL=YES/NO                     9 RESTART 1=YES/NO
5 STOP=YES/NO                   10 POWER=YES/NO

FO SEQ       11 1A-870:16:14    14 2B-801:41:48
             12 1B-411:21:23    15 2C-958:46:50
             13 2A-582:49:10    16 03-391:35:21
08 675:48:58
19 PAO=28        23 AMPER=12    27 SIGNL=YES/NO
20 PBO=40        24 HI VLT=2    28 FOV=7
21 PCO=26        25 LO VLT=4    29 MSG RELAY=61
                 26 HOLD OFF=1  30



WHAT IS THE VALUE OF ITEM 23 >
```

```
AEPI CMDS
1 BRKE ON=YES/NO
                             4 FUNC=YES/NG
                             5 HOLD=YES/NO
     2 SRT=YES/NO            6 EXIT=YES/NO
     3 FIL=YES/NO            7 UNPACK=YES/NO

          FO SEQ
                                      26:31
          12 2A-248:24:23
          13 2B-121:41:38
                                   TONE=21

     20 RV1=94    RAY FOC=31    23 PLT=YES/NO
     21 OPP=28                  24
     22 OPD=71                  25 ASK AGAIN=28



WHAT IS THE WORD BEFORE SEQ >
```

Figure 8.2: Three versions of screen layouts used in study of density by Dodson and Shields (1978). Version (a) is 70 percent characters, (b) is 50 percent, and (c) is 30 percent.

a percentage of available spaces in the circle and weighted by distance from the character.

3. Grouping: (1) Number of groups of "connected" characters, where a connection is any pair of characters separated by less than twice the mean of the distances between each character and its nearest neighbor; (2) Average visual angle subtended by groups (as defined above), weighted by number of characters in the group.

4. Layout complexity: The complexity, as defined in information theory, of the distribution of horizontal and vertical distances of each label and data item from a standard point on the display.

The argument for local density emerges from studies of visual perception indicating that concentration is focused in a 5-degree visual angle. At normal viewing distances from screens, this translates into a circle approximately 15 characters wide and 7 characters high. Lower local and overall densities should yield easier-to-read displays. The grouping metric was designed to yield an objective, automatable value that assesses the number of clusters of fields on a screen. Typically, clusters are formed by characters that are separated by no more than one intervening space horizontally and that are on adjacent lines. Layout complexity measures the variety of shapes that confront the user on a screen. Neat blocks of fields that start in the same column will have a lower layout complexity. These metrics do not account for coding techniques, upper versus lower case, continuous text, graphics, or multiscreen issues.

Ten Bell Laboratories employees did motel and airline information retrieval tasks on 520 different displays in a variety of formats (Figure 8.3). Performance times and subjective evaluations were collected. A multiple regression using the first three measures explained 48 percent of the variance (p < .01) in the performance times. Adding the layout complexity only marginally increased the explained variance. A multiple regression using all the measures explained 81 percent of the variance (p < .01) for the subjective ratings.

```
To: Atlanta, GA

    Departs    Arrives    Flight

Asheville, NC          First: $92.57    Coach: $66.85
    7:20a      8:05a      PI 299
   10:10a     10:55a      PI 203
    4:20p      5:00p      PI 259

Austin, TX             First: $263.00   Coach: $221.00
    8:15a     11:15a      EA 530
    8:40a     11:39a      DL 212
    2:00p      5:00p      DL 348
    7:15p     11:26p      DL 1654

Baltimore, MD          First: $209.00   Coach: $167.00
    7:00a      8:35a      DL 1767
    7:50a      9:32a      EA 631
    8:45a     10:20a      DL 1610
   11:15a     12:35p      EA 147
    1:35p      3:10p      DL 1731
    2:35p      4:16p      EA 141
```

```
To: Knoxville, TN
Atlanta, GA  Dp: 9:28a  Ar: 10:10a  Flt: DL 1704  1st: 97.00  Coach: 86.00
Atlanta, GA  Dp: 12:28p Ar: 1:10p  Flt: DL 152   1st: 97.00  Coach: 86.00
Atlanta, GA  Dp: 4:58p  Ar: 5:40p  Flt: DL 418   1st: 97.00  Coach: 86.00
Atlanta, GA  Dp: 7:41p  Ar: 8:25p  Flt: DL 1126  1st: 97.00  Coach: 86.00
Chicago, Ill. Dp: 1:45p Ar: 5:39p  Flt: AL 58    1st: 190.00 Coach: 161.00
Chicago, Ill. Dp: 6:30p Ar: 9:35p  Flt: DL 675   1st: 190.00 Coach: 161.00
Chicago, Ill. Dp: 6:50p Ar: 9:55p  Flt: RC 398   1st: 190.00 Coach: 161.00
Cincinnati, OH Dp: 12:05p Ar: 1:10p Flt: FW 453  1st: 118.00 Coach: 66.85
Cincinnati, OH Dp: 5:25p Ar: 6:30p Flt: FW 455   1st: 118.00 Coach: 66.85
Dallas, TX  Dp: 5:55p  Ar: 9:56p  Flt: AL 360   1st: 365.00 Coach: 215.00
Dayton, OH  Dp: 11:20a Ar: 1:10p  Flt: FW 453   1st: 189.00 Coach: 108.00
Dayton, OH  Dp: 4:40   Ar: 6:30p  Flt: FW 455   1st: 189.00 Coach: 108.00
Detroit, Mich. Dp: 9:10a Ar: 1:10p Flt: FW 453  1st: 183.00 Coach: 106.00
Detroit, Mich. Dp: 2:35p Ar: 6:30p Flt: FW 455  1st: 183.00 Coach: 106.00
```

Figure 8.3: Two versions of screens from the first experiment by Tullis (1984). Version (a) has a structured format that leads to superior performance and preference than version (b). The results led to predictive equations.

These strong results for the predictor equations were validated in a second study. Fourteen Bell Laboratories employees did author and book information retrieval tasks on 150 displays using 15 different display formats (Figure 8.4). Correlations between predicted and actual values were .80 for search times and .79 for subjective ratings.

```
Books

Author:        Aird, C
Author#:       33
Title:         Henrietta Who?
Price:         $5
Publisher:     Macmillan
#Pages:        253

Author:        Aird, C
Author#:       33
Title:         His Burial Too
Price:         $4
Publisher:     Macmillan
#Pages:        287

Author:        Aird, C
Author#:       33
Title:         Late Phoenix
Price:         $8
Publisher:     McGraw
#Pages:        362
```

```
Books

Silverberg,R    #112    Downward to the Earth    $8    McGraw     314p

Silverberg,R    #112    Dying Inside    $6    McGraw     284p

Silverberg,R    #112    Earth's Other Shadow    $4    Harper     295p

Silverberg,R    #112    Invaders from Earth    $3    McGraw     302p

Silverberg,R    #112    Lord Valentine's Castle    $12    Macmillan     354p

Silverberg,R    #112    Man in the Maze    $7    McGraw     322p

Springer, N     #204    Sable Moon    $3    Prentice     185p

Springer, N     #204    Silver Sun    $4    Norton     198p

Springer, N     #204    White Hart    $5    Prentice     215p

Stewart, M      #64     Crystal Cave    $11    McGraw     428p

Stewart, M      #64     Hollow Hills    $8    Macmillan     403p
```

Figure 8.4: Two versions of screens in the second experiment by Tullis (1984). Equations based on objective metrics accurately predicted performance and preference scores, indicating the superiority of version (a) over version (b).

This impressive result is encouraging, but unfortunately the metrics require a computer program to do the computations and they do not include coding techniques, user experience levels, or multiscreen considerations. Tullis is cautious in interpreting the results and emphasizes that displays that optimize search times do not necessarily optimize subjective ratings. Grouping of items led to fast performance, but high subjective ratings were linked to low local density and low layout complexity. A simple interpretation of these results might be that effective screen designs contain a middle number of groups (6 to 15) that are neatly laid out, surrounded by blanks, and similarly structured. This is a satisfying confirmation of a principle that, when stated, seems intuitively obvious but has not emerged explicitly in the numerous guidelines documents. Further study of human visual search strategies would be helpful in preparing design guidelines (Shields, 1980; Treisman, 1982).

8.4.4 Multiscreen design

Little is known about multiscreen design, but every guideline document implores the designer to preserve consistent location, structure, and terminology across screens. Supportive evidence for consistent location comes from a study of 40 inexperienced computer users of a menu system (Teitelbaum & Granda, 1983). The position of the title, page number, topic heading, instruction line, and entry area were varied across screens for half the subjects while the other half saw constant positions. Mean response time to questions about these items for subjects in the varying condition was 2.54 seconds and only 1.47 seconds for those seeing constant positions ($p < .001$).

Sequences of screens should be similar throughout the system for similar tasks, but exceptions will certainly occur. Within a sequence, users should be offered some sense of how far they have come and how far they have to go to reach the end. It should be possible to go backwards in a sequence to correct errors, review decisions, or try alternatives.

8.5 COLOR

Color displays are attractive to users and can often improve task performance, but the danger of misuse is high. Color can:

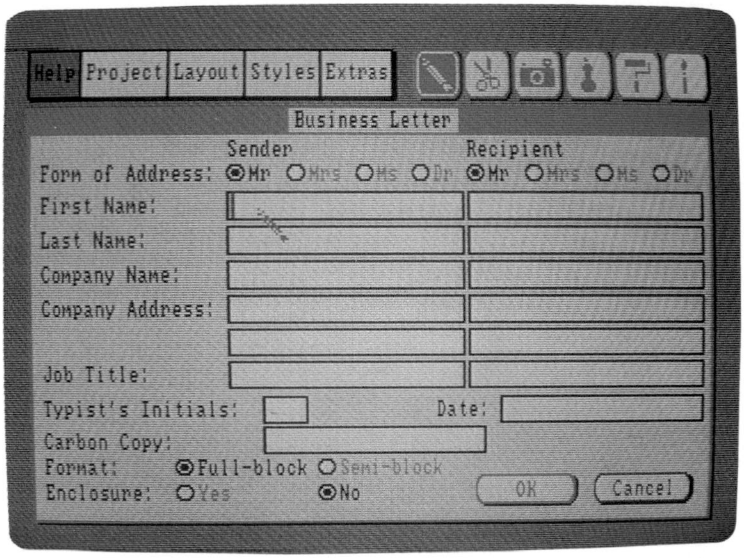

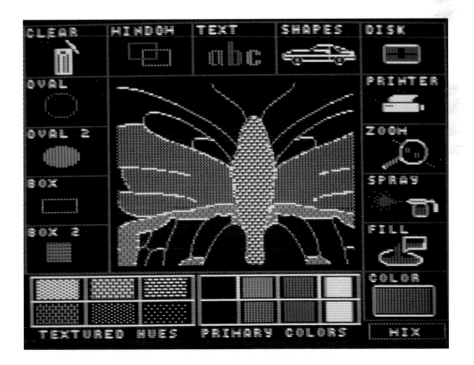

Color Plate 1: Subtle use of color can enliven a business form, indicate status, and help guide users to the necessary operations. (Copyright 1985–86 International Consumer Technologies Corp.)

Color Plate 2: Blazing Paddles, color graphics editing tool on the Apple II computers. (Courtesy of Baudville, Grand Rapids, MI)

Color Plate 3: The potential for computer art grows as higher resolution, better color, and improved graphics editors appears. (Copyright 1985 Island Graphics Corporation)

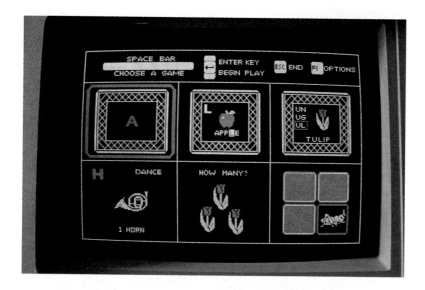

Color Plate 4: Color can add attraction and increase motivation for educational games. This educational game for 3- to 7-years olds uses color, graphics, animation, and sound to keep the users' attention. (Copyright © 1984 Paperback Software International, 2612 Eighth St., Berkeley, CA)

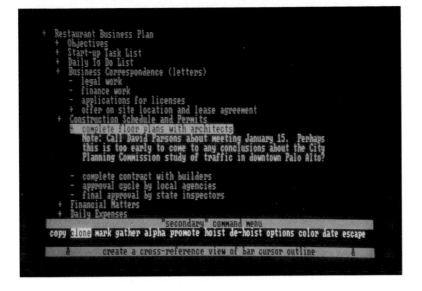

Color Plate 5: Color can be used to organize a text screen and draw attention to details. The light blue letters show the current focus of attention; other text is in green. The command menu is in white, and orange stripes contain additional guidance in ThinkTank for IBM PCs. This system was designed to operate on a monochrome display as well. (Courtesy Living Videotext, Inc., Mountain View, CA)

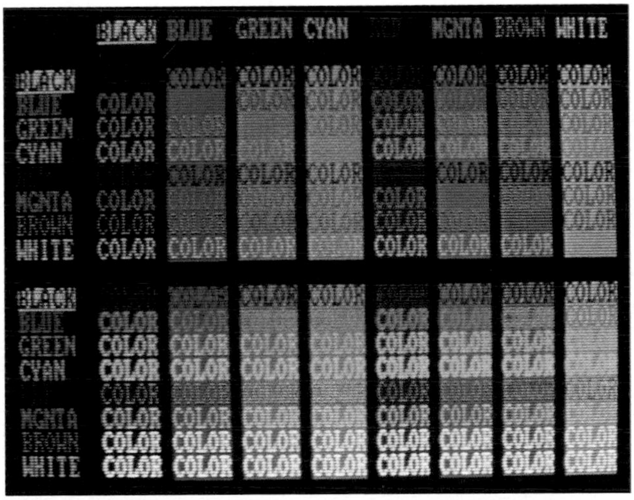

Color Plate 6: Some combinations of color text and background are easier to read than others. The dramatic color pairs can draw attention with phrases but may be difficult to read when used for full screen of text.

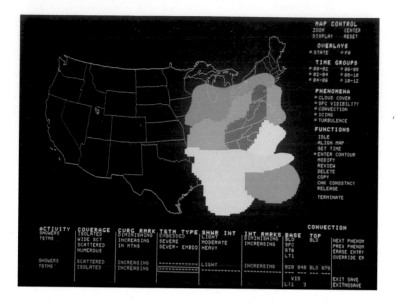

Color Plate 7: An engineering model of an interactive workstation used for entering weather forecasts graphically. (Courtesy of Jeff Mittelman, The MITRE Corporation, McLean, Virginia)

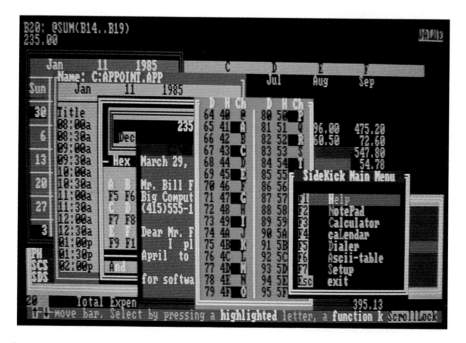

Color Plate 8: Multiple colors are used in Sidekick to show different pop-up windows with appointments, a calendar, notepads, a calculator, etc. (Photo courtesy of Borland International, Inc.)

- be soothing or striking to the eye
- add accents to an uninteresting display
- facilitate subtle discriminations in complex displays
- emphasize the logical organization of information
- draw attention to warnings
- evoke more emotional reactions of joy, excitement, fear, or anger.

The principles developed by graphic artists for using color in books, magazines, highway signs, and television are now being adapted for computer displays (Marcus, 1983, 1984). Programmers and interactive systems designers are quickly learning how to create effective computer displays and avoid the pitfalls (Robertson, 1980; Galitz, 1980; Durrett & Trezona, 1982; Weitzman, 1985; Brown, 1986) (Color plates 3 and 4).

There is no doubt that color makes videogames more attractive to users, conveys more information on power plant or process control diagrams, and is necessary for realistic images of people, scenery, or three dimensional objects (Foley & Van Dam 1982; Kron & Rosenfeld, 1983; Bobko, Bobko, & Davis, 1984). These applications require color. Greater controversy exists about the benefits of color for alphanumeric displays.

No simple set of rules governs use of color, but a number of guidelines can become the starting point for designers:

- Use color conservatively: Many programmers and novice designers are eager to use color to brighten up their displays, but the results are often counterproductive. One videotext system had the seven letters in its name in large letters, each with a different color. At a distance, the display appeared inviting and eye-catching; but up close, it was difficult to bring all the letters together to read the system name.

Instead of showing meaningful relationships, inappropriately colored fields mislead users into searching for relationships that don't exist. In one poorly designed screen, white lettering was used for input fields and for explanations of PF keys, leading users to think that they had to type the letters "PF3" or "PF9."

Using a different color for each of twelve items in a menu produces an overwhelming effect. Using four colors, such as red, blue, green and yellow, for the twelve items will still mislead users into thinking that all the similarly colored items are related. An appropriate strategy would be to show all the menu items in one color, the title in a second color, the instructions in a third color, and error messages in a fourth color. Even this strategy can be overwhelming if the colors are too striking visually.

Some suggested guidelines for using color are:

- Limit the number of colors: Many design guides suggest limiting the number of colors in a single alphanumeric display to four, with a limit of seven colors in the entire sequence of screens. Experienced users may be able to benefit from a larger number of color codes.

- Recognize the power of color as a coding technique: Color speeds recognition for many tasks, but it can inhibit performance of tasks that go against the grain of the coding scheme. For example, in an accounting application, if data lines with accounts overdue more than thirty days are coded in red, they will be readily visible among the nonoverdue accounts coded in green. In air traffic control, high flying planes might be coded differently from low flying planes to facilitate recognition. In programming workstations, newly added programming language statements might be coded differently from the old statements, to show progress in writing or maintaining programs.

- Color coding should support the task: If in the accounting application with color coding by days overdue, the task is now to locate accounts with balances of more than $55, the coding by days overdue may inhibit performance on the second task. In the programming application, the coding of recent additions may make it more difficult to read the entire program. Designers should attempt to make a close linkage between the users' tasks and the color coding.

- Color coding should appear with minimal user effort: In general, the color coding should not have to be assigned by the users each time they perform a task but should appear because they initiate the program to check for accounts overdue by more than 30 days. When the users perform the task of locating accounts with balances of more than $55, the new color coding should appear automatically.

- Color coding is under user control: When appropriate, the users should be able to turn off the color coding. For example, if a spelling checker color codes possibly misspelled words in red, then the user should be able to accept the spelling and turn off the coding. The presence of the highly visible red coding is a distraction from reading the text for comprehension.

- Design for monochrome first: The primary goal of a screen designer should be to lay out the contents in a logical pattern. Related fields can be shown by contiguity or by similar structural patterns; for example, successive employee records may have the same indentation pattern. Related fields can also be grouped by drawing a box around the group. Unrelated fields can be kept separate by blank space —at least one blank line vertically or three blank characters horizontally. Monochrome displays should be seriously considered as the primary format because approximately 8 percent of males in European and North American communities have some form of color blindess. It may be advantageous to design for monochrome because color displays may not be universally available. Monochrome designs may increase the consumer audience of a product or permit operation when a color monitor fails.

- Color can help in formatting: In densely packed displays where screen space is at a premium, similar colors can be used to group related items (Color plate 5). For example, in a police dispatcher's tabular display of assignments, the police cars on emergency calls might be coded in red and the police cars on routine calls might be coded in green. Then, when a new emergency arises, it will be relatively easy to identify the cars on routine calls and assign one to the emergency. Dissimilar colors can be used to distinguish physically close but logically distinct fields. In a block-structured programming language, the nesting levels could be shown by coding the statements in a progression of colors, for example, dark green, light green, yellow, light orange, dark orange, red, and so on.

- Be consistent in color coding: Use the same color coding rules throughout the system. If error messages are in red, then make sure that every error message appears in red; a change to yellow may be interpreted as a change in importance of the message. If colors are used differently by several designers of the same system, then users will hesitate as they attempt to assign meaning to the color changes. A set of color coding standards should be written down for the benefit of every designer.

- Be alert to common expectations about color codes: The designer needs to speak to operators to determine what color codes are applied in the task domain. From automobile driving experience, red is commonly considered to indicate stop or danger, yellow is a warning, and green is go. In investment circles, red is a financial loss and black is a gain. For chemical engineers, red is hot and blue is cold. For mapmakers, blue means water, green means forests, and yellow means deserts. These multiple conventions can cause problems for designers. A designer might consider using red to signal that an engine is warmed up and ready, but a user might understand the red coding as an indication of danger. A red light is often used to indicate power on for electrical equipment, but some users are made anxious by this decision since red has a strong association with danger or stopping. When appropriate, put the color code interpretations on the screen or in a help panel.

- Be alert to problems with color pairings: If saturated (pure) red and blue appear on a screen at the same time, it may be difficult for users to absorb the information. Red and blue are on the opposite ends of the spectrum, and the muscles surrounding the human eye will be strained by attempts to produce a sharp focus for both colors simultaneously. The blue will appear to recede and the red will appear to come forward. Blue text on a red background would be an especially difficult challenge for users. Similarly, other combinations will appear to be garish and difficult to read —for example, yellow on purple, magenta on green. Too little contrast is also a problem. Imagine yellow letters on a white background or brown letters on a black background. On each color monitor, the color appears differently, and careful tests with various text and background colors is necessary. Pace (1984) tested twenty-four color combinations on an Amdek monitor connected to an IBM PC, using thirty-six undergraduate subjects. He found errors rates ranged from approximately one to four errors per thousand characters read. Black on blue and blue on white were two colors with low error rates in both tasks, and magenta on green and green on white were two colors with high error rates. Tests with other monitors and tasks are necessary to reach a general conclusion about the most effective color pairs (Color plate 6).

- Use color changes to indicate status changes: If an automobile speedometer had a digital readout of the driving speed, it might be helpful to change from green numbers below the speed limit to red above the speed limit to act as a warning. Similarly, in an oil refinery, pressure indicators might change color as the value went above or below acceptable limits. In this way, color acts as an attention-getting method. This is potentially very valuable when there are hundreds of values continuously displayed.

- Use color in graphic displays for greater information density: In graphs with multiple plots, color can be helpful in showing which line segments form the full graph. The usual strategies for differentiating lines in black on white graphs, such as dotted lines, thicker lines, and dashed lines, are not as effective as using separate colors for each line. Architectural plans benefit from color coding of electrical, phone, hot water, cold water, and natural gas lines. Similarly, mapmakers can have greater information density when color coding is used (Color plate 7).

• Beware of the loss of resolution with color displays: Many color displays have poorer resolution than do monochrome displays. The benefits of color coding must be weighed against the loss of resolution. Color displays may also be more costly, heavier, less reliable, hotter, and larger than monochrome displays.

Christ (1975) reports on forty-one studies of the benefits of color, but few of these studies were conducted on CRTs. Tullis (1981, see Section 8.4.2) describes an experiment that used color in one of four versions of a CRT display. The color graphics display did not yield significantly improved performance, but user reactions were positive: "Color highlights important parts. High speed and very clear," and "Color adds to what might otherwise be a boring task."

In summary, with color display quality increasing and cost decreasing, designers are tempted to use color in system designs. There are undoubtedly benefits of increased user satisfaction and often increased performance; however, there are real dangers in misusing color. Care should be taken to make appropriate designs and conduct thorough evaluations.

8.6   WINDOW DESIGNS

With some exceptions, early computer systems depended on line printers or teletype printers for user interfaces. Output was seen as a linear sequence of printed pages or lines. As display screens became the more common peripheral device, designers more frequently applied highlighting and two-dimensional interactions. Sections of the screen were devoted to such specific fields as a title, error messages, instructions, online help, or data blocks. It is hard to trace the first explicit description of windows, but many designers discovered that meaningful groups of information could be assigned to specific windows. The next steps were to have independent windows in which separate processes could be executed and to permit windows to overlap. The Xerox Star (see Figure 5.8) and later the Apple Lisa and Macintosh (see Figure 3.2) brought the concept of overlapping windows to widespread popularity.

On small screens with poor resolution, the opportunities for using multiple overlapped windows are limited. With higher resolution screens and careful design, multiple windows can become practical (Figure 8.5). The window borders can consume a substantial fraction of the screen, and small windows on large fields of information lead to annoying horizontal

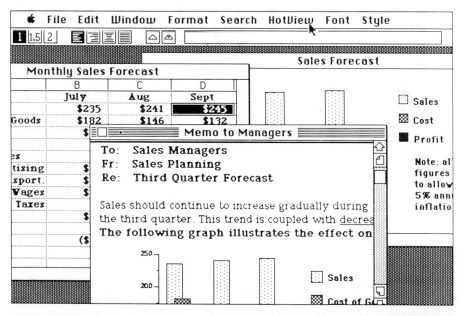

Figure 8.5: Several windows can provide useful information; with careful design, they can be made readable on a small display. On this Jazz Desktop, several documents can be viewed simultaneously. (Courtesy of © Lotus Development Corporation 1985. Used with permission.)

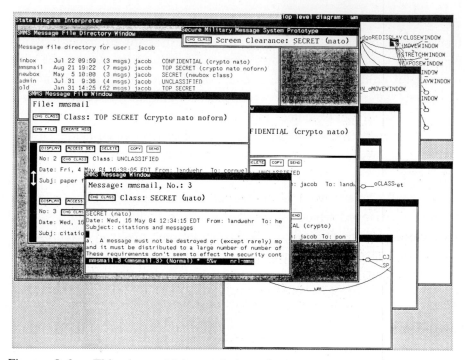

Figure 8.6a: This large high resolution display shows multiple windows containing a mock-up of a military messaging system. The security classifications shown are simulated for demonstration purposes. (Courtesy of Robert J. K. Jacob, Naval Research Laboratory, Washington, DC)

and vertical scrolling. On larger, high resolution screens (Figure 8.6), windows become more attractive, but the manipulation of windows can be a distraction from the user's task. Opening windows, moving them around, changing their size, or closing them are the most common operations supported (Card et al., 1984; Weiser, 1985). The visual nature of window use has led many designers to apply a direct manipulation strategy (see Chapter 5) to window actions. Instead of typing a command to stretch, move, and scroll a window, users can point at appropriate icons on the window border and simply click down on the mouse button.

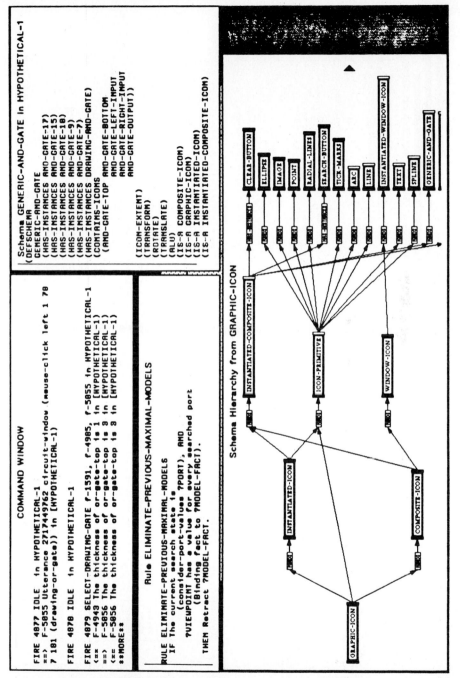

Figure 8.6b: A Symbolics 3600 supports the Automated Reasoning Tool (ART, from Inference Corporation, Los Angeles, CA). This display shows the root menu of commands, a portion of the fact database, a command window with the command history, and a large window with the viewpoint lattice.

345

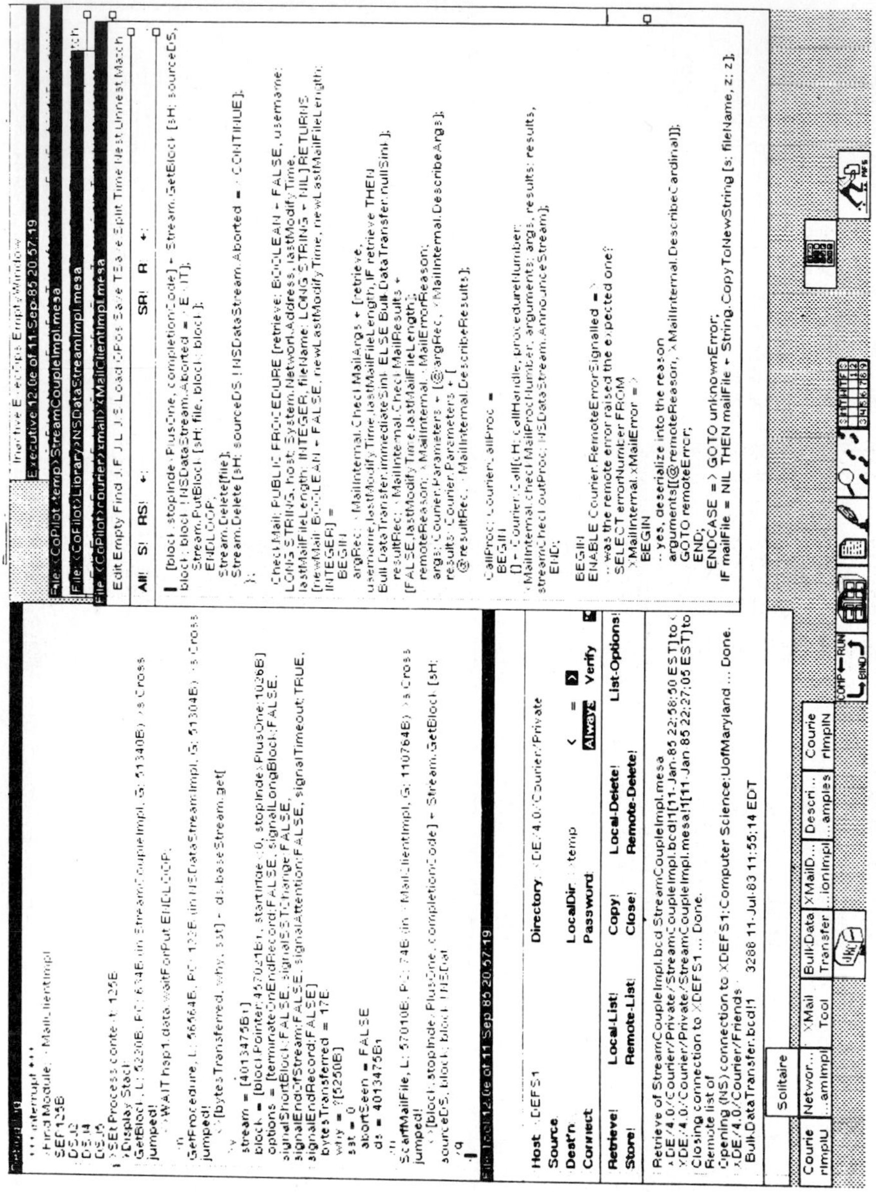

Figure 8.6c: A debugging session for the Mesa language using the Xerox Development Environment running on a Xerox Dandelion workstation. The Debug.log window has commands to open files, display variable values, show local and global variables, and show control positions in files. Files contain source code for modules. (Prepared by Jack Callahan, University of Maryland)

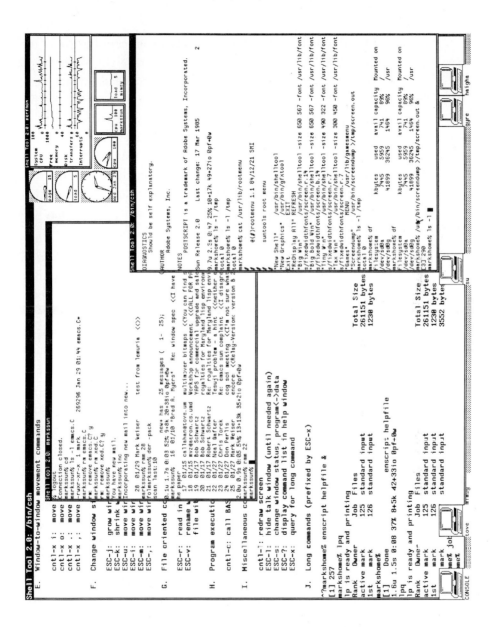

Figure 8.6d: Working session showing online help, electronic mail, and text editing on a Sun workstation. (Prepared by Mark Weiser, University of Maryland)

The extra effort of manipulating windows can distract users from the task they are accomplishing. In an empirical test with eight experienced users, the windowed environment of a system produced longer task completion times than the nonwindowed environment (Bury et al., 1985). The multiple smaller windows led to more time arranging information on the screen and more scrolling activity to bring necessary information into view. However, after eliminating the time to arrange the screen, the task solution times were lower for the windowed environment. Fewer errors were made in the windowed environment. These results suggest that there are advantages to using windows, but these advantages may be compromised unless automatic window arrangement is provided.

Windows can be advantageous if independent tasks are being carried out. For example, in the middle of using a word processor, the user decides to send a piece of electronic mail or consult a personal schedule. The user can pop-up a new window, take care of the task, and return to the main task without losing context or restarting the work. The Sidekick program from Borland, and its imitators, provide a variety of personal services in a rapid and convenient manner (Color plate 8).

The manipulation of windows is an activity related to the computer domain and not directly related to the user's task. An advantage may be gained by developing coordinated windows, in which windows appear, change contents, and disappear as an indirect result of user activity in the task domain (Norman et al., 1985; Shneiderman et al., 1985). For example, in medical insurance claims processing, when the agent retrieves information about a client, such fields as the address, phone numbers, and membership numbers should appear on the screen. Simultaneously, and with no additional effort, the medical history might appear in a second window and the record of previous claims could appear in a third window. A fourth window might contain a form for the agent to complete to indicate payment or exceptions. Scrolling the medical history screen might produce a synchronized scroll of the previous claims window to show related information.

Another application of coordinated windows is hierarchical browsing (Figure 8.7). If one window contains the table of contents of a document or a list of program modules, selection of an item by a pointing device should lead to display, in an adjoining window, of the chapter or module

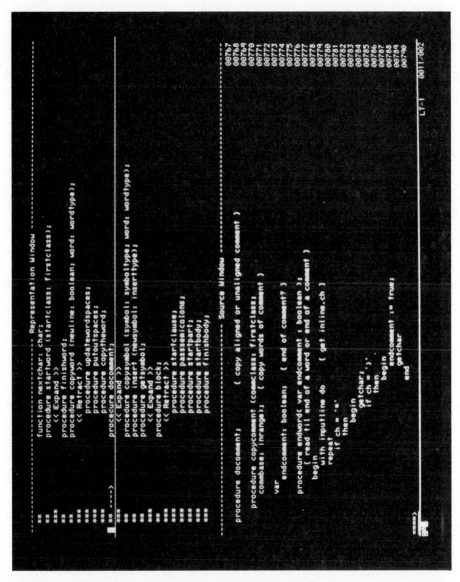

Figure 8.7a: The cursor in the upper Representation Window points at procedure docomment. A function key has been pressed to produce the text of the procedure docomment in the lower Source Window. The <<Expand>> markers in the Representation Window indicate that lower levels of the program can be seen if the marker is selected. The <<Retract>> marker can be selected to eliminate the lower level of procedures. (Courtesy of Digitalk, Inc., Los Angeles, CA)

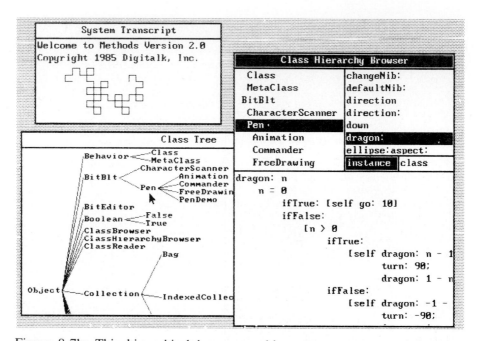

Figure 8.7b: This hierarchical browser enables users to see several levels of indexes and detailed descriptions. Moving the reverse video bar to dragon, in the alphabetically-organized list, produces the associated dragon program. The Class Tree gives a two-dimensional view of the organization of objects. (Used with permission of Digitalk, Inc., Los Angeles, CA)

contents. A third application might be direct selection, in which pointing at a word in the text or a variable name in a program produces a window with the word definition or the variable declaration.

Windows provide visually appealing possibilities and intriguing opportunities for designers, but the advantages and disadvantages of design features are still poorly understood.

8.7 PRACTITIONER'S SUMMARY

The wording of system messages may have an impact on performance and attitudes of users, especially novices whose anxiety and lack of knowledge put them at a disadvantage. Improvements might be made by merely using more specific diagnostic messages, offering constructive guidance rather than focusing on failures, employing user-centered phrasing, choosing a suitable physical format, and avoiding vague terminology or numeric codes.

When giving instructions, focus on the user and the user's tasks. Avoid anthropomorphic phrasing and use the YOU form to guide the novice user. Avoid judging the user. Simple statements of the status are more succinct and usually more effective.

Pay careful attention to screen design, and develop a local set of guidelines for all designers. Use spacing, indentation, columnar formats, and field labels to organize the screen for users. Color can improve some screens and lead to more rapid task performance with higher satisfaction; but improper use of color can mislead users.

Multiple window displays can be helpful for some tasks, but the additional effort of opening, moving, sizing, and deleting windows can be time consuming and distracting from the user's task. Attempt to make window use automatic and provide coordinated windows where possible.

Organizations can benefit by careful study of screen design guidelines documents and the creation of their own set of guidelines tailored to local needs. This should also include a list of local terminology and abbreviations. Consistency and thorough testing are critical.

8.8   RESEARCHER'S AGENDA

Experimental testing could refine the proposed error message guidelines and identify the source of user anxiety or confusion. Message placement, highlighting techniques, and multiple level message strategies are candidates for exploration. Improved parsing strategies to provide better messages automatically would be useful.

There is a great need for testing to validate screen, color, and window design concepts. Basic understanding and cognitive models of visual perception of screen displays would be a dramatic contribution. Do users follow a scanning pattern from the top left? Does color coding reorganize the pattern of scanning? Can users deal easily with rapid shifts among multiple windows? Is a rapid scrolling non-windowed environment better than a windowed environment? Can automatic placement, sizing, and deletion of windows be accomplished?

Performance and preference data for multiple tasks and user communities would help make the case for improved screen, color, and window design. Such studies would be likely to yield clues to improved strategies.

REFERENCES

Bobko, P., Bobko, D. J., and Davis, M. A., A multidimensional scaling of video games, *Human Factors 26*, (1984), 477–482.

Brown, C. Marlin, *Human-Computer Interface Design Guidelines*, Ablex Publishing Co., Norwood, NJ, (1986).

Bury, Kevin F., Davies, Susan E., and Darnell, Michael J., Window management: A review of issues and some results from user testing, IBM Human Factors Center Report HFC–53, San Jose, CA, (June 1985), 36 pages.

Card, Stuart K., Pavel, M., and Farrell, J. E., Window-based computer dialogues, *INTERACT '84, First IFIP Conference on Human-Computer Interaction*, London, (September 1984), 355–359.

Christ, R. E., Review and analysis of color coding research for visual displays, *Human Factors 17*, (1975), 542–570.

Conway, R. W., and Maxwell, W. L., CORC the Cornell computing language. *Communications of the ACM 6*, 6, (1963), 317–324.

Conway, R. W., and Wilcox, T. R., Design and Implementation of a Diagnostic Compiler for PL/I. *Communications of the ACM 16*, 3, (1973), 169–179.

Cress, P., Dirksen, P, and Graham, J. W., *FORTRAN IV with WATFOR and WATFIV*, Prentice-Hall, Inc., Englewood Cliffs, NJ (1970).

Dean, M., How a computer should talk to people, *IBM Systems Journal 21*, 4, (1982), 424–453.

Dodson, D. W., and Shields, N. L., Jr., Development of user guidelines for ECAS display design, Vol. 1, Report No. NASA-CR–150877, Huntsville, AL, Essex Corp., (1978).

Durrett, John, and Trezona, Judi, How to use color displays effectively, *BYTE*, (April 1982), 50–53.

Dwyer, B., Programming for users: A bit of psychology. *Computers and People 30*, Nos.1 and 2, (1981a), 11–14, 26.

Dwyer, B., A user friendly algorithm, *Communications of the ACM 24*, 9, (September 1981b), 556–561.

Foley, James, and Van Dam, Andries, *Fundamentals of Interactive Computer Graphics*, Addison-Wesley Publishing Co., Reading, MA, (1982), 664 pages.

Fulton, Margaret A., A research model for studying the gender/power aspects of human-computer interaction, *International Journal of Man-Machine Studies 23*, (1985), 369–382.

Galitz, Wilbert O., *Screen Format Designers Handbook*, CNA, Chicago, (1978).

Galitz, Wilbert O., *Human Factors in Office Automation* Life Office Management Assn., Atlanta, (1980), 237 pages.

Golden, D., A plea for friendly software. *Software Engineering Notes 5*, No.4, (1980).

Hahn, K. W., and Athey, J. G., Diagnostic messages, *Software—Practice and Experience 2*, (1972), 347–352.

Heaps, H. S., and Radhakrishnan, T., Compaction of diagnostic messages for compilers. *Software—Practice and Experience 7*, (1977), 139–144.

Isa, Barbara S., Boyle, James M., Neal, Alan S., and Simons, Roger M., A methodology for objectively evaluating error messages, *Proc. ACM SIGCHI '83 Human Factors in Computing Systems*, (1983), 68–71.

Jones, P. F., Four principles of man-computer dialog, *IEEE Transactions on Professional Communication PC–21*, 4, (December 1978), 154–159.

Kron, Hildegard, and Rosenfeld, Edward, *Computer Images: State of the Art*, Stewart, Tabori & Chang Publishers, New York, (1983), 200 pages.

Marcus, Aaron, Graphic design for computer graphics, *IEEE Computer Graphics and Applications*, (July 1983), 63–70.

Marcus, Aaron, Corporate identity for iconic interface design: The graphic design perspective, *IEEE Computer Graphics and Applications*, (December 1984), 24–32.

Mosteller, W., Job entry control language errors, *Proceedings of SHARE 57*, SHARE, Inc., Chicago, IL, (1981), 149–155.

Moulton, P. G., and Muller, M. E., DITRAN—a compiler emphasizing diagnostics, *Communications of the ACM 10*, (1967), 45–52.

Norman, Kent L., Weldon, Linda J., and Shneiderman, Ben, Cognitive representation of windows and multiple screen layouts of computer interfaces, *International Journal of Man-Machine Studies*, (to appear, 1986).

Pace, Bruce J., Color combinations and contrast reversals on visual display units, *Proceedings of the Human Factors Society 28th Annual Meeting*, Human Factors Society, Santa Monica, CA, (1984), 326–330.

Pakin, S. E., and Wray, P., Designing screens for people to use easily, *Data Management*, (July 1982), 36–41.

Quintanar, Leo R., Crowell, Charles R., and Pryor, John B., Human-computer interaction: A preliminary social psychological analysis, *Behavior Research Methods & Instrumentation 14*, 2, (1982), 210–220.

Robertson, P. J., A guide to using color on alphanumeric displays, IBM Technical Report G320–6296, IBM White Plains, NY, (1980).

Shields, Nicholas, Jr., Spacelab display design and command usage guidelines, NASA Report MSFC-PROC–711A, Huntsville, AL, (April 1980).

Shneiderman, Ben, System message design: Guidelines and experimental results, In Badre, A., and Shneiderman, B. (Editors), *Directions in Human/Computer Interaction*, Ablex Publishers, Norwood, NJ, (1982), 55–78.

Shneiderman, Ben, Shafer, Phil, Simon, Roland, and Weldon, Linda, Display strategies for program browsing, *Proc. IEEE Conference on Software Maintenance*, Silver Spring, MD, (1985).

Smith, Sidney L., and Mosier, Jane N., Design guidelines for user-system interface software, Report ESD-TR–84–190, The Mitre

Corp., Bedford, MA, (September 1984), 448 pages.

Spiliotopoulos, V. and Schackel, B., Towards a computer interview acceptable to the naive user, *International Journal of Man-Machine Studies 14*, (1981), 77–90.

Teitelbaum, Richard C., and Granda, Richard F., The effects of positional constancy on searching menus for information, *Proc. ACM CHI '83 Human Factors in Computing Systems*, ACM, Baltimore, MD, (1983), 150–153.

Treisman, Anne, Perceptual grouping and attention in visual search for features and for objects, *Journal of Experimental Psychology: Human Perception and Performance 8*, 2, (1982), 194–214.

Tullis, T. S., An evaluation of alphanumeric, graphic and color information displays, *Human Factors 23*, (1981), 541–550.

Tullis, T. S., Predicting the usability of alphanumeric displays, Ph.D. dissertation, Available from The Report Store, Lawrence, KS, (1984), 172 pages.

Weiser, Mark, CWSH: The windowing shell of the Maryland window system, *Software: Practice and Experience*, (May 1985), 515–519.

Weitzman, Donald O., Color coding re-viewed, *Proc. Human Factors Society—29th Annual Meeting*, Santa Monica, CA, (1985), 1079–1083.

Woody, C. A., Fitzgerald, M. P., Scott, F. J., and Power, D. L., A Subject-Content-Retriever-for-Processing-Information-On-Line (SCORPIO). *AFIPS Conference Proceedings 46*, (1977).

Zelkowitz, M. V., *PL/1 Programming with PLUM*, Paladin House, Geneva, IL., (1976).

© CAROL WN

CHAPTER 9

PRINTED MANUALS, ONLINE HELP, AND TUTORIALS

What is really important in education is...that the mind is matured, that energy is aroused.

Sören Kierkegaard, *Either/Or*, Volume II.

9.1 INTRODUCTION

All users of interactive computer systems require some training. Many users can learn from another person who knows the system, but training materials are often necessary. Traditional printed manuals are sometimes poorly written, but this medium can be very effective if properly prepared (Price, 1984). Many designers are enticed by the notion of online help facilities and tutorials that use the same interactive system to provide training and reminders about specific features and syntax.

Learning anything new is a challenge. Although the challenge is usually joyous and satisfying, when it comes to learning about computer systems many people experience anxiety, frustration, and disappointment. Much of the difficulty flows directly from the poor design of the commands, menus, display formats, or prompts that lead to error conditions or simply from the inability of the user to know what to do next.

Even though increasing attention is being paid to improving the user interface design, there will always be a need for supplemental materials that aid the user. These materials include:

1. Traditional user manual: a paper document that describes the features of the system. Many variations on this theme include:

    a. alphabetic listing and description of the commands

    b. quick reference card with a concise presentation of the syntax

    c. novice user introduction or tutorial

    d. conversion manual that teaches the features of the current system to users who are knowledgeable about some other system.

2. Computer-based material, such as the:

    a. online user manual—an electronic version of the traditional user manual. The simple conversion to electronic form may make the text more readily available but more difficult to read and absorb.

    b.   online help facility—the most common form of online help is the hierarchical presentation of keywords in the command language, akin to the index of a traditional manual. The user selects or types in a keyword and is presented with one or more screens of text about the command.

    c.   online tutorial—this potentially appealing and innovative approach uses the electronic medium to teach the novice user by showing simulations of the working system, by attractive animations, and by interactive sessions that engage the user.

Other forms of instruction or information acquisition include classroom instruction, personal training and assistance, telephone consultation, videotapes, instructional films, and audio tapes (Francas et al., 1982). These forms are not discussed here, but many of the same instructional design principles apply.

9.2. PAPER VERSUS SCREENS: A COMPARISON

The technology of printing text on paper has been evolving for more than 500 years. The paper surface and color, font design, character width, letter sharpness, text contrast with the paper, width of the text column, size of margins, spacing between lines, and even room lighting have all been explored to produce the most appealing and readable format.

In the last 30 years, the cathode ray tube (CRT), often called the visual display unit or tube (VDU or VDT), has emerged as an alternate medium for presenting text, but researchers have only begun the long process of optimization (Cakir et al., 1980; Shurtleff, 1980; Grandjean & Vigliani, 1982; Helander et al., 1984) to meet user needs. Serious concerns about radiation or other health hazards have lessened as manufacturers, labor unions, and government agencies have applied major efforts in this area. The widespread reports about visual fatigue have been confirmed, but this condition disappears with proper rest. But even before users are aware of visual fatigue, their capacity to work with CRTs is below their capacity to work with printed materials.

Hansen et al. (1978) found that seven students who were asked to take examinations on paper and on PLATO terminals took almost twice as long online. Much of the increased time could be attributed to system delays, poor software design, and slower output rates, but 37 percent of the longer time on PLATO could not be accounted for. Hansen et al. conjecture that the 37 percent of additional time might be attributed to uncertainty about how to control the medium, what the system will do, and what the system has done.

Wright and Lickorish (1983) studied proofreading of 134-line texts that contained 39 typographical errors, spelling errors, missing words, and repeated words. Thirty-two subjects read from an Apple II using an 80-column display on a 12-inch black-and-white display or from hardcopy generated from an Epson MX–80 printer. There was a modest, but significant (p < .05) increase in detected errors with the printed text. There was also a 30 to 40 percent (p < .001) advantage in speed with the printed text.

Gould and Grischkowsky (1983) studied proofreading for typographic errors on IBM 3277 displays and output from an APS5 computer-controlled photocomposer. Both the screens and the hardcopy texts had 23 lines per page with about 9 words per line. Twenty-four subjects spent one full day reading in each format. The reading rate was significantly faster (p < .01) on hardcopy (200 words per minute) than on the screens (155 words per minute). Accuracy was slightly, but reliably, higher on hardcopy. The subjective ratings of readability were similar in both formats.

Similar results were reported by Muter et al. (1982), who found 28.5 percent longer times for subjects reading from a white-on-blue background monitor than from paper. Muter and Kruk (1983) report 24.1 percent slower reading from a green monochrome monitor than from paper.

Designers of displays with textual information must be alert to the impact of other factors, such as upper case only versus upper and lower case letters, right and left justification, margin space, display rate, flicker, phosphor color, and scrolling versus painting. Unfortunately, the interaction among these factors makes it very difficult to isolate the contribution of each (Heines, 1984).

Moskel et al. (1984) studied upper case only versus upper-and-lower case and three presentation formats. There was a typewritten format and screen presentations using black letters on a white background and white letters on a black background. Thirty-five undergraduates worked for six minutes on two of the six conditions (Table 9.1), proofreading for spelling errors and answering comprehension questions. The screen displays were generated by a Commodore 64 computer with a 15-inch monitor that produced 25 lines of 40 characters. No paging or other commands were required; the full text remained on the screen. The results show a 25 to 30 percent advantage for typewritten text (independent of case) and a somewhat larger advantage for

COMPREHENSION AND PROOFREADING SCORES

	Mean Scores for Comprehension		
	Black letters on white	White letters on black	Typewritten
Upper Case	.44	.45	.56
Lower and Upper Case	.63	.66	.62

	Mean Scores for Proofreadings		
	Black letters on white	White letters on black	Typewritten
Upper Case	.15	.18	.23
Lower and Upper Case	.29	.20	.37

Table 9.1: Data from an empirical study of screen versus paper readability (Moskel, Erno, & Shneiderman, 1984).

upper-and-lower case. No difference emerged for the black-on-white versus white-on-black versions.

In another pilot study, experienced users of white-on-black screens performed more poorly when they had to switch to black on white. Novice users performed equally on both versions.

Recent results from Gould and others (Haas & Hayes, 1985) suggest that higher resolution screens and anti-aliasing techniques to produce sharper characters may improve readability. Another interesting recent conjecture is that the difference in readability is also a function of task type (Koubek & Janardan, 1985).

9.3.   PREPARING PRINTED MANUALS

Traditionally, training and reference materials for computer systems were printed manuals. Writing these manuals was often left to the most junior member of the development team as a 5 percent effort at the end of the project. As a result, the manuals were often poorly written, not suited to the background of the users, delayed or incomplete, and inadequately tested.

There is a growing awareness that users are not like designers, that system developers might not be good writers, that it takes time to write an effective manual, that testing and revisions must be done before widespread dissemination, and that the success of a system may be closely coupled to the quality of the documentation (Sohr, 1983).

In one experiment, Foss, Rosson, and Smith (1982) modified a standard text editor manual. The standard manual presented all the details about a command; the modified manual offered a progressive, or spiral, approach to the material by presenting subsets of the concepts. The standard manual used an abstract formal notation to describe the syntax of the commands; the modified manual showed numerous examples. Finally, the standard manual had terse technical prose; the modified manual had readable explanations with less technical terminology.

During the experiment, subjects took 15 to 30 minutes to study the manuals and were then asked to complete nine complex text-editing or

	Standard Manual	Modified Manual
Tasks Completed	7.36	8.77
Average Minutes/Task	26.63	16.00
Average Exit Errors/Task	1.36	.27
Average Commands/Task	23.63	13.04
Average Requests for Verbal Help	5.50	2.55

Table 9.2: Results from a study comparing standard manual with a modified manual (spiral approach, numerous examples, more readable explanations) (Foss, Rosson, & Smith, 1982).

creation tasks within a three-hour period. On all five dependent measures, the subjects with the modified manual had superior performance (Table 9.2). The results make a strong case for the impact of the manual on the success of the user.

The iterative process of refining a text editor manual and evaluating its effectiveness is described by Sullivan and Chapanis (1983). They rewrote a manual for a widely used text editor, conducted a walk-through test with colleagues, and performed a more elaborate test with five temporary secretaries. Subjective and objective metrics showed substantial benefits from the rewriting.

9.3.1 Using the syntactic/semantic model to design manuals

The syntactic/semantic model offers insight to the learning process providing guidance to instructional materials designers.

If the reader knows the task, such as letter writing, but not the computer-related concepts in text editing and syntactic details (Figure

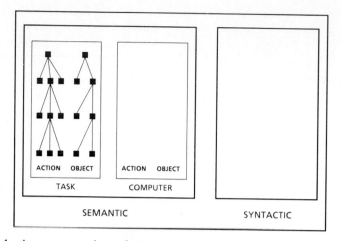

Figure 9.1: A representation of a user who knows the task domain but not the computer domain or syntactic details. Educational materials for this community should start with the task domain, explain the computer concepts, and then show the syntax. If the system conveniently represents the task domain, then learning can be simplified.

9.1), then the instructional materials should start from the familiar concepts and tasks in letter writing, link them to the computer-related concepts, and then show the syntax needed to accomplish each task (Morariu, 1985).

If the reader is knowledgeable about letter writing and computerized text editing but must learn a new text editor, then all that is needed is a brief presentation of the relationship between the syntax and the computer-related semantics (Figure 9.2).

Finally, if the reader knows letter writing, computerized text editing, and most of the syntax on this text editor, then all that is needed is a concise syntax reminder.

These three scenarios demonstrate the three most popular forms of printed materials: the introductory tutorial, the command reference, and the quick review (or "cheat sheet"). The VisiCalc documentation from VisiCorp follows this approach. Similarly, *A CMS Primer* from IBM was a welcome tutorial for the many users who had to struggle through the *CMS User's Guide* with its detailed, highly technical descriptions of

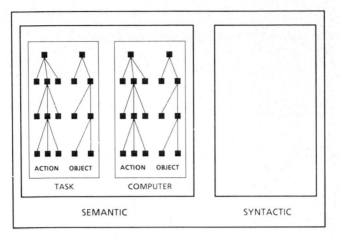

Figure 9.2: Users who are knowledgeable about the task and computer domains need only learn the syntax of this specific system. For example, someone who knows about writing scientific articles and is familiar with at least one word processor will find it relatively easy to acquire the syntax of another word processor.

each command. The Apple Macintosh manuals are appealing because of their graphic layout, use of color and photos, ample illustrations, and task orientation.

The syntactic/semantic model can also help map the current levels of knowledge in learning systems. For example, a user who is learning about database management systems for Congressional voting patterns might have some knowledge about the database and its manipulation, the query language concepts, and the syntax needed. This user would benefit from seeing typical queries that would demonstrate the syntax and serve as templates for other queries. In fact, complete sample sessions are extremely helpful in giving a portrait of the system features and interaction style (Figure 9.3). Many users will work through these sessions to verify their understanding, gain a sense of competence in using the system, and test to see if the system and the manual match.

Another helpful guide to using a system is an overall flow diagram of activity from log-on to log-off (Figure 9.4). This high-level representation provides a map that orients users by presenting a visual

---

TASK 1
RETRIEVE DOCUMENTS CONTAINING A WORD OR ACRONYM;
VIEW FULL TEXT

Retrieve FSD Management Instructions (MIs) that reference subcontracting; page through the retrieved MIs, viewing the words in context.

You can substitute another query for **subcontract$**, a different manual for "MGTI". To retrieve all FSD instructions and procedures that reference subcontracting, use the manual named "OMIR".

USER		RESPONSE
• Type **QPROC** □		WELCOME TO STAIRS
• Type option number ==> **1** manual name ==> ***** □		List of manuals
• Move cursor next to "MGTI", Type **s** □		MGTI LOGO
• □		SEARCH mode, ready for first query
• Type **subcontract$**		Words starting with "subcontract", Number of times each word appears; Number of MIs retrieved
• Type **..brw** □	(PF4)	First page of first MI
• □		Next page
• Type **p*** □	(PF11)	Next page containing a word starting with "subcontract"
• Type **doc+1** □	(PF8)	First page of next MI
• Type **..search** □	(PF2)	SEARCH mode, ready for next query
• Type **..end** □	(PF3)	WELCOME TO STAIRS
• Return to PROFS	(PF4)	PROFS menu

□ = press ENTER

Figure 9.3: A sample session is often a convenient way to show system usage. Many users try the sample session and then make variations to suit their needs. This sample session shows the use of a text retrieval system meant for nontechnical users. (Published with the permission of the International Business Machines Corporation)

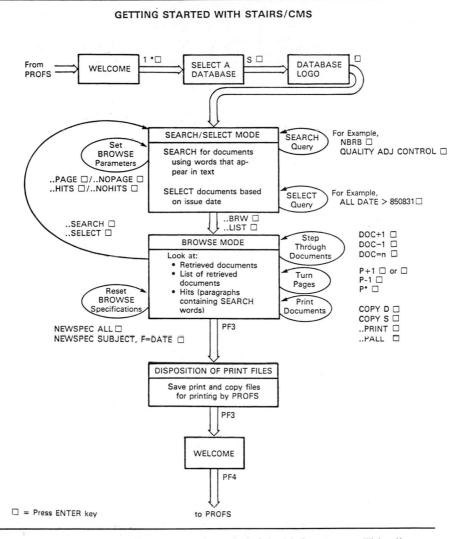

Figure 9.4: A transition diagram can be a helpful aid for users. This diagram shows user actions on the arrows and computer responses in the boxes, for the same system as Figure 9.3. (Courtesy Barbara Young, International Business Machines, Inc., Federal Systems Division, Bethesda, MD)

representation of transitions from one activity to another. Similarly, if the system uses a complex model of data objects, a diagram may help sort out the details (Figure 9.5).

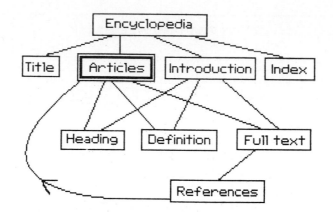

Figure 9.5: Often the relationship among data objects is difficult for users to grasp. This diagram shows the relationship among the components of The Interactive Encyclopedia System (TIES). An encyclopedia consists of a title, a collection of articles, an introductory article, and an index to the articles. Articles consist of a heading, definition, and the full text. The text of articles contains references to other articles.

9.3.2 Organization and writing style

Designing instructional materials is a challenging endeavor. The author must be knowledgeable about the technical content; sensitive to the background, reading level, and intellectual ability of the reader; and skilled in writing lucid prose. Assuming that the author has acquired the technical content, the primary job in creating a manual is to understand the readers and the tasks they must perform.

A precise statement of the educational objectives (Mager, 1962) is an invaluable guide to the author and the reader. The sequencing of instructional content is governed by the reader's current knowledge and ultimate objectives. Precise rules are hard to identify, but the author should attempt to present concepts in a logical sequence with increasing order of difficulty to insure that each concept is used in subsequent sections, to avoid forward references, and to construct sections with approximately equal amounts of new material. In addition to these structural requirements, the manual should have sufficient examples and complete sample sessions.

Within a section that presents a concept, the author should begin with the motivation for the concept, describe the concept in task-domain semantic terms, then show the computer-related semantic concepts, and, finally, offer the syntax.

The choice of words and their phrasing is as important as the overall structure. A poorly written sentence mars a well-designed manual, just as an incorrect note mars a beautifully composed sonata. The classic book on writing, *The Elements of Style* (Strunk & White, 1979) is a valuable resource. Another classic is the article by Chapanis (1965) titled "Words, words, words."

Style guides for organizations are worthy attempts at insuring consistency and high quality (see *Documentation Style Manual* from General Electric [1981] for a good example). The *Ease-of-Use Reference* from IBM (undated) offers this advice:

Make Information Easy to Find
- include entry points
- arrange information to be found

Make Information Easy to Understand
- keep it simple
- be concrete
- put it naturally

Make Information Task-Sufficient
- include all that's needed
- make sure it's correct
- exclude what's not needed

Of course, no set of guidelines can turn a mediocre writer into a great writer. Writing is a highly creative act; effective writers are national treasures.

One study focused on the impact of writing style and reading ability in learning to use a computer terminal (Roemer & Chapanis, 1982). A tutorial was written at the 5th-, 10th-, and 15th-grade levels. Then, 54 technical and nontechnical subjects were divided into low, middle, and high reading ability. Increased reading ability led to significant differences in the completion time, number of errors, and scores on a concepts test. Increased complexity of the writing style did not lead to significant differences on the performance variables, but subjective preferences significantly favored the 5th-grade version. For this task, subjects could overcome the complex writing style, but the authors conclude that "the most sensible approach in designing computer dialogue is to use the simplest language."

Thinking-aloud studies (see Section 10.2.4) of subjects who were learning word processors revealed the enormous difficulties that most novices have and the strategies they adopt to overcome them (Carroll & Mack, 1984). Learners are actively engaged in trying to make the system work, read portions of the manual, understand the screen displays, explore the function of keys, and overcome the many problems they encounter. Learners apparently prefer trying things out on the computer rather than reading lengthy manuals. They want to perform meaningful, familiar tasks immediately and see the results for themselves. They apply real-world knowledge, experience with other computer systems, and frequent guesswork, as opposed to the stereotypic image of the new user patiently reading through and absorbing the contents of a manual.

These observations led to the design of "minimal manuals" that drastically cut verbiage, encouraged active involvement with hands-on experiences, supported error recovery, focused on realistic tasks, and promoted "guided exploration" of system features (Carroll, 1984). Results of field trials and empirical studies are encouraging; they suggest that learning time can be substantially reduced and user satisfaction increased.

9.3.3 Nonanthropomorphic descriptions

The metaphors used in describing computer systems can influence the user's reactions. Some writers are attracted to an anthropomorphic style that suggests that the computer is close to human in its powers. This suggestion can anger some users; more likely, it is seen as cute the first time, silly the second, and an annoying distraction the third time.

Many designers prefer to focus attention on the users and the tasks they must accomplish. In introductory sections of user manuals and online help, use of second person singular pronouns ("you") seems appropriate. Then, in later sections, simple descriptive sentences place the emphasis on the user's tasks.

In a transportation network system, the user might have to establish the input conditions on the screen and then invoke the program to perform an analysis.

> POOR: The expert system will discover the solution when the F1 key is pressed
>
> BETTER: You can get the solution by pressing F1
>
> BETTER: To solve, press F1

The first description emphasizes the computer's role, the second focuses on the user and might be used in an introduction to the system. In later sections, the briefer third version is less distracting from the task.

Evidence is sparse and individual differences will be important, but there may be an advantage to clearly distinguishing human abilities from computer powers.

In discussing computers, writers might be well advised to avoid such verbs as:

> POOR: know, think, understand, have memory.

In their place, use more mechanical terms, such as:

> BETTER: process, print, compute, sort, store, search, retrieve.

When describing what a user does with a computer, avoid such verbs as:

> POOR: ask, tell, speak to, communicate with.

In their place, use such terms as:

> BETTER: use, direct, operate, program, control.

Still better is to eliminate the reference to the computer and concentrate on what the user is doing, such as writing, solving a problem, finding an answer, learning a concept, or adding up a list of numbers.

> POOR: The computer can teach you some Spanish words.
>
> BETTER: You can use the computer to learn some Spanish words.

Make the user the subject of the sentence.

> POOR: The computer will give you a printed list of employees.

> POOR: Ask the computer to print a list of employees.
>
> BETTER: You can get the computer to print a list of employees.
>
> BETTER: You can print a list of employees.

The last sentence puts the emphasis on the user and eliminates the computer.

> POOR: The computer needs to have the disk in the disk drive to boot the system.
>
> BETTER: Put the disk labeled A2 in the disk drive before starting the computer.
>
> BETTER: To begin writing, put the Word Processer disk in the drive.

The last form emphasizes the function or activity that the user is going to perform.

> POOR: The computer knows how to do arithmetic.
>
> BETTER: You can use the computer to do arithmetic.

Focus on the user's initiative, process, goals, and accomplishments.

9.3.4 Development process

Recognizing the difference between a good and bad manual is a necessary precursor to being able to produce a successful manual on-time within a reasonable budget. Manual writing, like any project, must be properly managed, staffed with suitable personnel, and monitored with appropriate milestones (Table 9.3).

Getting started early is invaluable. If the manual-writing process begins before the implementation, then there is adequate time for review, testing, and refinement. Furthermore, the user's manual can act as an alternate that is sometimes more complete and comprehensible to the formal specification for the software. Implementers may miss or misunderstand some of the design requirements when reading a formal specification, but a well-written user manual may clarify the design. The manual writer becomes an effective critic, reviewer, or question-asker who can stimulate the implementation team. Early development of the manual enables pilot testing of the software's learnability even before it is built. For the months before the software is completed, the manual is the

USER MANUAL GUIDELINES

Product

- User's tasks guide organization (outside in)
- User's learning process shapes sequencing
- Present semantics before syntax
- Keep writing style clean and simple
- Show numerous examples
- Offer meaningful and complete sample sessions
- Draw transition diagrams
- Try advance organizers and summaries
- Provide table of contents, index, and glossary
- Include list of error messages
- Give credits to all project participants

Process

- Seek professional writers and/or copy writers
- Prepare user manuals early (before implementation)
- Review drafts thoroughly
- Field test early editions
- Provide a feedback mechanism for readers
- Revise to reflect changes regularly

Table 9.3: User manual guidelines based on practice and some empirical studies.

best way to convey the designers' intentions to potential customers and users, as well as to system implementers and project managers.

Ample lead time in the development of the manual allows for reviews and suggestions by designers, other technical writers, potential customers, the intended users, copy editors, graphic artists, lawyers, marketing personnel, instructors, telephone consultants, and product testers (Wagner, 1980).

Beyond informal reviews by people with different backgrounds, there are other strategies for evaluating the manual. Checklists of features have been developed by many organizations based on their experience with previous manuals. Automated indexes of reading level or difficulty are available to help isolate complex sections of text. Computerized style evaluations and spelling checkers are useful tools in refining any document.

Informal walkthroughs with users are usually an enlightening experience for software designers and manual writers. Potential users are asked to read through the manual and to describe aloud what they are seeing and learning. More controlled experiments with groups of users may help make design decisions about the manual. In such studies, subjects are assigned tasks, and their time to completion, error rates, and subjective satisfaction are the dependent variables.

Field trials with moderate numbers of users are a further process for identifying problems with the user manual and the software. Field trials can range from a half an hour with a half-dozen people to several months with thousands of users. One effective and simple strategy is for field trial users to mark up the manual while they are using it. They can rapidly indicate typos, misleading information, and confusing sections.

Software and their manuals are rarely completed. Rather, they go into a continuous process of evolutionary refinement. Each version eliminates some errors, adds refinements, and extends the functionality. If the users can communicate with the manual writers, then there is a greater chance of rapid improvement. Most manuals offer a tear-out sheet for sending comments to the manual writers. This device can be effective, but other routes should also be explored: electronic mail, interviews with users, debriefing of consultants and instructors, written surveys, group discussions, and further controlled experiments or field studies.

9.4. PREPARING ONLINE FACILITIES

There is a great attraction to making technical manuals available on the computer. The positive reasons for doing so are that:

1.   Information is available whenever the computer is available. There is no need to locate the correct manual—a minor

disruption if the proper manual is close by or a major disruption if the manual must be retrieved from another building or person.

2. The user does not need to allocate work space to opening up manuals. Paper manuals can become clumsy and clutter up a workspace.

3. Information can be electronically updated rapidly and at low cost. Electronic dissemination of revisions ensures that out-of-date material cannot be inadvertently retrieved.

4. Specific information necessary for a task can be located rapidly if the online manual offers electronic indexing or text searching. Searching for one page in a million can usually be done more quickly on a computer than through printed material.

5. The computer screen can show graphics and animations that may be very important in explaining complex actions.

However, these positive attributes can be compromised by several potentially serious negative side effects:

1. Screens are not as readable as printed materials (see Section 9.2).

2. Screens display substantially less information than a sheet of paper, and the rate of paging through screens is slow compared to the rate of paging through a manual. The resolution of screens is poor compared to the resolution of paper; this is especially important when showing pictures or graphics.

3. The command language of screens may be novel and confusing to novices. By contrast, most people are thoroughly familiar with the "command language" of paper manuals. The extra mental effort in navigating through screens may interfere with concentration and learning.

4. If the screen is used for other work, it becomes a severe burden on the user's short-term memory to have to switch

between the work and the online manual. Users lose their context of work and have difficulty remembering what they read in the online manual. Multiple screens or windows are potential resolutions to this problem.

Still, the online environment opens the door to a variety of helpful facilities that might not be practical in printed form. Relles and Price (1981) offer this list:

1. Successively more detailed explanations of a displayed error message.
2. Successively more detailed explanations of a displayed question or prompt.
3. Successive examples of correct input or valid commands.
4. Explanation or definition of a specified term.
5. A description of the format of a specified command.
6. A list of allowable commands.
7. A display of specified sections of documentation.
8. A description of the current value of various system parameters.
9. Instruction on the use of the system.
10. News of interest to users of the system.
11. A list of available user aids.

Houghton (1984) reviews online help facilities and points out the great difficulty in helping the novice user get started as well as helping the expert user who needs one specific piece of information.

9.4.1 Experimental results

The contrast between novice and expert users was demonstrated in Relles's (1979) experiment with a simple bank account management system that had a 37-page user manual. In a pilot study, six computer-naïve subjects were all given 30 minutes to read the manual.

The subjects then had to carry out a set of tasks using the command language. The online aids group had "exceptionally poor performance" as compared to the group that had only the printed manual. Apparently, the former group of subjects had difficulty using the online aids and their existence was a distraction from the task. "The provision of online aids did have an adverse effect on user performance, and subjects who used the aids had significantly less confidence in their ability to use the system without a manual."

Relles then used 30 subjects who had interactive computer experience for his main experiment. After all subjects read the manual for twenty minutes, they carried out a set of tasks. Those without online aids took 42 minutes; those with carefully designed online aids took only 30 minutes ($p < .05$). The availability of online aids significantly increased users' confidence that they could use the system without a manual ($p < .01$).

Dunsmore (1980) also found that novice users had difficulty with online aids. The online group was shown a complete description of the system online and then could call up this material at any time with a one-character command. The printed group received this material on two printed pages. A third group (the brief group) received a "cryptic description of system capabilities" online at the start, but they could not retrieve this information. All subjects had to search a database using menu selection. The median number of successful searches (out of a maximum of thirty) for the twelve subjects in each group were:

Online - 7
Printed - 13.5
Brief - 12

There was a statistically significant difference ($p = .02$) across groups. Apparently, the printed version could be accessed more quickly, whereas the online version interrupted and delayed problem solving in this menu-searching environment. The use of system features was clear enough that subjects did not need much explanation and could work effectively with only the brief text.

Watley and Mulford (1983) prepared a simple interactive drawing program with a seven-screen instruction manual available online or on paper in identical formats. Subjects could learn the commands and carry

	Minutes Spent Using Help	
	Novice	Experienced
Online	7.2	6.6
Hardcopy	3.9	2.3
	Post-Test Comprehension	
	Novice	Experienced
Online	51.3	52.8
Hardcopy	55.6	63.2

Table 9.4: Results from an experimental comparison of online and hardcopy help for a simple interactive drawing system with seven pages or screens (Watley & Mulford, 1983).

out the tasks with less time (p < .001) using the hardcopy version (Table 9.4). Posttest comprehension scores were also reliably higher (p < .001) for the hardcopy groups.

Further results about the efficacy of online help facilties come from a study with 72 novice users of a text editor (Cohill & Williges, 1982). A control group receiving no online help facilities was compared with eight experimental conditions formed from all combinations of initiation (user vs. computer causes the help session to begin), presentation (printed manual vs. online), and selection of topics (user vs. computer selects which material is displayed). The control group with no online facilities did significantly more poorly than the experimental groups (Table 9.5). Of the eight experimental groups, the best performance (significantly different at the p < .05 level) was achieved by the user-initiated, user-selected, and printed manual group.

A well-designed help facility may be more beneficial than a poorly designed help facility. Magers (1983) revised an online help facility to offer context-sensitive help instead of keyword indexed help, wrote

HELP CONFIGURATIONS

Init-iation	Presentation	Selection	Time in Subtask	Errors per Subtask	Commands /Subtask	Subtasks Completed
User	Manual	User	293.1	0.4	8.4	5.0
User	Manual	System	442.2	2.0	17.7	4.9
User	Online	User	350.9	1.1	13.5	5.0
User	Online	System	382.2	1.8	17.6	4.9
System	Manual	User	367.9	1.3	13.1	4.8
System	Manual	System	399.1	0.9	13.8	4.9
System	Online	User	425.9	2.8	15.1	5.0
System	Online	System	351.5	1.2	13.7	4.9
Control: No HELP Available			679.1	5.0	20.2	3.4

Table 9.5: Results from a study comparing nine styles of online help facilities (Cohill & Williges, 1982).

tutorial screens in addition to the reference material, reduced computer jargon, used examples instead of a mathematical notation, provided an online dictionary of command synonyms, and wrote task-oriented rather than computer-oriented help screens. Thirty computer novices (mean age thirty-three years) were split into two groups; half received the original and half the modified help facility. The subjects with the revised help achieved a task score of 90.6 compared with 43.0 for the other subjects ($p < .001$). Time was reduced from 75.6 to 52.0 minutes with the improved help facility ($p < .01$). Subjective satisfaction scores also strongly favored the revised help facility.

Borenstein (1985) studied sixteen novices and twelve expert computer users peforming 22 tasks that required online help. The standard UNIX *man* system for manual reading was compared with improved texts delivered by Borenstein's ACRONYM system, a hybrid using *man* texts delivered by ACRONYM, a simulated natural language system, and an ever-present human tutor. The human tutor led to significantly faster times, and the content of the texts appeared to be a more important factor than the format of the delivery system. The standard *man* system produced the poorest performance.

In summary, the experiments reveal that online help is not necessarily better than hardcopy manuals; in fact, it may be worse. Paper manuals are more familiar, can be examined without disrupting computer use, are faster to use, and do not require learning additional commands. A second screen or window may be necessary to make online help attractive when compared with paper manuals. Still, the advantage of having helpful information available online is considerable when compared with the absence of any manual. Since users may not have access to printed manuals, some online facility is strongly recommended. The form and content of the online help facility make a profound difference (Figure 9.6). Good writing, task-orientation, context-sensitivity, and command examples may all contribute to improved online help.

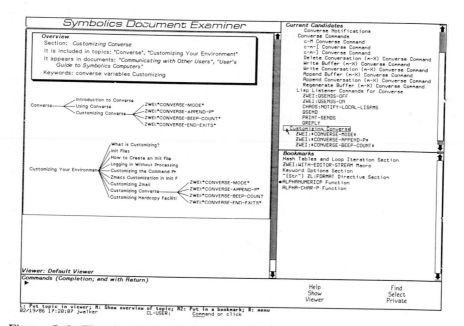

Figure 9.6: The Symbolics Document Examiner enables users to display full pages of text and to select topics by pointing at them. The bookmarks window keeps references to recently viewed topics. (Courtesy of Symbolics Corporation, Cambridge, MA)

9.4.2 Online tutorials

Online help that offers concise descriptions of the command syntax and semantics is probably most effective for intermittent knowledgeable users but difficult for novices who need more of a tutorial. Natural language dialog was proposed (Shapiro & Kwasny, 1975) for interactive learning about an operating system command language. The prototype was engaging and occasionally successful in helping users, but this strategy has not yet been refined sufficiently for widespread use.

Another approach is to design an interactive tutorial environment in which the computer instructs the user to carry out commands right on the system. One introductory tutorial for the LOTUS 1–2–3 package displays the exact keystrokes the user must type and then carries out the commands. The user can type the exact keystrokes or just keep pressing the space bar to speed through the demonstration. Some users find this very attractive; others are put off by the restrictive sequencing that prevents errors and exploration.

Online tutorials can be effective because the user (Al-Awar et al., 1981):

- does not have to keep shifting attention between the terminal and the instructional material
- practices the skills needed to use the system
- can work alone at an individual pace and without the embarrassment of mistakes made before a human instructor or fellow students.

Creators of interactive tutorials must deal with the usual questions of instructional design and also with the novelty of the computer environment. Repeated testing and refinement is highly recommended (Al-Awar et al., 1981).

9.5.   PRACTITIONER'S SUMMARY

Paper manuals, online help, and tutorials play an important role in the success or failure of a software/hardware product. Sufficient personnel, money, and time should be assigned to these support materials. A user manual should be developed before the implementation. Online manuals and help are attractive, but the poor readability, small size, and slow display rate of most screens are serious limitations. At this stage of technology, paper manuals are still preferred, with good cause, by many users. Online help and tutorials are potentially appealing, but ample effort must be expended to take advantage of this new medium. Online help should be written with a specific user community in mind to accomplish specific goals (offering task concepts, computer concepts, or syntactic knowledge), while avoiding the difficulties of using online help (too many extra commands to learn, losing the context of work, requiring memorization of information from the help screen, flooding with irrelevant information, etc.). However, even excellent manuals or tutorials cannot be relied on to overcome the problems of a poorly designed user interface. Online help should be written lucidly, access should be offered conveniently, and its contents should be carefully reviewed and tested. Quality manuals, online help, and tutorials have a profound effect on users' success and their impressions of most interactive systems.

9.6. RESEARCHER'S AGENDA

One important problem in human factors of computer systems is understanding why screens are more difficult to read than paper. When the contributions of the two dozen factors are understood, it will become possible to create more readable screens. Some designers may even dream of making screens more readable than paper. The main advantage of screens is the potential for rapid retrieval and traversal of large databases, but very little is known about how to offer this advantage conveniently without overwhelming the user. The cognitive model of turning pages in a book is too simple, but users can easily get lost if more elaborate networks or trees are used. Multiple windows or screens can help users by allowing them to see the problem and the online help or tutorial at the same time, but the strategies are only beginning to be explored. Cognitive models of learning to use computer systems could aid designers of tutorials, manuals, and online help.

REFERENCES

Al-Awar, J., Chapanis, A., and Ford, W. R., Tutorials for the first-time computer user, *IEEE Transactions on Professional Communication, PC–24*, (1981), 30–37.

Barnard, P., and Hammond, N., Usability and its multiple determination for the occasional user of interactive systems, In Williams, M. B., *Pathways to the Information Society*, North-Holland Publishers, Amsterdam, (1982), 543–548.

Borenstein, Nathaniel S., The design and evaluation of on-line help systems, Ph.D. dissertation, Carnegie-Mellon University, Pittsburgh, PA, (1985).

Cakir, A., Hart, D. J., and Stewart, T. F. M., *Visual Display Terminals: A Manual Covering Ergonomics, Workplace Design, Health and Safety, Task Organization*, John Wiley and Sons, New York, (1980).

Carroll, J. M., Minimalist training, *Datamation 30*, 18, (1984), 125–136.

Carroll, J. M., and Mack, R. L., Learning to use a word processor: By doing, by thinking, and by knowing, In Thomas, J. C., and Schneider, M., (Editors), *Human Factors in Computing Systems*, Ablex Publishing Corporation, Norwood, NJ, (1984), 13–51.

Chapanis, Alphonse, Words, words, words. *Human Factors, 7*, (1965), 1–17.

Cohill, A. M., and Williges, Robert C., Computer-augmented retrieval of HELP information for novice users, *Proc. Human Factors Society— 26th Annual Meeting*, (1982), 79–82.

Dunsmore, H. E., Designing an interactive facility for non-programmers, *Proc. ACM National Conference*, (1980), 475–483.

Foss, D., Rosson, M. B., and Smith, P., Reducing manual labor: An experimental analysis of learning aids for a text editor, *Proc. Human*

Factors in Computer Systems, Washington, DC, Chapter of ACM, (March 1982).

Francas, M., Goodman, D., and Dickinson, J., Command-set and presentation method in the training of Telidon operators, *Proc. of the Human Factors Society — 26th Annual Meeting*, Human Factors Society, Santa Monica, CA, (1982), 752–755.

General Electric Information Services Company, *Documentation Style Manual*, (December 1981), 72 pages.

Gould, John, and Grischkowsky, Nancy, Doing the same work with hardcopy and with cathode ray tube (CRT) terminals, IBM Research Report RC 9849, (January 20, 1983).

Grandjean, E., and Vigliani, E., Editors, *Ergonomic Aspects of Visual Display Terminals*, Taylor and Francis, Ltd., London, (1982).

Haas, Christine, and Hayes, John R., *Effects of text display variables on reading tasks: Computer screen versus hardcopy, Communications Design Center*, Report No. 3, Carnegie-Mellon University, Pittsburgh, PA, (March 1985).

Hansen, Wilfred J., Doring, Richard, and Whitlock, Lawrence R., Why an examination was slower on-line than on paper, *International Journal of Man-Machine Studies 10*, (1978), 507–519.

Heines, Jesse M., *Screen Design Strategies for Computer-Assisted Instruction*, Digital Press, Bedford, MA, (1984).

Helander, Martin G., Billingsley, Patricia A., and Schurick, Jane M., An evaluation of human factors research on visual display terminals in the workplace, In Muckler, Fred A., *Human Factors Review 1984*, Human Factors Society, Santa Monica, CA, (1984), 55–130.

Houghton, Raymond C., Online help systems: A conspectus, *Communications of the ACM 27*, 2, (February 1984), 126–133.

IBM Santa Teresa Laboratory, Ease-of-Use Reference, (undated), 8 pages.

Koubek, Richard J., and Janardan, Chaya Garg, A basis for explaining the conflicting results in performance on CRT and paper displays, *Proc. of the Human Factors Society—29th Annual Meeting*, Human Factors Society, Santa Monica, CA, (1985), 1102–1105.

Mager, Robert F., *Preparing Instructional Objectives*, Fearon, Palo Alto, CA, (1962).

Magers, Celeste S., An experimental evaluation of on-line HELP for non-programmers, *Proc. CHI'83 Conference: Human Factors in Computing Systems*, Available from ACM, P. O. Box 64,145, Baltimore, MD, 21264 (1983), 277–281.

Morariu, Janis, Human factors for design and evaluation of software, *ASIS Bulletin*, (October/November 1985), 18–19.

Moskel, Sonya, Erno, Judy, and Shneiderman, Ben, Proofreading and comprehension of text on screens and paper, University of Maryland Computer Science Technical Report, (June 1984).

Muter, Paul, and Kruk, Richard, Reading of continuous text on video screens, Department of Psychology, University of Toronto, (1983).

Muter, Paul, Latremouille, S. A., Treurniet, W. C., and Beam, P., Extended reading of continuous text on television screens, *Human Factors 24*, (1982), 501–508.

Price, Jonathan, and staff, *How to Write a Computer Manual*, Benjamin/Cummings Publication, Addison-Wesley Publishing Company, Reading, MA, (1984), 293 pages.

Relles, Nathan, The design and implementation of user-oriented systems, Ph. D. dissertation, Technical Report 357, University of Wisconsin, Madison, WI, (July 1979).

Relles, Nathan, and Price, Lynne A., A user interface for online assistance, *Proc. Fifth International Conference on Software Engineering*, Available from IEEE, Silver Spring, MD, (1981).

Relles, N., Sondheimer, N., and Ingargiola, G., A unified approach to online assistance, *Proceedings of AFIPS National Computer Conference 50*, AFIPS Press, Arlington, VA, (1981), 383–388.

Roemer, Joan M., and Chapanis, Alphonse, Learning performance and attitudes as a function of the reading grade level of a computer-presented tutorial, *Proc. Human Factors in Computer Systems*, Washington, DC, Chapter of the ACM, (1982), 239–244.

Shapiro, Stuart C., and Kwasny, Stanley C., Interactive consulting via natural language, *Communications of the ACM, 18*, 8, (August 1975), 459–462.

Shurtleff, D. A., *How to Make Displays Legible*, Human Interface Design, La Mirada, CA, (1980).

Sohr, Dana, Better software manuals, *BYTE Magazine*, (May 1983), 286–294).

Strunk, William, Jr., and White, E. B., *The Elements of Style*, third edition, Macmillan, New York, (1979).

Sullivan, Marc A., and Chapanis, Alphonse, Human factoring a text editor manual, *Behaviour and Information Technology 2*, 2, (1983), 113–125.

Wagner, Carl B., Quality control methods for IBM computer manuals, *Journal of Technical Writing and Communication 10*, 2, (1980), 93–102.

Watley, Charles, and Mulford, Jay, A comparison of commands' documentation: Online vs. hardcopy, Unpublished student project, University of Maryland, (December 8, 1983).

Williges, Robert C., and Williges, Beverly H., Human-computer dialogue design considerations, In Johannsen, G., and Rijnsdorp, J. E., Editors, *Analysis, Design, and Evaluation of Man-Machine Systems*, VDI/VDE-Gesellschaft Mess-und Regelungstechnik, Dusseldorf, Germany, (1982), 273–280.

Wright, P., and Lickorish, A., Proof-reading texts on screen and paper, *Behaviour and Information Technology 2*, 3, (1983), 227–235.

PART IV

ASSESSMENT AND REFLECTION

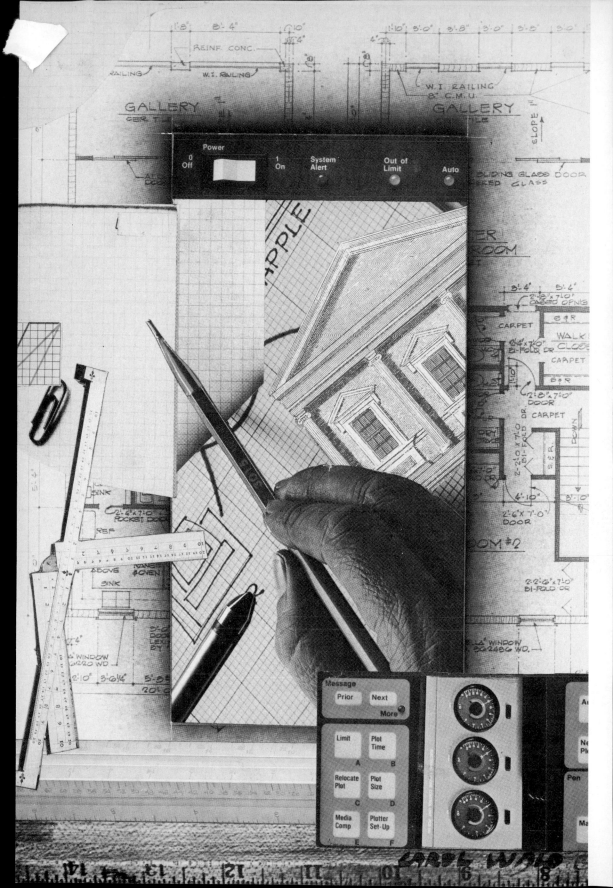

CHAPTER 10

ITERATIVE DESIGN, TESTING, AND EVALUATION

Quality is the continuing stimulus which causes us to create the world in which we live. All of it. Every last bit.

Quality is the track that directs the train.

Robert Pirsig, *Zen and the Art of Motorcycle Maintenance*, 1974.

10.1   INTRODUCTION

In the first decades of computer software development, senior programmers designed text editors, operating system control languages, programming languages, and applications packages for themselves and their peers. Now, the user population for control rooms, office automation, home and personal computing, and point-of-sales terminals is so vastly different that the experience and intuition of senior programmers may be inappropriate. Designs must be validated through pilot and acceptance tests that can also provide a finer understanding of user skills and capabilities.

The egocentric style of the past must yield to humility and a genuine desire to accommodate to the user's skills, wishes, and orientation. Designers must seek more direct interaction with the users during the design phase, development process, and throughout the system lifecycle. Iterative design methods that allow early testing of prototypes, revisions based on feedback from users, and incremental refinements suggested by test administrators are all necessary to arrive at a successful system.

Corporate marketing departments are aware of these issues and are a source of constructive encouragement. When more than two hundred suppliers provide similar word-processing packages, human engineering is vital for product acceptance. Many organizations have created usability laboratories to conduct videotaped tests of products during development. Typical users are brought in to try out the system, perform benchmark tasks, and suggest improvements (Hirsch, 1981).

Many organizations maintain a human factors group that is a source of experience and expertise in testing techniques (Thomas, 1984). In some cases, this resource is not used because the group members are not familiar with the application area, are seen as outsiders, or must be paid as if they were external consultants. Development projects might be better served if a human factors role were assigned to a team member or to several members if the project is large. The human factors coordinator for a project would develop the necessary skills for the project and would be more effective in communicating with external human factors professionals when further expertise, references to the literature, or experimental tests were required. This dual strategy balances the needs for centralized expertise and decentralized application. It enables professional growth in the human factors area and in the application domain.

As projects grow in complexity, size, and importance, role specialization will emerge, as it has in architectural, aircraft, and book design. Eventually, individuals will become highly skilled in such specific problems as dialog management techniques, graphic display algorithms, voice and audio tone design, writing of messages and menus, or online tutorial writing. Consultation with graphic artists, book designers, advertising copy writers, instructional text book authors, or film animation creators may be useful. Perceptive system developers will recognize and employ psychologists for experimental testing, sociologists for evaluating organizational impact, educational psychologists for refining training procedures, and social workers for guiding user consultants or customer service personnel.

10.2   ITERATIVE DESIGN DURING DEVELOPMENT

Design is inherently creative and unpredictable. Interactive system designers must blend a thorough knowledge of technical feasibility with a mystical esthetic sense of what will be attractive to users. Carroll & Rosson (1985) characterize design this way:

- Design is a *process*; it is not a state and cannot be adequately represented statically.
- The design process is *nonhierarchical*; it is neither strictly bottom-up nor strictly top-down.
- The process is *radically transformational*; it involves the development of partial and interim solutions that may ultimately play no role in the final design.
- Design intrinsically involves the *discovery of new goals*.

These characterizations of design convey the dynamic nature of the process. But in every creative domain, there can also be discipline, refined techniques, wrong and right ways, and measures of success. The techniques described in this section are meant to help structure and channel the design process.

10.2.1 Establishing guidelines

During the early design stages, data about current performance should be collected as a baseline. Information about similar systems can be gathered and interviews can be conducted with interested parties, such as users and managers. Several design teams might make independent proposals from which the final design will emerge. At this early stage, the design team should debate among themselves and generate a set of working guidelines. Guidelines should be proposed for such items as:

- menu selection formats
- wording of prompts and feedback messages
- terminology and abbreviations
- character set
- keyboard, display, and cursor control devices
- audible sounds, touch input, and other special devices
- screen layout and use of multiple windows
- response times and display rates
- use of color, highlighting, blinking, inverse video, etc.
- data entry and display formats for items and lists
- command syntax, semantics, and sequences
- use of programmed function keys
- error messages and recovery procedures
- online assistance and tutorials
- training and reference materials.

Controversial guidelines can be reviewed by colleagues or empirically tested. Procedures must be established to distribute the guidelines, permit amendments, allow exceptions, and ensure enforcement. A three-level approach of rigid standards, more flexible guidelines, and suggested practices may be useful to clarify which items are firmer and which items are easily changed.

The creation of a guidelines document at the beginning of an implementation project focuses attention on the interface design and provides an opportunity for discussion of controversial issues. When the guideline is adopted by the development team, the implementation proceeds quickly and with few design changes.

10.2.2 Participatory design

Many authors have urged participatory design strategies (Olson & Ives, 1981; Mumford, 1983; Ives & Olson, 1984; Gould & Lewis, 1985), but their positive impact is not validated. The arguments in favor of user involvement include more accurate information about task performance, an opportunity to argue over design decisions, the sense of participation that builds ego investment in successful implementation, and the potential for increased user acceptance of the final system. Recent results provide increased evidence of the benefits of user involvement (Baroudi et al., 1986).

On the other hand, extensive user involvement may be more costly and may lengthen the implementation period, build antagonism with those who are not involved or whose suggestions are rejected, force designers to compromise their design to satisfy incompetent participants, and simply build opposition to implementation (Ives & Olson, 1984).

The social and political environment surrounding the implementation of a complex information system is not amenable to study by controlled experimentation. Social and industrial psychologists are interested in these issues, but dependable strategies may never emerge. The sensitive project leader must judge each case on its merits and decide on the right level of user involvement. The personalities of the design team and the users are such a critical determinant that experts in group dynamics and social psychology may be useful as consultants.

The experienced project leader knows that organizational politics and the preferences of individuals may be more important than the technical issues in governing the success of an interactive system. The warehouse managers who see their position threatened by an interactive system that provides senior managers with up-to-date information through their terminals will ensure that the system fails by delaying data entry or by being less than diligent in guaranteeing data accuracy. Proper system design should take into account the impact on users and solicit their participation to ensure that all concerns are made explicit early enough to avoid "counterimplementation" (Keen, 1981).

10.2.3 Pilot studies

Theatrical producers know that extensive rehearsals are necessary to ensure a successful opening night. Early rehearsals require only one or two performers wearing street clothes; but as opening night approaches, dress rehearsals with props and lighting are expected. Aircraft designers carry out wind tunnel tests, build plywood mockups of the cabin layout, construct complete simulations of the cockpit, and thoroughly flight test the first prototype. Similarly, interactive system designers are now recognizing that they must carry out many small and some large pilot tests of system components before release to customers.

Early pilot studies can be conducted using typewritten versions of screen displays to assess user reactions to wording, layout, and sequencing. A test administrator plays the role of the computer by flipping the pages while asking a potential user to carry out a set of tasks. This informal testing is inexpensive, rapid, and usually very productive.

Pilot tests can be run to compare design alternatives, to contrast with current manual procedures, or to evaluate competitive products. Data can be collected informally or, more precisely, to suit circumstances.

Instructional materials and command language designs can be evaluated with paper-and-pencil tests on typical users. As prototype versions become available, testing can be more elaborate. These preliminary tests help build confidence that the stringent acceptance test can be satisfied when the implementation is complete.

10.2.4 Rapid prototype systems

One difficulty in designing interactive systems is that the customer and the user may not have a clear idea of what the system will look like when it is done. Since interactive systems are novel in many situations, the users may not realize the implications of design decisions. Unfortunately, it is difficult, costly, and time consuming to make major changes to systems once they have been implemented.

Even though this problem has no complete solution, some of the more serious difficulties can be avoided if the customers and users can be given a realistic impression of what the final system will look like at an early stage (Clark, 1981; Savage et al., 1982; Gould & Lewis, 1985). A typewritten display of the screens used in pilot tests is helpful, but an on-the-screen display with an active keyboard is more realistic. For some applications, a text editor-generated display may be sufficient; but in other situations, it may be useful to write some programs to drive a series of displays. The simulation or prototype of a menu system may only have one or two paths active instead of the thousands of paths in the final system. In a command language situation, the simulation may support the command for a minute fraction of the available options. An imaginative approach in testing a speech input device was to create a mockup of the system with a person simulating the hoped-for computer's performance (Gould et al., 1983).

Since rapid prototyping is increasingly recognized as a valuable approach, there are a growing number of software support tools (Squires et al., 1982; Wasserman & Shewmake, 1985). In some cases, the framework built for the prototype can become the basis for the actual implementation. Dialog management systems (Roach et al., 1982) that permit quick partial system implementations are another approach. The potential for creating executable formal specifications for interactive systems is stimulating several research efforts (Jacob, 1985; Yunten & Hartson, 1985).

An effective technique during prototype testing is to invite users to perform a few well-chosen tasks and to "think aloud" about what they are doing (Lewis, 1982). The designer/tester should be supportive to the user, not taking over or giving instructions, but prompting and listening for clues to how the user is dealing with the system. After a suitable time period, possibly an hour or two, the user can be invited to make general comments or suggestions or to respond to specific questions. The informal atmosphere of a thinking aloud session is pleasant for both parties and often leads to many suggestions for improvements. As the system is refined, more ambitious tests can be conducted with users who are doing real work. Videotaping users performing tasks is often valuable for later review and for showing designers or managers the problems that users encounter (Lund, 1985). At each stage, the design can be iteratively refined (Carroll & Rosson, 1985).

Support for the iterative development of interactive systems comes from a project to develop a natural language interaction for a personal calendar system (Kelley, 1984). As subjects used the system, the word dictionary was increased from about 50 to more than 200 terms, reflecting the diverse usage patterns. A similar strategy, termed *user-derived interface,* was used to develop a command language for an electronic mail facility (Good et al., 1984). Users were encouraged to guess at possible commands, and their terms and structures were used to refine the system. As the number of parser rules and words increased from 120 to 330, the percentage of user commands accepted by the system increased from almost 0 to more than 90. It seems appealing to try to use commands that users invent; but other evidence suggests that users do not always invent the best strategy. Especially as the command sets grow large, there may be an advantage to providing a more structured facility to start with and then adding refinements to deal with problems.

10.2.5 Acceptance tests

For large implementation projects, the customer or manager usually sets objective and measurable goals for hardware and software performance. Many authors of requirements documents are even so bold as to specify mean time between failures and mean time to repair for hardware and in some cases for software. More typically, a set of test cases is specified for the software, with possible response time requirements for the hardware/software combination. If the completed product fails to meet these acceptance criteria, the system must be reworked until success is demonstrated.

Now, these notions can be extended to the human interface. Explicit acceptance criteria should be established when the requirements document is written or when a contract is offered. Measurable criteria for the human interface can be established for the:

1. Time to learn specific functions.
2. Speed of task performance.
3. Rate of errors.
4. Subjective user satisfaction.
5. Human retention of commands over time.

An acceptance test might specify that:

> Thirty typical users will be trained in using the system for 45 minutes. These users will be given 15 minutes to carry out the enclosed benchmark set of tasks. The average completion rate must be above 80 percent and the average number of errors must be below 3.

In a modest sized system, there may be eight or ten such tests to carry out on different components of the system and different user classes. An important test might be for speed of performance of typical tasks after one week of regular use. Other issues, such as subjective satisfaction or retention of commands after a week, may also be tested.

By establishing precise acceptance criteria, both the customer and the system developer can benefit. Arguments about the user friendliness of the system are avoided, and contractual fulfillment can be demonstrated in a more objective manner.

The goal of early pilot studies, prototypes, and acceptance tests is to force as much of the evolutionary development as possible into the prerelease phase, when change is relatively easy and inexpensive.

10.3   EVALUATION DURING ACTIVE USE

A carefully designed and thoroughly tested system is a wonderful asset, but successful active use requires constant attention from dedicated managers, user services personnel, and the maintenance staff. Everyone involved in supporting the user community can contribute to system refinements that provide ever higher levels of service. You can't please all of the users all of the time, but an earnest effort will be rewarded by the appreciation of a grateful user community. Perfection is not attainable, but percentage improvements are possible and worth pursuing.

Gradual system dissemination is useful so that problems can be repaired with minimal impact. As more and more people use the system, further changes should be limited to an annual or semi-annual system revision that is adequately announced. If system users can anticipate the change, then resistance will be reduced, especially if they have positive expectations of improvement.

10.3.1 Surveys

There are many productive avenues for assessing user performance and attitudes (Hiltz, 1983). Written user surveys are an inexpensive and generally acceptable approach with both management and users. A survey form should be prepared, reviewed among colleagues, and tested with a small sample of users before a large-scale survey is conducted.

Online surveys avoid the cost of printing and the extra effort in distribution and collection. Many people prefer answering a brief survey displayed on a screen instead of filling in and returning a printed form. To keep costs low, the survey might be administered to only a fraction of the user community.

In one survey, users were asked to respond to eight questions according to the following scale:

1 - strongly agree
2 - agree
3 - neutral
4 - disagree
5 - strongly disagree

The questions in the survey were:

1. The system commands are easy to use.

2. I feel competent with and knowledgeable about the system commands.

3. When writing a set of system commands for a new application, I am confident that they will be correct on the first run.

4. When I get an error message, I find that it is helpful in identifying the problem.

5. There are too many options and special cases.

6. I feel that the commands could be substantially simplified.

7. I have trouble remembering the commands and options and must consult the manual frequently.

8. When a problem arises, I go ask someone who really knows the system for assistance.

This list of questions can help identify problems users are having and is useful in demonstrating improvement to the interface as changes are made to training, online assistance, command structures, and so on. As changes are made, progress can be demonstrated by improved scores on subsequent surveys.

In a study of error messages in text-editor usage, we asked users to rate the messages on 1 to 7 scales:

Hostile 1 2 3 4 5 6 7 Friendly
Vague 1 2 3 4 5 6 7 Specific
Misleading 1 2 3 4 5 6 7 Beneficial
Discouraging 1 2 3 4 5 6 7 Encouraging

If precise, as opposed to general, questions are used in surveys, then there is a greater chance that the results will provide useful guidance in taking action (Lyons, 1980; Root & Draper, 1983).

Williges (1985) developed a set of bipolar semantically anchored items that asked users to describe their reactions to using a word processor. Another approach is to ask users to evaluate aspects of the interface design, such as the readability of characters, meaningfulness of command

USER EVALUATION OF INTERACTIVE COMPUTER SYSTEMS (SHORT FORM)

Please circle the numbers that most appropriately reflect your impressions about using this computer system.

Please add your written comments about any item.

Does Not Apply = NA

Characters in the displays	unreadable readable 0 1 2 3 4 5 6 7 8 9 10	NA
Highlighting facilitates task	poorly very well 0 1 2 3 4 5 6 7 8 9 10	NA
Terminology relates to the task domain	distantly closely 0 1 2 3 4 5 6 7 8 9 10	NA
Terminology	inconsistent consistent 0 1 2 3 4 5 6 7 8 9 10	NA
Instructions describing tasks	confusing clear 0 1 2 3 4 5 6 7 8 9 10	NA
Instructions are consistent	never always 0 1 2 3 4 5 6 7 8 9 10	NA
Operations relate to tasks	distantly closely 0 1 2 3 4 5 6 7 8 9 10	NA
Informative feedback is appropriate	never always 0 1 2 3 4 5 6 7 8 9 10	NA
Display layouts simplify tasks	never always 0 1 2 3 4 5 6 7 8 9 10	NA
Sequence of displays	confusing clear 0 1 2 3 4 5 6 7 8 9 10	NA
Pace of the interaction	too slow fast enough 0 1 2 3 4 5 6 7 8 9 10	NA
Error messages are helpful	never always 0 1 2 3 4 5 6 7 8 9 10	NA
Error correction is	confusing clear 0 1 2 3 4 5 6 7 8 9 10	NA
Online help	confusing clear 0 1 2 3 4 5 6 7 8 9 10	NA

	difficult	easy	
Learning the operation	0 1 2 3 4 5 6 7 8 9 10		NA
	not accommodated	accomodated	
Use by different levels of experience	0 1 2 3 4 5 6 7 8 9 10		NA
	overwhelmed	are respected	
Human memory limitations	0 1 2 3 4 5 6 7 8 9 10		NA
	confusing	clear	
Supplemental reference materials	0 1 2 3 4 5 6 7 8 9 10		NA
	discouraged	encouraged	
Exploration of features	0 1 2 3 4 5 6 7 8 9 10		NA
	terrible	wonderful	
Overall reactions	0 1 2 3 4 5 6 7 8 9 10		NA
	frustrating	satisfying	
	0 1 2 3 4 5 6 7 8 9 10		NA
	uninteresting	interesting	
	0 1 2 3 4 5 6 7 8 9 10		NA
	dull	stimulating	
	0 1 2 3 4 5 6 7 8 9 10		NA
	difficult	easy	
	0 1 2 3 4 5 6 7 8 9 10		NA
	inadequate power adequate power		
	0 1 2 3 4 5 6 7 8 9 10		NA

Table 10.1: Short form for subjective user evaluation of interactive systems.

names, or helpfulness of error messages. If users rate one aspect of the interactive system poorly, the designers have a clear indication of what needs to be redone.

Table 10.1 contains the short form of a generic user evaluation questionnaire for interactive systems. The long form (Table 10.2) was designed to have two levels of questions: general and detailed. If participants are willing to respond to every item, then the long form questionnaire can be used. If participants are not likely to be patient, then only the general questions in the short form need be asked.

USER EVALUATION OF INTERACTIVE COMPUTER SYSTEMS (LONG FORM)

Please circle the numbers that most appropriately reflect your impressions about using this computer system.

Please add your written comments about any item.

Does Not Apply = NA

	unreadable	readable	
Characters in the displays	0 1 2 3 4 5 6 7 8 9 10		NA

	fuzzy	sharp	
Character definition	0 1 2 3 4 5 6 7 8 9 10		NA

	poor	excellent	
Character contrast with background	0 1 2 3 4 5 6 7 8 9 10		NA

	unreadable	readable	
Character shapes (fonts)	0 1 2 3 4 5 6 7 8 9 10		NA

	inadequate	adequate	
Space surrounding characters	0 1 2 3 4 5 6 7 8 9 10		NA

	poorly	very well	
Highlighting facilitates task	0 1 2 3 4 5 6 7 8 9 10		NA

	hard to see	clear	
Levels of intensity or boldfacing	0 1 2 3 4 5 6 7 8 9 10		NA

	hard to see	clear	
Letter or shape size changes	0 1 2 3 4 5 6 7 8 9 10		NA

	inappropriate	appropriate	
Underscoring	0 1 2 3 4 5 6 7 8 9 10		NA

	inappropriate	appropriate	
Reverse video	0 1 2 3 4 5 6 7 8 9 10		NA

	inappropriate	appropriate	
Blinking	0 1 2 3 4 5 6 7 8 9 10		NA

	inappropriate	appropriate	
Color changes	0 1 2 3 4 5 6 7 8 9 10		NA

	distantly	closely	
Terminology relates to the task domain	0 1 2 3 4 5 6 7 8 9 10		NA

	too frequently	appropriately	
Computer-related terms are used	0 1 2 3 4 5 6 7 8 9 10		NA

	ambiguous precise	
Terms on the screen are	0 1 2 3 4 5 6 7 8 9 10	NA

	confusing clear	
Abbreviations	0 1 2 3 4 5 6 7 8 9 10	NA

	inconsistent consistent	
Terminology	0 1 2 3 4 5 6 7 8 9 10	NA

	inconsistent consistent	
Task terms	0 1 2 3 4 5 6 7 8 9 10	NA

	inconsistent consistent	
Computer terms	0 1 2 3 4 5 6 7 8 9 10	NA

	inconsistent consistent	
Abbreviations	0 1 2 3 4 5 6 7 8 9 10	NA

	confusing clear	
Instructions describing tasks	0 1 2 3 4 5 6 7 8 9 10	NA

	confusing clear	
Instructions for commands or choices	0 1 2 3 4 5 6 7 8 9 10	NA

	confusing clear	
Instructions for correcting errors	0 1 2 3 4 5 6 7 8 9 10	NA

	confusing clear	
Instructions for getting more help	0 1 2 3 4 5 6 7 8 9 10	NA

	never always	
Instructions are consistent	0 1 2 3 4 5 6 7 8 9 10	NA

	never always	
Instructions have consistent position	0 1 2 3 4 5 6 7 8 9 10	NA

	never always	
Instructions use consistent grammar	0 1 2 3 4 5 6 7 8 9 10	NA

	never always	
Instructions use consistent tone	0 1 2 3 4 5 6 7 8 9 10	NA

	distantly closely	
Operations relate to tasks	0 1 2 3 4 5 6 7 8 9 10	NA

	many few	
Number of operations per task	0 1 2 3 4 5 6 7 8 9 10	NA

	distantly closely	
Operations related to tasks	0 1 2 3 4 5 6 7 8 9 10	NA

Operations prevent mistakes	never always 0 1 2 3 4 5 6 7 8 9 10	NA
Informative feedback is appropriate	never always 0 1 2 3 4 5 6 7 8 9 10	NA
Link between operations and results	confusing clear 0 1 2 3 4 5 6 7 8 9 10	NA
Amount of feedback	too much adequate 0 1 2 3 4 5 6 7 8 9 10	NA
Amount of feedback	too little adequate 0 1 2 3 4 5 6 7 8 9 10	NA
Amount of feedback is user-controlled	never always 0 1 2 3 4 5 6 7 8 9 10	NA
Display layouts simplify tasks	never always 0 1 2 3 4 5 6 7 8 9 10	NA
Displays	cluttered uncluttered 0 1 2 3 4 5 6 7 8 9 10	NA
Displays	disorderly orderly 0 1 2 3 4 5 6 7 8 9 10	NA
A title identifies the display	never always 0 1 2 3 4 5 6 7 8 9 10	NA
Work proceeds from top to bottom	never always 0 1 2 3 4 5 6 7 8 9 10	NA
Sequence of displays	confusing clear 0 1 2 3 4 5 6 7 8 9 10	NA
Next screen in a sequence	unpredictable predictable 0 1 2 3 4 5 6 7 8 9 10	NA
Maintain a sense of position	impossible easy 0 1 2 3 4 5 6 7 8 9 10	NA
Going back to previous display	impossible easy 0 1 2 3 4 5 6 7 8 9 10	NA
Beginnings, middles, and ends of tasks are marked	confusingly clearly 0 1 2 3 4 5 6 7 8 9 10	NA
Pace of the interaction	too slow fast enough 0 1 2 3 4 5 6 7 8 9 10	NA

	too slowly	quickly enough	
Data entry operations are echoed	0 1 2 3 4 5 6 7 8 9 10		NA

	too slowly	quickly enough	
Response time for most operations	0 1 2 3 4 5 6 7 8 9 10		NA

	too slowly	quickly enough	
Error messages appear	0 1 2 3 4 5 6 7 8 9 10		NA

	too slowly	quickly enough	
Display rate for most displays	0 1 2 3 4 5 6 7 8 9 10		NA

	never	always	
Error messages are helpful	0 1 2 3 4 5 6 7 8 9 10		NA

	never	always	
Error messages clarify the problem	0 1 2 3 4 5 6 7 8 9 10		NA

	never	always	
Error messages indicate actions to be taken	0 1 2 3 4 5 6 7 8 9 10		NA

	never	always	
Error messages are specific	0 1 2 3 4 5 6 7 8 9 10		NA

	nasty	pleasing	
Error messages are	0 1 2 3 4 5 6 7 8 9 10		NA

	confusing	clear	
Error correction is	0 1 2 3 4 5 6 7 8 9 10		NA

	complex	simple	
Correcting typos or complex slips	0 1 2 3 4 5 6 7 8 9 10		NA

	complex	simple	
Going back to change values	0 1 2 3 4 5 6 7 8 9 10		NA

	complex	simple	
Undoing operations	0 1 2 3 4 5 6 7 8 9 10		NA

	confusing	clear	
Online help	0 1 2 3 4 5 6 7 8 9 10		NA

	complex	simple	
Accessing online help	0 1 2 3 4 5 6 7 8 9 10		NA

	confusing	clear	
Organization of online help	0 1 2 3 4 5 6 7 8 9 10		NA

	confusing	clear	
Contents of online help	0 1 2 3 4 5 6 7 8 9 10		NA

Learning the operation	difficult easy 0 1 2 3 4 5 6 7 8 9 10	NA
Getting started	difficult easy 0 1 2 3 4 5 6 7 8 9 10	NA
Learning more features	difficult easy 0 1 2 3 4 5 6 7 8 9 10	NA
Relearning after intermittent use	difficult easy 0 1 2 3 4 5 6 7 8 9 10	NA
Use by different levels of experience	not accommodated accommodated 0 1 2 3 4 5 6 7 8 9 10	NA
Novices can use a subset	with difficulty conveniently 0 1 2 3 4 5 6 7 8 9 10	NA
Experts can add features/shortcuts	with difficulty conveniently 0 1 2 3 4 5 6 7 8 9 10	NA
User can tailor the interface	with difficulty conveniently 0 1 2 3 4 5 6 7 8 9 10	NA
Human memory limitations	overwhelmed are respected 0 1 2 3 4 5 6 7 8 9 10	NA
Syntactic details	overwhelming are limited 0 1 2 3 4 5 6 7 8 9 10	NA
Information to complete tasks	must be memorized is visible 0 1 2 3 4 5 6 7 8 9 10	NA
Information patterns	obscure recognizable 0 1 2 3 4 5 6 7 8 9 10	NA
Supplemental reference materials	confusing clear 0 1 2 3 4 5 6 7 8 9 10	NA
Novice tutorial	confusing clear 0 1 2 3 4 5 6 7 8 9 10	NA
Reference manuals	confusing clear 0 1 2 3 4 5 6 7 8 9 10	NA
Video or audio tapes	confusing clear 0 1 2 3 4 5 6 7 8 9 10	NA
Exploration of features	discouraged encouraged 0 1 2 3 4 5 6 7 8 9 10	NA

	not protected protected 0 1 2 3 4 5 6 7 8 9 10	NA
Destructive operations		
	not provided provided 0 1 2 3 4 5 6 7 8 9 10	NA
Meaningful prompts		
	difficult easy 0 1 2 3 4 5 6 7 8 9 10	NA
Learning new features		
	terrible wonderful 0 1 2 3 4 5 6 7 8 9 10	NA
Overall reactions		
	frustrating satisfying 0 1 2 3 4 5 6 7 8 9 10	NA
	dull stimulating 0 1 2 3 4 5 6 7 8 9 10	NA
	difficult easy 0 1 2 3 4 5 6 7 8 9 10	NA
	inadequate power adequate power 0 1 2 3 4 5 6 7 8 9 10	NA

Table 10.2: Long form for subjective user evaluation of interactive systems

10.3.2 Interviews and group discussions

Interviews with individual users can be productive because the interviewer can pursue specific issues of concern. After a series of individual discussions, group discussions are valuable to ascertain the universality of comments. Interviewing can be costly and time consuming so usually only small fractions of the user community are involved. On the other hand, direct contact with users often leads to very specific constructive suggestions (Lieff & Allwood, 1985).

A large corporation conducted 45-minute interviews with 66 of the 4,300 users of an internal message system. The interviews revealed that the users were very happy with some aspects of the functionality, such as the capacity to pick up messages at any site, legible printed messages, and the convenience of after-hours access. However, the interviews also revealed that 23.6 percent of the users had concerns about reliability,

20.2 percent felt the system was confusing, 18.2 percent said convenience and accessibility could be improved, whereas only 16.0 percent expressed no concerns. Later questions in the interview explored specific features. As a result of this interview effort, a set of 42 enhancements to the system was proposed and implemented. The designers of the system had earlier proposed a set of enhancements, but the results of the interviews led to a changed set of priorities that more closely reflected the users' needs.

10.3.3 Online or telephone consultants

Online or telephone consultants are an extremely effective idea for providing assistance to users who are experiencing difficulties. Many users feel reassured if they know there is a human being to whom they can turn when problems arise. The consultants are an excellent source of information about problems users are having, suggestions for improvement, and potential extensions.

Several systems offer a toll-free 800 number by which the users can reach a knowledgeable consultant. On the PLATO computer-based instruction system, the consultants can monitor the user's terminal and see the same displays the user sees while maintaining telephone voice contact. This service can be very reassuring; the users know that someone can walk them through the correct sequence of screens to complete their tasks.

The Electronic Information Exchange System (EIES) allows users to send a message to a designated mailbox, called HELP, and receive a response immediately or within a few minutes in most cases (Hiltz & Turoff, 1981). The Dartmouth College Kiewit Computer Center, known for its attempts to provide good service to the university community, offers these instructions:

Typing JOIN CONSULT will connect you with Kiewit's Public Room Assistant, who is on duty 8 a.m. to midnight Monday through Saturday and noon to midnight Sunday. You can carry on a conversation with the assistant; you type in your questions and the assistant's responses are printed at your terminal.

Type /OLD SUGGEST***/RUN if you don't need an immediate response. Your questions will be recorded and, in the morning of the next working day, answers will be supplied in a file in your user number.

10.3.4 Online suggestion box or trouble reporting

Electronic mail can be employed to allow users to send messages to the maintainers or designers. Such an online suggestion box encourages some users to make productive comments, since writing a letter may be seen as requiring too much effort.

At the University of Maryland Computer Science Center, users can type the command GRIPE and they will receive a prompt for a comment to be sent to the systems programming staff. A typical comment is:

**** Message from user ****

I am having trouble with the editor when using a 132 character display. I occasionally lose the character typed in the last position.

Gwen User

**** Response from User Services ****

Several users have reported this erratic problem that has been traced to a bug in the new communications interface. It has been fixed as of October 29—please let us know if you are still encountering this problem.

Sharon Staff

A large corporation installed a full screen fill-in-the-blanks form for user problem reports and received ninety comments on a new internal system within three months. The user's identification number and name were entered automatically, and the user moved a cursor to indicate which subsystem was causing a problem and the seriousness (showstopper, annoyance, improvement, other). Each problem received a dated and signed response that was stored on a file for public reading.

10.3.5 Online bulletin board

Some users may have a question about the suitability of a software package for their application or may be seeking someone with experience using a system feature. They do not have any individual in mind so that electronic mail does not serve their needs. Many systems designers offer users an electronic bulletin board to permit posting of open messages and invitations. Many bulletin boards cover such technical topics as programming languages or hardware problems; others deal with tennis advice or film reviews.

Some professional societies offer bulletin boards by way of networks such as The Source, CompuServe, or through inexpensive one-user-at-a-time microcomputers with a modem to permit dialup access. These bulletin boards may offer information services or permit downloading of software by way of the telephone.

Bulletin board software systems usually offer a list of item headlines, allowing the user the opportunity to select items for display. New items can be added by anyone, but usually someone monitors the bulletin board to insure that offensive, useless, or repetitious items are removed.

10.3.6 User newsletters and conferences

When there are a substantial number of users who are geographically dispersed, managers may have to work harder to create a sense of community. Newsletters that provide information about novel system facilities, suggestions for improved productivity, requests for assistance, case studies of successful applications, or stories about individual users can promote user satisfaction and greater knowledge. Printed newsletters are more traditional and have the advantage that they can be carried away from the terminal workstation. A printed newsletter has an appealing air of respectability. Online newsletters may be less expensive and more rapidly disseminated.

Personal relationships established by face-to-face meetings also increase the sense of community among users. Conferences allow workers to exchange experiences with colleagues, promote novel approaches, stimulate greater dedication, encourage higher productivity, and develop a deeper relationship of trust. Ultimately, it is the people who matter, and human needs for social interaction should be satisfied. Every technical system is also a social system that needs to be encouraged and nurtured.

By soliciting user feedback in any of these ways, the system managers can gauge user attitudes and elicit useful suggestions. Furthermore, users may have a more positive attitude toward the system if they see that the system managers genuinely desire comments and suggestions.

10.4   QUANTITATIVE EVALUATIONS

Scientific and engineering progress is often stimulated by improved techniques for precise measurement. Rapid progress in interactive systems design will occur as soon as researchers and practitioners evolve suitable human performance measures and techniques. We have come to expect that automobiles will have miles-per-gallon reports pasted to the window, appliances will have energy efficiency ratings, and textbooks will be given grade level designations; soon, we will expect software packages to show learning time estimates and user satisfaction indices from appropriate evaluation sources.

10.4.1 Controlled psychologically oriented experimentation

Academic and industrial researchers are discovering that the power of the traditional scientific method can be fruitfully employed in studying interactive systems. They are conducting numerous experiments that are uncovering basic design principles. The outline of the scientific method is to:

- begin with a lucid and testable hypothesis
- explicitly state the independent variables that are to be altered
- carefully choose the dependent variables that will be measured

- judiciously select and assign subjects to groups
- control for biasing factors
- apply statistical methods to data analsyis.

The classic experimental methods of psychology are being refined to deal with the complex cognitive tasks of human performance with information and computer systems. The transformation from Aristotelian introspection to Galilean experimentation that took two millenia in physics is being accomplished in two decades in the study of human-computer interaction.

The reductionist approach required for controlled experimentation yields small but reliable results. Through multiple replications with similar tasks, subjects, and experimental conditions, reliability and validity can be enhanced. Each small experimental result acts as a tile in the mosaic of human performance with computerized information systems.

Managers of actively used systems are also coming to recognize the power of controlled experiments in fine tuning the human-computer interface. As proposals are made for new command syntax, different menu tree structures, novel cursor control devices, and reorganized display formats, a carefully controlled experiment can provide data to support a management decision.

Fractions of the user population could be given proposed improvements for a limited time and then performance could be compared with the control group. Dependent measures could include performance times, user-subjective satisfaction, error rates, and user retention over time.

Experimental design and statistical analysis are complex topics. Novice experimenters would be well advised to collaborate with experienced social scientists. A beginning text is by Runyon and Haber (1984) and a more advanced text is by Hays (1973).

10.4.2 Continuous user performance data collection

The software architecture should make it easy for system managers to collect data about the patterns of system usage, speed of user performance, rate of errors, or frequency of request for online assistance.

Specific data provide guidance in the acquisition of new hardware, changes in operating procedures, improvements to training, plans for system expansion, and so on (Good, 1985).

For example, if the frequency of each error message is recorded, then the highest frequency error is a candidate for attention. The message might be rewritten, training materials could be revised, the software could be changed to provide more specific information, or the command syntax might be simplified. Without specific data, the system maintenance staff has no way of knowing which of the many hundreds of error message situations is the biggest problem for users. Similarly, messages that never appear should be examined to see if there is an error in the code or if users are avoiding use of some facility.

If usage data for each command, each help screen, and each database record are available, then changes to the human-computer interface can be made to simplify access to frequently used features. Unused or rarely used facilities should also be examined to understand why users are avoiding them. A major benefit of usage frequency data is the guidance they provide to system maintainers in optimizing performance and reducing costs for all participants. This latter argument may yield the clearest advantage to a cost-conscious management, but the increased quality of the human-computer interface is an attraction to service-oriented managers.

10.5   DEVELOPMENT LIFE-CYCLE

Designers, implementers, and managers want to build a high-quality system, but they may not have a clear vision of what steps to take. The following life-cycle for interactive systems development is a framework that can be adapted to meet the widely varying needs of specific projects (Rouse, 1984). The life-cycle is presented in an orderly step-by-step manner, but the reality is often iterative, requiring a return to earlier stages for some parts of the system design.

1.   Collect information.
     Organize the design team

Obtain management and customer participation
Conduct interviews with users
Submit written questionnaires to users
Perform detailed task and task frequency analysis
Read professional and academic literature
Speak with designers and users of similar systems
Estimate development, training, usage, and maintenance
    costs
Prepare a schedule with observable milestones and reviews
Design the testing strategy

2.   Define requirements and semantics.

Define high-level goals and middle-level requirements
Consider task flow sequencing alternatives
Organize operations into transaction units
Create task and computer objects
Create task and computer actions
Determine reliability and availability needs
Specify security, privacy, and integrity constraints
Obtain management and customer agreement on goals,
    requirements, and semantic design

3.   Design syntax and support facilities.

Compare alternative display formats
Create syntax for operations
Design informative feedback for each operation
Develop error diagnostics
Specify system response times and display rates
Plan user aids, help facilities, and tutorials
Write user and reference manuals
Review, evaluate, and revise design specifications
Carry out paper-and-pencil pilot tests or field studies with
    an online mock-up or prototype

4.   Specify physical devices.

Choose hard- or softcopy devices
Specify keyboard layout
Select audio, graphics, or peripheral devices

    Establish requirements for communications lines
    Consider work environment noise, lighting, table space, etc.
    Carry out further pilot tests and revise design

5.   Develop software.

    Use dialog management tools where available
    Produce top-down modular design
    Emphasize modifiability and maintainability
    Ensure reliability and security
    Enable user and system performance monitoring
    Provide adequate system documentation
    Conduct thorough software test with realistic usage load

6.   Integrate system and disseminate to users.

    Assure user involvement at every stage
    Conduct acceptance tests and fine tune the system
    Field test printed manuals, online help, and tutorials
    Implement a training subsystem or simulator
    Provide adequate training and consultation for users
    Follow phased approach to dissemination and provide time
      and resources to make modest revisions in response to
      user feedback

7.   Nurture the user community.

    Provide on-site or telephone consultants
    Offer online consultant
    Develop online suggestion box
    Offer online subjective evaluation
    Perform interviews with users

    Make user news and bulletin boards available online
    Publish newsletter for users
    Organize group meetings
    Respond to user suggestions for improvements
    Conduct subjective and objective evaluations of the current
      system and proposed improvements
    Monitor usage frequencies and patterns
    Track user error frequencies

8. Prepare evolutionary plan.

   Design for easy repair and refinement
   Measure user performance regularly
   Improve error handling
   Carry out experiments to assess suggested changes
   Sample feedback from users by questionnaires and
      interviews
   Schedule revisions regularly and inform users in advance.

It's easy to build an ordinary system, but to build a good interactive system requires substantial effort during the design phase. The investments in time and money during design can dramatically reduce the development time and cost. Well-designed systems have lower lifetime costs, enable rapid task performance, substantially reduce error rates, shorten learning times, and bring satisfaction to the user community. Users who experience the competence of mastery, the confidence to explore novel features, the satisfaction of being able to perform their work, and the joyous sense of accomplishment will celebrate the role of the system designers, maintainers, and managers.

10.6 PRACTITIONER'S SUMMARY

Basic research in industrial and academic centers is beginning to yield guidelines for interactive systems designers. Industrial and governmental system developers employ empirical techniques by conducting informal pilot studies, evaluations of early prototypes, more careful studies of system components, rigorous acceptance tests, and continuous performance evaluation during the system's active use. If you are not measuring, you are not doing human factors!

Successful system managers understand that they must work hard to establish a relationship of trust with the user community. In addition to providing a properly functioning system, computer center managers and information systems directors recognize the need to create social mechanisms for feedback, such as online surveys, interviews, discussions, consultants, suggestion boxes, bulletin boards, newsletters, and conferences.

10.7 RESEARCHER'S AGENDA

Human interface guidelines are often based on best-guess judgments rather than on experimental data. More experimentation could lead to refined standards that are more complete and dependable and to more precise knowledge of how much improvement can be expected from a design change. It will take several decades to establish a stable and complete set of guidelines, but the benefits will be enormous in terms of the reliability and quality of the human interface.

Researchers can also contribute their experience with experimentation to developing techniques of system evaluation. Guidance in conducting pilot studies, acceptance tests, surveys, interviews, and discussions would benefit commercial development groups. Psychological test construction experts would be extremely helpful in preparing a validated and reliable test instrument for subjective evaluation of interactive systems. Such a standardized test would allow independent groups to compare the acceptability of their systems.

Clinical psychologists, psychotherapists, and social workers could contribute to training online or telephone consultants—after all, helping troubled users is a human relationship issue. Finally, more input from experimental, cognitive, and clinical psychologists would help computer specialists recognize the importance of the human aspects of computer use.

REFERENCES

Baroudi, Jack J., Olson, Margrethe H., Ives, Blake, An empirical study of the impact of user involvement on system usage and information satisfaction, *Communications of the ACM 29*, 3, (March 1986), 232–238.

Carroll, John M., and Rosson, Mary Beth, Usability specifications as a tool in iterative development, In Hartson, H. Rex (Editor), *Advances in Human-Computer Interaction 1*, Ablex Publishing Corporation, Norwood, NJ, (1985), 1–28.

Clark, I. A., Software simulation as a tool for usable product design, *IBM Systems Journal 20*, 3, (1981), 272–293.

Good, Michael, The use of logging data in the design of a new text editor, *Proc. CHI'85—Human Factors in Computing Systems*, Available from ACM, P. O. Box 64145, Baltimore, MD, 21264, (1985), 93–97.

Good, Michael D., Whiteside, John A., Wixon, Dennis R., and Jones, Sandra J., Building a user-derived interface, *Communications of the ACM 27*, 10, (October 1984), 1032–1043.

Gould, John D., Conti, J., and Hovanyecz, T., Composing letters with a simulated listening typewriter, *Communications of the ACM 26*, 4, (1983), 295–308.

Gould, John D., and Lewis, Clayton, Designing for usability: Key principles and what designers think, *Communications of the ACM 28*, 3, (March 1985), 300–311.

Hays, William L., *Statistics for the Social Sciences*, second edition, Holt, Rinehart and Winston, Inc., New York, (1973), 954 pages.

Hiltz, Starr Roxanne, *Online Communities: A Case Study in the Office of the Future*, Ablex Publishing Co., Norwood, NJ, (1983).

Hiltz, Starr Roxanne, and Turoff, Murray, The evolution of user behavior in a computer conferencing system, *Communications of the ACM*, 24, 11, (November 1981), 739–751.

Hirsch, Richard S., Procedures of the Human Factors Center at San Jose, *IBM Systems Journal 20*, 2, (1981), 123–171.

Ives, Blake, and Olson, Margrethe H., User involvement and MIS success: A review of research, *Management Science 30*, 5, (May 1984), 586–603.

Jacob, Robert J. K., An executable specification technique for describing human-computer interaction, In Hartson, H. Rex (Editor), *Advances in Human-Computer Interaction 1*, Ablex Publishing Corporation, Norwood, NJ, (1985), 211–242.

Keen, Peter G. W., Information systems and organizational change, *Communications of the ACM 24*, 1, (January 1981), 24–33.

Kelley, J. F., An interative design methodology for user-friendly natural language office information applications, *ACM Transactions on Office Information Systems 2*, 1, (March 1984), 26–41.

Lewis, Clayton, Using the "thinking aloud" method in cognitive interface design, IBM Research Report RC–9265, Yorktown Heights, NY, (1982).

Lieff, Ed, and Allwood, Carl-Martin, Empirical methods in the Better Terminal Use project, In Agrawal, Jagdish C., and Zunde, Pranas (Editors), *Empirical Foundations of Information and Software Science*, Plenum Press, New York and London, (1985), 157–168.

Lund, Michelle A., Evaluating the user interfaces: The candid camera approach, *Proc. CHI'85—Human Factors in Computing Systems*, Available from ACM, P. O. Box 64145, Baltimore, MD, 21264, (1985), 93–97.

Lyons, Michael, Measuring user satisfaction: The semantic differential technique, *Proceedings of the 17th Annual Computer Personnel Research Conference*, ACM SIGCPR, (1980), 79–87.

Mumford, Enid, *Designing Participatively*, Manchester Business School, England, (1983).

Olson, Margrethe H., and Ives, Blake, User involvement in system design: An empirical test of alternative approaches, *Information and Management 4*, (1981), 183–195.

Roach, J., Hartson, H. R., Ehrich, R., Yunten, T., and Johnson, D., DMS: A comprehensive system for managing human-computer dialogues, *Proc. Iluman Factors in Computer Systems Conference*, Gaithersburg, MD, (March 1982), 102–105.

Root, Robert W., and Draper, Steve, Questionnaires as a software evaluation tool, *Proc. ACM CHI'83 Human Factors in Computing Systems*, Available from ACM, (1983), 83–87.

Rouse, William B., Design and evaluation of computer-based decision support systems, In Salvendy, A. (Editor), *Human-Computer Interaction*, Elsevier Science Publishers, B. V. Amsterdam, (1984), 229–246.

Runyon, Richard P., and Haber, Audrey, *Fundamentals of Behavioral Statistics*, Fifth Edition, Random House, New York, (1984), 494 pages.

Savage, Ricky E., Habinek, James K., and Barnhart, Thomas W., The design, simulation, and evaluation of a menu driven user interface, *Proc. Human Factors in Computer Systems Conference*, Gaithersburg, MD, (March 1982), 36–40.

Squires, S. L., Zelkowitz, M., and Branstad, M., (Editors), Special issue on Rapid Prototyping, *ACM SIGSOFT Software Engineering Notes 7*, 5, (December 1982).

Thomas, John C., Organizing for human factors, In Vassiliou, Y. (Editor), *Human Factors in Interactive Computer Systems*, Ablex Publishing Co., Norwood, NJ, (1984), 29–46.

Wasserman, Anthony I., and Shewmake, David T., The role of prototypes in the User Software Engineering (USE) methodology, In Hartson, Rex (Editor), *Advances in Human-Computer Interaction 1*, Ablex Publishing Corporation, Norwood, NJ, (1985), 191–210.

Williges, Robert, *Proc. Human Factors Society—29th Annual Meeting*, Santa Monica, CA, (1985).

Yunten, Tamer, and Hartson, H. Rex, A SUPERvisory Methodology: A Notation (SUPERMAN) for human-computer system development, In Hartson, Rex (Editor), *Advances in Human-Computer Interaction 1*, Ablex Publishing Corporation, Norwood, NJ, (1985), 243–282.

CHAPTER 11

SOCIAL AND INDIVIDUAL IMPACT

People who are so fascinated by the computer's lifelike feats—it plays chess! it writes "poetry"!—that they would turn it into the voice of omniscience, betray how little understanding they have of either themselves, their mechanical-electrical agents or the potentialities of life.

Lewis Mumford, *The Myth of the Machine*, 1970

11.1 HOPES AND DREAMS

Why are many people enthusiastic about computers? For some, there is immediate gratification in using new technology and gadgets. In others, the opportunity for financial success or professional advancement must be appealing. Other motives are the sense of power computers offer to users and the feeling of godlike creation they convey to programmers (Turkle, 1984). These strong forces generate intense engagement for some people.

Beyond these motivations, what benefits to individuals and society might accrue from the widespread use of computers (Birnbaum, 1985)? Each person forms an individual answer, but here is a starting list.

Productivity enhancement: The most natural way to promote computers in organizations and also for individuals is to suggest that the users will become more productive. Enthusiasts claim that time to complete tasks and task costs can be reduced by employing computers. For well-defined tasks in which information processing is prominent, there is little doubt that computers can produce benefits. Accounting, inventory, reservations, mathematical computations, library information retrieval, insurance claims, banking, student registration, and factory automation are only some of the areas in which successful applications of computers increase productivity. More difficult questions are: Who are the beneficiaries of the productivity gains and, How are these gains distributed?

Quality improvement: Since productivity is improved and the tedious parts of some work can be reduced by using computers, there is an opportunity to improve quality of work. Word processor users can take the time to ensure that consistent terminology is used, that spelling is correct, that the best references are included in scientific articles, and that comments from colleagues can be easily applied. Hotel or airline reservations systems can help ensure that individual physical or dietary needs are accommodated and that the lowest rate is offered. Automated factories can deliver custom-designed and thoroughly tested products.

Individual opportunity: In the 1960s, the popular phrase was "[computer] power to the people," and in the 1970s many people talked about "self actualization." In the 1980s, it seems more appropriate to focus on individual growth or opportunity. Indeed, in the 1960s computers were available primarily to big business and big government, creating an imbalance. By the 1980s, personal computers had become widely, although not universally, available, thus offering many people the chance to be entrepreneurs and to develop a business or other interest of their own. The power of the computer enables individuals more easily to publish newsletters, provide investment or accounting services, develop educational materials, write novels, run mail-order businesses, or develop a consulting company. Other information-intensive tasks that can be aided by personal computers include political campaigning, community organizing, maintaining family histories, and managing religious groups, parent-teacher associations, performing arts troupes, or museums. Personal applications, such as home finance, tax preparation, automobile maintenance, health records, or vacation planning, are certain to expand.

Exploration: Easy access to computing can encourage exploration of new ideas and individual self-expression. These ideas include the chemist who can easily try new mathematical models, the political scientist who can conveniently trace voting patterns, the corporate planner who can rapidly generate multiple business strategies, or the artist who can experiment with a new medium for visual, aural, or tactile compositions.

Learning: Computer facilitation of learning is still in its early stages. The familiar computer-assisted instruction with drill and practice strategies are simple, first applications of computers for rote memorization or forced learning. Some educational games offer role-playing fantasies that attempt to portray realistic situations, such as emergency-room decision-making or a pioneer's wagon trip across the plains in the 1800s. Lively environments for learning are emerging in which the learner sets goals, encounters problems, formulates plans, measures progress, searches databases, performs computations, interacts with others, and derives satisfaction from accomplishments (Bork, 1981, 1985).

Entertainment: Never underestimate the importance of entertainment, sports, and leisure time activities as potential applications of computers. The videogame phenomenon is well reported; computers also allow sports enthusiasts to manage Little League schedules; enable collectors to maintain stamp, music, or book collections; and permit students to explore mathematical puzzles.

Cooperation: Increasingly, computers and communication networks offer the possibility of cooperation among people. Network facilities allow electronic mail between individuals, computer conferencing within organizations, interactive game playing, group decision-making, or information sharing.

11.2   FEARS AND NIGHTMARES

It would be naïve to assume that widespread use of computers brings only benefits. There are legitimate reasons to worry that increased dissemination of computers might lead to a variety of oppressions—personal, organizational, political, or social. People who fear computers have good reason for their concerns. Computer system designers have an opportunity and a responsibility to be alert to the dangers and to make thoughtful decisions about reducing the dangers they perceive.

Here, then, is a personal list of potential and real dangers from use of computer systems:

TEN PLAGUES OF THE INFORMATION AGE

1.   *Anxiety*: Many people avoid the computer or use it with great anxiety; they suffer from "computer shock," "terminal terror," or "network neurosis." Their anxieties include the fear of breaking the machine, worry over losing control to the computer, trepidation about appearing foolish or incompetent ("computers make you feel so dumb"), or the common concern about something new. These anxieties are real, should be acknowledged rather than dismissed, and can often be overcome with positive experiences.

2.   *Alienation*: As people spend more time using computers, they may become less connected to other people (Sheridan, 1980). Computer users as a group are more introverted than average, and increased time with the computer may increase their isolation. One psychologist (Brod, 1984) fears that computer users come to expect rapid performance,

yes-no or true-false responses, and a high degree of control not only from their machines but also from their friends, spouses, and children. The dedicated videogame player who rarely communicates with another person is an extreme case, but what happens to the emotional relationships of a person who spends two hours a day doing electronic mail rather than chatting with colleagues? Studies of households with personal computers reveal that family time watching television is reduced and that individuals spend more time using the computer or doing other projects alone (Vitalari et al., 1985).

3. *Information-poor minority*: Although some utopian visionaries believe that computers will eliminate the distinctions between rich and poor or right social injustices, often computers are just another way for the disadvantaged to be disadvantaged. Those people without computer skills may have a new reason for not succeeding in school or not getting a job offer. Already great disparity exists in the distribution of educational computers. The high-income school districts are more likely to have computer facilities than are the poorer school districts. Access to information resources is also disproportionately in the hands of the wealthy and established social communities.

4. *Impotence of the individual*: Large organizations can become impersonal because the cost of handling special cases is great. Individuals who are frustrated in trying to receive personal treatment and attention may vent their anger at the organization, the personnel they encounter, or the technology that limits rather than enables. People who have tried to find out the current status of their social security accounts or tried to have banks explain accounting discrepancies are aware of the problems, especially if they have language, hearing, or physically disabling handicaps. Interactive computer systems can be used to increase the impact of individuals or provide special treatment, but this requires alert committed designers and sympathetic managers.

5. *Bewildering complexity and speed*: The tax, welfare, and insurance regulations developed by computerized bureaucra-
   cies are so complex and fast changing that it is extremely
   difficult for individuals to keep up and make informed
   choices. Even knowledgeable computer users are often
   overwhelmed by the torrent of software packages, each with
   hundreds of features and options. The presence of computers and other technologies can mislead managers into believing that they can deal with the complexities they are
   creating. Rapid computer systems become valued, speed
   dominates, and more features seem "better." This situation
   is apparent in nuclear reactor control rooms, where
   hundreds of lighted annunciators overwhelm operators when
   indicating failures. Simplicity is a simple, but too often ignored, principle.

6. *Organizational fragility*: As organizations come to depend
   on more complex technology, they can become fragile.
   When breakdowns occur, they can propagate rapidly and
   halt the work of many people. With computerized airline
   ticketing or department store sales, computer failures can
   mean immediate shutdowns of service. A more subtle example is that computerized inventory control may eliminate
   or dramatically reduce stock on hand so that disruptions
   spread rapidly. For example, a strike in a ball bearing plant
   can force the closing of a distant automobile assembly line
   within a few days. Computers can cause concentration of
   expertise so that a small number of people can disrupt a
   large organization.

7. *Invasion of privacy*: This widely reported threat is worri-
   some because the concentration of information and powerful
   retrieval systems makes it possible to violate the privacy of
   many people easily and rapidly. Of course, well-designed
   computer systems have the potential of becoming more safe
   than paper systems if management is dedicated to privacy
   protection. Airline, telephone, bank, and employment records can reveal much about an individual if confidentiality
   is compromised.

8. *Unemployment and displacement*: As automation spreads, productivity and overall employment may increase, but some jobs may become less valued or eliminated. Retraining can help some employees, but others will have a difficult time changing lifetime patterns of work. This happens to low-paid clerks or highly paid typesetters whose work is automated as well as to the bank vice-president whose mortgage loan decisions are now done by an "expert system."

9. *Lack of professional responsibility*: Faceless organizations may respond impersonally and deny responsibility for problems. The complexity of technology and organizations provides ample opportunities for employees to pass the blame on to others or to the computer; "Sorry, the computer won't let us accept the library book without the machine-readable card." Will users of medical diagnostic or defense-related systems be able to escape responsibility for decisions? Will computer printouts become more trusted than a person's word or a professional's judgment?

10. *Deteriorating image of people*: With the presence of "intelligent terminals," "smart machines," and "expert systems," it seems that the machines have indeed taken over human abilities. These misleading phrases not only generate anxiety about computers, but they also may undermine the image we have of people and their abilities. Some behavioral psychologists suggest that we are little more than machines; some artificial intelligence workers believe that the automation of many human abilities is within reach. The rich diversity of human skills, the generative or creative nature of daily life, the emotional or passionate side, and the idiosyncratic imagination of each child seem lost or undervalued (Rosenbrock, 1982).

Undoubtedly, more plagues and problems also exist. Each situation is a small warning for the designer. Each design is an opportunity to apply computers in positive, constructive ways that avoid these dangers.

11.3   PREVENTING THE PLAGUES

There is no set formula for preventing these plagues. Even well-intentioned designers can inadvertently spread them, but alert, dedicated designers whose consciousness is raised can reduce the dangers. The strategies for preventing the plagues and reducing their impact include:

Human-centered design: Concentrate attention on the users and the tasks they must accomplish. Make the user the center of attention and build feelings of competence, mastery, clarity, and predictability. Construct well-organized menu trees, provide meaningful structure in command languages, present specific and constructive instructions and messages, develop uncluttered displays, offer informative feedback, enable easy error handling, ensure appropriate display rates and response time, and produce comprehensible learning materials.

Organizational support: Beyond the software design, the organization must also support the user. Explore strategies for participatory design and elicit frequent evaluation and feedback from users. Techniques include personal interviews, focus groups, online surveys, paper questionnaires, and online consultants or suggestion boxes. A robust user community can be supported by meetings, newsletters, and an impartial ombudsman (Kling, 1980).

Job design: European labor unions have been active in setting rules for terminal users to prevent the exhaustion, stress, or burn-out of an *electronic sweatshop*. Rules might be set to limit hours of use, to guarantee rest periods, to facilitate job rotation, and to support education. Similarly, negotiated measures of productivity or error rates can help to reward exemplary workers and guide training. Monitoring or metering of work must be done cautiously, but both management and employees can be beneficiaries of a thoughtful plan. Responsibility for failures and the benefits of success should be explicitly shared among designers, users, and managers.

Education: The complexity of modern life and computer systems demands that education be critical. Schools and colleges as well as employers all play a role in training. Special attention should be paid to continuing education, on-the-job training, and teacher education.

Feedback and rewards: User groups can be more than passive partici-pants. They can ensure that system failures are reported, that design im-provements are conveyed to managers and designers, and that manuals and online aids are reviewed. Similarly, excellence should be acknowl-edged by awards within organizations and through public presentations. Professional societies in computing might promote awards, similar to the awards of the American Institute of Architects, the Pulitzer Prize Committee, or the Academy of Motion Picture Producers.

Public consciousness raising: Informed consumers of personal comput-ers and users of commercial systems can benefit the entire community. Professional societies such as the Association for Computing Machinery or the IEEE, and user groups such as the Washington Apple Pi or the Capitol IBM PC User's Group can play a key role through public rela-tions, consumer education, and professional standards of ethics.

Legislation: Much progress has been made with legislation concerning privacy, right of access to information, and computer crime, but more work remains. Cautious steps toward regulation, work rules, and stan-dardization can be highly beneficial. Dangers of restrictive legislation do exist, but thoughtful legal protection will stimulate development and pre-vent abuses.

Advanced research: Individuals, organizations, and governments can support research to develop novel ideas, minimize the dangers, and spread the advantages of interactive systems. Theories of user-cognitive behavior, individual differences, acquisition of skills, visual perception, and organizational change would be helpful in guiding designers and implementers.

11.4   OVERCOMING THE OBSTACLE OF ANIMISM

The emergence of computers is one of the fundamental historical changes. Alvin Toffler describes this *third wave* (1980) as the successor to the agricultural and then the industrial revolutions. Such upheavals are neither all good nor all bad, but the amalgam of many individual deci-sions about how a technology is applied. Each designer plays a role in shaping the direction. The computer revolution has passed its infancy, but there is still tremendous opportunity for change.

The metaphors, images, and names chosen for systems play a key role in the designers' and the users' perceptions. It is not surprising that many computer system designers still derive their inspiration by mimicking human or animal forms. The first attempts at flight were to imitate birds, and the first designs for microphones followed the shape of the human ear. Eventually, human needs and the underlying technology shape products to maximize service and reduce cost. Such primitive visions may be useful starting points, but success comes most rapidly to people who move beyond these fantasies and apply scientific analyses. Except for amusement, the goal is never to mimic human form but to provide effective service to the users in accomplishing their tasks.

Lewis Mumford, in his classic book, *Technics and Civilization* (1934), characterized the problem of "dissociation of the animate and the mechanical" as the "obstacle of animism." He describes Leonardo da Vinci's attempt to reproduce the motion of birds' wings, then Ader's bat-like airplane as late as 1897, and Branca's steam engine in the form of a human head and torso. Mumford wrote (page X3–33):

> the most ineffective kind of machine is the realistic mechanical imitation of a man or another animal...for thousands of years animism has stood in the way of...development.

Choosing human or animal forms as the inspiration for some projects is understandable, but significant advances will come more quickly by recognizing the goals that serve human needs and the inherent attributes of the technology that is employed. Hand calculators do not follow human forms but serve effectively for doing arithmetic. Designers of championship chess playing programs no longer imitate human strategies. Vision systems researchers realized the advantages of radar or sonar rangefinders and retreated from using human-like stereo depth recognition.

Robots provide an informative case study. Beyond stone idols and voodoo dolls, we can trace modern robots back to the devices built by Pierre Jacquet-Droz, a Swiss watchmaker, from 1768 to 1774. The first child-sized mechanical robot, called The Scribe, could be programmed to write any message up to forty characters long. It had commands to

change lines, skip a space, or dip the quill in the inkwell. The second, called The Draughtsman, had a repertoire of four pencil sketches: a boy, a dog, Louis XV of France, and a pair of portraits. The third robot, The Musician, performed five songs on a working pipe organ and could operate an hour and a half on one winding. These robots made their creators famous and wealthy since they were in great demand at the court of the kings and in public showings. Printing presses became more effective than The Scribe and The Draughtsman, and tape players and phonographs superior to The Musician.

Robots of the 1950s included electronic components and a metallic skin, but their designs were also strongly influenced by the human form. Robot arms were of the same dimension as human arms and the hands had five fingers. Designers of modern robots have finally overcome the obstacle of animism and now construct arms whose dimensions are appropriate for the steel and plastic technology. Two fingers are more common than five on robot hands, and the hands can often rotate more than 270 degrees. Where appropriate, fingers have been replaced by rubber suction cups with vacuum pumps to pick up parts.

In spite of these improvements, the metaphor and terminology of human form can still mislead the designers and users of robots. Programmers of one industrial robot were so disturbed by the labels "upper arm" and "lower arm" on the control panel that they had scratched them out. They felt that the anthropomorphic term misled their intuitions about how to program the robot (McDaniel & Gong, 1982). The term *programmable manipulators* or the broader *flexible manufacturing systems* are less exciting but more accurately describe the newer generation of robot-like systems.

The banking machines offer a simple example of the evolution from anthropomorphic imagery to a service orientation. Early systems had such names as Tillie the Teller or Harvey Wallbanker and were programmed with such phrases as "How can I help you?" These deceptive images rapidly gave way to a focus on the computer technology with such names as The Electronic Teller, CompuCash, Cashmatic, or CompuBank. Over time, the emphasis moves towards the service provided to the user: CashFlow, Money Exchange, 24-Hour Money Machine, All-Night Banker, and Money Mover.

The computer revolution will be judged not by the complexity or power of technology but by the service to human needs. By focusing on the user, researchers and designers will generate powerful yet simple systems that permit users to accomplish their tasks. These tools will enable short learning times, rapid performance, and low error rates. Putting the user's needs first will lead to more appropriate choices of system features, a greater sense of mastery and control, and the satisfaction of achievement. At the same time, the user will feel increased responsibility and may be more motivated to learn about the tasks and the interactive system.

Sharpening the boundaries between people and computers will lead to a clearer recognition of computer powers and human reason (Weizenbaum, 1976). Rapid progress will occur when designers accept that human-human communication is a poor model for human-computer interaction. People are so different from computers, and human operation of computers is vastly different from human relationships. Vital factors that distinguish human behavior include the diversity of skills and background across individuals; the creativity, imagination, and inventiveness incorporated in daily actions; the emotional involvement in every act; the desire for social contact; and the power of intention.

Ignoring these primitive but enduring aspects of humanity leads to inappropriate technology and a hollow experience. Embracing these aspects can bring about powerful tools, joy in learning, the capacity to realize goals, a sense of accomplishment, and increased social interaction.

11.5 IN THE LONG RUN

Successful interactive systems will bring ample rewards to the designers, but widespread use of effective tools is only the means to reach higher goals. A computer system is more than a technological artifact: interactive systems, especially when linked by computer networks, create human social systems. As Marshall McLuhan pointed out, "the medium is the message," and therefore each interactive system is a message from the designer to the user. That message has often been a harsh one, with the underlying implication that the designer does not care about the user.

The nasty error messages are obvious manifestations; complex commands, cluttered screens, and confusing sequences of operations are also part of the harsh message.

Most designers want to send a more kind and caring message. Designers, implementers, and researchers are learning to send warmer greetings to the users with effective and well-tested systems. The message of quality is compelling to the recipients and can instill good feelings, appreciation for the designer, and the desire to excel in their own work. The capacity for excellent systems to instill compassion and connection was noted by Sterling (1974) at the end of his guidelines for information systems:

> In the long run what may be important is the *texture* of a system. By texture we mean the *quality* the system has to evoke in users and participants a feeling that the system increases the kinship between men.

At first, it may seem remarkable that computer systems can instill a kinship among people, but every technology has the potential to engage people in cooperative efforts. The same message emerges from Robert Pirsig's *Zen and the Art of Motorcyle Maintenance* (1974). Each act of quality is noticed and spreads like waves on the water. Each designer can play a role, not only of fighting for the user, but also of nurturing, serving, and caring for the user.

REFERENCES

Birnbaum, Joel S., Toward the domestication of microelectronics, *IEEE Comupter 18*, 11, (November 1985), 128–140.

Bork, Alfred, *Learning with Computers*, Digital Press, Bedford, MA, (1981).

Bork, Alfred, *Personal Computers for Education*, Harper and Row, Publishers, New York, NY, (1985).

Brod, Craig, *Technostress: The human cost of the computer revolution*, Addison-Wesley Publishing Company, Reading, MA, (1984).

Kling, Rob, Social analyses of computing: Theoretical perspectives and recent empirical research, *ACM Computing Surveys 12*, 1, (March 1980), 61–110.

McDaniel, Ellen, and Gong, Gwendolyn, The language of robotics: Use and abuse of personification, *IEEE Transactions on Professional Communications PC–25*, 4, (December 1982), 178–181.

Mumford, Lewis, *Techniques and Civilization*, Harcourt Brace Jovanovich, New York, (1934).

Pirsig, Robert, *Zen and the Art of Motorcycle Maintenance*, Morrow and Co., New York, (1974).

Rosenbrock, H. H., Robots and people, *Measurement and Control 15*, (March 1982), 105–112.

Sheridan, Thomas B., Computer control and human alienation, *Technology Review 83*, 1, (October 1980), 51–73.

Sterling, T. D., Guidelines for humanizing computerized information systems: A report from Stanley House, *Communications of the ACM 17*, 11, (November 1974), 609–613.

Toffler, Alvin, *The Third Wave*, William Morrow and Company, New York, (1980).

Turkle, Sherry, *The Second Self*, Simon and Schuster, New York, (1984).

Vitalari, Nicholas P., Venkatesh, Alladi, and Gronhaug, Kjell, Computing in the home: Shifts in the time allocation patterns of households, *Communications of the ACM 28*, 5, (May 1985), 512–522.

Weizenbaum, Joseph, *Computer Power and Human Reason*, W. H. Freeman and Company, San Francisco, CA, (1976).

NAME INDEX

Abrahamson, David S., 107, 131, 302, 307
Agrawal, Jagdish C., 419
Al-War, J., 381, 383
Albert, Alan E., 245, 247, 266
Allen, S. I., 269
Allwood, Carl-Martin, 407, 419
Alty, J. L., 38
Anderson, Matt, 267
Arkin, Michael D., 280, 308
Arnheim, Rudolf, 199, 220
Athey, J. G., 315, 353

Badre, Albert, 38
Bailey, Robert W., 9, 19, 35, 45, 79
Banks, William W., 33, 34
Barber, Raymond E., 63, 79, 298, 304, 305
Barnard, Phil, 150, 151, 159, 160, 174, 175, 383
Barnes, Vincent, 267
Barnhart, Thomas W., 132, 419
Baroudi, Jack J., 393, 417
Beam, P., 385
Bean, Carl, 107
Benbasat, Izak, 160, 162, 174
Bergman, Hans, 301, 306
Berman, Melvyn L., 267
Bevan, Nigel, 279, 306
Bewley, William L., 219, 220
Billingsley, Patricia A., 130, 268, 384
Bird, J. M., 245, 269
Birnbaum, Joel S., 424, 435
Black, J., 174
Blackman, Harold S., 34
Blaser, A., 38
Bobko, D. J., 337, 352
Bobko, P., 337, 352
Boehm, Barry W., 305, 306
Boggs, George, 308
Boies, S. J., 295, 296, 297, 306
Bolt, Richard A., 35
Bonar, Jeffrey, 81
Borenstein, Nathaniel S., 379, 383
Bork, Alfred, 425, 435
Boyle, James M., 123, 132, 353
Branstad, M., 420
Briggs, Amy, 266

Brinkman, Albert, 306
Brod, Craig, 426, 435
Brown, C. Marlin, 69, 76, 79, 123, 130, 266, 337, 352
Brown, James W., 97, 130
Brown, O., Jr., 269
Bruner, James, 199, 220
Brunner, Hans, 233, 266
Bubis, Gad, 269
Budge, Bill, 192
Burr, B. J., 266
Bury, Kevin F., 348, 352
Butler, T. W., 296, 299, 302, 306
Buxton, William, 237, 266

Cakir, A., 35, 256, 266, 359, 383
Callahan, Jack, 346
Calotti, K. M., 175–176
Carbonell, J. R., 273, 306
Card, Stuart K., 35–36, 44, 49, 63, 79, 105, 130, 245, 247, 248, 266, 344, 352
Carroll, John M., 143, 153, 154, 155, 174, 175, 184, 192, 199, 201, 220, 370, 383, 391, 396, 418
Chan, Peggy, 267
Chapanis, Alphonse, 363, 369, 383, 385, 386
Christ, Richard E., 260, 266, 342, 352
Clark, I. A., 174, 395, 418
Clarke, Arthur C., 249
Clauer, Calvin Kingsley, 97, 130
Cohill, A. M., 378, 379, 383
Conti, J., 418
Conway, R. W., 313, 352
Coombs, M. J., 38, 39
Copeland, Richard W., 203, 220
Cotton, Ira W., 281, 306
Cress, P., 313, 352
Crowell, Charles R., 354
Curtis, Bill, 38

Dannenbring, Gary L., 295, 306
Darnell, Michael J., 352
Davies, Susan E., 362
Davis, M. A., 337, 352
Dean, M., 352
Dickinson, J., 384

437

SUBJECT INDEX